OXFORD MANAGEMENT READ



# LEADERSHIP

The OXFORD MANAGEMENT READERS series reflects the interdisciplinary nature of much teaching of management. The aim of this series is to bring together carefully selected contributions on particular issues. The volumes will be based around either key themes or topics on the management curriculum.

# LEADERSHIP

## Classical, Contemporary, and Critical Approaches

Edited by

**Keith Grint**

OXFORD UNIVERSITY PRESS

**OXFORD**
UNIVERSITY PRESS

Great Clarendon Street, Oxford OX2 6DP

Oxford University Press is a department of the University of Oxford.
It furthers the University's objective of excellence in research, scholarship,
and education by publishing worldwide in

Oxford New York

Auckland Cape Town Dar es Salaam Hong Kong Karachi
Kuala Lumpur Madrid Melbourne Mexico City Nairobi
New Delhi Taipei Toronto Shanghai

With offices in

Argentina Austria Brazil Chile Czech Republic France Greece
Guatemala Hungary Italy Japan South Korea Poland Portugal
Singapore Switzerland Thailand Turkey Ukraine Vietnam

Published in the United States
by Oxford University Press Inc., New York



ISBN 978-0-19-878182-0 (Hbk.)
ISBN 978-0-19-878181-3 (Pbk.)

Printed in Great Britain
on acid-free paper by
Biddles Ltd., King's Lynn, Norfolk

For Sandra, Katy, Beki, and Kris

# Preface and Acknowledgements

I would like to thank David Musson at Oxford University Press and Hilary Walford for their help with this project and the staff of the Information Centre at Templeton College for their usual forbearance and support with securing the materials. I would also like to thank the IT staff, especially Chris Farmer for help with scanning of the texts, and Elaine Pullin, Doreen Hirons, and especially Val Martin for their tireless attempts to translate the hieroglyphics of the scanner into recognizable English. Many students and executives have suffered the consequences of my leadership lectures over the last five years and I would like to acknowledge their help in revealing the many holes in my arguments. David Feeny, Karl Moore, Janine Nahapiet, Richard Pascale, and Sue Vickers-Thompson have been involved in a wider debate about leadership at Templeton which I have found extremely useful in consolidating my ideas. Finally, my thanks go to: Katy for lessons in copy editing and driving; Beki for lessons in humour and language; Kris for lessons in computing and organizational resistance, and Sandra for lessons in life.

# Acknowledgements

© Robin Waterfield 1993. Reprinted from Plato, *The Republic*, translated by Robin Waterfield (World's Classics, 1993) by permission of Oxford University Press.

Extracts from Sun Tzu, *The Art of War*, translated by Samuel B. Griffith (Oxford University Press, 1971). Reprinted by permission.

© Peter Bondanella and Mark Musa 1979. Reprinted from Machiavelli, *The Prince*, edited by Peter Bondanella, translated by Peter Bondanella and Mark Musa (World's Classics, 1984) by permission of Oxford University Press.

From Pareto, 'Foxes and Lions', in S. Finer (ed.), *Sociological Writings*. Reprinted by permission of Dawson UK Ltd.

Chester I. Barnard, 'The Nature of Leadership', reprinted by permission of the publisher from *Organization and Management: Selected Papers* by Chester Barnard, Cambridge, Mass: Harvard University Press. Copyright © 1948 by the President and Fellows of Harvard College.

R. M. Stogdill, 'Leadership, Membership, and Organization', *Psychological Bulletin*, 47 (1950), 1–14. Material in public domain.

Fred E. Fiedler, 'Situational Control and a Dynamic Theory of Leadership', in Bert King, Siegfried Streufert, and Fred E. Fiedler (eds.), *Managerial Control and Organizational Democracy* (Winston and Sons, 1976), 107–31. Reprinted by permission.

John Gastil, 'A Definition and Illustration of Democratic Leadership', *Human Relations*, 47/8 (1994), 953–75. Reprinted by permission of the author and Plenum Publishing Corporation.

Andrew Kakabadse *et al*, 'Top Management Styles in Europe', *European Business Journal*, 7/1 (1995), 17–27. Reprinted by permission of Whurr Publishers Ltd, London.

B. M. Bass and B. J. Avolio, 'Shatter the Glass Ceiling: Women May Make Better Managers', *Human Resource Management*, 33/4 (1994), 549–60. Copyright © 1994 by John Wiley & Sons. Reprinted by permission of John Wiley & Sons, Inc.

'Sexual Static' in Judy B. Rosener, *America's Competitive Secret: Utilizing Women as a Management Strategy* (Oxford University Press, 1995), 67–83. Copyright © 1995 by Oxford University Press, Inc. Reprinted by permission.

Iain Pears, 'The Gentleman and the Hero: Wellington and Napoleon in the Nineteenth Century', in R. Porter (ed.), *Myths of the English* (Polity, 1992), 216–36. Reprinted by permission of Blackwell Publishers.

M. F. R. Kets de Vries, 'The Leadership Mystique', *Academy of Management Executive*, 8/3 (1994), 73–92. Reprinted by permission of the Academy of Management.

Gary Gemmill and Judith Oakley, 'Leadership: An Alienating Social Myth?', *Human Relations*, 45/2 (1992), 113–29. Reprinted by permission of the authors and Plenum Publishing Corporation.

D. M. Hosking, 'Organizing, Leadership and Skilful Process', *Journal of Management Studies*, 25/2 (1988), 147–66. Reprinted by permission of Blackwell Publishers.

Stephen J. Lilley and Gerald M. Platt, 'Correspondents' Images of Martin Luther King, Jr: An Interpretive Theory of Movement Leadership', in T. R. Sarbin and J. I. Kitsuse (eds.), *Constructing the Social* (Sage, 1994), 65–83. Reprinted by permission of Sage Publications Ltd.

Marta B. Calás and Linda Smircich, 'Voicing Seduction to Silence Leadership', *Organization Studies*, 12/4 (1991), 567–602. Reprinted by permission of the authors.

# Contents

# List of Figures

# List of Tables

# Abbreviations

| | |
|---|---|
| ANT | Actor-Network Theory |
| CEO | chief executive officer |
| GM | General Managers |
| INSEAD | European Institute of Business Management |
| LPC | Least Preferred Co-worker |
| MIA | Montgomery Improvement Association |
| MLQ | Multifactor Leadership Questionnaire |
| MPI | Minnesota Multiphasic Personality Inventory |
| NAACP | National Association for the Advancement of Colored People |
| NACLO | National Association of Community Leadership Organizations |
| NASA | National Aeronautics and Space Administration |
| NIF | National Issues Forums |
| ROTC | Reserve Officer Training Corps |
| SCLC | Southern Christian Leadership Conference |

# List of Contributors

| | |
|---|---|
| **Bruce Avolio** | Center for Leadership Studies, Binghampton University, USA |
| **Bernard Bass** | Center for Leadership Studies, Binghampton University, USA |
| **Chester Barnard** | Former President of the New Jersey Bell Telephone Co.; he subsequently led the Rockefeller Foundation |
| **Marta Calás** | University of Massachusetts, USA |
| **Fred Fiedler** | University of Washington, USA |
| **John Gastil** | University of Wisconsin-Madison, USA |
| **Gary Gemmill** | Syracuse University, USA |
| **Dian Hosking** | Aston University, UK |
| **Andrew Kakabadse** | Cranfield University, UK |
| **Manfred Kets de Vries** | European Institute of Business Administrations (INSEAD), France |
| **Stephen Lilley** | Sacred Heart University, USA |
| **Tim McMahon** | University of Houston, USA |
| **Niccolò Machiavelli** | 1469–1527, Florentine politician and writer |
| **Andrew Myers** | Cranfield University, UK |
| **Judith Oakley** | Syracuse University, USA |
| **Vilfredo Pareto** | 1848–1923, Italian economist and political philosopher |
| **Ian Pears** | Author of *The Discovery of Paintings: The Growth of Interest in the Arts in England, 1680–1760* (1988): he is currently working on a history of nineteenth-century Paris |
| **Plato** | 428–347 BC, Greek philosopher, student of Socrates, and teacher of Aristotle |
| **Gerald Platt** | University of Massachusetts, USA |
| **Judy Rosener** | University of California, Irvine, USA |
| **Linda Smircich** | University of Massachusetts, USA |
| **Gilles Spony** | Cranfield University, UK |
| **Ralph Stogdill** | Former Professor Emeritus of Management Sciences at Ohio State University, USA |
| **Sun Tzu** | ?400–320 BC, Chinese military philosopher and strategist |

# Introduction

> In whatever direction a ship moves the flow of waves it cuts will always be noticeable ahead of it . . . When the ship moves in one direction there is one and the same wave ahead of it, when it turns frequently the wave ahead of it also turns frequently. But wherever it may turn there always will be the wave anticipating its movement. Whatever happens it appears that just that event was foreseen and decreed. Wherever the ship may go, the rush of water which neither directs nor increases its movement foams ahead of it, and at a distance seems not merely to move of itself but to govern the ship's movement also.
>
> (Tolstoy 1991: 1289)

## Reading Tolstoy's Wave

What is leadership? Tolstoy's bow-wave metaphor for leadership is an extremely fruitful but enigmatic answer: it suggests that leaders are mere figureheads, propelled by events which are beyond their control, even though it appears that events are controlled by them. It also suggests that views about leaders may themselves be subject to fashion and fads—that is, that we may consider certain kinds of leadership more appropriate for certain conditions or that what counts as leadership itself changes across space and time. One thing is clear: leaders are in front of those they lead—but the enigma surrounds the issue of whether they are pulling or being pushed by those behind them. The distinction is not just concerned with what leaders are doing but also with what followers are doing. Can you be a leader without followers? Do followers make leaders by acting as followers? Is the relationship between leading and following a virtuous/vicious circle or is it possible to specify that an action by one of the parties involved must logically precede the other? Bow waves/leaders may not have anything to do with the direction and speed of the vessel/organization, but does that mean that ships/organizations can move without creating a bow-wave leader? Leaders may not be logically necessary to organizational success, but have we become so accustomed to their existence that we can no longer think them away, even in a thought experiment? Even Dilbert's (Adams 1996) satirical view on leadership—nature's way of removing morons from the productive flow—implies that leadership is an essential element of life. Current research certainly suggests that leaders can make a difference to the performance of business organization, perhaps by as much as 10 per cent in annual earnings either way—which also suggests that 90 per cent has little to do with the particular leader in place. However, a 10 per cent change in fortunes for a business, hospital, charity, sports team, or army may be a considerable amount, particularly when the going gets tough (Useem 1996).

This collection of articles on leadership provides views on Tolstoy's enigmatic bow wave from different periods in time, different cultures, and different assumptions. It does not provide the answer to Tolstoy's enigma but it does provide a range of different ways of reading the question—or perhaps that should read 'riding the wave'. It is organized along thematic waves in order to develop—that is, impose—a degree of consistency upon the material. Anyone who has been studying leadership will know that it is an exponentially accelerating arena, though this does not mean we are getting ever nearer understanding what leadership is. In the 1980s there were, very roughly, five articles a day being published on leadership in the English language; by the 1990s this had doubled to ten a day. If this increase persists we shall run out of wood before we can see the tree.

The irony is that so many leaders appear to have led very well without ever reading a book on leadership. One implication of this is that leadership cannot be taught: either you can do it or you cannot. It would be strange if leadership was the only human skill that could not be enhanced through understanding and practice. Perhaps a reflection on musical talent can be considered as an equivalent; are not musical talent and leadership talent both innate gifts? Well, the former is not according to Howe, Davidson, and Sloboda (1996), for, despite the common assumption that some children are naturally talented and others simply incapable of ever learning a note, their research on 200 young musicians suggests that practice, not innate talent, makes perfect. Granted, we are not all going to be turned into professional musicians by a music course, nor world leaders through a leadership course, but this does not mean that one's skill as a leader cannot be improved, notably through practice. Granted some children do seem to be self-evidently better leaders than others from a very early age, though this does not mean they are born leaders, since it may derive from childhood experiences. Nor does it mean that such children grow up to retain whatever leadership skills they appear to have; we simply do not know enough about this to come down on one side of the debate or the other. Indeed, since what counts as leadership appears to change quite radically across time and space, as the waves of fortune and fashion wash across the world, even some kind of systematic and objective research at this point in time and space would not solve Tolstoy's enigmatic wave problem.

An initial reading of leadership material might tend to produce a list of traits, characteristics, and behaviours that leaders are supposed to have—though my preliminary attempt to reproduce the 'ideal' leader ran out of space on one side of paper after I had passed number 127 on the 'necessary-aspects-of-leadership' list. Another approach might be to list the polarities that tend to be generated in such an exercise. For example, such a list might contain any or all of the following binary opposites:

| | | |
|---|---|---|
| management | vs. | leadership |
| leadership | vs. | followership |
| task-oriented | vs. | people-oriented |
| born leaders | vs. | made leaders |
| theory X | vs. | theory Y |
| transactional | vs. | transformational |
| one best way | vs. | contingent |
| how to do it | vs. | what to do |
| doing the right things | vs. | doing the things right |
| essentialist | vs. | non-essentialist |
| taught | vs. | experiential learning |
| charismatic | vs. | ordinary |
| forceful | vs. | enabling |
| people | vs. | people and things |

Such lists are potentially infinite and I make no pretence that this one is either representative or even valid; the point is that we may well tend to perceive leadership in such oppositional terms and this may not be the most appropriate way to analyse or develop leadership (see Kaplan 1996 for an interesting approach to this issue).

An alternative to the 'bipolar-shopping-list' approach is to resort to the familiar $2 \times 2$ in an attempt to keep the variables down to a minimum so that some progress in understanding might be made at the cost of losing a considerable amount of data and complexity. Some of the $2 \times 2$s are reproduced in the articles below, but I want to generate yet another model so that the reader may have some grasp of where current research seems to be leading. The most significant divisions at present appear, at least to me, to be twofold. First, around the significance allocated to the individual, as opposed to the situation or context the individual is in. Secondly, and cross-cutting this division, is one rooted in the traditional split between objective and subjective assumptions about knowledge and data. The resulting model—which is grounded in positions along a continuum rather than opposites—does not encompass all positions nor all the current approaches, but it does represent a useful approach to leadership based on ideal types—heuristic extremes not typical cases. In other words, this is not the *best* way to see leadership, because it seems to me impossible to validate the claim that such a things exists. Rather, I am suggesting that this model encompasses epistemologically and methodologically different perspectives on leadership that should facilitate a greater understanding of the readings that follow. Since the readings are not based on the model, it would be foolhardy to assume that they fit neatly into any of the quadrants. However, it should be possible to make greater sense of the readings once the model is understood. In this instance the term 'essentialist' implies that we can acquire a definitive/objective account of the phenomenon under investigation; the term 'non-essentialist' implies this is not possible.

In the *trait* approach the 'essence' of the individual leader is critical but the context is not. In short, a leader is a leader under any circumstances, and it is more than likely that such traits are part of the individual's genetic make-up—otherwise the circumstances of the situation that faced the individual at some time in his or her life would have had an influence upon his or her leadership 'traits'. This kind of model implies that organizations should concern themselves with the selection of leaders rather than their develop-

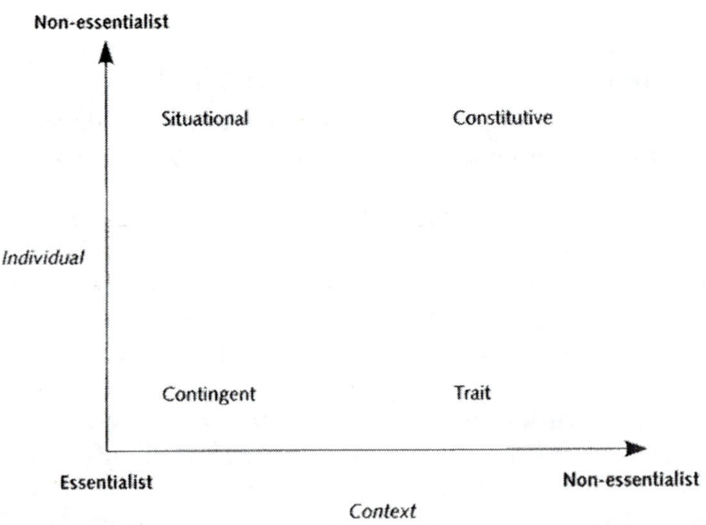


**Fig. 0.1.** Essentialist and non-essentialist leadership.

ment, though traits can, presumably, be honed, just as one's singing can be improved through training or one's athletic ability can be improved. However, since—in this approach—you cannot 'make a silk purse out of a sow's ear', there is no hope for those of us not born with certain gifts or talents for leadership.

In the *contingency* approach both the essence of the individual and the content are knowable and critical. Here one would expect individuals to generate an awareness of their own leadership skills and of the context so that they can compute the degree of alignment between themselves and the context. Where the permutation of the two suggests a high level of alignment—for instance, where a strong leader and a crisis situation coincide—then the leader should step into the breach, only to step out when the situation changes and the context is no longer conducive to their vigorous style. Self-awareness and situational analysis are the two developmental areas for such approaches to concentrate upon.

The third variant, the *situational* approach, reproduces the essentialist position with regard to the context—certain contexts demand certain kinds of leadership; however, in this model the leader may be flexible enough to generate a repertoire of styles to suit the particular situation. In effect, the leader's actions and behaviour change to suit the situation. The consequent development work required is both in terms of situational analysis and in terms of expanding the variety or versatility of the leader.

The final, and most recent, model here, the *constitutive* approach, receives most attention because it is the newest and least understood (see Grint 1995: 124–61). It is derived from constructivist theories in social science and, in its most radical formats, rejects the notion of essences entirely (see Grint and Woolgar, forthcoming). That is to say, it rejects the idea that we can ever have an objective account of either individual or situation because all such accounts are derived from linguistic reconstructions; they are not, in effect, transparent reproductions of the truth. Instead the approach suggests that what the situation and the leader actually are is a consequence of various accounts and interpretations, all of which vie for domination. Thus we know what a leader or situation is actually like only because some particular version of him, her, or it has secured prominence. The relativism at the heart of the approach does not mean that all interpretations are equal—and that what the leader/context is, is wholly a matter of the whim of the observer—but that some interpretations appear to be more equal than others. For example, my account of a popular individual may be that he or she is an incompetent charlatan, but if the popularity of this person rests upon the support of more powerful 'voices' (including material resources), then my negative voice will carry little or no weight. The critical issue for this approach, then, is not what the leader or the context is 'really' like, but what are the processes by which these phenomena are constituted into successes or failures, crises or periods of calm, and so on. For example, when the chief executive officer (CEO) declares an impending crisis based on information that must remain confidential to prevent the crisis deepening, how are we mere ignorant subordinates to evaluate the claim? When governments declare military 'incidents' to be 'the mother of all victories', how are we to judge? Do we ever really know what happened? When the media represent leaders as villains or heroes, do we really know enough about them to agree or disagree? The point of this approach, therefore, is to suggest that we may never know what the true essence of the leader or the situation actually is and must often base our actions and beliefs on the accounts of others from whom we can (re)constitute our version of events. This does not mean that leaders are simply at the hands of their followers who attribute to their leader whatever they want. It may be that leaders 'fail' to deliver the charismatic performance we expect from them—but what counts as a charismatic performance is still an issue for debate. Nor does it mean that the powerful institutions that control information in our societies can promote and sustain individuals who are blatantly incompetent—though a quick look at the current crop suggests I may be completely wrong here. But it does mean we may only ever achieve an opaque account of 'the truth'. In terms of leadership development, the approach suggests that the ancient study of rhetoric provides one significant element of leadership training since it may be persuasive powers that hold the key to leadership success. Political networking, interpersonal skills, material wealth, and negotiating skills are the hallmark of this approach, and it should be no surprise that it is with Plato, allegedly an arch-exponent of rhetorical skill, that this reader begins, and with some of the theoretical developments from this kind of approach that the reader ends.

However, before we enter the core of the book proper, it is worth reconsidering in a little detail the work of Heifetz, since it is this work that is probably stimulating the most interest today. Heifetz, both in his book *Leadership Without Easy Answers* (1994), and in his leadership courses at Harvard, combines a relatively novel theme—about forcing subordinates to reflect upon their influence in the achievement of goals—and a relatively old theme—about the difference between situations that require mechanistic responses (technical issues) and those that require 'adaptive' responses (leadership). In so far as Heifetz also distinguishes between the exercise of 'authority' and the exercise of 'leadership'—sometimes labelled power derived from formal role and power derived from informal role—Heifetz also hinges his ideas on a distinction familiar to Weber and many others since. Hence, for Heifetz, the critical issue is whether people have the ability and skill or whatever to intervene in situations that are not routine and in which the answer cannot be derived from previous experience, and where part of the role of the leader is to reflect the problem-solving back into the followers. In sum, the leader must not take on the mantle of magician him or herself. Heifetz is one of the few leadership writers that has made a significant contribution to the debate, and I have no doubt that the refusal of leaders to own the problem is simultaneously the best way to create organizational learning and responsibility, and the best way for leaders to make themselves unpopular with followers whose expectations are premised upon more traditional notions of leadership. Storr (1996), for example, notes how 'gurus'—such as Bhagwan Shree Rajneesh, Jim Jones, and Shoko Asahara—appear to own the problem of purpose and provide meaning for their followers in a way that galvanizes their physical and mental power as well as enervating their critical moral faculties. On the other hand, if we pursue the constitutive model of leadership then it should be apparent that what counts as a situation requiring adaptive or technical work is not something that inheres in the situation itself but is, rather, the consequence of persuasive accounts of the situation. In other words, it may not be that leadership is required when the situation demands it—a derivative of the situational and contingency approaches we have already discussed—but that it is leadership which constitutes the situation as one requiring adaptive or technical work. Hence, the question is less one of being able to analyse the situation and take whatever action is necessary and more one of taking action to provide an analysis of the situation in which adaptive or technical work appears the most appropriate. Let us explore an example to clarify this problem.

Suppose to a tribe that was constantly at war with its neighbour a new invader appeared. Should the response be such that the invader is deemed to have been beaten back by conventional means then we have what Heifetz would call an exercise in authority rather than leadership and in technical rather than adaptive work—the tried-and-tested contingency plan for invaders which has always worked in the past, worked again. Now suppose that the following year the invader reappears and the leader of the tribe fails to respond appropriately—manifest in a successful incursion by the invaders—this is the point at which an exercise of leadership is needed, quite possibly from someone without formal authority, and where adaptive rather than technical work is required. In this scene William Wallace now emerges from an obscure position to lead the Scottish nation against the invading English after the conventional figures of Scottish authority failed. So what was initially a form of technical work moved into a form of adaptive work *when the situation required it*. Thus, in Heifetz's approach, it is the *situation* which deems whether technical or adaptive work is required—though whether the appropriate work is executed depends upon the individuals not upon the situation: there is no situational determinism in here.

Now let us rerun the film to see where the constitutive models offer a different perspective on the scene. In this case we have—to the Scots—the all-too-familiar English invasion. But this time it is not the situation that self-evidently cries out for adaptive work; instead it is the participants who persuade their colleagues that either adaptive work or technical work is necessary. In short, we see William Wallace persuading his Scottish colleagues that the situation is a crisis, and a novel crisis at that, where adaptive not technical work is needed. At this point one hears the all-too-common division between: 'Crisis? What crisis?' and the oppositional cry of 'Run' or 'Fight' and so on. On the one hand, the calmness of the technical approach steadies the fears of the troops as the enemy approaches. On the other hand, the very same calmness instils a degree of misplaced confidence that merely increases the likelihood of defeat. To reiterate, the point here is whether the situation determines what the action should be or whether the rhetorical action of the participants constitutes the situation—from which further action may follow. Thus Dunkirk, during the Second World War, is either a situation of gross incompetence and a humiliating defeat for the British army or it is a miraculous example of true British character in the face of impossible odds. The point is not that the situation of Dunkirk must, objectively, have been one or the other but that what Dunkirk was is a consequence of the way leaders constituted the events. In effect, Churchill's rhetoric, combined with close control over the media—including patriotic self-control—ensured that the Dunkirk 'situation' became the Dunkirk 'miracle' and not the Dunkirk 'humiliation'.

Let us now take an opposite tack and consider a business situation that was 'obviously' one where certain kinds of leadership were appropriate but were not taken. We now travel forward fifty years to 1991 and we have left Churchill's 'Never before have so many owed so much to so few' rhetoric at the nadir of British hopes, to pick up Gerald Ratner, owner and CEO of what was then the largest jewellery chain in the world with 34 per cent of the market. Here is Ratner talking about Ratner's business philosophy at the apex, rather than the nadir, of his organization's fortunes:

> We also do this nice sherry decanter, it's cut glass and it comes complete with six glasses on a silver plated tray that your butler could bring you in and serve you drinks on. And it only costs £4.95. People say to me: 'how can you sell this for such a low price?' I say: 'Because it's total crap' (laughter) . . . We even sell a pair of earrings for under a pound; gold earrings as well. Some people say: 'that's less than a prawn sandwich at Marks and Spencers', but I have to say that the sandwich will probably last longer!' (laughter) (BBC2 1995)

Now the point might be that the situation—a speech to business leaders—is not the place to deliver self-mocking humour of this variety; indeed, it seems an act of consummate folly, of appalling leadership, that, in Ratner's words, 'cost the company a few hundred million pounds, £100 million, £200 million? Personally it cost me everything' (ibid.). Assuming this is not the consequence of some kind of commercial death wish, is there anything that the constitutive variant can explain which 'common sense' and situational analysis cannot? Well perhaps. After all, it is the case that Ratner had told these jokes on numerous occasions to similar audiences for the previous four years and they had been printed in the *Financial Times* in December 1987—over three years before his leadership 'mistake'. It may be, therefore, that what is critical is not what the situation is but what it is made into by those with the power to make it—in this case the popular newspaper writers and editors who deemed it appropriate to splash the jokes on the front of their papers for several days after. Here, then, is a situation that appears to be identical—Ratner has used these jokes before in public but this time it backfires, not because the situation is *actually* different, but because powerful people make the situation different through their actions; in effect, to misquote a current insurance advert, they make a crisis out of a drama.

To sum up, the constitutive approach does not involve doubts about the moral basis of Heifetz's approach—leaders do appear to make unpopular decisions that, often with hindsight, can be justified as necessary. Nor does it deny the importance of leadership. However, it does assert that an epistemological question mark hangs over all of the issues. Thus, whether the situation is a crisis, whether the actions of the authority figure are appropriate actions for the situation, whether acts taken by anyone are acts of 'leadership' or not, and so on are issues that are contingent on the power of persuasive accounts and not contingent on objective or rational analysis. The consequence of this approach is to return us back to the beginning of the debate: it suggests that leadership is essentially interwoven with acts of persuasion; it does not offer a definitive account on the ethical aspects of leadership; indeed, it denies the plausibility of any account that deems itself to be definitive. It suggests we concentrate not just on what leaders do and what the situation is, but on the formative issues that lie behind these phenomena: how do we know what a leader does, and how are we persuaded that a situation is *X* and that a leader should do *Y* in such a situation? Finally, let me reaffirm that this does not mean that leadership is whatever anyone wants it to be; it is what certain powerful 'voices' make it. All voices may be equal but some are more equal than others. To resume our ride with Tolstoy, it is not that leaders are those who identify the wave and ride it; rather, leaders are those that persuade us a wave is coming, who go out of their way to appear the most visible surfers to the onlookers, and whose actions are taken by the onlookers as actions appropriate for leaders to take.

In what follows the subject is sliced up into five different waves. These waves represent substantive or temporal seas of thought but they are by no means representative of all the many thousands of readings about leadership. Rather, they are intended to provide the reader with a cross-section of quite different theoretical and substantive approaches to the topic to demonstrate the wide diversity but also to impose some degree of coherence upon the diversity. Recently some excellent books on leadership have appeared but not in formats suitable for reconstruction within this edited collection. Readers seeking good single-authored introductions to leadership are advised to consider any or all of the following: Kouzes and Posner's *The Leadership Challenge* (1987), Heifetz's *Leadership Without Easy Answers* (1994), Gardner's *Leading Minds* (1995), and Wright's *Managerial Leadership* (1996).

## Reading the Leadership Silences

Inevitably in a collection like this only a minute proportion of material can be represented and several aspects of the debate have been omitted for reasons of length, cost, or direct relevance. However, before moving on to the selections proper I want to take a little time to 'speak for the silences'.

Much of our knowledge and many of our models of leadership are, like Sun Tzu's, drawn from the military. Precisely how such models relate to the world of business leadership or the leadership of nations or hospitals or schools is moot, and there have been many arguments that the military world of physical coercion and corporal punishment is simply irrelevant to an area where coercion is absent and volition is everything. However, military leadership is itself constrained by both of these. Dixon (1976: 214) notes that military officers 'are required to fulfil incompatible roles. They are expected to show initiative, yet remain hemmed in by regulations. They must be aggressive, yet never insubordinate. They must be assiduous in caring for their men, yet maintain an enormous social distance. They must know everything about everything, yet never appear intellectual.' Despite all these problems some military leaders are more successful than others, so what makes for this differentiation? For Dixon, timing is a critical issue, as is the leaders' catalytic effect upon followers, but a crucial difference between military and civilian leaders is the ability of the former to call upon a much greater level of legitimate, and sometimes illegitimate, sanctions to coerce followers who disobey. Yet, as I have argued elsewhere (Grint 1995: 222–5), individuals are almost always free to disobey authority—and suffer the consequences—but Dixon's point is that for the most part individuals do not recognize any freedom in some circumstances. The consequences of such authoritarian forms of leadership are not just that subordinate compliance may be secured but also that communication is very limited, to the extent that a considerable amount of information may never reach the decision-making authorities.

Despite the drawbacks of military leadership, Dixon still has to explain how a system that seems destined to fail actually succeeds. How can an amateur and autocratic leadership style have worked at all? His answer lies partly in the context of war: 'when the going gets tough, the tough get going' is the shorthand version of this situation in which the stress of combat induces a high level of dependency on the part of subordinates towards their leaders. Such an exchange relationship forms the basis of some versions of the transactional approach to leadership; in the military or crisis case this usually implies followers exchanging their own feelings of insecurity in return for the leader's securing high levels of power and status (see Burns 1978, Bass 1985). It is also the case that risk-takers are more likely to generate acquiescence amongst followers—a point confirmed by the casualty rate of front-line officers in most combat zones, which is almost inevitably higher than that of either their own subordinates or indeed their superior officers back at base camp. Thirdly, Dixon stresses the utility of status differences between officers and troops as the latter follow traditional patterns of social subordination to their 'betters'. Thus, while line officers 'walk the talk' and take risks in an attempt to generate loyalty from below, the opposite, paradoxically, can secure the reputation of more senior officers, whose patent incompetence is masked by their invisibility. Of course, such methods for securing successful leadership may also operate in reverse, as 'risk-takers' are promoted beyond the point at which failure outweighs potential reward; or where blind obedience by subordinates leads to suicidal behaviour.

None of these points is restricted to military leadership. It is clear that leadership patterns under 'crisis' conditions are perceived differently from those that operate under 'normal' conditions, but it is not clear what counts as a crisis. It is also evident that successful leaders enhance their reputation by their visibility and less successful ones should adopt the opposite ploy. This is precisely Machiavelli's point written 500 years earlier, for 'men in general judge more by their eyes than their hands; for everyone can see but few can feel. Everyone sees what you seem to be, few touch upon what you are, and those few do not dare to contradict the opinion of the many who have the majesty of the state to defend them.' If, as Dixon implies, Haig could facilitate the elimination of a substantial proportion of the British army in the

First World War, and still not face condemnation from those he condemned, there must surely be something in the case for invisibility. Perhaps some leaders should 'talk the talk' rather than walk it.

Having distinguished between 'social specialist' and 'task specialist', Dixon goes on to consider how the combination of the two is both rare in the military and also extraordinarily effective when it does occur. Hence Wellington, Nelson, and Slim are hailed as twin specialists, while others, like Montgomery, can improvise by talking directly to troops whilst ignoring the best part of the officers. Dixon's notion of the 'contrived bonhomie' secured by Montgomery with 'cigarettes and numerous cap badges' is very reminiscent of Napoleon's claim that 'it was with such baubles [that] men are led. You imagine that an enemy is defeated by analysis? Never!' (quoted in Cronin 1971: 205).

However, Dixon takes the issue of leadership away from the individual and sets it firmly back in the lap of the institution. When the penalty for failure far exceeds the reward for success, the system induces a high level of anxiety that inhibits decision-making and risk-taking. We can see this not just in the military but in management everywhere. Whatever the rhetoric of risk-taking, most managers know only too well that risk-taking does not pay—the odds against it are simply too great. Even Japanese management systems struggle with this issue, for when the system of promotion is premised upon selecting out a minority of 'failures', rather than promoting a minority of 'successes', most players in the promotion game will recognize the utility of keeping 'your head down, your nose clean and your mistakes secret'.

But perhaps the most significant role model derived from the military is that of the superhero—the charismatic knight on a white charger in many European versions.

The approach taken by Manz and Sims (1991), despite their alternative label 'SuperLeadership', which actually suggests a return to the superhero, is roughly in the same arena as that of Bass and Avolio (this volume, Chapter 10), in that it seeks to establish whether a form of leader quite distinct from the 'white knight on a charger', beloved of unreconstructed male leaders, is appropriate. Suggesting there are four types of leadership model in existence, they begin by outlining the most traditional, or 'strong-man', view of leadership, in which the autocratic John Wayne character knocks a few heads together to coerce followers into line. This is contrasted to the 'transactor' type, a subsequent form that uses the powers of exchange, especially reward, to ensure subordinate compliance in a model drawn explicitly upon F. W. Taylor. The third form is the 'visionary hero', whose motivational vision ensures subordinate allegiance, rather than compliance—though we have already seen such charismatics in various formats before, and Manz and Sims accept some of these problems. Finally, they suggest that 'Superleadership' is the most appropriate form, in that it releases the energy and skills of the workforce and establishes a pattern of self-leadership that ensures that the problems of charismatic styles are avoided.

The rest of their argument is a prescriptive series of steps designed to show the reader, or at least putative superleader, how to acquire such skills. The first step, perhaps naturally, is to sort oneself out by adopting an array of self-oriented mechanisms to improve self-performance, such as self-goal-setting, self-reward, self-criticism, and so on, and by reconstructing one's approach to management in alignment with the overall strategy of superleadership. The second step is to model this form of behaviour, to 'walk the talk', and to demonstrate the tight link between rhetoric and deed to others. Thirdly, one should apply this to one's subordinates, embracing them in their own goal-setting and providing positive strokes (point four) wherever possible. Fifth is the development of reward and reprimand systems that encourage self-reward through intrinsic systems—not just, I assume, because extrinsic rewards actually cost money, but because such extrinsic rewards seem to deteriorate rather quicker than internally generated rewards. It is also important to discourage punishment for mistake-making, since this inhibits the organization learning from such errors and teaches the individual responsible for the error to bury it wherever possible. Finally, Manz and Sims suggest that teamwork and a self-leading culture need to be promoted if the system is to become self-sustaining. The whole message is summarized in the poem by Lao-tzu:

> A leader is best
> When people barely know he exists
> Not so good when people obey and acclaim him
> Worse when they despise him
> But of a good leader, who talks little,
> When his work is done, his aim fulfilled,
> They will say:
> We did it ourselves.
>
> (Quoted in Manz and Sims 1991: 35)

Or, as Frank Sinatra sang in a more individualistic culture, and 1,300 years later: 'I did it my way.'

This apparent devolvement (or desertion—depending on your perspective) of responsibility has become the new standard in contemporary models of leadership, but this contrasts very sharply with what is perhaps the most traditional model of all—the charismatic leader. Charismatics have long been the focus of much research into leadership, with Max Weber (1968: 241–55), the eminent German sociologist, providing the basic framework. During the 1980s, charismatic leadership returned with a vengeance, complete with all the accoutrements of biblical charismatics, including: visions, missions, and zealot-like disciples. Bryman's (1992) review of charismatic authority refers to this contemporary form of leadership which articulates a 'vision' and relentlessly pursues it despite resistance. Securing commitment to such a vision is a principle aim of leaders, but Bryman is quick to point out the dangers of such visions becoming nightmares as the relentless pursuit proceeds irrespective of claims that the vision is either unachievable or not worth achieving. This is a particularly difficult issue for leaders who, having been weaned on the notion of 'relentless pursuit', are now asked to consider whether a degree of circumspection might be in order to prevent a relentless pursuit turning into an obsessive and pointless rendition.

Bryman raises a different issue to resolve the 'relentless leader' and it involves a much greater emphasis on teamwork, especially amongst managers and leaders. Accepting that leadership and management are the opposite sides of the same coin, he argues that many visions can be achieved only through the actions of many managers and not simply through the exhortations of individual leaders. One reason why the individual leader's role has been overemphasized is, according to Bryman, the significance of the research method used. For instance, if researchers insist on focusing upon individuals and ignore the role of the team, then it is hardly surprising that the team's significance is devalued. This is an example where knowledge 'constitutes', rather than 'discovers', the subject.

Continuing in this vein, Bryman argues that, while the contingency theories of the 1980s were atheoretical and empirically suspect, the new leadership studies seem to be reverting to the 'one-best-way' approach of Scientific Management, as universal principles for success flow from the likes of Peters and Waterman (1982). The latter is certainly the case; however, it should be noted that at the root of the contingency approach is simply a more sophisticated 'one-best-way' approach, because each contingency should, in theory, generate not a series of potential leadership styles but the 'one' style deemed most appropriate by the situation. Of course, the emphasis then shifts to an accurate interpretation of the situation, but the point remains the same: there is only one best way for each situation.

The assumption that crisis generates a requirement for a charismatic leader is, of course, anything but new—as the Churchill case demonstrates. However, in pursuit of the constitutive model, we still have to ask: what counts as a crisis? At what point does the glass move from being half full to half empty? If Britain's wartime crisis thrust Churchill to the leadership position, why did this happen in May 1940 and not September 1939; and what crisis was it that brought him back to power in 1951? Bryman suggests, in his account of Roberts and Bradley's (1988) research, that charisma is not a personal possession but is dependent upon the production of certain 'effects' that are themselves dependent upon conditions and social relationships. If this is not the case, if charisma really is an attribute of individuals (though how one can demonstrate charisma in the absence of another person is difficult to comprehend), then even the charismatics should be approached only from a distance because they can disempower other (non-charismatic) people.

It is also worth considering the way leader behaviour is affected by external normative pressures. Adopting an institutional model of organizations, Bryman suggests that leaders incorporate actions and behaviours from which they believe they can derive legitimacy. For example, in a world driven by 'visions' and 'mission statements', no leader could possibly operate in today's environment without a vision. That the vision may prove to be unachievable or irrelevant or positively counter-productive is not important; what matters is that leaders perceive that the wider community requires such actions on the part of leaders (see Scott and Meyer 1994; cf. Donaldson 1995). Thus, for example, we ordinarily expect leaders to be confident rather than diffident, and there are frequent press stories that attempt to relate successful leadership amongst humans to the apparent equivalent in non-human societies. For example, in June 1996, 'Monkey scientists' found the 'answer' to the problem then facing the Republicans in the USA: why do Americans appear to prefer Clinton to Dole, despite the investigations into Clinton's character that implied voters should support Dole rather than the Clinton? The answer, according to the aforementioned eminent monkey scientists, relates to the chemical stimulation that dominant and confident males secure from appearing before their followers. In effect, it is the public presentation of confidence by leaders, which is itself derived from the positive feedback received from followers, that operates in a virtuous circle (Nethaway 1996).

Finally, Bryman returns to reconsider Weber's account of charisma in which only the remarkable and exceptional devotion of the followers to a leader counted as charisma. Within this tighter definition all notions of 'degrees of charisma' are disposed of, for either a leader is charismatic or he or she is not. However, it may be significant to note that most alleged charismatics have a habit of dying young—before their charisma wears out, or rather, before their followers decide that they were mistaken. The trick for budding charismatics is not to proclaim themselves as such but to take high-level risks—and to be successful. This surely is the golden rule of all leaders: you can be whatever you want—as long as you are successful first.

The final 'silence' I want to address takes the latter point and considers its implications for leadership in a very practical sense: what do you have to do and be to achieve leadership? In other words, if we accept that being successful is the golden rule, how do you get to be successful, and does this mean we must follow Machiavelli into the abyss of immorality if we want immortality?

Latour (1988) takes issue with those who criticize leaders for their 'immoral' acts but praise the achievements of the very same leaders, and asserts that the rules Machiavelli sets up transcend the (contested) difference between moral and immoral action by placing the end—continuing power—as the arbiter of action. Hence, since the world that Machiavelli inhabits is immoral, the only way to maintain a modicum of morality is to use whatever means are necessary to retain power. In effect, the distinction between moral and immoral actions is imposed upon the action by the observer; it does not inhere within the acts themselves. This, of course, is a similar kind of externalist approach to leadership as that considered by Lilley and Platt's account (this volume, Chapter 16) of Martin Luther King. But Latour takes the analysis one stage further by considering how Machiavelli could have achieved power in the face of such duplicitous 'allies'. Latour's approach, known as Actor-Network Theory (see Grint and Gill 1995; Grint and Woolgar, forthcoming 1997), suggests that Machiavelli's position would be much stronger were he to recruit more non-humans to his cause. Indeed, Latour argues that the very division between humans and non-humans is itself derived from the duplicity of the analyst and is not an element appertaining to the 'real' world (see Latour 1995 for a longer statement along these lines). The consequence is that leaders must weave a 'seamless web' of heterogeneous allies so that the weaknesses of all are constrained by the strength of the relationship. In other words, the issue is not how strong are the various elements on each side but how strong are the relationships which keep the side together?

Latour then takes this model and deploys it against the likes of Marx (1954) and Braverman (1974), whose class-based model of social change inevitably assumed that all technical developments would be contrary to the interests of the working class and favourable to the interests of the capitalists' class. The problem for this entire approach is that it is overly concerned with one aspect of the relationship: capitalists are concerned not with class wars but with individual survival. Hence, the modern prince, as Latour calls the individual capitalist, has to fight enemies on several fronts simultaneously; resistant workers, competing capitalists, demanding stockholders, and so on. So while Marx praises capitalists for their technical inventiveness, he decries them for their exploitive social relationships. For Latour's modern princes, technology is just one more temporary and recalcitrant ally in the war of competition against other capitalists. The consequence, therefore, may be that workers' lives are lightened by technology—*if* it appears that such a strategy will secure a competitive advantage for one capitalist over another. Of course, the opposite may also occur and workers' lives may be ruined by technology, but the issue is determined not by the technology but by the strategic intent of the capitalists as they weave their web of alliances to secure their ultimate aim. To do that a series of 'fronts' have to be opened and sustained simultaneously, including the class front, but also involving their own collaborators, other princes, consumers, and non-humans.

Latour's ultimate point is to deny the utility of postulating either social strategies or technical strategies as critical, since every strategy necessarily embodies both: naked, friendless, money-less, and technology-less leaders are unlikely to prove persuasive. However, even with all the necessary accoutrements of leadership, the particular project may end up seriously different from the original project envisaged as leaders are forced to make compromises and trade-offs with various 'enrolled' actors (usually called 'actants' in Actor-Network Theory to include non-human actors) to ensure some form of progress. In effect, then, leadership should not be reduced to the actions of the leader, nor even to the relations between the leader and the led. Instead, leadership should be concerned with the mobilization of resources of all forms. If the word 'leader' means to move in a new direction, then let it end this particular journey through leadership by setting off anew with a different perspective: don't trace the leader, don't even trace the followers; trace the mobilization.

# I. CLASSICAL LEADERSHIP

In temporal terms the first, or Classical Leadership,wave, reproduces selections from four of the most influential writers from widely separated times: Plato, Sun Tzu, Machiavelli, and Pareto. Only Sun Tzu appears to embody anything recognizably liberal and humanitarian in his writings, though perhaps the most despised writer of all, Machiavelli, was neither as authoritarian as some have suggested nor as hostile to the participation of followers. However, one thing is clear: all four write against backgrounds of war or conflict or impending strife, and it is crucial to remember that no authors write in a political vacuum. The implication is not necessarily that these people are only relevant to understanding leadership under crisis conditions but rather that our interpretations of their messages tend to change across time. This is particularly appropriate for writers such as Machiavelli, long regarded as either an immoralist or as a writer whose ideas should be read only against a backdrop of immorality. However, it is also possible to read writings in quite different ways.

The first reading is taken from Plato's *The Republic*, probably the first serious attempt to construct a systematic theory of politics and leadership. Why start a book about contemporary leadership with a work that is well over 2,000 years old? Well there are some interesting resonances that are immediately apparent.

First, Plato thought the concept of a democratic society was irredeemably problematic and developed a critique that would not look out of place in the speeches of some of today's business leaders, especially those intent on resisting moves to introduce works councils and any other forms of participative management. Plato introduces one of the most enduring of anti-democratic images in the 'large and dangerous animal' otherwise known as the ship's crew, or the mob: the majority. Plato attempts to persuade us that it is self-evident that the captain of the boat is the only one to be trusted with its control, since only the captain has the necessary knowledge. The crew, without the expertise to recognize a true expert, are easily corrupted and, inevitably, the ship will founder as impostor after impostor assumes the helm on the grounds of public popularity rather than navigational skill. In Plato's alternative, the subordinate groups would not be allowed to challenge the philosopher rulers, or guardians, to ensure the safety of the 'ship'.

Secondly, women are noticeable in Ancient Athens by their virtual absence or their presence in particular occupations deemed suited to their 'natural' affectations. In other words, women act as service providers to the male leaders and citizens of Ancient Athens. Democratic or otherwise, Athenian women were not citizens of the state and therefore not held to be in contention for positions of leadership. Plato, however, did argue that some women might become guardians of his alternative society (if any appeared with 'suitable' characteristics).

Thirdly, Plato's justifications for the selection of leadership are similar in form, if not content, to the current development of managerial expertise and generate a particularly significant debate concerning the nature of leadership as a skill to be learned. In particular, Plato argued that, although the general (male) citizenry seemed to think it rational to bow before economic and occupational expertise—such as shipbuilders or doctors, for example—they simultaneously deemed it rational that no one, and therefore everyone, was an expert in moral knowledge. Hence the issue that Plato held dearest—the philosopher's knowledge of truth, justice, morality, and so forth—constituted a free for all where the loudest, but not the clearest, voices prevailed. We may see here a similar line of argument to today's educational sceptic for whom leadership cannot be acquired through knowledge but can be demonstrated only through the Darwinian forum for the survival of the fittest. Yet, paradoxically, Plato is particularly disparaging about the Sophists and Isocrates for whom training in Rhetoric, the art of public speaking, was a foremost virtue. The issue, then, was not over *whether* leadership skills could be taught but what they were being taught *for*. For Plato the teaching of superficial skills like public speaking merely made the possibility of the wrong leader securing even greater control. This was even more dangerous given that the leader's role was not just to protect the ship but to establish where it should go. Far better to develop the base for a wise ruler than to inculcate the tricks of the trade to potential malcontents.

Fourthly, the consequence of the success of Isocrates and his ilk is that society is controlled, not just by non-philosophers—unwise but popular fools—but by those who, in other circumstances, would prove to be philosopher kings themselves. Here Plato asserts that the social aspects of organizations are sufficient to swamp any individual aspect, such that where a particular culture prevails it will not be possible to generate leadership premised upon an alternative and contradictory culture. Hence, when the individual with the requisite qualities for leadership (courage, self-discipline, and a philosophical approach) is connected to what we normally consider 'the good things of life' (good looks, wealth, physical strength, being well connected, and all the rest) within an environment that professes to please the mob, the consequence is fatal for all. For:

What do you imagine he'll do in this situation . . . especially if he happens to come from a wealthy and noble family within a powerful state, and is also good looking and well built? Don't you think he'll be filled with unrealizable hopes, and will expect to be one day capable of managing the affairs not only of Greece, but of the non-Greek world as well? In these circumstances won't he get ideas above his station and puff himself up with affectation and baseless, senseless pride? . . . Those are the powerful factors which ruin and corrupt anyone who is, by nature, best suited for the best occupation—and such people are rare anyway, as we said. Moreover, these are the men who have the potential to do the greatest harm to communities and individuals, and the greatest good, if that's the course they happen to take. An insignificant person, however, never has any effect of any significance on any individual or society.

From such a sceptical position Plato asserts that only two alternatives exist: either 'true' philosophers must keep their heads down and refuse to be drawn into political life (a position Plato regarded as inevitable after the democratically inspired execution of Socrates for impiety—encouraging disaffection amongst the young—although Plato did serve in the Athenian army and as a member of the Council of 500 which organized the meetings of the general Assembly.) or the whole of society must be reconstructed such that philosophers become the rulers, while a military class protects society, and a third class engages in economic production. However, this alternative would indeed drag many of today's business (and political) leaders under, for the only way to maintain integrity is to seek pleasures 'the mind feels of its own accord, and has nothing to do with the pleasure which reach the mind through the agency of the body'. In this brave new world the philosopher rulers would have no property and hold wives and children in common.

While Plato wrestled with leadership during a period of internecine conflict between Greek city states, Sun Tzu contemplated very similar problems at about the same time but on the other side of the world. Like Plato, Sun Tzu regarded the principle of one person, one job as crucial to success—hence his attack upon political leaders who interfere with military strategy. Sun Tzu's *The Art of War* was written sometime during the so-called 'Warring States' period of ancient China, between the fifth and the third centuries BC, as the Chou Dynasty disintegrated amidst civil war. In other words, it is, more or less, a direct contemporary of Plato's work. The oldest known military text, its aphorisms are attributed to Sun Tzu but may not have been written by him but by his subsequent pupils and admirers, some of whom make up the other voices in the text. As a successful military philosopher, Sun Tzu embodied a Taoist approach to war in which apparent paradoxes are reconciled within an approach rooted in balance. Although widely read in China, and translated into Japanese by the eighth century AD, the first European translation was in French in 1772, and the first English version was published in 1905.

The aphorisms are, on the whole, simultaneously and unambiguously sensible as well as being obscure. Overall the doctrine does not glorify war but denounces those who seek it; it details not tactics to promote it but strategies to avoid it—or to conclude it as quickly as possible. It promotes, therefore, the kind of philosophy popularized by David Carradine in the Kung Fu movies, where the way of peace is always sought in preference to violence—but, when there is no option, the violence is executed with the minimum effort and maximum effect. Indeed, one of the voices in the text, Li Ch'üan, was himself a famous martial artist living in the same area as Bodhidharma who allegedly brought the martial art to the Shaolin Temple, where it is still practised today. This underlying philosophy generates a hierarchy of strategies which are always premised on avoidance as the first strategy and face-to-face violence as the last. Thus, the best way to defeat an enemy is to foil the enemy's plots. If this fails, one should ruin their alliances. If this cannot succeed, one must attack the enemy, and only if this is impossible should one engage in the most expensive form of warfare: sieges. The links between conflict and medicine in this philosophy are demonstrated not just in the combination of the two in Tai Chi but also in the hierarchy of approaches to medicine. Given the choice, one should keep healthy to avoid medical problems, but if this is insufficient one should avoid coming into contact with diseases. If disease has already taken hold, then medicines should be taken and surgery should be used only as a last resort.

Beyond the links to medicine there are many business lessons drawn from *The Art of War*. The most recent addition to the interpreters of Sun Tzu is Donald G. Krause's *The Art of War for Executives* (1995); Krause reduces the work to 'ten principles for competitive success: learn to fight; do it right; expect the worse; burn the bridges; pull together; show the way; know the facts; seize the day; do it better; and keep them guessing'. As ever there is rather more to it than the list, but the significant point is how fresh and appropriate some of the aphorisms seem to be today. Many of these are not covered in the quoted extract but they include such points as 'seeking victory in the shortest possible time with the least effort and least cost in casualties to the *enemy*'. At first this seems a strange piece of advice, whether for war or for business: if you have your enemy/competitor on the run, then why let up? Sun Tzu, however, is clear that, unless you can eliminate your enemy—and need not fear reprisals of any kind—then one should provide a golden bridge to allow your enemy to escape. In the words of Tu Mu: 'It is a military doctrine that an encircling force must leave a gap to show the surrounded troops there is a way out, so that they will not be determined to fight to the death' (*The Nine Varieties of Ground*, 22). This is most appropriate for those negotiations between unions and management, or between managers, where it is certain (a) that you cannot remove the opponent completely, and (b) that, when the wheel of fortune turns, then they will have the upper hand. At that point, if you have not demonstrated magnanimity in victory, if you have prevented them from saving face in defeat, they will surely come looking for revenge.

The opposite of this holds for your own side, and images of burning boats are replete within the text. In the same paragraph Tu Mu continues: 'Now, if I am in encircled ground, and the enemy opens a road in order to tempt my troops to take it, I close this means of escape so that my officers and men will have a mind to fight to the death' (ibid.). One might interpret this as implying that the development of a crisis is a necessary (but not sufficient) step to generate the high levels of commitment currently sought by management. Only where one can construct what Cole (1980) called a 'community of fate' is it likely that subordinates will be willing to exert themselves above and beyond the call of the wage packet. Relatedly, this commitment from subordinates must be based on perceived justice and reasonableness on their part, not commitment constructed through terror. Only the former kind of commitment will ensure loyalty to the organization when times are difficult, but this form of commitment also includes a commitment to speak out against injustices and inefficiencies; it is not blind obedience to an ideal body or a body of ideals. Yet the central message of the *Art of War* is fundamentally about the role of leadership for: 'The responsibility for a martial host of a million lies in one man. He is the trigger of its spirit' (*Manœuvre*, 20).

At first glance it looks as though Machiavelli and Sun Tzu have absolutely nothing in common, except an interest in leadership and direct experience of war. However, it is often the case that we treat those people who hold a mirror up to our own behaviour with the utter contempt that would have Shakespeare mumble that '(she) doth protest too much, methinks' (*Hamlet*, III. 2. ii. 240). 'A handbook for gangsters' is how Bertrand Russell described Machiavelli's *The Prince*, and we might take Napoleon's comment, that it was 'the only book worth reading', as confirmation of Russell's position. Yet Machiavelli's aim was not to provide the veritable mobsters' bible but to get his readers, and leaders in particular, to look more carefully at what they did and how success was achieved and failure avoided in a way that Sun Tzu would clearly have recognized, if not necessarily approved of.

The first draft of *The Prince* was written in 1513 so Machiavelli's text needs to be contextualized against a background of civil war, external military intervention, and the need to impress his potential employers. It is, just as much as Marx and Engels's *Communist Manifesto*, a polemic, not a cool and detached review of the world. In this immoral world Machiavelli's plea to leadership is not to act immorally but to consider the inefficacy of acting morally in an immoral world. It is an attack upon the pacifist in a world at war, not a celebration of tyranny: 'for a man who wishes to profess goodness at all times will come to ruin among so many who are not good. Hence it is necessary for a prince who wishes to maintain his position to learn how not to be good, and to use this knowledge or not to use it according to necessity.' In this context he praises Cesare Borgia, who 'was considered cruel; none the less, his cruelty had brought order to Romagna, united it, restored it to peace and obedience. If we examine this carefully, we shall see that he was more merciful than the Florentine people, who, in order to avoid being considered cruel, allowed the destruction of Pistoia'. For Machiavelli it might seem that a leader must do whatever is necessary to protect him or herself, but this is far from his intention. His advice is not that the end justifies the means but that 'one must consider the final result'. As his more detached work, *The Discourses*, makes considerably clearer, leadership should be concerned with leading the corporate body of the state not the body of the corporate leader. Moreover, it is not the case that the end justifies any means but that a good end justifies any means. The question, of course, is what is a good end? In *The Discourses* this appears to be the good of the citizens but in *The Prince* it often seems to be more akin to whatever the prince thinks is good. Of course, since the prince is in a better position than most to determine what counts as good the prince has an immediate advantage and Machiavelli is keen to point out the role that appearances play in the development of a strong leader. While 'everyone sees what you seem to be, few touch upon what you are, and those few do not dare to contradict the opinion of the many who have the majesty of the state to defend them'. Leaders, then, must be proactive in the construction of their own image.

Machiavelli's approach to leadership does not swirl around the leader alone but is critically located in the body politic itself. For all his concern that 'it is much safer to be feared than to be loved when one of the two must be lacking', he is keen for leaders to avoid being hated. And although he appears to despise the strength of the bonds of love, he is well aware that 'the goodwill' of the people is of immense significance, partly because leaders cannot trust mercenaries whose loyalty is merely tied by the cash nexus (an interesting reflection on the long-term significance of outsourcing perhaps?), and partly because a prince alone has no strength. Only by forging alliances with other princes (partnerships?) and by the use of technology (forts and artillery), and only by disorganizing the competition, will the prince survive.

Five other points are worth remembering when trying to examine the significance of Machiavelli's writings in contemporary society. First, that only expanding communities are likely to survive—an argument for economic growth that clashes with radical green assumptions about equilibrium. Secondly, that princes should avoid injuring those who are critical to their own survival (too late to take heed, Mrs Thatcher). Thirdly, that the significance of religion (corporate culture) lies not in the truth of the ideas but in their effects in maintaining control. Fourthly, his perception of nature 'as a woman' who must be forcefully controlled is clearly at odds with the contemporary shifts with regard to both nature and women. Finally, Machiavelli rails against determinists and fatalists of all varieties in favour of free will, or at least the free will of the brave and able, those with *virtù*, for *virtù vince fortuna* (bravery/ ability wins over fortune). However, he does not imply that we are free to do whatever we like, because another force provides a counter-effect: for 'fortune is the arbiter of one half of our actions, but that still leaves the control of the other half, or almost that, to us . . . From this results that which I have said, that two men, working in opposite ways, can produce the same outcome, and of two men working in the same fashion one achieves his goal and the other does not'. This admission of luck as a crucial distributor of success and failure (an issue on which most management writers are notoriously silent) is linked to, but not subverted by, the importance of contextually contingent behaviour. This also explains why, 'if a man governs himself with caution and patience, and the times and conditions are turning in such a way that his policy is a good one, he will prosper; but if the time and conditions change he will be ruined because he does not change his method of procedure'. Here Machiavelli introduces the dual strategies of the lion and the fox: the (animal-like) lion succeeds by force but force is insufficient against traps and here the (human-like) fox succeeds—but the fox is defenceless against the wolf. The prince, therefore, must approximate the ways of the centaur—half-beast and half-man—if he is to survive. But beware all leaders: the dice are loaded against you.

Pareto adopted Machiavelli's distinctions between lions and foxes to develop what was called 'a gargantuan retort to Marx' (quoted in Hamilton 1975: 112)—that is, amongst other things, a denial of Marx's claim about the possibility of an egalitarian society. Élites not 'the people' were an inevitable part of human society for Pareto, and we can untangle in his argument strong resonances of the claims by Plato to the necessarily non-democratic essence of all organizations and the specific role and strategies of leaders—claims that Michels was later to expand into an 'Iron law of oligarchy': 'Who says organization says oligarchy.'

As Pareto bluntly puts it: 'Discounting exceptions, which are few and of short duration, there is everywhere a governing class, not large in membership, which maintains itself in power partly by force and partly by consent of the governed, who are very numerous . . . whatever the form of political system—the men who govern have, as a rule, a definite tendency to use their power to keep control of affairs and to abuse it in order to obtain personal advantages.'

Pareto argues that most of human action is irrational, or non-logical as he terms it, and can be traced to the *residues* or instinctual reflections which are psychological in location. Residues are common to all human societies and unchanging across space or time. However, *derivations*, the meanings which people give to their actions, are different across space and time, hence the apparent differences between societies.

The different forms of society, or, more particularly, the different forms of élite control, are rooted in two oppositional forms of residues: Class I and Class II. The mass tend to have Class II residues ('the instinct of the persistence of aggregates' is the clumsy phrase normally used); they are conservative and collective in nature, seeking stability. The élite tend to have Class I residues; those with the 'instinct of combination', they combine new ideas and are change-seekers. However, since societies do change Pareto argues that the change is derived from the changing composition of the élite, as élites with Class I attributes, the equivalent of Machiavelli's foxes, are ousted by élites with Class II attributes, Machiavelli's lions, and vice versa in a continuing cycle. Foxes achieve power by the wily manipulation of the mass and through the incremental attrition of the support for the inflexible lions' government. In contrast, lions come to power in swift and bloody *coups*, usually in an apparent defence of some particular moral system, but their very lack of imagination forces them to recruit foxes who, in turn, begin the erosion of the lions.

Beyond these divisions Pareto also divides the élites into A types who are idealists and B types who are self-promoters, with the subgroups B-*a* as power-hungry and B-*b* as money-hungry. The crucial aspect for Pareto is not just that élites always rule—and hence leadership is an inevitable element of all human organizations—but what kind of elites/leaders are in control? Once their sentiments are identified, then their opponents may begin to plan their (inevitable) downfall. Here Pareto touches another raw nerve in his description of the scandals that regularly precede the downfall of leaders. He is scathing of the way 'irrelevant' personal actions topple major figures as their behaviour is compared not to what the entire élite is doing but to the morale high ground which all élites claim to be theirs. 'It is not by fortuitous circumstance that such a man is raised to a position of power; it is by selection at the dictates of the very nature of the system.' For Pareto, therefore, the 'warts' of the system are not unfortunate excesses that can be eradicated by more moral behaviour on the part of leaders; they are the way individuals get to be leaders. But, unlike Machiavelli and Plato, Pareto has no utopian alternative; the only question is which élite is in control and how might it be sustained or undermined.

# The Republic

**Plato**

Adeimantus spoke up. 'Socrates,' he said, 'no one's going to take you up on this point; but that may be due to the fact that there's a particular experience which people who hear you speak on any occasion always have. They get the impression that, because they lack expertise at the give and take of discussion, they're led a little bit astray by each question, and then when all the little bits are put together at the end of the discussion, they find that they were way off the mark and that they've contradicted their original position. They're like unskilled backgammon players, who end up being shut out by skilled ones and incapable of making a move: they too end up being shut out and incapable of making an argumentative move in this alternative version of backgammon, which uses words rather than counters, since they feel that this is not necessarily a certain route to the truth. From my point of view, what I'm saying is relevant to our current situation. You see, someone might object that his inability to find the words to challenge you doesn't alter the evident fact that the majority of the people who take up philosophy and spend more than just their youth on it—who don't get involved in it just for educational purposes and then drop it—turn out to be pretty weird (not to say rotten to the core), and that the effect of this pursuit you're praising, even on those of its practitioners who are supposed to be particularly good, is that they become incapable of performing any service to their communities.'

I responded by asking, 'Do you think this view is right?'

'I don't know,' he replied. 'But I'd be happy to hear what you have to say on the matter.'

'What you'd hear from me is that I think they're telling the truth.'

'Then how can it be right', he said, 'to say that there'll be no end to

Plato, *The Republic* (Oxford: Oxford University Press, 1993), 207–19.

political troubles until philosophers have power in their communities, when we agree that philosophers are no use to them?'

'It'll take an analogy to answer your question,' I said.

'And you never use analogies, of course,' he said.

'What?' I exclaimed. 'It's hard enough to prove my point without you making fun of me as well as forcing me to try. Anyway, here's my analogy: now you'll be in a better position to see how inadequate it is. I mean, what society does to the best practitioners of philosophy is so complex that there's no other single phenomenon like it: in order to defend them from criticism, one has to compile an analogy out of lots of different elements, like the goat-stags and other compound creatures painters come up with.

Imagine the following situation on a fleet of ships, or on a single ship. The owner has the edge over everyone else on board by virtue of his size and strength, but he's rather deaf and short-sighted, and his knowledge of naval matters is just as limited. The sailors are wrangling with one another because each of them thinks that he ought to be the captain, despite the fact that he's never learnt how, and can't name his teacher or specify the period of his apprenticeship. In any case, they all maintain that it isn't something that can be taught, and are ready to butcher anyone who says it is. They're for ever crowding closely around the owner, pleading with him and stopping at nothing to get him to entrust the rudder to them. Sometimes, if their pleas are unsuccessful, but others get the job, they kill those others or throw them off the ship, subdue their worthy owner by drugging him or getting him drunk or something, take control of the ship, help themselves to its cargo, and have the kind of drunken and indulgent voyage you'd expect from people like that. And that's not all: they think highly of anyone who contributes towards their gaining power by showing skill at winning over or subduing the owner, and describe him as an accomplished seaman, a true captain, a naval expert; but they criticize anyone different as useless. They completely fail to understand that any genuine sea-captain has to study the yearly cycle, the seasons, the heavens, the stars and winds, and everything relevant to the job, if he's to be properly equipped to hold a position of authority in a ship. In fact, they think it's impossible to study and acquire expertise at how to steer a ship (leaving aside the question of whether or not people want you to) and at the same time be a good captain. When this is what's happening on board ships, don't you think that the crew of ships in this state would think of any true captain as nothing but a windbag with his head in the clouds, of no use to them at all?'

'They definitely would,' Adeimantus replied.

'I'm sure you don't need an analysis of the analogy to see that it's a metaphor for the attitude of society towards true philosophers,' I said. 'I'm sure you take my point.'

'I certainly do,' he said.

'You'd better use it, then, in the first instance, to clarify things for that person who expressed surprise at the disrespect shown to philosophers by society, and try to show him how much more astonishing it would be if they were respected.'

'All right, I will,' he said.

'And that you're right to say that the best practitioners of philosophy are incapable of performing any public service. But you'd better tell him to blame their uselessness on the others' failure to make use of them, rather than on the fact that they are accomplished philosophers. I mean, it's unnatural for the captain to ask the sailors to accept his authority and it's unnatural for wise men to dance attendance on rich men; this story is misleading. The truth of the matter is that it makes no difference whether you're rich or poor: if you feel ill, you're bound to dance attendance on a doctor, and if you need to accept authority, you must dance attendance on someone in authority who is capable of providing it. If he is really to serve any useful purpose, it's not up to him to ask those under him to accept his authority. And you won't be mistaken if you compare present-day political leaders to the sailors in our recent tale, and the ones they call useless airheads to the genuine captain.'

'You're absolutely right,' he said.

'Under these conditions and circumstances, it's not easy for the best of occupations to gain a good reputation, when reputations are in the hands of people whose occupations are incompatible with it. But by far the worst and most influential condemnation of philosophy comes about as a result of the people who claim to practise it—the ones the critic of philosophy was talking about, in your report, when he described the majority of the people who take up philosophy as rotten to the core (although the best of them are merely useless). And I agreed that you were telling the truth, didn't I?'

'Yes.'

'Well, we've described the reasons for the uselessness of the good practitioners, haven't we?'

'We certainly have.'

'Shall we next describe why the corruption of most philosophers is inevitable, and try to explain why this shouldn't be blamed on philosophy either, if we can?'

'Yes.'

'Let's start our discussion by reminding ourselves of the fundamental points in our description of the kind of character a truly good person will inevitably have. If you remember, above all he was led by truth: if he didn't pursue truth absolutely and wholeheartedly, he was bound to be a specious impostor, with nothing whatsoever to do with true philosophy.'

'That's what we said.'

'Well, that in itself is diametrically opposed to current opinion about philosophers, isn't it?'

'It certainly is,' he said.

'Now, our response will be to point out that a genuine lover of knowledge innately aspires to reality, and doesn't settle on all the various things which are assumed to be real, but keeps on, with his love remaining keen and steady, until the nature of each thing as it really is in itself has been grasped by the appropriate part of his mind—which is to say, the part which is akin to reality. Once he has drawn near this authentic reality and united with it, and thus fathered intellect and truth, then he has knowledge; then he lives a life which is true to himself; then he is nourished; and then, but not before, he finds release from his love-pangs. Would this be a reasonable response for us to make?'

'Nothing could be more reasonable,' he said.

'And will he be the sort of person to love falsehood or will exactly the opposite be the case, and he'll loathe it?'

'He'll loathe it,' he said.

'I'm sure we'd insist that no array of evils could follow leadership of truth.'

'Of course we would.'

'But rather, a character imbued with health and morality, and the self-discipline that accompanies them.'

'Right,' he said.

'Anyway, there's no need for us to have the whole array of the philosopher's characteristics line up all over again. I'm sure you remember how we found that philosophers naturally have courage, broadness of vision, quickness at learning, and a good memory. You interrupted by saying that, although argument was absolutely incontrovertible, it was still possible for someone to leave arguments out of it and look at the actual people we were talking about, and to conclude that, while some philosophers are evidently merely useless, the majority of them are bad through and through. We're trying to uncover the reasons for their bad name, and so we're now up against the question why the majority are bad. That's why we brought the true philosopher's characteristics back in again and felt compelled to provide a clear statement of them.'

'True,' he said.

'What we have to do', I said, 'is see how this philosophical nature is corrupted and why it is often completely ruined, while immunity from corruption is rare—and these escapees are the people who get called useless, rather than bad. After that, we'll turn to pseudo-philosophical natures and the kinds of people who take up the occupation which is proper to a philosophical nature, and we'll try to discern what it is in the make-up of their minds which drives them towards an occupation which is too good and too sublime for them, so that they commit a wide variety of offences and make everyone, all over the world, think of philosophy in the way that you've mentioned.'

'What sources of corruption do you have in mind?' he asked.

'I'll do my best to explain,' I replied. 'I suppose it's indisputable that a fully philosophical nature—of the kind we've described, with the whole array of qualities we lined up not long ago—is a rare human phenomenon: there aren't going to be very many of them. Don't you agree?'

'Definitely.'

'Well, look how heavily these few people are outnumbered by powerful sources of corruption.'

'What are they, though?'

'The most astounding thing of all is that there isn't one of their commendable characteristics which doesn't ruin a mind which possesses it and cause a rift between it and philosophy. I'm talking about courage, self-discipline, and all the qualities we went through.'

'It's not easy to make sense of this idea,' he said.

'And that's not all,' I said. 'Every single one of the acknowledged good things of life is a factor in its corruption and the rift—good looks, affluence, physical fitness, influential family relationships in one's community, and so on and so forth. I've cut the list short, because you can see what I'm saying.'

'I can,' he said. 'And I wouldn't mind hearing a more detailed explanation.'

'If you grasp the general principle of the matter,' I said, 'everything will fall into place and what I've already said will start to make sense.'

'What are you getting at?' he asked.

'We know', I said, 'that if any plant or creature, at the stage when it is a seed or a new growth, fails to get the right nourishment or weather or location, then the number of its deficiencies, in respect to properties it should have, is proportionate to its vigour. I mean, bad is the opposite of good, rather than of not-good.'

'Of course.'

'So I suppose it's plausible to think that a very good thing will end up in a worse state than a second-rate thing if the conditions of its nurture are less suited to its nature.'

'Yes.'

'Well, by the same token, Adeimantus,' I asked, 'won't we claim that if the most gifted minds are subjected to a bad education, they become exceptionally bad? I mean, do you imagine that horrendous crimes and sheer depravity stem from a second-rate nature, rather than from a vigorous one which has been ruined by its upbringing? Could significant benefit or significant harm conceivably proceed from innate weakness?'

'No, you're right,' he said.

'Now, in my opinion, if it receives a suitable education, the philosophical nature we proposed is bound to grow and arrive at perfect goodness. However, if its germination and growth take place in an unsuitable educational environment, then without divine intervention its destination will inevitably be completely the opposite. Or do you follow the masses and believe that there are members of the younger generation who are corrupted by professional teachers, and that there are professional teachers who, despite being private citizens, can be a source of corruption to any degree worth mentioning? Don't you think, rather, that it is the very people who make this claim who are the most influential teachers, and who provide the most thorough education and form men and women of all ages into any shape they want?'

'When do they do this?' he asked.

'When a lot of them huddle together on seats in the assembly or law court or theatre,' I said, 'or when they convene for military purposes, or when there's any other general public gathering, and the boos and applause of their criticism or praise (excessive in both cases) of whatever is being said or done make a terrible din, and it's not only them—the rocks and their surroundings double the noise of their approval and disapproval by echoing it. In a situation like this, how do you think a young man's heart, as they say, will be affected? How can the education he received outside this public arena stand up to it, do you suppose, without being overwhelmed by criticism or praise of this kind and swept away at the mercy of the current? Won't he end up just like them, with the same moral standards and the same habits as them?'

'He's bound to, Socrates,' he said.

'And we haven't yet mentioned the most irresistible pressure they bring to bear,' I said.

'What is it?' he asked.

'It's the concrete pressure these consummate professional educators apply when they turn to action, if their words have failed to indoctrinate someone. I mean, surely you're aware that they punish disobedience with forfeiture of rights, and with fines and death?'

'Yes, I'm certainly well aware of that,' he said.

'Can you think of any teacher or any kind of privately received instruction with the strength to hold out against these pressures?'

'I think it's impossible,' he said.

'Yes, and it's extremely stupid even to try to be that kind of teacher,' I said. 'You see, it's quite impossible, as the present and the past show, for any educational programme to alter anyone's character, as far as goodness is concerned, contrary to the conditioning he receives in the public arena—by 'anyone' I mean any human, of course, Adeimantus: as the proverb recommends, we'd better make an exception of divinity. I mean, I can tell you that you'd be quite right to see God at work when anything does retain its integrity and fulfil its potential within current political systems.'

'That's what I think too,' he said.

'And I wonder whether you agree with me on a further point as well,' I said.

'What?'

'Even though they call it knowledge, every one of those private fee-charging individuals—the ones who are called sophists and are regarded as rivals by these educators we've been talking about—teaches nothing but the attitudes the masses form by consensus. Imagine that the keeper of a huge, strong beast notices what makes it angry, what it desires, how it has to be approached and handled, the circumstances and conditions under which it becomes particularly fierce or calm, what provokes its typical cries, and what tones of voice make it gentle or wild. Once he's spent enough time in the creature's company to acquire all this information, he calls it knowledge, forms it into a systematic branch of expertise, and starts to teach it, despite total ignorance, in fact, about which of the creature's attitudes and desires is commendable or deplorable, good or bad, moral or immoral. His usage of all these terms simply conforms to the great beast's attitudes, and he describes things as good or bad according to its likes and dislikes—and can't justify his usage of the terms any further, but describes as right and good things which are merely indispensable, since he hasn't realized and can't explain to anyone else how vast a gulf there is between necessity and goodness. Wouldn't you really and truly find someone like this implausible as a teacher?'

'Yes, I would,' he said.

'Well, do you think there's anything to choose between him and someone who's noticed what makes the motley masses collectively angry and happy and thinks he has knowledge—whether it's in the field of painting or music or government? I mean, whenever someone's relationship with the masses consists of displaying his composition (or whatever product it may be) or his political service to them, and giving them power over him—or rather, more power than they need have—then the proverbial necessity of Diomedes forces him to compose things of which they approve. Sometimes one of the sophists might argue that what the masses like coincides with what is genuinely good and fine, but this argument always comes across as utterly absurd, don't you think?'

'It always has and it always will, in my opinion,' he said.

'So, against this background, please remember what we were saying before. Is it possible for the masses to accept or conceive of the existence of beauty itself, rather than the plurality of beautiful things? Or anything in itself, rather than the plurality of instances of each thing?'

'Not at all,' he said.

'It's impossible, then, for the masses to love knowledge,' I said.

'Yes, it is.'

'They're bound to run philosophers down, then, as well.'

'That's inevitable.'

'And so are those individuals whose relationship with the masses consists of wanting to please them.'

'Obviously.'

'In this context, can you see how any innate philosopher will preserve the integrity of his nature, and consequently stay with the occupation and see it through to the end? Look at it in the context of what we were saying earlier. We agreed that a philosopher has quickness at learning, a good memory, courage, and broadness of vision.'

'Yes.'

'From his earliest years, then, he'll outclass other children at everything, especially if he's as gifted physically as he is mentally, won't he?'

'Of course,' he answered.

'So when he grows up, his friends and fellow citizens will want to make use of him for their own affairs.'

'Naturally.'

'They'll be a constant presence, then, with their requests and courtesies, as they flatter him and try to get him on their side in anticipation of the influence that will one day be his.'

'Yes, that's what invariably happens,' he said.

'What do you imagine he'll do in this situation,' I asked, especially if he happens to come from, a wealthy and noble family within a powerful state, and is also good-looking and well built? Don't you think he'll be filled with unrealizable hopes, and will expect to be capable one day of managing the affairs not only of Greece, but of the non-Greek world as well? In these circumstances, won't he get ideas above his station and puff himself up with affectation and baseless, senseless pride?'

'He certainly will,' he said.

'Now, suppose someone gently approaches him while he's in this frame of mind and tells him the truth—that he's taken leave of his senses and should try to dispel this inanity, but that he won't gain intelligence unless he works like a slave for it—do you think it's going to be easy for the message to penetrate all these pernicious influences and get through to him?'

'No, far from it,' he said.

'And,' I went on, 'supposing his innate gifts and his affinity with the rationality of what's being said do enable him to pay attention at all, and he is swayed and attracted towards philosophy, what reaction would you expect from those others, when they think they're losing his services and his friendship? Won't they do and say absolutely anything to stop him being won over? And as for the person who's trying to win him over, won't they come up with all kinds of private schemes and public court cases to stop him succeeding?'

'Inevitably,' he said.

'What chance does this young man have of becoming a philosopher?'

'No chance, really.'

'So, as you can see,' I went on, 'we were right to say that it is, in fact, the actual ingredients of a philosophical nature which are in a sense responsible (given a pernicious educational environment) for someone being deflected from his occupation, and that the acknowledged good things of life—affluence and similar resources—are also responsible. Do you agree?'

'Yes,' he said. 'We were quite right.'

'There we are, then, Adeimantus,' I said. 'Those are the powerful factors which ruin and corrupt anyone who is, by nature, best suited for the best occupation—and such people are rare anyway, as we said. Moreover, these are the men who have the potential to do the greatest harm to communities and to individuals, and the greatest good too, if that's the course they happen to take. An insignificant person, however, never has any effect of any significance on any individual or society.'

'You're quite right,' he said.

'So that's how the most appropriate people are deflected and desert philosophy, without consummating the relationship. They end up living a life which is inappropriate for them and which isn't true to their natures, and they leave philosophy, like an orphan with no relatives, to the mercy of others who aren't good enough for her, and who defile her and gain her the kind of tarnished reputation you say her detractors ascribe to her—for going about with people who are either worthless or obnoxious.'

'Yes, that's the usual view,' he said.

'And it's not unreasonable,' I said. 'You see, when the abandonment of this territory is noticed by others—inferior members of the human race—and when they also see how rich it is in renown and status, they behave like escaped convicts who take sanctuary in temples: they break away from their professions, with no regrets, and encroach on philosophy. In fact, they're the ones who do have some facility at their own paltry professions, because in spite of this treatment, philosophy still remains more prestigious than other occupations; and this prestige attracts a lot of people—immature people, who have been physically deformed by their jobs and work, and are mentally just as warped and stunted by their servile business. Don't you think that's inevitable?'

'It certainly is.'

'Do you think the impression they give', I went on, 'is any different from that of a small, bald metalworker who's come into some money? He's just got himself out of debtors' prison, he's had a bath and is wearing brand-new clothes and a bridegroom's outfit, and he's about to marry his master's daughter because she's hard up and has no one to look after her.'

'No, they're exactly the same, really,' he said.

'What sort of offspring are they likely to father, then? Second-rate half-breeds, don't you think?'

'Inevitably.'

'Now, when people who are unworthy of education force their presumptuous attentions on her, what sorts of ideas and thoughts do they produce, would you say? Isn't it perfectly appropriate to call them sophisms, and to claim that they are all illegitimate and lacking in true intelligence?'

'Absolutely,' he said.

'That leaves us with only a tiny number of people, Adeimantus,' I said, 'who have the right to consort with philosophy. A person of high character and sound education might fortuitously have been exiled, and so have remained true to his nature and faithful to philosophy by being out of the reach of corrupting influences; or occasionally a great mind is born in some backwater of a community and finds the politics petty and beneath him. And I suppose a few, because of their natural gifts, do have the right to find some other occupation demeaning and to turn from it to philosophy. Then there is also the bridle of our friend Theages, which can act as a curb: Theages was in all other respects well equipped to be deflected from philosophy, but he had to pamper his physical ailment and so he was curbed and prevented from taking up politics. It's not worth mentioning my own case—the communications I receive from my deity—because there's either very little or no precedent for the phenomenon.

'When the few members of this band have glimpsed the joy and happiness to be found in mastering philosophy and have also gained a clear enough impression of the madness of the masses; when they've realized that more or less every political action is pernicious and that if someone tries to assist morality there will be no one to back him up and see that he comes out unscathed, but it would be like an encounter between a human being and wild beasts; since he isn't prepared to join others in their immorality and isn't capable, all alone, of standing up to all those ferocious beasts, but would die before doing his community or his friends any good, and so would be useless to himself and to everyone else—once he has grasped all this with his rational mind, he lies low and does only what he's meant to do. It's as if he's taken shelter under a wall during a storm, with the wind whipping up the dust and rain pelting down; lawlessness infects everyone else he sees, so he is content if he can find a way to live his life here on earth without becoming tainted by immoral or unjust deeds, and to depart from life confidently, and without anger and bitterness.'

'If he could do that,' he said, 'he'd really have done something with his life.'

# 2 The Art of War

Sun Tzu

## Offensive Strategy

SUN TZU said:

1. Generally in war the best policy is to take a state intact; to ruin it is inferior to this.

   *Li Ch'üan*: Do not put a premium on killing.
2. To capture the enemy's army is better than to destroy it; to take intact a battalion, a company or a five-man squad is better than to destroy them.
3. For to win one hundred victories in one hundred battles is not the acme of skill. To subdue the enemy without fighting is the acme of skill.
4. Thus, what is of supreme importance in war is to attack the enemy's strategy;[1]

   *Tu Mu*: . . . The Grand Duke said: 'He who excels at resolving difficulties does so before they arise. He who excels in conquering his enemies triumphs before threats materialize.'

   *Li Ch'üan*: Attack plans at their inception. In the Later Han, K'ou Hsün surrounded Kao Chun.[2] Chun sent his Planning Officer, Huang-fu Wen, to parley. Huang-fu Wen was stubborn and rude and K'ou Hsün beheaded him, and informed Kao Chun: 'Your staff officer was without propriety. I have beheaded him. If you wish to submit, do so immediately. Otherwise defend yourself' On the same day, Chun threw open his fortifications and surrendered.

Sun Tzu, *The Art of War* (Oxford: Oxford University Press, 1971), 77–84, 102–15, 130–40.

All K'ou Hsün's generals said: 'May we ask, you killed his envoy, but yet forced him to surrender his city. How is this?'

K'ou Hsün said: 'Huang-fu Wen was Kao Chun's heart and guts, his intimate counsellor. If I had spared Huang-fu Wen's life, he would have accomplished his schemes, but when I killed him, Kao Chun lost his guts. It is said: "The supreme excellence in war is to attack the enemy's plans."'

All the generals said: 'This is beyond our comprehension.'

5. Next best is to disrupt his alliances:[3]

*Tu Yu*: Do not allow your enemies to get together.

*Wang Hsi*: . . . Look into the matter of his alliances and cause them to be severed and dissolved. If an enemy has alliances, the problem is grave and the enemy's position strong; if he has no alliances the problem is minor and the enemy's position weak.

6. The next best is to attack his army.

*Chia Lin*: . . . The Grand Duke said: 'He who struggles for victory with naked blades is not a good general.'

*Wang Hsi*: Battles are dangerous affairs.

*Chang Yü*: If you cannot nip his plans in the bud, or disrupt his alliances when they are about to be consummated, sharpen your weapons to gain the victory.

7. The worst policy is to attack cities. Attack cities only when there is no alternative.[4]

8. To prepare the shielded wagons and make ready the necessary arms and equipment requires at least three months; to pile up earthen ramps against the walls an additional three months will be needed.

9. If the general is unable to control his impatience and orders his troops to swarm up the wall like ants, one-third of them will be killed without taking the city. Such is the calamity of these attacks.

*Tu Mu*: . . . In the later Wei, the Emperor T'ai Wu led one hundred thousand troops to attack the Sung general Tsang Chih at Yu T'ai. The Emperor first asked Tsang Chih for some wine.[5] Tsang Chih sealed up a pot full of urine and sent it to him. T'ai Wu was transported with rage and immediately attacked the city, ordering his troops to scale the walls and engage in close combat. Corpses piled up to the top of the walls and after thirty days of this the dead exceeded half his force.

10. Thus, those skilled in war subdue the enemy's army without battle. They capture his cities without assaulting them and overthrow his state without protracted operations.

*Li Ch'üan*: They conquer by strategy. In the Later Han the Marquis of Tsan, Tsang Kung, surrounded the 'Yao' rebels at Yüan Wu, but during a succession of months was unable to take the city.[6] His officers and men were ill and covered with ulcers. The King of Tung Hai spoke to Tsang Kung, saying: 'Now you have massed troops and encircled the enemy, who is determined to fight to the death. This is no strategy! You should lift the siege. Let them know that an escape route is open and they will flee and disperse. Then any village constable will be able to capture them!' Tsang Kung followed this advice and took Yüan Wu.

11. Your aim must be to take All-under-Heaven intact. Thus your troops are not worn out and your gains will be complete. This is the art of offensive strategy.
12. Consequently, the art of using troops is this: When ten to the enemy's one, surround him;
13. When five times his strength, attack him; *Chang Yü*: If my force is five times that of the enemy I alarm him to the front, surprise him to the rear, create an uproar in the east and strike in the west.
14. If double his strength, divide him.[7]

*Tu Yu*: . . . If a two-to-one superiority is insufficient to manipulate the situation, we use a distracting force to divide his army. Therefore the Grand Duke said: 'If one is unable to influence the enemy to divide his forces, he cannot discuss unusual tactics.'

15. If equally matched you may engage him.

*Ho Yen-hsi*: . . . In these circumstances only the able general can win.

16. If weaker numerically, be capable of withdrawing;

*Tu Mu*: If your troops do not equal his, temporarily avoid his initial onrush. Probably later you can take advantage of a soft spot. Then rouse yourself and seek victory with determined spirit.

*Chang Yü*: If the enemy is strong and I am weak, I temporarily withdraw and do not engage.[8] This is the case when the abilities and courage of the generals and the efficiency of troops are equal.

If I am in good order and the enemy in disarray, if I am energetic and he careless, then, even if he be numerically stronger, I can give battle.

17. And if in all respects unequal, be capable of eluding him, for a small force is but booty for one more powerful.[9]

*Chang Yü*: . . . Mencius said: 'The small certainly cannot equal the large, nor can the weak match the strong, nor the few the many.'[10]

18. Now the general is the protector of the state. If this protection is all-embracing, the state will surely be strong; if defective, the state will certainly be weak.

*Chang Yü*:. . . . The Grand Duke said: 'A sovereign who obtains the right person prospers. One who fails to do so will be ruined.'

19. Now there are three ways in which a ruler can bring misfortune upon his army:[11]
20. When ignorant that the army should not advance, to order an advance or ignorant that it should not retire, to order a retirement. This is described as 'hobbling the army'.

    *Chia Lin*: The advance and retirement of the army can be controlled by the general in accordance with prevailing circumstances. No evil is greater than commands of the sovereign from the court.
21. When ignorant of military affairs, to participate in their administration. This causes the officers to be perplexed.

    *Ts'ao Ts'ao*: . . . An army cannot be run according to rules of etiquette.

    *Tu Mu*: As far as propriety, laws, and decrees are concerned, the army has its own code, which it ordinarily follows. If these are made identical with those used in governing a state, the officers will be bewildered.

    *Chang Yü*: Benevolence and righteousness may be used to govern a state but cannot be used to administer an army. Expediency and flexibility are used in administering an army, but cannot be used in governing a state.
22. When ignorant of command problems to share in the exercise of responsibilities. This engenders doubts in the minds of the officers.[12]

    *Wang Hsi*: . . . If one ignorant of military matters is sent to participate in the administration of the army, then in every movement there will be disagreement and mutual frustration and the entire army will be hamstrung. That is why Pei Tu memorialized the throne to withdraw the Army Supervisor; only then was he able to pacify Ts'ao Chou.[13]

    *Chang Yü*: In recent times court officials have been used as Supervisors of the Army and this is precisely what is wrong.
23. If the army is confused and suspicious, neighbouring rulers will cause trouble. This is what is meant by the saying: 'A confused army leads to another's victory.'[14]

    *Meng*:. . . The Grand Duke said: 'One who is confused in purpose cannot respond to his enemy.'

    *Li Ch'üan*: . . . The wrong person cannot be appointed to command . . . Lin Hsiang-ju, the Prime Minister of Chao, said: 'Chao Kua is merely able to read his father's books, and is as yet ignorant of correlating changing circumstances. Now Your Majesty, on account of his name, makes him the commander-in-chief. This is like gluing the pegs of a lute and then trying to tune it.'
24. Now there are five circumstances in which victory may be predicted:
25. He who knows when he can fight and when he cannot will be victorious.
26. He who understands how to use both large and small forces will be victorious.

*Tu Yu*: There are circumstances in war when many cannot attack few, and others when the weak can master the strong. One able to manipulate such circumstances will be victorious.

27. He whose ranks are united in purpose will be victorious.

*Tu Yu*: Therefore Mencius said: 'The appropriate season is not as important as the advantages of the ground; these are not as important as harmonious human relations.'[15]

28. He who is prudent and lies in wait for an enemy who is not, will be victorious.

*Ch'en Hao*: Create an invincible army and await the enemy's moment of vulnerability.

*Ho Yen-hsi*: . . . A gentleman said: 'To rely on rustics and not prepare is the greatest of crimes; to be prepared beforehand for any contingency is the greatest of virtues.'

29. He whose generals are able and not interfered with by the sovereign will be victorious.

*Tu Yu*: . . . Therefore Master Wang said: 'To make appointments is the province of the sovereign; to decide on battle, that of the general.'

*Wang Hsi*: . . . A sovereign of high character and intelligence must be able to know the right man, should place the responsibility on him, and expect results.

*Ho Yen-hsi*: . . . Now in war there may be one hundred changes in each step. When one sees he can, he advances; when he sees that things are difficult, he retires. To say that a general must await commands of the sovereign in such circumstances is like informing a superior that you wish to put out a fire. Before the order to do so arrives, the ashes are cold. And it is said one must consult the Army Supervisor in these matters! This is as if in building a house beside the road one took advice from those who pass by. Of course the work would never be completed![16]

## The Nine Variables

SUN TZU said:

1. In general, the system of employing troops is that the commander receives his mandate from the sovereign to mobilize the people and assemble the army.[17]
2. You should not encamp in low-lying ground.

3. In communicating ground, unite with your allies.
4. You should not linger in desolate ground.
5. In enclosed ground, resourcefulness is required.
6. In death ground, fight.
7. There are some roads not to follow; some troops not to strike; some cities not to assault; and some ground which should not be contested.

   *Wang Hsi*: In my opinion, troops put out as bait, élite troops, and an enemy in well-regulated and imposing formation should not be attacked.

   *Tu Mu*: Probably this refers to an enemy in a strategic position behind lofty walls and deep moats with a plentiful store of grain and food, whose purpose is to detain my army. Should I attack the city and take it, there would be no advantage worth mentioning; if I do not take it the assault will certainly grind down the power of my army. Therefore I should not attack it.

8. There are occasions when the commands of the sovereign need not be obeyed.[18]

   *Ts'ao Ts'ao*: When it is expedient in operations, the general need not be restricted by the commands of the sovereign.

   *Tu Mu*: *The Wei Liao Tzu* says: 'Weapons are inauspicious instruments; strife contrary to virtue; the general, the Minister of Death, who is not responsible to the heavens above, to the earth beneath, to the enemy in his front, or to the sovereign in his rear.'

   *Chang Yü*: Now King Fu Ch'ai said: 'When you see the correct course, act; do not wait for orders.'

9. A general thoroughly versed in the advantages of the nine variable factors knows how to employ troops.

   *Chia Lin*: The general must rely on his ability to control the situation to his advantage as opportunity dictates. He is not bound by established procedures.

10. The general who does not understand the advantages of the nine variable factors will not be able to use the ground to his advantage even though familiar with it.

    *Chia Lin*: . . . A general prizes opportune changes in circumstances.

11. In the direction of military operations one who does not understand the tactics suitable to the nine variable situations will be unable to use his troops effectively, even if he understands the 'five advantages'.[19]

    *Chia Lin*: . . . The 'five variations' are the following: A road, although it may be the shortest, is not to be followed if one knows it is dangerous and there is the contingency of ambush.

    An army, although it may be attacked, is not to be attacked if it is in desperate circumstances and there is the possibility that the enemy will fight to the death.

A city, although isolated and susceptible to attack, is not to be attacked if there is the probability that it is well stocked with provisions, defended by crack troops under command of a wise general, that its ministers are loyal and their plans unfathomable.

Ground, although it may be contested, is not to be fought for if one knows that, after getting it, it will be difficult to defend, or that he gains no advantage by obtaining it, but will probably be counter-attacked and suffer casualties.

The orders of a sovereign, although they should be followed, are not to be followed if the general knows they contain the danger of harmful superintendence of affairs from the capital.

These five contingencies must be managed as they arise and as circumstances dictate at the time, for they cannot be settled beforehand.

12. And for this reason, the wise general in his deliberations must consider both favourable and unfavourable factors.[20]

*Ts'ao Ts'ao*: He ponders the dangers inherent in the advantages, and the advantages inherent in the dangers.

13. By taking into account the favourable factors, he makes his plan feasible; by taking into account the unfavourable, he may resolve the difficulties.[21]

*Tu Mu*:. . . If I wish to take advantage of the enemy I must perceive not just the advantage in doing so but must first consider the ways he can harm me if I do.

*Ho Yen-hsi*: Advantage and disadvantage are mutually reproductive. The enlightened deliberate.

14. He who intimidates his neighbours does so by inflicting injury upon them.

*Chia Lin*: Plans and projects for harming the enemy are not confined to any one method. Sometimes entice his wise and virtuous men away so that he has no counsellors. Or send treacherous people to his country to wreck his administration. Sometimes use cunning deceptions to alienate his ministers from the sovereign. Or send skilled craftsmen to encourage his people to exhaust their wealth. Or present him with licentious musicians and dancers to change his customs. Or give him beautiful women to bewilder him.

15. He wearies them by keeping them constantly occupied, and makes them rush about by offering them ostensible advantages.

16. It is a doctrine of war not to assume the enemy will not come, but rather to rely on one's readiness to meet him; not to presume that he will not attack, but rather to make one's self invincible.

*Ho Yen-hsi*: . . . The 'Strategies of Wu' says: 'When the world is at peace, a gentleman keeps his sword by his side.'

17. There are five qualities which are dangerous in the character of a general.
18. If reckless, he can be killed;

*Tu Mu*: A general who is stupid and courageous is a calamity. Wu Ch'i said: 'When people discuss a general they always pay attention to his courage. As far as a general is concerned, courage is but one quality. Now a valiant general will be certain to enter an engagement recklessly and if he does so he will not appreciate what is advantageous.'

19. If cowardly, captured;

*Ho Yen-hsi*: *The Ssu-ma Fa* says: 'One who esteems life above all will be overcome with hesitancy. Hesitancy in a general is a great calamity.'

20. If quick-tempered you can make a fool of him;

*Tu Yu*: An impulsive man can be provoked to rage and brought to his death. One easily angered is irascible, obstinate and hasty. He does not consider difficulties.

*Wang Hsi*: What is essential in the temperament of a general is steadiness.

21. If he has too delicate a sense of honour you can calumniate him;

*Mei Yao-ch'en*: One anxious to defend his reputation pays no regard to anything else.

22. If he is of a compassionate nature you can harass him. *Tu Mu*: He who is humanitarian and compassionate and fears only casualties cannot give up temporary advantage for a long-term gain and is unable to let go this in order to seize that.
23. Now these five traits of character are serious faults in a general and in military operations are calamitous.
24. The ruin of the army and the death of the general are inevitable results of these shortcomings. They must be deeply pondered.

# The Nine Varieties of Ground

SUN TZU said:[22]

1. In respect to the employment of troops, ground may be classified as dispersive, frontier, key, communicating, focal, serious, difficult, encircled, and death.[23]
2. When a feudal lord fights in his own territory, he is in dispersive ground.

*Ts'ao Ts'ao*: Here officers and men long to return to their nearby homes.

3. When he makes but a shallow penetration into enemy territory, he is in frontier ground.[24]
4. Ground equally advantageous for the enemy or me to occupy is key ground.[25]
5. Ground equally accessible to both the enemy and me is communicating.

*Tu Mu*: This is level and extensive ground in which one may come and go, sufficient in extent for battle and to erect opposing fortifications.

6. When a state is enclosed by three other states, its territory is focal. He who first gets control of it will gain the support of All-under-Heaven.[26]
7. When the army has penetrated deep into hostile territory, leaving far behind many enemy cities and towns, it is in serious ground.

*Ts'ao Ts'ao*: This is ground difficult to return from.

8. When the army traverses mountains, forests, precipitous country, or marches through defiles, marshlands, or swamps, or any place where the going is hard, it is in difficult ground.[27]
9. Ground to which access is constricted, where the way out is tortuous, and where a small enemy force can strike my larger one is called 'encircled'.[28]

*Tu Mu*: . . . Here it is easy to lay ambushes and one can be utterly defeated.

10. Ground in which the army survives only if it fights with the courage of desperation is called 'death'.

*Li Ch'üan*: Blocked by mountains to the front and rivers to the rear, with provisions exhausted. In this situation it is advantageous to act speedily and dangerous to procrastinate.

11. And therefore, do not fight in dispersive ground; do not stop in the frontier borderlands.
12. Do not attack an enemy who occupies key ground; in communicating ground do not allow your formations to become separated.[29]
13. In focal ground, ally with neighbouring states; in deep ground, plunder.[30]
14. In difficult ground, press on; in encircled ground, devise stratagems; in death ground, fight.
15. In dispersive ground I would unify the determination of the army.[31]
16. In frontier ground I would keep my forces closely linked. *Mei Yao-ch'en*: On the march the several units are connected; at halts the camps and fortified posts are linked together.
17. In key ground I would hasten up my rear elements. *Ch'ên Hao*: What the verse means is that if . . . the enemy, relying on superior numbers, comes to contest such ground, I use a large force to hasten into his rear.[32]

*Chang Yü*:. . . Someone has said that the phrase means 'to set out after the enemy and arrive before him'.[33]

18. In communicating ground I would pay strict attention to my defences.
19. In focal ground I would strengthen my alliances.

*Chang Yü*: I reward my prospective allies with valuables and silks and bind them with, solemn covenants. I abide firmly by the treaties and then my allies will certainly aid me.

20. In serious ground I would ensure a continuous flow of provisions.
21. In difficult ground I would press on over the roads.
22. In encircled ground I would block the points of access and egress.

*Tu Mu*: It is military doctrine that an encircling force must leave a gap to show the surrounded troops there is a way out, so that they will not be determined to fight to the death. Then, taking advantage of this, strike. Now, if I am in encircled ground, and the enemy opens a road in order to tempt my troops to take it, I close this means of escape so that my officers and men will have a mind to fight to the death.[34]

23. In death ground I could make it evident that there is no chance of survival. For it is the nature of soldiers to resist when surrounded; to fight to the death when there is no alternative, and when desperate to follow commands implicitly.
24. The tactical variations appropriate to the nine types of ground, the advantages of close or extended deployment, and the principles of human nature are matters the general must examine with the greatest care.[35]
25. Anciently, those described as skilled in war made it impossible for the enemy to unite his van and his rear; for his elements both large and small mutually to cooperate; for the good troops to succour the poor, and for superiors and subordinates to support each other.[36]
26. When the enemy's forces were dispersed they prevented him from assembling them; when concentrated, they threw him into confusion.

*Meng*: Lay on many deceptive operations. Be seen in the west and march out of the east; lure him in the north and strike in the south. Drive him crazy and bewilder him so that he disperses his forces in confusion.

*Chang Y'ü*: Take him unaware by surprise attacks where he is unprepared. Hit him suddenly with shock troops.

27. They concentrated and moved when it was advantageous to do so;[37] when not advantageous, they halted.
28. Should one ask: 'How do I cope with a well-ordered enemy host about to attack me?' I reply: 'Seize something he cherishes and he will conform to your desires.'[38]

29. Speed is the essence of war. Take advantage of the enemy's unpreparedness; travel by unexpected routes and strike him where he has taken no precautions.

    *Tu Mu*: This summarizes the essential nature of war . . . and the ultimate in generalship.

    *Chang Y'ü*: Here Sun Tzu again explains . . . that the one thing esteemed is divine swiftness.

30. The general principles applicable to an invading force are that when you have penetrated deeply into hostile territory your army is united, and the defender cannot overcome you.
31. Plunder fertile country to supply the army with plentiful provisions.
32. Pay heed to nourishing the troops; do not unnecessarily fatigue them. Unite them in spirit; conserve their strength. Make unfathomable plans for the movements of the army.
33. Throw the troops into a position from which there is no escape and even when faced with death they will not flee. For if prepared to die, what can they not achieve? Then officers and men together put forth their utmost efforts. In a desperate situation they fear nothing; when there is no way out they stand firm. Deep in a hostile land they are bound together, and there, where there is no alternative, they will engage the enemy in hand to hand combat.[39]
34. Thus, such troops need no encouragement to be vigilant. Without extorting their support, the general obtains it; without inviting their affection, he gains it; without demanding their trust, he wins it.[40]
35. My officers have no surplus of wealth but not because they disdain worldly goods; they have no expectation of long life but not because they dislike longevity.

    *Wang Hsi*: . . . When officers and men care only for worldly riches they will cherish life at all costs.

36. On the day the army is ordered to march the tears of those seated soak their lapels; the tears of those reclining course down their cheeks.

    *Tu Mu*: All have made a covenant with death. Before the day of battle the order is issued: 'Today's affair depends upon this one stroke. The bodies of those who do not put their lives at stake will fertilize the fields and become carrion for the birds and beasts.'

37. But throw them into a situation where there is no escape and they will display the immortal courage of Chuan Chu and Ts'ao Kuei.
38. Now the troops of those adept in war are used like the 'Simultaneously Responding' snake of Mount Ch'ang. When struck on the head its tail attacks; when struck on the tail, its head attacks, when struck in the centre both head and tail attack.[41]
39. Should one ask: 'Can troops be made capable of such instantaneous

co-ordination?' I reply: 'They can.' For, although the men of Wu and Yüeh mutually hate one another, if together in a boat tossed by the wind they would cooperate as the right hand does with the left.'

40. It is thus not sufficient to place one's reliance on hobbled horses or buried chariot wheels.[42]

41. To cultivate a uniform level of valour is the object of military administration.[43] And it is by proper use of the ground that both shock and flexible forces are used to the best advantage.[44]

*Chang Yü*: If one gains the advantage of the ground then even weak and soft troops can conquer the enemy. How much more so if they are tough and strong! That both may be used effectively is because they are disposed in accordance with the conditions of the ground.

42. It is the business of a general to be serene and inscrutable, impartial and self-controlled.[45]

*Wang Hsi*: If serene he is not vexed; if inscrutable, unfathomable; if upright, not improper; if self-controlled, not confused.

43. He should be capable of keeping his officers and men in ignorance of his plans.

*Ts'ao Ts'ao*: . . . His troops may join him in rejoicing at the accomplishment, but they cannot join him in laying the plans.

44. He prohibits superstitious practices and so rids the arm of doubts. Then until the moment of death there can be no troubles.[46]

*Ts'ao Ts'ao*: Prohibit talk of omens and of supernatural portents. Rid plans of doubts and uncertainties.

*Chang Yü*: *The Ssu-ma Fa* says: 'Exterminate superstitions.'

45. He changes his methods and alters his plans so that people have no knowledge of what he is doing.

*Chang Yü*: Courses of action previously followed and old plans previously executed must be altered.

46. He alters his campsites and marches by devious routes, and thus makes it impossible for others to anticipate his purpose.[47]

47. To assemble the army and throw it into a desperate position is the business of the general.

48. He leads the army deep into hostile territory and there releases the trigger.[48]

49. He burns his boats and smashes his cooking pots; he urges the army on as if driving a flock of sheep, now in one direction, now in another, and none knows where he is going.[49]

50. He fixes a date for rendezvous and, after the troops have met, cuts off their return route just as if he were removing a ladder from beneath them.

51. One ignorant of the plans of neighbouring states cannot prepare alliances

in good time; if ignorant of the conditions of mountains, forests, dangerous defiles, swamps, and marshes, he cannot conduct the march of an army; if he fails to make use of native guides, he cannot gain the advantages of the ground. A general ignorant of even one of these three matters is unfit to command the armies of a Hegemonic King.[50]

*Ts'ao Ts'ao*: These three matters have previously been elaborated. The reason Sun Tzu returns to the subject is that he strongly disapproved of those unable to employ troops properly.

52. Now when a Hegemonic King attacks a powerful state he makes it impossible for the enemy to concentrate. He overawes the enemy and prevents his allies from joining him.[51]

*Mei Yao-ch'en*: In attacking a great state, if you can divide your enemy's forces your strength will be more than sufficient.

53. It follows that he does not contend against powerful combinations nor does he foster the power of other states. He relies for the attainment of his aims on his ability to overawe his opponents. And so he can take the enemy's cities and overthrow the enemy's state.[52]

*Ts'ao Ts'ao*: By 'Hegemonic King' is meant one who does not ally with the feudal lords. He breaks up the alliances of All-under-Heaven and snatches the position of authority. He uses prestige and virtue to attain his ends.[53]

*Tu Mu*: The verse says if one neither covenants for the help of neighbours nor develops plans based on expediency but in furtherance of his personal aims relies only on his own military strength to overawe the enemy country then his own cities can be captured and his own state overthrown.[54]

54. Bestow rewards without respect to customary practice; publish orders without respect to precedent.[55] Thus you may employ the entire army as you would one man.

*Chang Yü*: . . . If the code respecting rewards and punishments is clear and speedily applied then you may use the many as you do the few.

55. Set the troops to their tasks without imparting your designs; use them to gain advantage without revealing the dangers involved. Throw them into a perilous situation and they survive; put them in death ground and they will live. For when the army is placed in such a situation it can snatch victory from defeat.

56. Now the crux of military operations lies in the pretence of accommodating one's self to the designs of the enemy.

57. Concentrate your forces against the enemy and from a distance of a thousand *li* you can kill his Generals.[57] This is described as the ability to attain one's aim in an artful and ingenious manner.

58. On the day the policy to attack is put into effect, close the passes, rescind

the passports,[58] have no further intercourse with the enemy's envoys and exhort the temple council to execute the plans.[59]

59. When the enemy presents an opportunity, speedily take advantage of it.[60] Anticipate him in seizing something he values and move in accordance with a date secretly fixed.
60. The doctrine of war is to follow the enemy situation in order to decide on battle.[61]
61. Therefore at first be shy as a maiden. When the enemy gives you an opening be swift as a hare and he will be unable to withstand you.

## Notes

1. Not, as Giles translates, 'to balk the enemy's plans'.
2. This took place during the first century AD.
3. Not, as Giles translates, 'to prevent the junction of the enemy's forces'.
4. In this series of verses Sun Tzu is not discussing the art of generalship, as Giles apparently thought. These are objectives or policies — *cheng* — in order of relative merit.
5. Exchange of gifts and compliments was a normal preliminary to battle.
6. Yao connotes the supernatural. The Boxers, who believed themselves impervious to foreign lead, could be so described.
7. Some commentators think this verse means 'to divide one's own force', but that seems a less satisfactory interpretation, as the character *chih* used in the two previous verses refers to the enemy.
8. Tu Mu and Chang Yü both counsel 'temporary' withdrawal, thus emphasizing the point that offensive action is to be resumed when circumstances are propitious.
9. Lit. 'The strength of a small force is . . .'. This apparently refers to its weapons and equipment.
10. II (Mencius), i, ch. 7.
11. Here I have transposed the characters meaning 'ruler' and 'army', otherwise the verse would read that there are three ways in which an army can bring misfortune upon the sovereign.
12. Lit. 'Not knowing [or understanding or ignorant of] [where] authority [lies] in the army'; or 'ignorant of [matters relating to exercise of] military authority. . .'. The operative character is 'authority' or 'power'.
13. The 'Army Supervisors' of the T'ang were in fact political commissars. Pei Tu became Prime Minister in AD 815 and in 817 requested the throne to recall the supervisor assigned him, who must have been interfering in army operations.
14. 'Feudal Lords' is rendered 'neighbouring rulers'. The commentators agree that a confused army robs itself of victory.

15. II (Mencius), ii, ch. 1, p. 85.
16. A paraphrase of an ode which Legge renders:
    They are like one taking counsel with wayfarers about building a house
    Which consequently will never come to completion. (IV, ii, P. 332, Ode I)
17. As Sun Tzu uses almost identical words to introduce chapter vii, Yang P'ing-an would drop this. He would also drop vi. 2–6 inclusive, as they occur later in discussion of the 'Nine Grounds', and replace them with vi. 26–32 inclusive from chapter vii. Where Sun Tzu uses a negative in vi. 2–6, it is not the peremptory form he used previously. Hence I do not feel justified in accepting the emendations proposed. The 'Nine Variables' are then expressed in vi. 2–7 inclusive.
18. A catch-all which covers the variable circumstances previously enumerated.
19. A confusing verse which baffles all the commentators. If Chia Lin is correct, the 'five advantages' must be the situations named in vi. 2–6 inclusive.
20. Sun Tzi says these are 'mixed'.
21. Sun Tzu says that by taking account of the favourable factors the plan is made 'trustworthy' or 'reliable'. 'Feasible' (or 'workable') is as close as I can get it.
22. The original arrangement of this chapter leaves much to be desired. Many verses are not in proper context; others are repetitious and may possibly be ancient commentary which has worked its way into the text. I have transposed some verses and eliminated those which appear to be accretions.
23. There is some confusion here. The 'accessible' ground of the preceding chapter is defined in the same terms as 'communicating' ground.
24. Lit. 'Light' ground, possibly because it is easy to retire or because the officers and men think lightly of deserting just as the expedition is getting under way.
25. This is contestable ground, or, as Tu Mu says, 'strategically important'.
26. The Empire is always described as 'All-under-Heaven'.
27. The commentators indulge in some discussion respecting the interpretation of the character rendered 'difficult'. Several want to restrict the meaning to ground susceptible to flooding.
28. The verb may be translated as 'tie down' rather than 'strike'.
29. Ts'ao Ts'ao says they must be 'closed up'.
30. Li Ch'üan thinks the latter half should read 'do not plunder', as the principal object when in enemy territory is to win the affection and support of the people.
31. This and the nine verses which immediately follow have been transposed to this context. In the text they come later in the chapter.
32. The question is, whose 'rear' is Sun Tzu talking about? Ch'ên Hao is reading something into the verse as it stands in present context.
33. The 'someone' is Mei Yao-ch'ên, who takes *hou* to mean 'after' in the temporal sense.
34. A long story relates that Shen Wu of the Later Wei, when in such a position, blocked the only escape road for his troops with the army's livestock. His forces then fought desperately and defeated an army of two hundred thousand.
35. This verse is followed by seven short verses which again define terms previously defined in vi. 2– 10 inclusive. This appears to be commentary which has worked its way into the text.

36. The implication is that, even were the enemy able to concentrate, internal dissensions provoked by the skilled general would render him ineffective.
37. Lit. 'They concentrated where it was advantageous to do so and then acted. When it was not advantageous, they stood fast.' In another commentary Shih Tzu-mei says not to move unless there is advantage in it.
38. Comments between question and answer omitted.
39. There are several characters in Chinese which basically mean 'to fight'. That used here implies 'close combat'.
40. This refers to the troops of a general who nourishes them, who unites them in spirit, who husbands their strength, and who makes unfathomable plans.
41. This mountain was anciently known as Mt Hêng. During the reign of the Emperor Hên (Liu Hêng) of the Han (179–159 BC) the name was changed to 'Ch'ang' to avoid the taboo. In all existing works 'Hêng' was changed to 'Ch'ang'.
42. Such 'Maginot Line' expedients are not in themselves sufficient to prevent defending troops from fleeing.
43. Lit. 'To equalize courage [so that it is that of] one [man] is the right way of administration.'
44. Chang Yü makes it clear why terrain should be taken into account when troops are disposed. The difference in quality of troops can be balanced by careful sector assignment. Weak troops can hold strong ground, but might break if posted in a position less strong.
45. Giles translated: 'It is the business of a general to be quiet and thus ensure secrecy; upright and just and thus maintain order.' The commentators do not agree, but none takes it in this sense, nor does the text support this rendering. I follow Ts'ao Ts'ao and Wang Hsi.
46. The character at the end of this sentence is emended to mean a natural or 'heaven-sent' calamity. Part of Ts'ao Ts'ao's comment which is omitted indicates that various texts were circulating in his time.
47. Or perhaps, 'makes it impossible for the enemy to learn *his* plans'. But Mei Yao-ch'en thinks the meaning is that the enemy will thus be rendered incapable of laying plans. Giles infers that the general, by altering his camps and marching by devious routes, can prevent the enemy 'from anticipating his purpose', which seems the best. The comments do not illuminate the point at issue.
48. 'Release' of a trigger, or mechanism, is the usual meaning of the expression *fa chi*. The idiom has been translated: 'puts into effect his expedient plans.' Wang Hsi says that when the trigger is released 'there is no return' (of the arrow or bolt). Lit. this verse reads: 'He leads the army deep into the territory of the Feudal Lords and there releases the trigger' (or 'puts into effect his expedient plans'). Giles translates the phrase in question as 'shows his hand', i.e. takes irrevocable action.
49. Neither his own troops nor the enemy can fathom his ultimate design.
50. Emending '[these] four or five [matters]' to read 'these three [matters]'
51. This verse and the next present problems. Chang Yü thinks the verse means that, if the troops of a Hegemonic King (or a ruler who aspires to such status) attack

hastily (or recklessly, or without forethought), *his* allies will not come to *his* aid. The other commentators interpret the verse as I have.

52. The commentators differ in their interpretations of this verse. Giles translates: 'Hence he does not strive to ally himself with all and sundry nor does he foster the power of other states. He carries out his own secret designs, keeping his antagonists in awe. Thus he is able to capture their cities and overthrow their kingdoms.' But I feel that Sun Tzu meant that the 'Hegemonic King' need not contend against 'powerful combinations' because he isolates his enemies. He does not permit them to form 'powerful combinations'.
53. Possibly Giles derived his interpretation from this comment.
54. Also a justifiable interpretation, which illustrates how radically the commentators frequently differ.
55. This verse, obviously out of place, emphasizes that the general in the field need not follow prescribed procedures in recognition of meritorious service but should bestow timely rewards. The general need not follow customary law in respect of administration of his army.
56. Possibly too free a translation, but the commentators agree that this is the idea Sun Tzu tries to convey. I follow Tu Mu.
57. I follow Ts'ao Ts'ao here. A strategist worthy of the name defeats his enemy from a distance of one thousand *li* by anticipating his enemy's plans.
58. Lit. 'Break the tallies'. These were carried by travellers and were examined by the Wardens of the Passes. Without a proper tally no one could legally enter or leave a country
59. The text is confusing. It seems literally to read: 'From [the rostrum of] the temple, exhort [the army?] [the people?] to execute the plans.' The commentators are no help.
60. Another difficult verse. Some commentators think it should read: 'When the enemy sends spies, imediately let them enter.' The difficulty is the idiom *k'ai ho*, literally in, 'to open the leaf of a door', thus, 'to present an opportunity [to enter]'. Ts'ao Ts'ao says the idiom means 'a cleavage', 'a gap', or 'a space'. Then, he goes on, 'you must speedily enter'. Other commentators say the idiom means 'spies' or 'secret agents'. I follow Ts'ao Ts'ao.
61. The commentators again disagree: v. 58-61 are susceptible to varying translations or interpretations.

# 3 The Prince

Niccolò Machiavelli

## Chapter XII. On the Various Kinds of Troops and Mercenary Soldiers

Having treated in detail all the characteristics of those principalities which I proposed to discuss at the beginning, and having considered, to some extent, the reasons for their success or shortcomings, and having demonstrated the ways by which many have tried to acquire them and to maintain them, it remains for me now to speak in general terms of the kinds of offence and defence that can be adopted by each of the previously mentioned principalities. We have said above that a prince must have laid firm foundations; otherwise he will of necessity come to grief. And the principal foundations of all states, the new as well as the old or mixed, are good laws and good armies. And since there cannot exist good laws where there are no good armies, and where there are good armies there must be good laws, I shall leave aside the treatment of laws and discuss the armed forces.

Let me say, therefore, that the armies with which a prince defends his state are made up of his own people, or of mercenaries, or auxiliaries, or of mixed troops. Mercenaries and auxiliaries are useless and dangerous. And if a prince holds on to his state by means of mercenary armies, he will never be stable or secure; for they are disunited, ambitious, without discipline, disloyal; they are brave among friends; among enemies they are cowards; they have no fear of God, they keep no faith with men; and your downfall is deferred only so long as the attack is deferred; and in peace you are plundered by them, in war by

Niccolò Machiavelli, *The Prince*, (Oxford: Oxford University Press, 1984), chs. XII, XV, XVII, XVIII, XXII, XXV.

your enemies. The reason for this is that they have no other love nor other motive to keep them in the field than a meagre wage, which is not enough to make them want to die for you. They love being your soldiers when you are not making war, but when war comes they either flee or desert. This would require little effort to demonstrate, since the present ruin of Italy is caused by nothing other than her dependence for a long period of time on mercenary forces. These forces did, at times, help some get ahead, and they appeared courageous in combat with other mercenaries; but when the invasion of the foreigner came they showed themselves for what they were; and thus, Charles, King of France, was permitted to take Italy with a piece of chalk.[1] And the man who said that our sins were the cause of this disaster spoke the truth;[2] but they were not at all those that he had in mind, but rather these that I have described; and because they were the sins of princes, the princes in turn have suffered the penalty for them.

I wish to demonstrate more fully the sorry nature of such armies. Mercenary captains are either excellent soldiers or they are not; if they are, you cannot trust them, since they will always aspire to their own greatness either by oppressing you, who are their masters, or by oppressing others against your intent; but if the captain is without skill, he usually ruins you. And if someone were to reply that anyone who bears arms will act in this manner, mercenary or not, I would answer that armies have to be commanded either by a prince or by a republic: the prince must go in person and perform the duties of a captain himself; the republic must send its own citizens; and when they send one who does not turn out to be an able man, they must replace him; if he is capable, they ought to restrain him with laws so that he does not go beyond his authority. And we see from experience that only princes and armed republics make very great advances, and that mercenaries do nothing but harm; and a republic armed with its own citizens is less likely to come under the rule of one of its citizens than a city armed with foreign soldiers.

Rome and Sparta for many centuries stood armed and free. The Swiss are extremely well armed and are completely free. An example from antiquity of the use of mercenary troops is the Carthaginians; they were almost overcome by their own mercenary soldiers after the first war with the Romans, even though the Carthaginians had their own citizens as officers. Philip of Macedonia[3] was made captain of their army by the Thebans after the death of Epaminondas,[4] and after the victory he took their liberty from them. The Milanese, after the death of Duke Philip, employed Francesco Sforza to war against the Venetians; having defeated the enemy at Caravaggio, he joined with them to oppress the Milanese his employers. Sforza, his father, being in the employ of Queen Giovanna of Naples,[5] all at once left her without defences; hence, in order not to lose her kingdom, she was forced to throw herself into the lap of the King of Aragon. And if the Venetians and the Florentines have in the past increased their possessions with such soldiers, and their captains have not yet made themselves princes but have instead defended them, I answer that the Florentines have been favoured in this matter by luck; for among their able captains whom they could have had reason to fear, some did not win, others met with opposition, and others turned their ambition elsewhere. The one who did not win was John Hawkwood,[6] whose loyalty, since he did not succeed, will never be known; but anyone will admit that, had he succeeded, the Florentines would have been at his mercy. Sforza always had the Bracceschi[7] as enemies so that each checked the other. Francesco turned his ambition to Lombardy, Braccio against the Church and the Kingdom of Naples.

But let us come to what has occurred just recently. The Florentines made Paulo Vitelli[8] their captain, a very able man and one who rose from private life to achieve great fame. If this man had taken Pisa, no one would deny that the Florentines would have had to become his ally; for, if he had become employed by their enemies, they would have had no defence, and if they had kept him on, they would have been obliged to obey him. As for the Venetians, if we examine the course they followed, we see that they operated securely and gloriously as long as they fought with their own troops (this was before they started fighting on land); with their nobles and their common people armed, they fought courageously. But when they began to fight on land, they abandoned this successful strategy and followed the usual practices of waging war in Italy. As they first began to expand their territory on the mainland, since they did not have much territory there and enjoyed a high reputation, they had little to fear from their captains; but when their territory increased, which happened under Carmagnola,[9] the Venetians had a taste of this mistake; for, having found him very able, since under his command they had defeated the Duke of Milan, and knowing, on the other hand, that he had lost some of his fighting spirit, they judged that they could no longer conquer under him, for he had no wish to do so, yet they could not dismiss him for fear of losing what they had acquired; so in order to secure themselves against him, they were forced to execute him. Then they had as their captains Bartolomeo da Bergamo, Roberto da San Severino, the Count of Pitigliano,[10] and the like; with such as these they had to fear their bosses, not their acquisitions, as occurred later at Vailà,[11] where, in a single day, they lost what had cost them eight hundred years of exhausting effort to acquire. From these soldiers, therefore, come only slow, tardy, and weak conquests and sudden and astonishing losses. And because with these examples I have begun to treat of Italy, which has for many years been ruled by mercenary soldiers, I should like to discuss the matter more thoroughly, in order that once their origin and developments are revealed they can be more easily corrected.

You must, then, understand how in recent times, when the Empire began to be driven out of Italy and the Pope began to win more prestige in temporal affairs, Italy was divided into many states; for many of the large cities took up arms against their nobles, who, at first backed by the Emperor, had kept them under their control; and the Church supported these cities to increase its temporal power; in many other cities citizens became princes. Hence, Italy having come almost entirely into the hands of the Church and of several republics, those priests and other citizens who were not accustomed to bearing arms began to hire foreigners. The first to give prestige to such troops was Alberigo of Conio,[12] a Romagnol. From this man's school emerged, among others, Braccio and Sforza, who in their day were the arbiters of Italy. After them came all the others who, until the present day, have commanded these soldiers. And the result of their ability has been that Italy has been overrun by Charles, plundered by Louis, violated by Ferdinand, and insulted by the Swiss. Their method was first to increase the reputation of their own forces by taking away the prestige of the infantry. They did so because they were men without a state of their own who lived by their profession; a small number of foot soldiers could not give them prestige, and they could not afford to hire a large number of them; and so they relied completely upon cavalry, since for having only a reasonable number of horsemen they were provided for and honoured. And they reduced things to such a state that, in an army of twenty thousand troops, one could hardly find two thousand foot soldiers. Besides this, they had used every means to spare themselves and their soldiers hardship and fear, not killing each other in their battles but rather taking each other prisoner without demanding ransom; they would not attack cities at night; and those in the cities would not attack the tents of the besiegers; they built neither stockades nor trenches around their camps; they did not campaign in the winter. And all these things were permitted by their military code and gave them a means of escaping, as was stated, hardships and dangers: so that these condottieri have led Italy into slavery and humiliation.

## Chapter XV. On Those Things for which Men, and Particularly Princes, are Praised or Blamed

Now there remains to be examined what should be the methods and procedures of a prince in dealing with his subjects and friends. And because

I know that many have written about this, I am afraid that by writing about it again I shall be thought of as presumptuous, since in discussing this material I depart radically from the procedures of others. But since my intention is to write something useful for anyone who understands it, it seemed more suitable to me to search after the effectual truth of the matter rather than its imagined one[13]. And many writers have imagined for themselves republics and principalities that have never been seen nor known to exist in reality; for there is such a gap between how one lives and how one ought to live that anyone who abandons what is done for what ought to be done learns his ruin rather than his preservation: for a man who wishes to profess goodness at all times will come to ruin among so many who are not good. Hence it is necessary for a prince who wishes to maintain his position to learn how not to be good, and to use this knowledge or not to use it according to necessity.

Leaving aside, therefore, the imagined things concerning a prince, and taking into account those that are true, I say that all men, when they are spoken of, and particularly by princes, since they are placed on a higher level, are judged by some of these qualities which bring them either blame or praise. And this is why one is considered generous, another miserly (to use a Tuscan word, since 'avaricious' in our language is still used to mean one who wishes to acquire by means of theft; we call 'miserly' one who excessively avoids using what he has); one is considered a giver, the other rapacious; one cruel, another merciful; one treacherous, another faithful; one effeminate and cowardly, another bold and courageous; one humane, another haughty; one lascivious, another chaste; one trustworthy, another frivolous; one religious, another unbelieving; and the like. And I know that everyone will admit that it would be a very praiseworthy thing to find in a prince, of the qualities mentioned above, those that are held to be good; but since it is neither possible to have them nor to observe them all completely, because the human condition does not permit it, a prince must be prudent enough to know how to escape the bad reputation of those vices that would lose the state for him, and must protect himself from those that will not lose it for him, if this is possible; but if he cannot, he need not concern himself unduly if he ignores these less serious vices. And, moreover, he need not worry about incurring the bad reputation of those vices without which it would be difficult to hold his state; since, carefully taking everything into account, he will discover that something which appears to be a virtue, if pursued, will end in his destruction; while some other thing which seems to be a vice, if pursued, will result in his safety and his well-being.

## Chapter XVII. On Cruelty and Mercy, and whether it is Better to be Loved than to be Feared or the Contrary

Proceeding, to the other qualities mentioned above, I say that every prince must desire to be considered merciful and not cruel; nevertheless, he must take care not to misuse this mercy. Cesare Borgia was considered cruel; none the less, his cruelty had brought order to Romagna, united it, restored it to peace and obedience. If we examine this carefully, we shall see that he was more merciful than the Florentine people, who, in order to avoid being considered cruel, allowed the destruction of Pistoia.[14] Therefore, a prince must not worry about the reproach of cruelty when it is a matter of keeping his subjects united and loyal; for with a very few examples of cruelty he will be more compassionate than those who, out of excessive mercy, permit disorders to continue, from which arise murders and plundering; for these usually harm the community at large, while the executions that come from the prince harm particular individuals. And the new prince, above all other princes, cannot escape the reputation of being called cruel, since new states are full of dangers. And Virgil, through Dido, states: 'My difficult condition and the newness of my rule make me act in such a manner, and to set guards over my land on all sides.'[15]

Nevertheless, a prince must be cautious in believing and in acting, nor should he be afraid of his own shadow; and he should proceed in such a manner, tempered by prudence and humanity, so that too much trust may not render him imprudent nor too much distrust render him intolerable.

From this arises an argument: whether it is better to be loved than to be feared, or the contrary. I reply that one should like to be both one and the other; but since it is difficult to join them together, it is much safer to be feared than to be loved when one of the two must be lacking. For one can generally say this about men: that they are ungrateful, fickle, simulators and deceivers, avoiders of danger, greedy for gain; and while you work for their good they are completely yours, offering you their blood, their property, their lives, and their sons, as I said earlier,[16] when danger is far away; but when it comes nearer to you they turn away. And that prince who bases his power entirely on their words, finding himself completely without other preparations, comes to ruin; for friendships that are acquired by a price and not by greatness and nobility of character are purchased but are not owned, and at the proper moment they cannot be spent. And men are less hesitant about harming someone who makes himself loved than one who makes himself feared because love is held together by a chain of obligation which, since men are wretched creatures, is broken on every occasion in which their own interests are concerned; but fear is sustained by a dread of punishment which will never abandon you.

A prince must nevertheless make himself feared in such a manner that he will avoid hatred, even if he does not acquire love; since to be feared and not to be hated can very well be combined; and this will always be so when he keeps his hands off the property and the women of his citizens and his subjects. And if he must take someone's life, he should do so when there is proper justification and manifest cause; but, above all, he should avoid seizing the property of others; for men forget more quickly the death of their father than the loss of their patrimony. Moreover, reasons for seizing their property are never lacking; and he who begins to live by stealing always finds a reason for taking what belongs to others; on the contrary, reasons for taking a life are rarer and disappear sooner.

But when the prince is with his armies and has under his command a multitude of troops, then it is absolutely necessary that he not worry about being considered cruel; for without that reputation he will never keep an army united or prepared for any combat. Among the praiseworthy deeds of Hannibal[17] is counted this: that, having a very large army, made up of all kinds of men, which he commanded in foreign lands, there never arose the slightest dissension, neither among themselves nor against their leader, both during his good and his bad fortune. This could not have arisen from anything other than his inhuman cruelty, which along with his many other qualities, made him always respected and terrifying in the eyes of his soldiers; and without that, to attain the same effect, his other qualities would not have sufficed. And the writers of history, having considered this matter very little, on the one hand admire these deeds of his and on the other condemn the main cause of them.

And that it is true that his other qualities would not have been sufficient can be seen from the example of Scipio, a most extraordinary man not only in his time but in all recorded history, whose armies in Spain rebelled against him; this came about from nothing other than his excessive compassion, which gave to his soldiers more liberty than military discipline allowed. For this he was censured in the senate by Fabius Maximus,[18] who called him the corrupter of the Roman militia. The Locrians, having been ruined by one of Scipio's officers, were not avenged by him, nor was the arrogance of that officer corrected, all because of his tolerant nature; so that someone in the senate who tried to apologize for him said that there were many men who knew how not to err better than they knew how to correct errors. Such a nature would have, in time, damaged Scipio's fame and glory if he had continued to command armies; but, living under the control of the senate, this harmful characteristic of his not only was concealed but brought him glory.

I conclude, therefore, returning to the problem of being feared and loved, that, since men love at their own pleasure and fear at the pleasure of the prince, a wise prince should build his foundation upon that which belongs to him, not upon that which belongs to others: he must strive only to avoid hatred, as has been said.

## Chapter XVIII. How a Prince should Keep his Word

How praiseworthy it is for a prince to keep his word and to live by integrity and not by deceit everyone knows; nevertheless, one sees from the experience of our times that the princes who have accomplished great deeds are those who have cared little for keeping their promises and who have known how to manipulate the minds of men by shrewdness; and in the end they have surpassed those who laid their foundations upon loyalty.

You must, therefore, know that there are two means of fighting:[19] one according to the laws, the other with force; the first way is proper to man, the second to beasts; but because the first, in many cases, is not sufficient, it becomes necessary to have recourse to the second. Therefore, a prince must know how to use wisely the natures of the beast and the man. This policy was taught to princes allegorically by the ancient writers, who described how Achilles and many other ancient princes were given to Chiron the Centaur[20] to be raised and taught under his discipline. This can only mean that, having a half-beast and half-man as a teacher, a prince must know how to employ the nature of the one and the other; and the one without the other cannot endure.

Since, then, a prince must know how to make good use of the nature of the beast, he should choose from among the beasts the fox and the lion;[21] for the lion cannot defend itself from traps and the fox cannot protect itself from wolves. It is therefore necessary to be a fox in order to recognize the traps and a lion in order to frighten the wolves. Those who play only the part of the lion do not understand matters. A wise ruler, therefore, cannot and should not keep his word when such an observance of faith would be to his disadvantage and when the reasons which made him promise are removed. And if men were all good, this rule would not be good; but since men are a contemptible lot and will not keep their promises to you, you likewise need not keep yours to them. A prince never lacks legitimate reasons to break his promise. Of this one could cite an endless number of modern examples to show how many promises have been made null and void because of the infidelity of princes; and he who has known best how to use the fox has come to a better end. But it is necessary to know how to disguise this nature well and to be a great hypocrite and a liar: and men are so simple-minded and so controlled by their present needs that one who deceives will always find another who will allow himself to be deceived.

I do not wish to remain silent about one of these recent instances. Alexander VI did nothing else, he thought about nothing else, except to deceive men, and he always found the occasion to do this. And there never was a man who had more forcefulness in his oaths, who affirmed a thing with more promises, and who honoured his word less; nevertheless, his tricks always succeeded perfectly, since he was well acquainted with this aspect of the world.

Therefore, it is not necessary for a prince to have all of the above-mentioned qualities, but it is very necessary for him to appear to have them. Furthermore, I shall be so bold as to assert this: that having them and practising them at all times is harmful; and appearing to have them is useful; for instance, to seem merciful, faithful, humane, trustworthy, religious, and to be so; but his mind should be disposed in such a way that, should it become necessary not to be so, he will be able and know how to change to the contrary. And it is essential to understand this: that a prince, and especially a new prince, cannot observe all those things for which men are considered good, for, in order to maintain the state, he is often obliged to act against his promise, against charity, against humanity, and against religion. And, therefore, it is necessary that he have a mind ready to turn itself according to the way the winds of fortune and the changeability of affairs require him; and, as I said above, as long as it is possible, he should not stray from the good, but he should know how to enter into evil when necessity commands.

A prince, therefore, must be very careful never to let anything slip from his lips which is not full of the five qualities mentioned above: he should appear, upon seeing and hearing him, to be all mercy, all faithfulness, all integrity, all kindness, all religion. And there is nothing more necessary than to seem to possess this last quality. And men in general judge more by their eyes than their hands; for everyone can see but few can feel. Everyone sees what you seem to be, few touch upon what you are, and those few do not dare to contradict the opinion of the many who have the majesty of the state to defend them; and in the actions of all men, and especially of princes, where there is no impartial arbiter, one must consider the final result.[22] Let a prince therefore act to conquer and to maintain the state; his methods will always be judged honourable and will be praised by all; for ordinary people are always deceived by appearances and by the outcome of a thing; and in the world there is nothing but ordinary people; and there is no room for the few, while the many have a place to lean on. A certain prince of the present day,[23] whom I shall refrain from naming, preaches nothing but peace and faith, and to both one and the other he is entirely opposed; and both, if he had put them into practice, would have cost him many times over either his reputation or his state.

## Chapter XXII. On the Prince's Private Advisers

The choice of advisers is of no little import to a prince; and they are good or not, according to the wisdom of the prince. The first thing one does to evaluate the wisdom of a ruler is to examine the men that he has around him; and when they are capable and faithful one can always consider him wise, for he has known how to recognize their ability and to keep them loyal; but when they are otherwise one can always form a low impression of him; for the first error he makes is made in this choice of advisers.

There was no one who knew Messer Antonio da Venafro,[24] adviser of Pandoifo Petrucci, Prince of Siena, who did not judge Pandolfo to be a very worthy man for having him as his minister. For there are three types of intelligence: one understands on its own, the second discerns what others understand, the third neither understands by itself nor through the intelligence of others; that first kind is most excellent, the second excellent, the third useless; therefore, it was necessary that, if Pandolfo's intelligence were not of the first sort, it must have been of the second: for, whenever a man has the intelligence to recognize the good or the evil that a man does or says, although he may not have original ideas of his own, he recognizes the bad deeds and the good deeds of the adviser, and he is able to praise the latter and to correct the others; and the adviser cannot hope to deceive him and thus he maintains his good behaviour.

But as to how a prince may know the adviser, there is this way which never fails. When you see that the adviser thinks more about himself than about you, and that in all his deeds he seeks his own interests, such a man as this will never be a good adviser and you will never he able to trust him; for a man who has the state of another in his hand must never think about himself but always about his prince, and he must never be concerned with anything that does not concern his prince.

And, on the other hand, the prince should think of the adviser in order to keep him good—honouring him, making him wealthy, putting him in his debt, giving him a share of the honours and the responsibilities—so that the adviser sees that he cannot exist without the prince and so his abundant wealth will not make him desire more riches, or his many duties make him fear changes. When, therefore, advisers and princes are of such a nature in their dealings with each other, they can have faith in each other; and when they are otherwise, the outcome will always be harmful either to the one or to the other.

## Chapter XXV. On Fortune's Role in Human Affairs and how she can be Dealt with

It is not unknown to me that many have held, and still hold, the opinion that the things of this world are, in a manner, controlled by fortune and by God, that men with their wisdom cannot control them, and, on the contrary, that men can have no remedy whatsoever for them; and for this reason they might judge that they need not sweat much over such matters but let them be governed by fate. This opinion has been more strongly held in our own times because of the great variation of affairs that has been observed and that is being observed every day which is beyond human conjecture. Sometimes, as I think about these things, I am inclined to their opinion to a certain extent. Nevertheless, in order that our free will be not extinguished, I judge it to be true that fortune is the arbiter of one half of our actions,[25] but that she still leaves the control of the other half, or almost that, to us. And I compare her to one of those ruinous rivers that, when they become enraged, flood the plains, tear down the trees and buildings, taking up earth from one spot and placing it upon another; everyone flees from them, everyone yields to their onslaught, unable to oppose them in any way. But, although they are of such a nature, it does not follow that, when the weather is calm, we cannot take precautions with embankments and dikes, so that when they rise up again either the waters will be channelled off or their impetus will not be either so unchecked or so damaging. The same things happen where fortune is concerned: she shows her force where there is no organized strength to resist her; and she directs her impact there where she knows that dikes and embankments are not constructed to hold her. And, if you consider Italy, the seat of these changes and the nation, which has set them in motion, you will see a country without embankments and without a single bastion: for, if she were defended by the necessary forces, like Germany, Spain, and France, either this flood would not have produced the great changes that it has or it would not have come upon us at all. And this I consider enough to say about fortune in general terms.

But, limiting myself more to particulars, I say that one sees a prince prosper today and come to ruin tomorrow without having seen him change his character or any of the reasons that have been discussed at length earlier; that is, that a prince who relies completely upon fortune will come to ruin as soon as she changes; I also believe that the man who adapts his course of action to the nature of the times will succeed and, likewise, that the man who sets his course of action out of tune with the times will come to grief. For one can observe that men, in the affairs which lead them to the end that they seek—that is, glory and wealth—proceed in different ways; one by caution, another with impetuousness; one through violence, another with guile; one with patience, another with its opposite; and each one by these various means can attain his goals. And we also see, in the case of two cautious men, that one reaches his goal while the other does not; and, likewise, two men equally succeed using two different means, one being cautious and the other impetuous: this arises from nothing else than the nature of the times that either suit or do not suit their course of action. From this results that which I have said, that two men, working in opposite ways, can produce the same outcome; and of two men working in the same fashion one achieves his goal and the other does not. On this also depends the variation of what is good; for, if a man governs himself with caution and patience, and the times and conditions are turning in such a way that his policy is a good one, he will prosper; but, if the times and conditions change, he will be ruined because he does not change his method of procedure. Nor is there to be found a man so prudent that he knows how to adapt himself to this, both because he cannot deviate from that to which he is by nature inclined and also because he cannot be persuaded to depart from a path, having always prospered by following it. And therefore the cautious man, when it is time to act impetuously, does not know how to do so, and he is ruined; but if he had changed his conduct with the times, fortune would not have changed.

Pope Julius II acted impetuously in all his affairs, and he found the times and conditions so apt to this course of action that he always achieved successful results. Consider the first campaign he waged against Bologna while Messer Giovanni Bentivogli was still alive. The Venetians were unhappy about it; so was the King of Spain; Julius still had negotiations going on about it with France; and, nevertheless, he started personally on this expedition with his usual ferocity and lack of caution. Such a move kept Spain and the Venetians at bay, the latter out of fear and the former out of a desire to regain the entire Kingdom of Naples; and at the same time it drew the King of

France into the affair, for when the King saw that the Pope had already made this move, he judged that he could not deny him the use of his troops without obviously harming him, since he wanted his friendship in order to defeat the Venetians. And therefore Julius achieved with his impetuous action what no other pontiff would ever have achieved with the greatest of human wisdom; for, if he had waited to leave Rome with agreements settled and things in order, as any other pontiff might have done, he would never have succeeded, because the King of France would have found a thousand excuses and the others would have aroused in him a thousand fears. I wish to leave unmentioned his other deeds, which were all similar and which were all successful. And the brevity of his life[26] did not let him experience the opposite, since, if times which necessitated caution had come, his ruin would have followed from it: for never would he have deviated from those methods to which his nature inclined him.

I conclude, therefore, that, since fortune changes and men remain set in their ways, men will succeed when the two are in harmony and fail when they are not in accord. I am certainly convinced of this: that it is better to be impetuous than cautious, because fortune is a woman,[27] and it is necessary, in order to keep her down, to beat her and to struggle with her. And it is seen that she more often allows herself to be taken over by men who are impetuous than by those who make cold advances; and then, being a woman, she is always the friend of young men, for they are less cautious, more aggressive, and they command her with more audacity.

## Notes

1. *a piece of chalk*: This expression refers to the practice Charles VIII followed in marking the homes to be used for quartering his troops during the invasion of Italy in 1494–5; the contemptuous tone of Machiavelli's remark underscores his belief that Italian resistance was virtually non-existent. This remark is attributed to Pope Alexander VI by the French historian Philippe de Commynes (*Mémoires*, vii, 14).
2. *And the man . . . spoke the truth*: Most probably, this is a reference to Girolamo Savonarola, whose sermon of 1 November 1494 interpreted the Italian invasion by Charles VIII as a punishment for the sins of Italy, Florence, and the Church.
3. *Philip of Macedonia*: King of Macedonia (359–336 BC) and father of Alexander the Great. Philip was not, strictly speaking, a mercenary.
4. *Epaminondas*: Theban general (d.362 BC) who defeated Sparta at the Battle of Leuctra (371 BC).

5. *Queen Giovanna of Naples*: Ruler of Naples (1414–35), who hired mercenaries (Sforza and others) to defend her kingdom.
6. *John Hawkwood*: An English knight who came to Italy in 1361 and served Florence as a mercenary until his death in 1393 (known in Italy as Giovanni Acuto).
7. *the Bracceschi*: mercenary troops commanded by Braccio da Montone (1368–1424) who opposed other mercenaries under Sforza in the service of Queen Giovanna of Naples.
8. *Paulo Vitelli*: Florentine mercenary executed by his employers in 1499 after an unsatisfactory performance at the Siege of Pisa, and the brother of Vitellozzo Vitelli, strangled by Cesare Borgia at Sinigaglia.
9. *Carmagnola*: Francesco Bussone, Count of Carmagnola (*c.*1380–1432), a Venetian soldier of fortune executed by Venice for suspected double-dealing with his Visconti opponents.
10. *Bartolomeo da Bergamo . . . the Count of Pitigliano*: Bartolomeo Colleoni (1400–75) fought in the service of Venice and is remembered by the magnificent equestrian statue Verrocchio erected in the city; Roberto da San Severino commanded Venetian troops in a war with Ferrara (1482–4); Niccolò Orsini, Count of Pitigliano (1442–1510), was the Venetian commander at the disastrous battle of Vailà against the forces of Pope Julius II.
11. *as occurred later at Vailà*: At the battle of Vailà or Agnadello in 1509, the Venetians were defeated by French troops.
12. *Alberigo of Conio*: Alberigo da Barbiano (d. 1409) was the founder of a famous company of mercenaries composed entirely of Italian rather than foreign troops.
13. *the effectual truth . . . rather than its imagined one*: Machiavelli has in mind here not only Plato but also the many abstract portraits of idealized rulers or Christian princes composed by the Latin humanists.
14. *the destruction of Pistoia*: When violent squabbles broke out between the Cancellieri and the Panciatchi factions of this Florentine subject-city in 1501–2, Machiavelli was sent there several times in an attempt to restore order.
15. *'My difficult condition . . . on all sides'*: Machiavelli cites the original Latin from Virgil's *Aeneid* (I.563–4).
16. *as I said earlier*: see chapter IX.
17. *Hannibal*: Commander of the Carthaginian army (249–183 BC) who was defeated by Scipio at the Battle of Zama in 202 BC, ending the Second Punic War.
18. *Fabius Maximus*: Roman consul and dictator in 217 BC (d. 203 BC), whose delaying tactics against Hannibal while his army was ravaging Italy were opposed by Scipio, who wished to wage a more aggressive offensive campaign.
19. *two means of fighting*: Machiavelli takes this argument from Cicero, *De officiis* (I.xi), but changes it quite drastically.
20. *Chiron the Centaur*: Machiavelli's strange allegorical interpretation of Chiron's dual nature has no apparent classical source and was probably a product of his own fantasy.
21. *the fox and the lion*: Machiavelli found this soon-to-become famous idea in Cicero's *De officiis* (I.xiii), but he changes Cicero's argument completely. Cicero

had maintained that both force and treachery were inhuman and, therefore, contemptible policies.

22. *one must consider the final result*: The Italian original, *si guarda al fine*, has often been misconstrued to imply that Machiavelli meant 'the end justifies the means', something he never said in *The Prince*. For another important statement concerning ends and means, see Machiavelli's discussion of Romulus in *The Discourses* (I.ix).
23. *a certain prince of the present day*: Probably Ferdinand II of Aragon.
24. *Messer Antonio da Venafro*: Antonio Giordani from Venafro (b. 1459) was one of Petrucci's most trusted advisers.
25. *fortune is the arbiter of one half of our actions*: Machiavelli's conception of the 'new prince', his *virtù*, and the important opportunities chance might provide him to achieve power, all presuppose a certain amount of human freedom. His discussion of fortune, however, owes more to his poetic inclinations than to a dispassionate philosophical discussion of the weighty issues involved in the conflict between human free will and determinism.
26. *And the brevity of his life*: Once again, as he had earlier done in discussing Pope Alexander VI (Chapter VII), Machiavelli is referring to the brevity of the pontificate of Julius II, not to the brevity of the man's life itself.
27. *fortune is a woman*: Here, Machiavelli clearly draws a parallel between the energy required for a violent sexual encounter and that which determines the drive for political power.

# 4 The Treatise on General Sociology

Vilfredo Pareto

## Political Forms

(2237) Among the various complex phenomena observable in a society, the regime or system of government is of very great importance, for it is intimately associated with the character of the governing class, and both of them are in a relationship of interdependence with other social phenomena.

(2239) Those for whom the form of government is of highest importance are much exercised by the question: 'What is the best form of governmental system?' But this question has little or no meaning unless the particular society is indicated to which the system is to be applied, and unless the term 'best' is explained, for it refers in a very indefinite way to the various individual and social utilities. Although now and then this has sometimes been discerned intuitively, consideration of forms of governmental system has begotten endless numbers of derivations which ultimately appear as various myths. Both myths and derivations are worth nothing at all from the logico-experimental viewpoint, but both of them (or rather the sentiments they manifest) may have effects of great significance in motivating human behaviour. It is certain that the sentiments manifested by belief in such political forms as monarchy, republic, oligarchy, and democracy have played, and continue to play, no small part in social phenomena—that they have in common with the sentiments manifested by other religions. 'Divine right', be it of prince, aristocracy, people, proletariat, majority, or any other

Vilfredo Pareto, 'The Treatise of General Sociology', in *Sociological Writings*, ed. S. Finer (London: Pall Mall Press, 1966), part two, pp. 265–75.

imaginable divine right, has not the least experimental validity. We must accordingly consider these forms of divine right only extrinsically, as facts, as manifestations of sentiments which, like other characteristics in the human beings composing a given society, operate to determine that society's ethos and form. In observing that such 'rights' have no experimental basis whatever, we are not in any way imputing invalidity to any social utility which may be attributed to any one of them. Certainly, if the observation were a derivation, then such an imputation would stick, since in such reasonings it is generally assumed automatically that 'what is not rational is harmful'. But the question of utility is not affected one way or the other when the proposition is strictly logico-experimental, since it makes no such assumption. The study of political forms properly belongs to *special* sociology. Here we are concerned with forms only for the purpose of ascertaining the substance underlying derivations and of studying the relationships between the various types of governing-class composition and other social phenomena.

(2240) As in other matters of this kind, we immediately come up against the stumbling block of terminology. This is to be expected, since the objective investigations we are making require an objective terminology, whereas the subjective discussions customary in these matters are served well enough by a subjective terminology drawn from everyday language. For example, everyone recognizes that, at the present time, 'democracy' is tending to become the political system of all civilized peoples. But what is the precise meaning of this term 'democracy'? It is even more vague than that vaguest of terms, 'religion'. We must, therefore, set it aside and turn to study the facts it covers.

## Agencies of Government

(2244) We will not linger over the fiction of 'popular representation'—fine words butter no parsnips. Let us rather see what is the substance beneath the various forms of power in the governing class. Discounting exceptions, which are few and of short duration, there is everywhere a governing class, not large in membership, which maintains itself in power partly by force and partly by consent of the governed, who are very numerous. Between one governing class and another the difference lies mainly, in regard to substance, in the ratio of force to consent, and, in regard to form, in the ways by which force is used and consent procured.

(2246) . . . Dominant peoples sometimes endeavour to assimilate their subject peoples. Success in achieving this assimilation is certainly the best way of ensuring their power. But often they fail because they seek to change residues violently instead of making use of existing residues. Rome brought the policy of assimilation to a fine art and was thereby able to extend and maintain its power over peoples in Latium, Italy, and the Mediterranean basin.

(2249) Utilizing the existing sentiments in a society is in itself neither useful nor harmful to society. The utility and the harm depend on the outcome. If this benefits society, there is utility; if it is detrimental, there is harm. Nor can it be said, when the governing class pursues an end which is to its own advantage and without concern whether this be advantageous for the subject class, that this is necessarily detrimental to the subject class. There are very many cases in which the governing class exclusively pursues its own best interests and yet in so doing also promotes the best interests of the subject class. In short, utilizing the existing residues of a society is only a means, and its value is determined by the value of its outcome.

(2250) Interests should be included with residues as agencies of government. Sometimes it is interests alone which are able to modify residues. Even so, although interests on their own, unalloyed with sentiments, can well be a powerful agency affecting individuals in whom residues of the instinct of combinations (Class 1) predominate—therein affecting many members of the governing class—we must take note that, on the other hand, interests on their own and unconnected with sentiments have very little effect on people in whom residues of aggregate-persistence predominate, which is to say the greater part of the subject class. Speaking generally and very roughly, it can be said that the governing class has a better view of its own interests because it wears thinner veils of sentiment, while the subject class has a less clear view of its interests because it is more heavily shrouded in veils of sentiment. As a result the governing class is able to gull the subject class into serving the interests of the governing class. Such interests are not necessarily opposed to those of the subject class; often the two sets of interests coincide to a degree which makes the deception advantageous to the subject class.

(2251) Throughout history, consent and force appear as agencies of government. . . .

(2252) In the same way that derivations are much more variable than the residues they manifest, so do the forms in which force and consent appear vary much more than the sentiments and interests originating in them; the differences in the proportions of force and consent largely arise from differences in the proportions of sentiments and interests. Both derivations and forms of government . . . have much less influence on the social equilibrium than the sentiments and interests sustaining them. . . .

## The Governing Class: Character and Methods

(2253) Everywhere there exists a governing class, even in a despotism, but the forms in which it appears vary. In absolute governments there is only one figure on the stage: the sovereign. In so-called democratic governments it is parliament. But all the time behind the scenes are people who have very important functions in the practical work of government. Certainly from time to time these have to bow the head to the caprices of ignorant and overbearing sovereigns or parliaments; but soon enough they return to their tenacious, patient, unwavering work, the effects of which are of much greater significance. We find in the Roman *Digesta* admirable constitutions bearing the names of quite deplorable emperors, just as in our own day tolerably good legal codes emanate from parliaments which, heaven knows, are stupid enough. In both cases the reason is the same: the sovereign gives a free hand to his legal advisers, in some cases being quite unaware of what he is being made to do. This is even more so the case with parliaments, which are apt to be even less discerning in these matters than some kings and potentates. Even less percipient is His Majesty Demos, and at times this has made it possible to achieve, against the current of his prejudices, improvements in social conditions, not to speak of timely measures for national defence. The worthy Demos thinks he is following his own wishes, whereas in fact he is following the behests of his rulers. But this very often serves only the interests of his rulers, for these, from the days of Aristophanes down to our own, have practised on a large scale the art of pulling the wool over the eyes of Demos. Like men of the same kidney at the end of the Roman Republic, our own plutocrats are absorbed in making money, either for themselves or to sate the greed of their partisans and accomplices. They give little or no thought to anything else. Among the various derivations they deploy to show the nation that their being in power is of benefit to it, there is the assertion that the people are better equipped to make decisions on general questions than on special questions. In fact, the exact reverse is the case. One has only to talk a little with uneducated people to discover that they can understand special questions, which are usually concrete, much better than general questions, which are usually abstract. But abstract questions have this merit for those in power: whatever the views of the public about them, political leaders will indubitably be able to make what they like of them. For example, the people elect members of parliament whose policy is to abolish interest on capital and 'surplus value' in industry and to check the 'greed' of the speculators. These are general questions. The elected representatives, directly or indirectly, make enormous increases in the public debt, and therefore in the interest paid to capital; they maintain and indeed increase the 'surplus value' enjoyed by manufacturers, many of whom grow rich on demagogy, and make over the government of the state to speculators. Some of the most prominent of these become diplomatists—like Volpi, who concluded the Peace of Lausanne—or ministers—like Caillaux and Lloyd George.

(2254) The governing class is not homogeneous; it has within itself a governing authority—a more exclusive class or a leader or a power group which exercises control in effect and practice. Sometimes the fact is obvious, as with the Ephors at Sparta, the Council of Ten at Venice, the favourite ministers of an absolute sovereign, or the political 'bosses' in parliament. At other times the centre of control is to some extent under cover, as with the 'caucus' in England, the party conventions in the USA, the wire-pulling financiers in France and Italy, and so on. The inclination to personify abstractions or even simply to give them an objective reality leads many people to think of the ruling class as a person, or at least as a concrete unit, and to suppose that it has a single will, implementing preconceived plans by logical procedures. Many anti-Semites think in this way of the Jews; likewise many socialists of the bourgeoisie—though others, approaching nearer to reality, see the bourgeoisie as a system for whose operations the individual bourgeois, to some extent, is not directly responsible. The governing class, like other groups in society, performs logical and non-logical actions. The main factor in the matter is really the system in which they subsist, not the conscious will of individuals, who may indeed in many cases be carried along by the system to positions they would never have arrived at by deliberate choice. . . .

(2257) To maintain its power, the governing class makes use of individuals from the subject class. These fall into two different categories which correspond to the two principal agencies for retaining power. In the first category, force is the instrument; it embraces soldiers, police, and the *bravi*—the hired cut-throats of former centuries. In the second, the instrument is artifice; from the days of the Roman clientele to the henchmen of modern politicians, individuals in this category exhibit similar characteristics. These two categories are always present in public life, but not in the same actual proportions and even less in the same visible proportions. Rome under the praetorians marks one extreme: here the main *de facto* instrument is armed force. The USA exemplifies the other extreme: here political cliques are the main actual—and to a somewhat lesser extent also the apparent—instruments. These cliques work in various ways. The principal way is the least obvious: the government 'looks after' the interests of the speculators, often without having any explicit understanding with them. A protectionist government, for example, wins the confidence and support of the manufacturers it protects without necessarily making an explicit agreement with all of them, although it may come to a direct understanding with leading individual manufacturers. . . . There are other more obvious ways, less important from the social viewpoint but which are held to be of great importance from the ethical viewpoint—for example, the bribing of voters, elected representatives, government officials and ministers, journalists, and similar people. This is the modern version of the bribery, under absolute governments, of courtiers, male and female favourites, government officials, generals and so on—nor has this older form of corruption entirely disappeared. . . .

(2259) There seems to be a very close correlation between 'democratic' evolution and the increasing use of that method of governing which resorts to artifice and clique politics as opposed to the method which has recourse to force. This opposition between the two agencies is observable in the history of the late Republican period in Rome; force finally emerged the victor in the shape of the Empire. It is even more evident at the present time. The political system of many 'democratic' countries could very well be defined as mainly an economic feudalism in which the skilful deployment of political cliques constitutes the main instrument of government. In this it differs from the military feudalism of the medieval period, the main instrument of which was force based on vassalage. A political system in which the 'people' expresses its 'will' (supposing it to have one, which is arguable) without cliques, intrigues, lobbies, and factions exists only as a pious wish of theorists. It is not observable in reality in the past or the present, either in the West or anywhere else.

(2260) These phenomena have attracted wide attention, but usually have been described as deviations or 'degenerations' of democracy. But when or where we are to find the perfect, or at least tolerably healthy, state of affairs from which these unpleasant things are a degeneration, this no one has ever been able to say. All one can say is that, when democracy was a political movement in opposition, it had fewer of the blemishes it now exhibits; but this is a characteristic common to almost all opposition parties, for these lack not so much the will as the opportunity for malpractice.

(2267) If we consider all these facts objectively, freeing our thinking as far as possible from the influence of sectarian passions and from the prejudices of country, party, perfectionist and idealist passions, and the like, we see that in reality—whatever the form of political system—the men who govern have, as a rule, a definite tendency to use their power to keep control of affairs and to abuse it in order to obtain personal advantages and gains, which sometimes they do not distinguish from party advantages and gains, and almost always identify with national advantages and gains. It follows that: (1) From this point of view, the various forms of political system do not differ markedly from one another. The differences existing between them lie not in the firm but in the substance; that is to say, in the sentiments of the people. The more—or less—honest the general population of a country, the more—or less—honest its government. (2) The uses and abuses of power will be the more considerable the greater the intervention of government in private affairs. As exploitable material increases, so do potential gains. . . . (3) The governing class sets itself to appropriate other people's goods and property not only for its own use but also to share its booty with individuals and groups in the subject class who defend it and support its power—as the client supports his patron—whether by force or guile. (4) Usually neither patrons nor clients are fully aware that their conduct transgresses the moral norms prevailing in their society, and even when they are so aware they readily find excuses either by arguing that, when all is said and done, other people would do just the same, or else by recourse to the convenient pretext that the end justifies the means—and for them there can be no more excellent end than maintaining themselves in power. (5) The government machine consumes in all sorts of ways a quantity of wealth which correlates not only with the total amount of wealth represented by the private interests which are subject to government intervention, but also with the relative proportions of Class I and Class II residues among the governors and the governed.

## Elements in the Governing Class

(2268) . . . We can divide these elements into two broad categories. Type A comprises the individuals who aim resolutely at ideal ends, adopting and strictly following certain rules of conduct. Type B comprises those whose aim is to promote the well-being of themselves and their dependants or henchmen. This general category is divisible into two subtypes. We will indicate as B-*a* those who are content with the enjoyment of power and honours, leaving the material benefits to their associates; and as B-*b* those who seek material benefits—generally money—both for themselves and for their adherents. People who favour a particular party call the A types in it 'honest men' and set them up for admiration. Opponents of that party term them fanatics and sectarians and hold them in odium. The men of the B-*a* sort are generally regarded as 'honest' by those well disposed to the party, and are viewed with indifference, in regard to honesty, by its opponents. When the existence of men of the B-*b* sort is discovered, everyone calls them 'dishonest', but the friends of the party try to cover up their existence, and to achieve this they are quite capable of saying that black is white. The B-*a* are usually much more costly to a country than the B-*b*, because their veneer of honesty makes possible all sorts of manœuvres directed towards transferring other people's property into the hands of their political cliques. Moreover, the B-*a* umbrella also covers a fair number of people who, while taking nothing for themselves, go to great lengths to enrich their families. The relative proportions of these two main categories A and B depend to a great extent on the relative proportions of Class I and Class II residues. Among the A, Class II residues greatly predominate and so, according to one's point of view, the A may be called 'honest' or 'fanatic and sectarian'. Class I residues prevail among the Bs; hence these are better fitted to rule. When the B attain power they find the A a heavy drag on their party, though they serve to give the party a tinge of respectability. But this purpose is better fulfilled by the B-*a*; these are a rather rare commodity and much sought after by parties. The relative proportions of Class I and Class II residues among the party's voters, active supporters, and those of its members not in government correspond, without being identical, to the relative proportions of these residues in the group which actually governs—the party's general staff. Only a party abundant in Class II residues can elect many individuals of the A category; but it also elects, without realizing it, some men of the B category, because these, being astute and circumspect and masters of the art of combinations, can easily pull wool over the eyes of ingenuous voters in whom Class II residues predominate.

In our western political systems, parties are divisible into two broad classes: (1) parties which alternate with one another in government; (2) intransigent, uncompromising parties which do not get into government. It therefore follows that in parties which alternate in power there will be a minimum of the A and a maximum of the B; in intransigent parties the relative proportions will be reversed. Another way of stating the same thing would be to say that the parties which do not get into government are often more honest, but also more fanatical and sectarian, than parties which do exercise power. Hence the French aphorism: 'The Republic was a fine thing under the Empire.' . . . In the parties which get into power, there is a first 'weeding-out' at the hustings. With few exceptions, a man cannot become a member of parliament unless he pays for the honour and unless he is prepared to dole out—and even more freely to promise—favours from the government. Very few of the A ever get beyond this hurdle. Yet candidates who are rich enough to buy parliamentary seats, regarding them as luxuries, come very near to being A, for, strange as it may first appear, they are next to the A the most honest of politicians. In our day their numbers are growing smaller owing to the enormous increase in the cost of buying votes. Those who meet the cost themselves aim at recouping the outlay by making money out of their political position, while those who will not or cannot find the money themselves get the administration to foot the bill in the form of various kinds of confessions and favours. The competition is tremendous and only those exceptionally well equipped with combination instincts can come out on top.

A second and more thorough test is the choice of ministers. Parliamentary candidates have to make promises to the electorate; ministerial candidates have to make promises to members of parliament and must be able to satisfy them that they and their political supporters will be well looked after. Ingenuous people are greatly mistaken in thinking that, to cope with these matters, it is enough for a man to be a knave. In fact, exceptional talents are required: shrewd intelligence and a marked aptitude for combinations of all kinds. Ministers do not have at their disposal great treasure chests which they can dip into at any time to scatter largesse among their adherents. They have to survey the world of business and industry with a shrewd eye to devise subtle combinations of economic favouritism, adroit ways of being agreeable to banks and business corporations, of promoting monopolies, of manipulating the incidence of taxation, and so forth. They have to know the ins and outs of bringing influence to bear on the law courts and of awarding titles and honours and such things to the benefit of those on whom they depend for continuation in power. And all along the A men in other parties must somehow be prevented from joining together. Those in a party who have a firm faith which is opposed to the firm faith of these A will not accomplish much in this direction. But if one has no faith or convictions whatever, with practically no residues save those of Class I (combinations), then it will not be too difficult to influence the A, or indeed profit from their very convictions to bring them over to one's own side, or at least to weaken the strength of their opposition. It is certain, therefore, that, in the parties which alternate in governing a country, Class I residues greatly preponderate. It is for this reason that our political system is tending to become more and more a demagogic plutocracy. The various parties continually accuse one another of dishonesty. . . . Since almost all parties contain B-*b* types in them, considering that element exclusively would justify an accusation of dishonesty against almost every party. Parties also have their B-*a*, so that, if one considers these exclusively, one may or may not accuse a party of dishonesty, depending on how one defines the term 'dishonesty'. Moreover, there are very few parties which do not have some A types; if one considers them exclusively, one may well say that a given party is honest. If instead we consider the relative proportions of A and B types in a party, we shall certainly find some parties in which the A predominate and which therefore may be called 'honest'. But in very many other cases it is not possible to determine whether there is any significant difference in the proportion of the A to the B. All one can say is that in the various parties which clash in the struggle for power, the A are remarkable for their rarity.

At the same time, since the lower classes are still rich in Class II residues, it behoves administrations which in reality are motivated solely by material interests at least to pretend that they are inspired by ideals. Politicians have to swaddle themselves in veils—often pretty diaphanous of honesty. When one of them is trapped with his finger in the till, the opposition raises a great clamour of indignation—which does not prevent it from doing all it can to turn the scandal to its own advantage. If the alleged culprit's party fails in its efforts to exculpate him, it will cast him off as a ship in a storm throws out ballast. The public watches the affair develop with the fascinated interest of an audience at the theatre, and it becomes high drama free of charge if by any chance there is in the affair an element of sex or human interest. Trivial minor issues push the main issues aside, and the real issue—the social and political system which begets such scandals—is entirely disregarded. . . . Moralists assume that it is the fortuitous rise to power and influence of a 'dishonest' man which has provoked the scandal, arguing as if it were equivalent to a cashier's embezzling his firm. But there is no parallel between the two cases. It is not by fortuitous circumstance that such a man is raised to a position of power; it is by selection at the dictates of the very nature of the system. For the comparison with the dishonest cashier to have point, we would have to assume that the cashier was not appointed in the normal way but that his employer deliberately recruited him from among potential till-pilferers with outstanding gifts for fraud and speculation.

## Typology of Government

(2274) . . . We must note that very often the governing class, aiming at certain ends, indirectly produces other results, some of which it neither foresaw nor desired. For example, governments which impose protective tariffs in order to favour the interests of their clique may unintentionally promote thereby the circulation of élites. From the ethical viewpoint, a measure may be judged independently of all other social phenomena, but from the viewpoint of social utility one cannot so judge matters; one has to consider how this measure affects the social equilibrium as a whole. . . . To gain a general notion of this aspect, let us consider certain types of government as revealed by history.

*Type I. Governments which rely mainly on physical force and on religious or other similar sentiments.* These include, for example, the governments of the Greek cities in the era of the 'tyrants', of Sparta, of Rome under Augustus and Tiberius, of the Venetian Republic in the last centuries of its existence, and of many European countries in the eighteenth century. In all there is a governing class in which Class II residues predominate over Class I residues. Élite-circulation generally speaking is slow. They are not expensive governments, but on the other hand they provide no stimulus to economic production, either because they have an innate repugnance for new things or because they set little value, in terms of élite circulation, on individuals with a marked propensity for economic combinations. If, however, such a propensity exists in the population as a whole, society may enjoy a fair degree of economic prosperity (as was the case with Rome under the High Empire), provided government sets no obstacles in the way. But often in the long run there proves to be a substantial obstacle arising from the fact that the ideal of governments of this type is a nation petrified in its institutions (Sparta, Rome during the Low Empire, Venice during its decadence). They may grow wealthy by conquests, but this wealth is necessarily precarious since conquest produces no new riches (Sparta, Rome). Moreover, such regimes have in the past often degenerated into rule by armed bands (praetorians, janissaries) which are fit only to squander wealth.

(2275) *Type II. Governments which rely mainly on intelligence and cunning.* Here we can distinguish two subtypes. II-*a*: If intelligence and cunning are mainly used to influence sentiments, the outcome is some kind of theocratic government. This type has disappeared in modern Europe and we need not linger over it. . . . II-*b:* If intelligence and cunning are mainly used to operate on interests (which is not to say that they neglect sentiments), the outcome is governments like Athenian demagogy, the Roman aristocracy at various periods during the Republic, many of the medieval republics, and finally—a very important variety—the 'speculator' governments of our own day.

(2276) In all governments of Type II, even those which play on sentiments, the governing class has a predominance of Class I over Class II residues . . .

The circulation of élites is normally slow in subtype II-*a* but rapid, sometimes very rapid, in subtype II-*b*, attaining its maximum rapidity under our 'speculator' governments. Regimes of the II-*a* subtype are usually not expensive, but neither are they productive. They lull their people into lassitude and stifle all stimulus to economic production. Not using force to any significant extent, they are unable to compensate for this lack of productivity by wealth gained through conquest, Indeed they become easy prey to neighbours who are adept in the use of force, and hence they disappear either by conquest or internal decadence. Regimes of the II-*b* subtype are expensive, sometimes very expensive indeed, but they are also productive of wealth, outstandingly so in some cases. There may therefore be such an excess of production of wealth over costs as to ensure great prosperity for the country, but it cannot by any means be assumed that, with increasing expenditure, the surplus will not become smaller, disappear, and perhaps even turn into a deficit. . . . Such regimes may degenerate into rule by astute but irresolute people who are easily overthrown by violence from within or without. Such was the fate of many democratic governments in Greek cities, and this factor played an appreciable part in the fall of the republics of Rome and Venice.

(2277) In actual experience one finds mixtures of these various types; sometimes one type predominates, sometimes another. Governments mainly of Type I mixed with an element of subtype II-*b* may endure for a long time, based on force and without reduction in economic prosperity. Rome under the High Empire provides an example. Such governments run the risk of the degeneration to which Type I is prone and of a serious reduction in the proportions of the II-*b* element in them. Governments which are mainly of subtype II-*b* mixed with an element of Type I may also endure for a long time because they combine sufficient strength to defend themselves with the ability to achieve considerable economic prosperity. They run the risk of the degeneration to which the II-*b* subtype is prone and of a serious reduction in the proportions of the Type I element in them, and this almost invariably entails the danger of foreign invasion. This factor can be seen contributing to the destruction of Carthage and the Roman conquest of Greece.

(2278) There may be a mixture of I and II-*b* in governments which rely mainly on force in international relations and on intelligence in internal affairs. The government of the aristocracy at the zenith of the Roman Republic was in many respects such a mixture.

# II. TRADITIONAL LEADERSHIP

The second wave of readings, Traditional Leadership, reflect very common assumptions about leadership in the USA of the post–1945 period. Barnard, Stogdill, and Fiedler provide quite distinct accounts of leadership, but all three are keen to ground their material in an analytic framework that mirrors the scientific pretensions of the day but ends up destroying much of the previous 'science' of leadership. Thus Barnard writes against the background of the Second World War and disputes the notion of a single form of leadership, paving the way for Stogdill's effective demolition of the previous forms of research that had suggested that the acquisition of certain personal characteristics would suffice to predict successful leadership, and supporting Fiedler's subsequent contingency approach. Of course, leadership theory does not develop in isolation from other theoretical constructions: contingency or situational approaches to leadership were reflected in similar developments in strategy (Chandler 1962), in the relationship between organizations and technology (Woodward 1965), and the relationship between organization and size (Williamson 1970). Another movement worth considering is how certain modes of interpreting leadership recur across time. Thus the early trait theories of leadership are currently undergoing something of a revival in the hands of Lord *et al.* (1986) and Kenny and Zaccaro (1983) (see Wright 1996: 169–93), while contingent approaches continue through the work of Hersey and Blanchard (1982).

Chester Barnard, President of the Rockerfeller Foundation and previously President of the New Jersey Bell Telephone Company, writing during the Second World War but before the entry of the USA, continues the concern for the links between leaders and followers and is as virulent in his condemnation of incompetence as Dixon. He begins by admitting his own ignorance of the subject but distinguishing between 'leadership' implying pre-eminence, and 'leadership' that implies governing or guiding the activities of others. Barnard sets out his views within a triangle of elements that include the individual leader, the followers, and the conditions. Critical to his approach is the assumption that it is the integration of these three that generates leadership and that the tendency to concentrate wholly on the role and capacity of the individual leader is a mistake. Presaging a concern for the Actor-Network Theory (ANT) links between people and things, he also asserts the importance of managing material resources, though these tend to be a subordinate point for reasons we shall come to shortly.

Part of the problem of analysing leadership, as Barnard sees it, is in the analytic form itself. Analysis requires the division of phenomena into their smallest elements, when in leadership these elements are 'not separate but closely interrelated, interdependent, and often overlapping and simultaneous'. Having said this, he is forced by the complexity of the subject to revert to an analytic approach and divides the notion of leadership itself into the determination of objectives, the manipulation of means, the control of the instrumentality of action, and the stimulation of coordinated action. Overall, Barnard is keen to promote the notion of a contingent approach to leadership: leaders must know how 'to steal the right ideas', to be 'properly stupid' when necessary, and to act 'in the particular concrete situation', but that situation may vary enormously from stable conditions, where calm and reflective behaviour suits a leader, to extreme conditions, where decisiveness and courage may be more valuable. Leaders also need a degree of technical competence—though he is at pains to point out that technical competence, in and of itself, is of limited utility as a prescription for leadership: it is necessary but not sufficient. Partly this 'insufficiency' derives from the holistic or systems approach to leadership that Barnard advocates, partly it is a reflection of the crucial value of 'persuasion' through which leaders get others to do what they require, and partly it is to do with his scepticism about the influence of intelligence.

Intellectual capacity is something that leaders must have but it remains fifth in Barnard's order of significance. Most influential is 'vitality and endurance' and one can perceive in Barnard's reflections on Mussolini and Hitler how the 'compelling' nature of a leader may be more influential than his or her 'intellectual' qualities. Leaders also need to be decisive, persuasive, and responsible. In an age where demagoguery, irresponsibility, and irrationality appeared to hold sway over large sections of Europe, Barnard remains suspicious of 'academic' cleverness. Intellectual sophistication, and what Barnard clearly regards as the related attributes, including the detailed and uncommitted examination of all sides in an argument, and a refusal to specify what must be done in the concrete circumstances, are a recipe for disastrous leadership. Indeed, in Barnard's 'digression on the importance of non-intellectual abilities', he specifically focuses on the 'use of voice and gestures (which) is of first importance', an issue he previously alluded to when considering 'the violent energy with which Mussolini throws his arms in the Fascist salute, or by the vehemence of Hitler's speech'. At a time when the prevarications of European appeasement seem to have encouraged rather than discouraged Hitler's adventurist expansion, Barnard's attack upon 'the limitations of intellectuals' with their 'irresponsible', 'non-decisive', and 'non-persuasive' leadership styles is itself a clearly contingent critique. Also important, though, is the industrial context of the USA when war production for the Allied side provided America with a valuable economic boost that was being threatened by industrial unrest. For Barnard, the unrest was the result of this same 'exaggerated intellectualism' in which there was a 'a propensity (amongst) educated people . . . to underestimate the intelligence and other important personal qualities of workmen . . . to blame failure to lack of brains in subordinates instead of to the stupidity of instructions . . . (and) in the desire of so many intellectuals to tell others how to eat, save money, dress, marry, raise families, take care of their own interests'.

Barnard's suggestions on the remedial action necessary to resolve the leadership problem include, as might be expected, a downplaying of the analytic intellectual focus on abstract principles and a shift towards an empathetic understanding of subordinates, preferably through actual field experience of leading. That experience need not be limited to the business world but, for Barnard, occurs in all social fields, voluntary, political, and even within labour unions; indeed, 'extracurricular' activities are also enrolled in the leadership training package.

Finally, Barnard raises the consequences of moving from leaders to followers, for:

> the test of the adequacy of leadership is the extent of co-operation, or lack of it, in relation to our ideals; and this is largely a matter of the disposition of the followers . . . (for) selection is made simultaneously by two authorities, the formal and the informal. That which is made by formal authority we may call appointment (or dismissal), the informal authority we may call acceptance (or rejection). *Of the two, the informal authority is fundamental and controlling*. It lies in or consists of the willingness and ability of followers to follow.

As Barnard concludes, 'the followers make the leader, though the latter also may affect and must guide the followers'.

Despite Barnard's attempt to instil some practical sense into leadership studies, it took Stogdill to undermine the desperate search for personal characteristics as predictors of leadership success. The early post-war period was denoted as a time of major expansion in the study of leadership, either through the Ohio State studies (see Hemphill 1949; Stogdill 1950) or through the more disparate research of many others who attempted to 'map and measure' leadership. Stogdill's 1948 survey of the literature demonstrated many of the problems associated with such topographical approaches: many of the traits and characteristics appear to be both positively *and* negatively correlated with leadership and one is left wondering whether the few undisputed characteristics remained so because fewer researchers had considered them. Certainly, variables such as age, height, and weight appear of marginal relevance, while appearance seems to depend upon the kind of organization being led—with role modelling, or a symmetry between leaders and followers of some import. As Barnard—and just about everyone else for that matter—would have expected, verbal fluency does correlate with leadership: one would hardly expect someone who was incoherent or mute to be able to lead anyone. However, as Peter Sellers playing Chancy Gardener in *Being There* suggests, it may well be that the interpretation of coherence lies in the attributions of the followers not the articulations of the leader.

One way of summarizing the research would be to suggest that the apparent confusion and complexity deepens as the research progresses: the kind of problem that Barnard expected but Socrates would have revelled in. On the other hand, one can say with some degree of certainty that those people regarded by others as unsuccessful loners, with no self-confidence, with speech impediments, a complete absence of social skills, no networking ability, low levels of intelligence, poor judgement, no ambition, and little cooperativeness or popularity would be unlikely to become a major leadership figure. This hardly seems to amount to a qualitative advance in understanding (and anyway I am sure we can all think of a 'leader' who fits all these categories). It is important though to note Ackerson's (1942) conclusion that leaders and followers are not opposite sides of the same coin because the 'indifferent' individual is the one that remains impervious to leaders and uninterested in leading.

Perhaps a rather more valuable conclusion to the survey would be to suggest that leadership is a very complex and contingent issue, that leadership qualities are not necessarily transferable across time and space, and that there may well be a large degree of pattern imposition here. By that I mean that the researchers may well bear considerable responsibility for deciding which traits are important by investigating some but not others. For instance, there is nothing about gendered forms of leadership here, nor whether there is a deeper contingent phenomena: not just that different situations require different forms of 'appropriate' leadership but that different cultures and different times project as 'appropriate' different things. That is, that what counts as the situation itself is highly dependent upon a particular form of 'reading'; or, in other words, what counts as an 'extreme' situation requiring 'extreme' forms of leadership is itself partly dependent on the way existing leaders can persuade followers that the existing situation is, indeed, 'extreme'. This relative approach also supports the 'devastating evidence' provided by Newstetter, Feldstein, and Newcomb (1938) that the concept of measurable traits in determining interactions is spurious because the very interactions themselves are socially contingent, they are accomplishments not determinants. In effect, leadership cannot be determined by the possession of characteristics but has to be 'brought off' on the day.

The Stogdill piece takes a closer look at the Ohio State Leadership Studies, a watermark in leadership studies which attempted to develop a set of objective methods by which leadership could be measured and evaluated. Set against the background of trait studies, the approach assumed that it would operate in all contexts, and that leadership, and indeed an organized group itself, was possible only where a marked division of responsibilities existed. The Ohio approach required the separation of variables that could be measured accurately, and these embodied both formal and informal variables. The approach was especially interested in the differences between formal responsibility and formal interaction, on the one hand, and the informal elements of tasks actually performed and people that one actually interacted with, on the other. Leadership was essentially concerned with closing the gap between these divergent notions of what should happen and what did happen.

The results from the research suggested that the lower in the formal hierarchy one was, the more detailed and routine the tasks became, and that the kind of tasks or function determined how much time one spent with subordinates, peers, or superiors. However, in a section that prefigures a considerable amount of phenomenological work later, Stogdill accepted that the allegedly objective structure of the organization did not determine such interaction because the interpretive accounts of individuals differed quite markedly. In effect, one could not predict degrees of participation—for example, simply by configuring a particular organizational structure.

The consequence seemed to be that leaders were much more constrained by the group and the external environment than had hitherto been appreciated. Indeed, the approach suggested that leadership itself was actually 'not so much an attribute of individuals as an aspect of organization'—an interactional process not a positional event. This also meant that leadership could derive from those without formal position in organizations and that it would be unlikely that a single individual would exert total domination in any organization.

This led the Ohio team to an apparent paradox, for, if leadership was to be measured by establishing the influence of *individuals* on the activities of the organization in different areas, whatever happened to the idea of leadership as a necessarily *social* process? The response was that individuals could have influence but that this influence would, to some degree or other, be constrained or advanced by the influence of others. In short, leadership was manifest in the actions of the individual—and these actions could be measured and compared to those of others—but those actions were embedded in social processes.

Fiedler, one of the leading authorities on contingency approaches to leadership, followed on from the kind of avenue carved out by Barnard and then Stogdill and makes a clarion call for practical relevance: 'The acid test of leadership theory obviously must be its ability to improve organizational performance.' He deals quickly with the weaknesses of the 'personality trait' and behavioural approaches to leadership which have failed to explain, never mind predict, leadership. He then launches into his own contingency model, which, though he subsequently refined it several times with other authors, remains at its heart a model where 'the context of an organizational environment . . . determines, in large part, the specific kind of leadership behaviour which the situation requires'. Asserting that the model 'can predict the relationship between certain leader attributes and organizational performance at a given point in time with a reasonable degree of accuracy', Fiedler begins to develop his model based on two different forms of leadership behaviour. The first centres on relationship-motivated leaders, the second on task-motivated leaders. We have seen this division before at the hands of Dixon, but Fielder's approach then suggests that, through the use of the Least Preferred Co-worker (LPC), a model of contingent leadership can be constructed. The LPC approach asks leaders to describe the person they would least like to work with and the resultant data are tabulated to develop a model where task-motivated leaders perform best where the situation is one of either high or low control, whereas relationship-motivated leaders work best when the control situation is neither extreme. There are, then, no universally 'good' leaders, but when the situation is one of extreme uncertainty or extreme certainty then task-related leaders are more successful than relationship-oriented leaders. The trick is to match up the personality characteristics of the leader with the situational characteristics.

The characteristics of the situation are not all externally impervious of course. Through securing greater training and experience, notably of routines and locally situated knowledge, leaders can reposition themselves within the situation. It is also the case, argues Fiedler, that the degree of organizational turbulence will have an impact upon the situation. Indeed, one might go further than this to suggest that, if the environment is constantly turbulent, then what may be an appropriate form of leadership today may also be inappropriate tomorrow.

So did Fiedler's claim to have developed a predictive theory of leadership resolve the problem? Yes and no. Yes, many subsequent accounts provided support to the basic model (Fiedler and Garcia 1987), but no, a large overview of the data suggests that a large minority of cases fall outside the predictive model (Nathan et al. 1986, quoted in Bass 1990). Partly this may be because the LPC method rests on a measure of personality not on a measure of behaviour; partly this may be because Fielder's model ignores the attributes of the subordinates; and partly it may be because his single variable of leadership is rooted in the task or person-oriented approach that may be a single, and singularly poor, attempt to contain the many complexities of leadership styles (see Wright 1996 for an extensive review). There is a further problem that has already been mentioned but is worth reiterating at this point. We *may* be able to measure leader's preferences for co-workers, but are we absolutely certain we can measure 'the situation' with any degree of accuracy? If not, then the whole contingency approach is premised upon very unstable foundations.

# 5 The Nature of Leadership

Chester Barnard

Leadership has been the subject of an extraordinary amount of dogmatically stated nonsense. Some, it is true, has been enunciated by observers who have had no experience themselves in coordinating and directing the activities of others; but much of it has come from men of ample experience, often of established reputations as leaders. As to the latter, we may assume that they know how to do well what they do not know how to describe or explain. At any rate, I have found it difficult not to magnify superficial aspects and catchphrases of the subject to the status of fundamental propositions, generalized beyond all possibility of useful application, and fostering misunderstanding.

Seeking to avoid such errors, I shall not tell you what leadership is or even how to determine when it is present; for I do not know how to do so. Indeed, I shall venture to assert that probably no one else knows. These statements may seem strange and extreme, but I hope to convince you that they are not expressions of false modesty or of ill-considered judgement. At any rate, what I intend to discuss is *the problem of understanding the nature of leadership.*

The need for wide consideration of this was most forcibly impressed upon me by two observations, made on a single occasion, which revealed the extent of public misunderstanding of it. Some time ago I attended a large joint conference of laymen and members of the faculty of an important university to consider the subject of educational preparation for leadership. At this meeting my first observation was that *leadership* was confused with *pre-eminence or extraordinary usefulness* both by speakers and by audience. In their view a leading writer, artist, pianist, mathematician, or scientist exemplifies leadership substantially, as does an executive or leader

C. Barnard, 'The Nature of Leadership', in C. Barnard, *Organization and Management* (Cambridge, Mass: Harvard University Press, 1948)

of an organization. No one appeared to be aware of the double meaning of 'leadership' and its implications for the discussion of the subject of preparing 'leaders'. Among the meanings of the verb 'to lead' we may say that one is: 'to excel, to be in advance, to be pre-eminent'; and another is 'to guide others, to govern their activities, to be head of an organization or some part of it, to hold command'. I think the distinction between these meanings is rather easy to see. Most individuals matured in a well-organized effort recognize it as a matter of course, so that it may be difficult for many who from long experience thoroughly understand the distinction to believe such a confusion common. I fear that it is common, however, and is making cooperation and adequate organization increasingly difficult.

My second observation at this meeting, further evidence of the same fact, was this: during the period of open discussion, a well-known engineer protested the subjection of engineers to supervision or management by those who are not engineers. The superiority of engineers in nearly all respects, especially in intellect, training, and science, was implied. Though the audience was not one of engineers, it expressed derision generally at the absurd state of affairs portrayed. Could there have been a more striking proof of the misconception of the subject these several hundred earnest, intelligent, educated people were discussing—how better to prepare people to be leaders?

These observations show the importance of public discussion of the problem. Mere knowledge of how to solve it would not be sufficient. Often, in similar matters, when a solution is available it will not be accepted unless the problem itself is either acknowledged as such by reliance upon a responsible authority or is recognized and accepted by agreement and understanding. Otherwise a correct solution is merely 'one man's idea, a little queer'; and a 'solution' is something that cannot be made effective because it *will* not be used. This seems often not to be adequately taken into account in the discussion of social and organization 'remedies'.

Now it seems to me evident that the problem of leadership, like some others which now obsess us, is not yet suitably formulated. For this reason, if for no other, it is not generally understood. This needs emphasis because within our own organizations we usually do not experience much difficulty on this account; for we already have an approximately common understanding or sense, coming from long interconnected experience, which is workably adequate. Such an understanding is a substitute, and a superior one, for abstract knowledge of the matter—at least for any I imagine being available for a long time. But outside these circles of intimate experiential knowledge, understanding fails, even among leaders.

Not only misunderstanding but a positive need for leaders warrants our attention to this subject. The large-scale integrations of our present societies—

the great nations, the immense organizations of war and peace, of culture and religion—make the needs of leadership relatively greater and its functions more complex than heretofore, so that the necessary proportion of leaders to the population has greatly increased. In other words, the 'overhead' of any organization or society clearly tends to expand more rapidly than its size. Moreover, technology and specialization make the arts of leadership even more complex than consideration of size alone would indicate. These facts suggest that scarcity of leaders of requisite quality may already limit the possibility of stable cooperation in our societies.

I think we may agree, then, that public misunderstanding and misinformation, and the need for provision of more adequate leadership, urge our effort to understand the nature of leadership. My present attempt to contribute to this end ought chiefly, I think, to make evident the obscurity of the subject and the complexity of the functions and conditions involved in it. This method of approach will surely try our patience and may be discouraging to some; but we shall be wise in this matter not to give answers before we have found out what are the questions. The attitude that I think we may best have has been admirably stated by T. S. Eliot:

> The fact that a problem will certainly take a long time to solve, and that it will demand the attention of many minds for several generations, is no justification for postponing the study. And, in times of emergency, it may prove in the long run that the problems we have postponed or ignored, rather than those we have failed to attack successfully, will return to plague us. Our difficulties of the moment must always be dealt with somehow; but our permanent difficulties are difficulties of every moment.[1]

In the light of these preliminary remarks it may be well for me to state the meaning of the word 'leadership'. As I use it herein it refers to the quality of the behaviour of individuals whereby they guide people or their activities in organized effort. This is its primary significance. Organized effort takes place, however, in systems of cooperation which often include property or plants. When this is so, the activities coordinated relate to, or are connected with, the property or plant, and the two are not separate. Hence, the management or administration of such properties, as distinguished from the command or supervision of personnel, is also included as a secondary aspect of leadership.

Whatever leadership is, I shall now make the much oversimplified statement that it depends upon three things: (1) the individual, (2) the followers, and (3) the conditions. We shall agree at once, no doubt; but, unless we are careful, I suspect that within an hour we shall be talking of the qualities, capacities, talents, and personalities of leaders as if the individual were the exclusive component of leadership. Therefore, let me emphasize the interdependence by restating it in quasi-mathematical language, thus: leadership appears to be a function of at least three complex variables—the individual, the group of followers, the conditions.

Now the points to note here are two. First, these are variables obviously within wide limits, so that leadership may in practice mean an almost infinite number of possible combinations. Secondly, if we are to have a good understanding of leadership we shall need a good understanding of individuals, of organizations, and of conditions, and of their interrelationships so far as they are relevant to our topic. Do we have that now? I am sure we do not. Yet I fear this may be thought an extreme theoretical view unless I give some demonstration of its correctness, and at the same time give some idea of how we might at least approach some better practical understanding.

In undertaking this, I shall depart from the scheme of the three variables and proceed along more everyday lines. To present my suggestions of possibilities as to the nature of leadership, I shall give the following: (i) a general description of what leaders have to do in four sectors of leadership behaviour; (ii) thoughts concerning certain differences of conditions of leadership; (iii) some remarks about the active personal qualities of leaders; (iv) a few notes on the problem of the development of leaders; and (v) observations about the selection of leaders.

## Four Sectors of Leadership Behaviour

Leaders lead. This implies activity, and suggests the obvious question: 'What is it that they have to do?' Now, I must confess that heretofore on the few occasions when I have been asked: 'What do you do?' I have been unable to reply intelligibly. Yet I shall attempt here to say generally what leaders do, dividing their work under four topics, which for present purposes will be sufficient. The topics I shall use are: the determination of objectives; the manipulation of means; the control of the instrumentality of action; and the stimulation of coordinated action.

Unfortunately it is necessary to discuss these topics separately. This is misleading unless it is remembered that, except in special cases or when specially organized, these kinds of action are not separate but closely interrelated, interdependent, and often overlapping or simultaneous. Therein lies one reason why it is so difficult for a leader to say what he does or to avoid misrepresenting himself. He does not know how to untangle his acts in a way suitable for verbal expression. His business is leading, not explaining his own behaviour, at which, though sometimes voluble, he is usually rather inept, as we doubtless all are. Indeed, as I shall show later, it is *impossible* for him to be aware of this behaviour in the sense necessary to explain it except very generally on the basis of his observations of others as well as of himself.

## *The First Sector: The Determination of Objectives*

An obvious function of a leader is to know and say what to do, what not to do, where to go, and when to stop, with reference to the general purpose or objective of the undertaking in which he is engaged. Such a statement appears to exhaust the ideas of many individuals as to a leader's *raison d'être.* But if they are able to observe the operations closely, it often disconcerts them to note that many things a leader tells others to do were suggested to him by the very people he leads. Unless he is very dynamic—too dynamic, full of his own ideas—or pompous or Napoleonic, this sometimes gives the impression that he is a rather stupid fellow, an arbitrary functionary, a mere channel of communication, and a filcher of ideas. In a measure this is correct. He has to be stupid enough to listen a great deal, he certainly must arbitrate to maintain order, and he has at times to be a mere centre of communication. If he used only his own ideas he would be somewhat like a one-man orchestra, rather than a good conductor, who is a very high type of leader.

However, one thing should make us cautious about drawing false conclusions from this description. It is that experience has shown it to be difficult to secure leaders who are able to be properly stupid, to function arbitrarily, to be effective channels of communication, and to steal the right ideas, in such ways that they still retain followers. I do not pretend to be able to explain this very well. It seems to be connected with knowing whom to believe, with accepting the right suggestions, with selecting appropriate occasions and times. It also seems to be so related to conditions that a good leader in one field is not necessarily good in others, and not equally good under all circumstances. But at any rate, to say what to do and when requires an understanding of a great many things 'on the whole', 'taking everything into account', in their relations to some purpose or intention or result—an understanding that leads to distinguishing effectively between the important and the unimportant *in the particular concrete situation,* between what can and what cannot be done, between what will probably succeed and what will probably not, between what will weaken cooperation and what will increase it.

**Chester Barnard**

## *The Second Sector: The Manipulation of Means*

There is undoubtedly an important difference between the kind of effort we have just considered and the direction of detailed activities that are parts of technical procedures and technological[2] operations as the subsidiary means and instruments of accomplishing specific objectives already determined. Sometimes an exceptional leader can effectively guide technical operations in which he has no special competence, whereas those of high competence are often not successful leaders. I shall not attempt a general explanation of these facts; but on the whole we may regard leadership without technical competence as increasingly exceptional, unless for the most general work. Usually leaders, even though not extraordinarily expert, appear to have an understanding of the technological or technical work which they guide, particularly in its relation to the activities and situations with which they deal. In fact, we usually assume that a leader will have considerable knowledge and experience in the specifically technical aspects of the work he directs. I need not say much about this, for it seems to me that at present we overestimate the importance of technical skill and competence and undervalue, or even exclude, the less tangible and less obvious factors in leadership.

Nevertheless, the technical and technological factors in leadership not only constitute a variable of great importance, but also introduce serious difficulties, which should be mentioned, especially in respect to (1) the development of types of leaders, and (2) the limitations these technical factors place upon the 'mobility' of the leaders in an organization or society, and also (3) because of the restrictive effect of technical study and experience on the *general* or 'social' development of individuals.

(1) It is almost a matter of course that leadership 'material' will be inducted into organization through some particular technical channel. Such channels are now highly specialized. When the course has been run, the man has been trained for leadership only with respect to a narrow range of activities. Otherwise he is untrained, and hence (2) the mobility of leadership resources may be seriously reduced because it is difficult to use a good leader of one narrow field in another field or in more general work—a fact which I suppose is now well recognized at least in all large organizations of industry and government and education. This difficulty, which is real, has become exaggerated in our minds, so that in my opinion we all—leaders and followers—tend to overlook superior leaders who at the moment may be lacking particular technical qualifications.

(3) Concerning the third difficulty—the effect of specialization upon the individual—it is only necessary to note that while men are concentrating upon techniques, machines, processes, and abstract knowledge, *they are*

*necessarily diverted to a considerable extent from experience with men, organizations, and the social situations, the distinctive fields of application of leadership ability.* Thus at the most impressionable period they become so well grounded in 'mechanical' attitudes towards non-human resources and processes that they transfer these attitudes, then and later, towards men also.

The technical sector of leadership behaviour is not a new thing in the world, but its importance has greatly increased. By technology and specialization we have accomplished much; but the resulting complexity of leadership functions and the restriction of the development and supply of general leaders seem to me to be the important problems of our times.

## *The Third Sector: The Instrumentality of Action*

Leadership obviously relates to the coordination of certain efforts of people. There is little coordination or cooperation without leadership, and leadership implies cooperation. Coordinated efforts constitute organization. *An organization is the instrumentality of action so far as leaders are concerned, and it is the indispensable instrumentality.* Many promising men never comprehend this because of early emphasis upon plants, structures, techniques, and abstract institutions, especially legal institutions such as the law of corporations.

The primary efforts of leaders need to be directed to the maintenance and guidance of organizations as whole systems of activities. I believe this to be the most distinctive and characteristic sector of leadership behaviour, but it is the least obvious and least understood. Since most of the acts which constitute organization have a specific function which superficially is independent of the maintenance of organization—for example, the accomplishment of specific tasks of the organization—it may not be observed that such acts at the same time also constitute organization and that this, not the technical and instrumental, is the primary aspect of such acts from the viewpoint of leadership. Probably most leaders are not ordinarily conscious of this, though intuitively they are governed by it. For any act done in such a way as to disrupt cooperation destroys the capacity of organization. Thus the leader has to guide all in such a way as to preserve organization as the instrumentality of action.[3]

Up to the present time, leaders have understood organization chiefly in an intuitive and experiential way. The properties, limitations, and processes of organization as systems of coordinated action have been little known in abstraction from concrete activities and situations; but the persistence and effectiveness of many organizations are evidence that leaders know how to behave with respect to them. On the other hand, we know that many very able, intelligent, and learned persons have neither understanding nor correct intuitions about concrete organizations.

### *The Fourth Sector: The Stimulation of Coordinated Action*

To repeat a commonplace, it is one thing to say what should be done, and quite another to get it done. A potential act lies outside organization, and it is one task of leaders to change potentiality into the stuff of action. In other words, one important kind of thing that leaders do is to induce people to convert abilities into coordinated effort, thereby maintaining an organization while simultaneously getting its work done. I need hardly say that this kind of activity of leaders is sometimes the most striking aspect of what they do. In a broad sense this is the business of persuasion. Nor need I say that the sorts of acts or behaviour by which executives 'persuade' to coordinated action are innumerable. They vary from providing the example in 'going over the top', or calm poise inspiring confidence, or quiet commands in tense moments, to fervid oratory, or flattery, or promises to reward in money, prestige, position, glory, or to threats and coercion. Why do they vary? Some obvious differences of combination in leaders, in followers, in organizations, in technology, in objectives, in conditions, will occur to you. But the effective combinations are often so subtle and so involved in the personalities of both leaders and followers that to be self-conscious about them, or for others to examine them when in process, would disrupt them.

My chief purpose in this brief account of four sectors of leadership behaviour has been to indicate how interconnected and interdependent they are and to suggest how great is the variation in what 'leadership' means specifically, depending upon the relative importance of the kinds of behavior required.

## The Conditions of Leadership

Already it has been necessary to allude at least by implication to differences in conditions of leadership, such, for example, as are involved in the degrees and kinds of technological operations. I shall now confine the discussion to differences of conditions of another sort, relating to the degree of tension of the action of leaders, followers, or both. It will be sufficient to consider only the two extremes.

The first is that which we may call stable conditions. These may be complex and of very large scale; but they are comparatively free from violent changes or extreme uncertainties *of unusual* character or implying important hazards. The behaviour of leaders under such conditions may be calm, deliberate, reflective, and anticipatory of future contingencies. Leadership then is lacking in the dramatic characteristics often observed at the other extreme, and this is one of its difficulties; for its function of persuasion must be carried on without the aid of emotional drives and of obvious necessities and against the indifference often accompanying lack of danger, excitement, and sentiment. Stable conditions call for self-restraint, deliberation, and refinement of technique, qualities that some men who are good leaders under tense conditions are unable to develop.

The other extreme is that of great instability, uncertainty, speed, intense action, great risks, important stakes, life-and-death issues. Here leaders must have physical or moral courage, decisiveness, inventiveness, initiative, even audacity; but I believe we tend to overstate the qualities required for this extreme, owing to its dramatic aspects and because the outcome of action is more easily judged.

This is enough to suggest that differences of conditions of this type—that is, differences in tension—are important factors in leadership behaviour. It should be apparent that we could expect only rarely to find men equally adapted to both extremes, and that quite different types of leaders are to be expected for this reason. Yet it is obvious that emergencies may be encountered in any kind of cooperative effort, and that leaders have to be adapted to function under wide ranges of conditions. Indeed, intermittent periods of severe stress are the rule in navigation, in military organizations, in some kinds of public-utility work, in political activity, to cite a few examples in which particular types of *flexibility* are necessary to continuous leadership. It may be apparent here, as perhaps it was in considering the sectors of leadership behaviour, that the practical problem in selecting specific leaders would be to ascertain *the balance of qualities* most probably adapted to the conditions or to the variations of conditions.

## The Active Personal Qualities of Leaders

I have already stated why I do not think it useful to discuss leadership exclusively in personal terms. Leaders, I think, are made quite as much by conditions and by organizations and followers as by any qualities and propensities which they themselves have. Indeed, in this connection, I should put much more emphasis upon the character of organizations than upon individuals. But this is not the common opinion; and I certainly could not fail to discuss that quite variable component, the individual.

I shall list and discuss briefly five fundamental qualities or characteristics of those who are leaders, in their order of importance as regarded for very *general* purposes. Probably I shall not include qualities that some think essential. I would not quarrel about what may be only a difference in name or emphasis. Perhaps, also, there will be disagreement about the order I have chosen. This I shall mildly defend, my chief purpose being to correct for a current exaggerated and false emphasis. The list follows: (i) vitality and endurance; (ii) decisiveness; (iii) persuasiveness; (iv) responsibility; and (v) intellectual capacity.

## *Vitality and Endurance*

We should not confuse these qualities with good health. There are many people of good health who have little or moderate vitality—energy, alertness, spring, vigilance, dynamic qualities—or endurance. Conversely, there are some who have poor health and even suffer much who at least have great endurance. Generally, it seems to me, vitality and endurance are fundamental qualities of leadership, though they may wane before leadership capacity does.

Notwithstanding the exceptions, these qualities are important for several reasons. The first is that they both promote and permit the unremitting acquirement of exceptional experience and knowledge which in general underlies extraordinary personal capacity for leadership.

The second is that vitality is usually an element in personal attractiveness or force which is a great aid to persuasiveness. It is sometimes even a compelling characteristic. Thus few can be unaffected by the violent energy with which Mussolini throws his arm in the Fascist salute, or by the vehemence of Hitler's speech, or by the strenuous life of Theodore Roosevelt. Similarly, we are impressed by the endurance of Franklin D. Roosevelt in campaign.

The third reason for the importance of vitality is that leadership often involves prolonged periods of work and extreme tension without relief, when failure to endure may mean permanent inability to lead. To maintain confidence depends partly on uninterrupted leadership.

## *Decisiveness*

I shall be unable to discuss here precisely what decision is, or involves as a process, but I regard it as the element of critical importance in all leadership, and I believe that all formal organization depends upon it. Ability to make decisions is the characteristic of leaders I think most to be noted. It depends upon a propensity or willingness to decide and a capacity to do so. I neglect almost entirely the appearance or mannerism of being decisive, which seems often to be a harmful characteristic, at least frequently misleading, usually implying an improper understanding and use of authority, and undermining confidence. Leadership requires making actual appropriate decisions and only such as are warranted.

For present purposes decisiveness needs to be considered in both its positive and negative aspects. Positively, decision is necessary to get the right things done at the right time and to prevent erroneous action. Negatively, failure to decide undoubtedly creates an exceedingly destructive condition in organized effort. For delay either to direct or to approve or disapprove, that is, mere suspense—checks the decisiveness of others, introduces indecisiveness or lethargy throughout the whole process of cooperation, and thus restricts experience, experiment, and adaptation to changing conditions.

## *Persuasiveness*

The fundamental importance of persuasiveness I have already mentioned. Here I refer to the ability in the individual to persuade, and the propensity to do so. Just what these qualities are defies description, but without them all other qualities may become ineffective. These other qualities seem to be involved, yet not to be equivalent. In addition, persuasiveness appears often to involve or utilize talents, such as that of effective public speaking or of exposition or special physical skills or even extraordinary physique, and many others. The relation of specific talents to leadership we cannot usefully consider further here. But at least we may say that persuasiveness involves a *sense* or understanding of the point of view, the interests, and the conditions of those to be persuaded.

## *Responsibility*

I shall define responsibility as an emotional condition that gives an individual a sense of acute dissatisfaction because of failure to do what he feels he is morally bound to do or because of doing what he thinks he is morally bound not to do in particular, concrete situations.[4] Such dissatisfaction he will avoid, and therefore his behaviour, if he is 'responsible' and if his beliefs or sense of what is right are known, can be approximately relied upon. That this stability of behaviour is important to leadership from several points of view will be recognized without difficulty; but it is specially so from that of those who follow. Capricious and irresponsible leadership is rarely successful.

### *Intellectual Capacity*

I have intentionally relegated 'brains' to the fifth place. I thereby still make it important, but nevertheless subsidiary to physical capacity, decisiveness, persuasiveness, and responsibility. Many find this hard to believe, for leaders especially seem to me frequently to be inordinately proud of their intellectual abilities, whatever they may be, rather than of their more important or effective qualities.

## A Digression on the Importance of the Non-Intellectual Abilities

This attitude may be due partly to a confusion between pre-eminence and leadership—an instance of which I gave in my introduction—and partly to the high social status now given to intellect, to which I shall refer later. Disagreement as to the subordinate place to which I here assign intellect may also be due partly to a matter of definition; for I think we usually confuse *acquirement* by intellectual processes with responsive, habitual, intuitive *expression or application* of what has been acquired, which I take to involve processes largely non-intellectual.

However, I believe sensitiveness about our intellects is often due especially to the fact that the part of behaviour *of which we are most conscious* is at least largely intellectual, whereas much of our most effective behaviour, such as reflects vitality, decisiveness, and responsibility, is largely matter of course, unconscious, responsive, and on the whole has to be so to be effective. Self-consciousness in these respects would at least often check their force, speed, or accuracy. Moreover, leaders, like others, are for the most part unaware of their most effective faculties in actual behaviour, for they cannot see themselves as others do.

This last point is so important both in theory and in practical administration that I think it worth further consideration here. The point is easy to prove, but its implications are difficult to explain. For the proof we may take, as an example, speaking and its accompanying gestures. It is well known that no one hears his own voice as it sounds to others chiefly because much of the vibrations of the speaker's voice are conducted within the structure and passages of the head. I believe that an individual without previous experience rarely recognizes his own voice from a good reproduction. Some are greatly surprised and often displeased at hearing such a reproduction for the first time. Obviously, too, an individual cannot see his own demeanour or many of his movements. Yet in all our relations to others the use of voice and gestures is of first importance and both are effectively controlled to a considerable extent so as to accomplish specific reactions in listeners. If we cannot hear and see ourselves as others do, how can we accomplish such control of our behaviour?

I think the explanation may be as follows. We learn to correlate our own speech and action, as we hear and feel them, with certain effects upon others. We are only approximately successful, and some are much more so than others. Listeners and observers, on the other hand, learn to correlate the entirely different thing, our observable behaviour, with our meanings and intentions. This is also only approximate, and is done more successfully by some than by others. Since leadership primarily involves the guidance of the conduct of others, in general, leaders need to be more effective than others both in conveying meanings and intentions and in receiving them.

These fundamental processes are certainly not to any great extent intellectual. We all know that the capacity to understand the logical significance of sentences, even when written or printed, is limited, and that repeatedly we understand by the manner of speaking. We can with some success teach by logical processes what to do in the operation of a machine or process, though even here we know that often to state a direction correctly in language is to mislead, whereas an incorrect statement especially with appropriate gesture or facial expression may well convey the precise meaning. But to teach by logical exposition how to behave with other people is a slow process of limited effectiveness at best. This is why I think it will be widely observed that good leaders seldom undertake to tell followers *how* to behave, though they tell what should be done, and will properly criticize the manner of its doing *afterward*. Whereas inferior leaders often fail by trying, as it were, to tell others how to live their lives.

## *The Limitations of Intellectuals*

Whatever may be the explanation of our strong predilection for our intellectual attainments, it is difficult to evade the emphasis I have placed on other qualities in leadership. We all know persons in and out of practical affairs of superior intellects and intellectual accomplishments who do not work well as leaders. In matters of *leadership,* for example, they prove to be irresponsible (absent-minded, non-punctual), non-decisive (ultra-judicial, see so many sides they can never make up their minds), non-persuasive (a little 'queer', not interested in people). Moreover, we can observe that intellectual capacity rarely rises above physiological disabilities in active life, that the utmost perspicacity is useless for leadership if it does not decide issues, that persuasive processes must take full account of the irrational by which all are largely governed, that responsibility is a moral or emotional condition.

## *The Importance of Intellectual Capacities*

Intellectual abilities of high order may achieve pre-eminent usefulness. They are sometimes an important element in leadership but not sufficient to maintain it. However, as a differential factor—that is, other qualities being granted and adequate—intellectual capacity is of unquestioned importance, and especially so in the age in which complex techniques and elaborate technologies are among the conditions of leadership. Leaders of the future, in my opinion, will generally need to be intellectually competent. However, the main point, which I wish greatly to emphasize, is that intellectual competency is *not* a substitute, at least in an important degree, for the other essential qualities of leadership.

## *Some Effects of Exaggerated Intellectualism*

Though it may be unpleasant to some, I have laid stress upon my opinion in this matter for two principal reasons. The first is that under present trends an excessive emphasis is placed upon intellectual (and pseudo-intellectual) qualifications by responsible 'selecting' authorities, which artificially limits the supply of leaders. The same excessive emphasis upon the intellectual is made by followers who are intellectuals. Thus it is often difficult for those (experts and professionals of many kinds) who have no administrative capacity (or interest) to follow even extraordinary leaders. This is a form of conceit frequently accompanied by exhibitions of temperament and disruptiveness, and by false, ruthless, and irresponsible professions of individualism and freedom, especially professional and academic freedom. All of this tends to a limitation of the supply of competent leaders, because it discourages men from undertaking the work of leadership, and it restricts their effectiveness.

My second reason is that a general condition amounting to intellectual snobbishness, it seems to me, has a great deal to do with industrial unrest. I see this in the propensity of educated people, whatever their economic status or social position, to underestimate the intelligence and other important personal qualities of workmen; in the tendency of some supervisors, quite honestly and sincerely, to blame failure to lack of brains in subordinates instead of to the stupidity of instructions; in the assumption of some men that 'pure bunk' dressed up in 'high brow' jargon is effective in dealing with people; in the excessive popularity of white-collar occupations; in the desire of so many intellectuals to tell others how to eat, save money, dress, marry, raise families, take care of their own interests. These are symptoms of attitudes and it is the latter, not the symptoms, which are important. They cause division of interest artificially and lack of sympathetic understanding that are destructive of cooperation and cannot be corrected by mere 'measures of good will'.

I am well aware that there are differences in the intellectual capacities of men and know that such differences are important, especially as respects the ability to acquire knowledge and understanding by study in those matters which can only be learned in this way. Nevertheless, after a fairly long experience in dealing with many classes of men and women individually and collectively, the destructive attitudes I am attacking seem to me to be unwarranted by anything I know about intellect, education, or leadership. Intellectual superiority is an obtrusive thing which even intellectuals dislike in others except as they *voluntarily* give it their respect.

## Our Ignorance of the Qualities of Leadership

After this long digression it may have been forgotten, though observed, that in this discussion of personal qualifications I have failed, with one exception, to define my terms. Though in a general way I am confident that my meaning is understood, greater precision of meaning seems quite impossible, at least without extended space, and is not needed here. Indeed, a significant fact to emphasize is that neither in science nor in practical affairs has there yet been attained a degree of understanding of these qualities now vaguely described which permits much clear definition even for special purposes.

It is worthwhile to illustrate this with reference to 'decisiveness'. The making of decisions is one of the most common of the events of which we are conscious both in ourselves and others. We believe that many decisions are momentous either to ourselves, to our enterprises, or to our society. We may agree that those incapable of making any decisions are at least morons if not insane. We are aware that to make decisions is a leading function of executives. We also know that decisions are made collectively, as in committees, boards, legislatures, juries, and that such work is one of the most characteristic features of our social life. Yet decisive behaviour, as contrasted with responsive behaviour, seems to have received little attention in the psychologies in the literature of logical operations, in sociology, and seldom in economics.[5] Moreover, in business I rarely hear appraisals of men in terms of their capacity for decision, except when they fail apparently for lack of ability to decide. It seems clear that we know so little of this quality or process that we do not discuss it as such, though 'decision', 'decisive', and 'decisiveness' are words frequently on our lips.

I am aware, as I said earlier, that I have omitted several qualifications of leadership which are commonly stated. In my intention, they are all comprehended in the five I have named or in some combination or derivation of them. Three omitted qualifications are great favourites: 'honesty' ('character'), 'courage', and 'initiative.' They may be added; but for myself I find them words which depend for their meaning in the specific case upon the *situation,* not merely the individual, as interpreted by either the actor or leader or others, and that his interpretation will often differ from the interpretations made by different observers. In any case, the important point is that the qualifications of leadership, however discriminated and however named, are interacting and interdependent. We do not assemble them as we would the ingredients of a compound, yet we may suppose that different combinations of qualities produce quite different kinds of leaders, and that the qualities and their combinations change with experience and with conditions.

## The Development of Leaders

I think I have now shown that my profession of ignorance of this subject and my doubts with respect to the knowledge of others concerning it were both justified. Yet I recognize that, however lacking in knowledge we may be, we nevertheless endeavour in our educational systems and at least in the larger organizations to increase the number of available leaders and their competence. It might be suggested that I should say something on this aspect of the subject in the light of my earlier remarks. I shall confine myself briefly to development methods and, in the next section, to the processes of selection.

Concerning the development of leaders, I shall in this section discuss the following topics: (i) training; (ii) balance and perspective; and (iii) experience.

## *Training*

As I understand it, the only qualification for leadership that is subject to specific preparatory training by formal processes is the intellectual, including therein the inculcation of general and special knowledge. My opinion as to the relative importance and status of intellectual qualities has already been stated to the effect that such qualities are increasingly necessary to effective leadership in technical and technological fields and also in large-scale organizations where complexity and the remoteness of concrete activities call for capacity in the handling of abstract material. The latter are the conditions in which leadership also usually involves management of extensive cooperative systems as well as of organizations.

Nevertheless, I believe it should be recognized that intellectual preparation by itself tends to check propensities indispensable to leadership. For example, study and reflection on abstract facts do not promote decisiveness and often seem to have the opposite effect. Analysis, which broadly is characteristic of intellectual processes especially in the early stages of education and experience, is the reverse of the process of combining elements, of the treatment of them as whole systems involved in concrete decisive action—for instance, in persuasion. As a result of intellectual training many prefer to recognize only what has been stated or is susceptible of statement and to disregard what has not been stated or is not susceptible of statement. The emphasis upon abstract facts characteristic now of the 'more intelligent' and dominant classes of our population has its results, in innumerable instances, in the 'fallacy of misplaced concreteness', the confusion of the fact with the thing and of *an aspect* with an indescribable whole, in the disregard of the interdependence of the known and the unknown.

An example of this or of its general effects may be found in the excessive emphasis upon knowledge as against skill in nearly all fields except sports and individual artistic performance. Yet but a moment's reflection is needed to acknowledge that many of the noteworthy efforts of scientist, teacher, lawyer, physician, architect, engineer, clergyman—to take professions in which intellectual discipline and experience are indispensable—are expressions not of intellect but of skills, the effective behaviour by which the appropriate adjustment to the infinite complexity of the concrete is accomplished. Indeed, we repeatedly confess the point in our practical emphasis upon experience, if not upon intuition, in every profession.

Nowhere is the emphasis upon fact to the exclusion of the thing to which it relates more harmful, it seems to me, than in the human side of industrial relations. We may think of employees as mechanics, clerks, labourers, or as members of an organization, but to lead requires to feel them as embodying a thousand emotions and relationships with others and with the physical environment, of which for the most part we can have no knowledge.

The dilemma which this state of affairs presents is, I think, concealed by the increasing extent to which prestige and status based on education are the basis of general social and industrial discrimination. I mean by this that a certain intellectual and educational status has become important, to the relative disregard of other qualifications, in getting a job, or at least a job generally regarded as desirable or distinctive. We can hardly help believing that an attitude is useful to society as a whole if we find that same attitude socially imposed upon us as individuals.[6]

## *Balance and Perspective*

It may be thought that changes in curricula might be sufficient to correct for the tendency towards distortion of judgement which I have described. This may be possible in the future but not yet. So far as I know there is not developed the basic material for such changes, and it is unlikely that there will be unless my view of this problem, assuming it to be correct, should be accepted widely. But at best I should expect such studies only to offset the prejudices inculcated, possibly excepting the humanities, by higher education.

Hence, for the present, it seems to me that balance, perspective, and proportion in the senses relevant to leadership are to be acquired almost exclusively from responsible experience in leading.

## *Experience*

In speaking of experience, it will be well to avoid the common error regarding it as primarily a matter of repetition through a period of time. When experience is merely repetition of action, it is better called practice to acquire patterns of behaviour. It is often convenient as a rough approximation to speak of hours, days, months, or years of experience, but we know that some men learn slowly, others quickly. Moreover, the possibility of learning depends upon activity. If nothing happens, little can be learned. Significant experience is secured largely by adapting one's self to varieties of conditions and by acquiring the sense of the appropriate in variations of action.

The acquirement of experience under modern conditions presents us with another dilemma, for the refined specialization and the technical complexity through which men are now introduced into the world of affairs give limited opportunity for general experience in leadership. The most 'natural' opportunities at present formally available seem to me to be the small *general* business, political party work in communities, perhaps to a less extent labour union leadership. These are insufficient sources for the supply of general leaders. Hence, we need to develop the artificial methods of giving wide experience which are now attempted to some extent in large organizations.

The effect of technical work is so strongly opposed to the acquirement of experience in the arts of leadership that I cannot forbear to add a suggestion that encouragement should be given in gaining experience informally in 'extracurricular' activities. In fact, though we can as yet apparently do little in a formal way to develop leaders, we can encourage potential leaders to develop themselves, to seek for themselves the occasions and opportunities when leadership is needed, to learn the ways of making themselves sought as leaders, to acquire experience in leading by doing it. I have myself been so encouraged and inspired in my youth and since then, as no doubt we all have, that to give such encouragement seems to me an important private and social duty; but I believe whatever we do in this respect will be harmful if not done in full realization that *there is no substitute for the experience of recognizing and seizing opportunities, or for making one's own place unaided and against interference and obstacles;* for these kinds of ability are precisely those that followers expect in leaders.

## The Selection of Leaders

Thus we have to recognize that leaders, almost blindly created by physiology, physical environments, social conditions, and experience, are now secured chiefly by selection, not by formal preparation. Our success is relative in the sense that we select as best we may of the quality that is presented but are little able to affect favourably that quality as a whole except as to the intellectual element. If this is a fact, it is admittedly difficult to observe, because to do so requires comparison of what we have with what we think we might have. Yet if we believe it to be a fact, it implies a precarious position; for the most perfect selection would not suffice to give adequate leadership if the supply of the 'raw material' were of inferior quality, any more, for example, than the best selection among untutored electricians would be likely to afford an adequate supply of superior electrical engineers.

The test of the adequacy of leadership is the extent of cooperation, or lack of it, in relation to our ideals; and this is largely a matter of the disposition of followers. Even in this brief discussion it should be stated that in all formal organizations selection is made simultaneously by two authorities: the formal and the informal. That which is made by formal authority we may call appointment (or dismissal), the informal authority we may call acceptance[7] (or rejection). *Of the two, the informal is fundamental and controlling.* It lies in or consists of the willingness and ability of followers to follow.

To many who have struggled and worried regarding appointment or dismissal of leaders, and to whom the maintenance of formal authority is the very keystone of cooperation, order, and efficiency, what I say may seem absurd or even subversive. But we have all many times proved it correct. For has not our first question always been in effect 'Can he lead and will they follow?' If our answer were 'No!' would we not appoint at the peril of our own leadership? And when there has been failure of followers to follow, writhe as we would, were not our only recourses to change the leader or possibly to change the followers?

If it is thought that this doctrine is subversive, this may be because it is thought to be what uninformed preachers of the vague thing called 'industrial democracy' want, and we suppose they know less of leadership and organization than even we do. But what they advocate and what we fear is the transfer of *formal* authority from leaders to voters, forgetting that the informal authority must finally determine, whatever be the nature of the formal authority. Indeed, this latter fact is the chief reason for our fear; for we recall the men who have been enthusiastically elected but never followed. As to most (but not all) leadership, *appointment* by responsible leaders has proved, and I believe will continue to prove, more effective and more satisfactory to followers than any other formal process.[8] And the followers make the leader, though the latter also may affect and must guide the followers.

I turn now to the process of selection, by formal authority of appointment or dismissal. In the selective process we eliminate for positive disqualification—bad health, lack of ability to decide, irresponsibility, lack of adequate intellectual or technical ability. Frequently this is all disregarded most conveniently by saying 'lack of experience' when what we mean is 'lack of successful experience'. For, although a few eliminations are made for positive disqualifications, the really important basis of selection is that of prior achievement. Since we know so little about the qualifications for leadership, this often proves a fallacious method, sometimes resulting in tragic errors and often in a great deal of foolish rationalization. Nevertheless, we must confess that the past record is the best basis of selection we have. Thirty years ago Mr Theodore N. Vail, a great leader and organizer in his day, and then President of the American Telephone and Telegraph Company, said to me: 'You can never tell what a man will do by what he has done; but it is the best guide you have.' I believe this still to be true; but I do not think it is an adequate basis for selection of leaders for our society of the future.

If leadership depends, as I have said, upon the individual, the followers, and the conditions, there must be many failures that are not the result of original errors of selection. For men, followers, and conditions all change. We are prone to forget this and to condemn, perhaps because it imposes upon us one of the most serious problems in the selective process. Failure of leadership if not corrected by replacement means the checking of the experience and development of potential leaders. Hence the elimination of superannuated, obsolete, and incompetent leaders is recognized as extremely important in most organizations, perhaps most systematically in the Army and Navy. But this process is extremely delicate; for, though followers cannot follow those who cannot lead, those who have been superior leaders embody or personify the spirit of an organization and represent the aspirations of their followers. Crude dismissal at any level of organization destroys morale and ambition and does violence to organization itself. In all types of organizations I believe this often means retaining a leader in the interest of everyone concerned after he has passed the peak of his capacities and sometimes even when the latter have become inadequate. When this is a matter of favouritism, there can be no good defence of it; but when it is a part of the process of *organizing leadership* involving the supplementing of incapacities by auxiliary leaders, it must be defended.

Here we are confronted with another problem of balance—another of the dilemmas of our subject. Who will say that we now know enough about it or are sufficiently successful with respect to it?

## Conclusion

In this short study of one aspect of life, I have tried to emphasize the extent of our limitations and the importance of overcoming them, both from the standpoint of the effect of public blindness to the nature of the problem—which results so often in obstruction and in destructive criticism—and from the standpoint of preparation to meet the future needs of leaders. These are ever increasing as the integrations of societies grow larger, and as specialization and technological progress continue. Whether such an account is depressing, perhaps appalling, or is challenging and inspiring, will depend, I suppose, upon one's philosophy, outlook, or temperament.

It is in the nature of a leader's work that he should be a realist and should recognize the need for action, even when the outcome cannot be foreseen, but also that he should be idealist and in the broadest sense pursue goals some of which can only be attained in a succeeding generation of leaders. Many leaders when they reach the apex of their powers have not long to go, and they press onward by paths the ends of which they will not themselves reach. In business, in education, in government, in religion, again and again, I see men who, I am sure, are dominated by this motive, though unexpressed, and by some queer twist of our present attitudes often disavowed.

Yet, 'Old men plant trees.' To neglect today for tomorrow surely reflects a treacherous sentimentalism; but to shape the present for the future by the surplus of thought and purpose which we now can muster seems the very expression of the idealism which underlies such social coherence as we presently achieve, and without this idealism we see no worthy meaning in our lives, our institutions, or our culture.[9]

## Notes

1. T. S. Eliot, *The Idea of a Christian Society* (New York: Harcourt, Brace & Co., 1940).
2. Throughout I use 'technological' exclusively to refer to conditions of physical technology (plants, machines, chemical processes); and 'technical' to refer either to systems of procedure in accounting, management, etc., or in a more general sense to cover both ideas.
3. The conception of the nature of organization—as a system of coordinated *activities*—involved in this paragraph is carefully developed and defended in 'The Theory of Formal Organization', ch. vii in *The Functions* (Cambridge, Mass.: Harvard University Press, 1938), and is made more explicit in the article 'Comments on the Job of an Executive', *Harvard Business Review* (Spring 1940), n. 1.
4. An extended exposition and an illustration of this definition are given in 'The Nature of Executive Responsibility', ch. xvii in *The Functions*.
5. While writing this sentence I have taken off the shelf at random more than a dozen books on psychology and social psychology. In only two is 'decision'

indexed (Lewin, *Principles of Topological Psychology,* and Guthric, *The Psychology of Human Conflict)* and in both cases the citations are few and quite secondary. Of course, perhaps all of the elements of the decisive processes may be covered in all these books, though from my recollection of them I doubt it. The fact is that one of the most conspicuous factors in common current observable behaviour simply has not been recognized as such, notwithstanding that decision is the culmination of whatever we mean by 'free will', 'will', 'voluntary', 'determined' (in some meanings). The situation recalls what one psychologist has said of others, though in another connection: 'All such explanations fail to explain why we think that *A* is *A*. For, even when the psychologists told us that *A* really was *B*, we stubbornly persisted in calling it *A* and not as *B* . . . For in the long run it has proved to be more profitable to accept an *A* as an *A* and explain it as such . . .' (K. Koffka, *Gestalt Psychology* (New York: Harcourt, Brace & Co., Inc., 1935), 179.)

6. 'An analogous problem is presented in 'oversaving' theories of depressions, in which it is asserted that it is possible for a society as a whole to oversave, whereas the desire to save is commendable as to individuals.
7. Under some, usually small or local, situations leaders are acclaimed spontaneously and are induced or forced to lead by pressure of social opinion. There is often some element of this even in large and institutionalized organizations, chiefly expressed on the negative side, i.e. it is socially or organizationally not countenanced to quit leading or to refuse promotion, and loss of 'caste' would be involved.
8. My reasons are developed at length in the lecture 'The Dilemmas of Leadership in the Democratic Process', repr. in *Human Factors in Management*, ed. Schuyler Hoslett (Kansas City: Park College Press, 1946).
9. This paper contains the substance of two similar addresses given on 24 Jan. 1940 before the Chemical Reserve Officers of the Second Corps Area, USA, under Colonel A. Gibson, CWS, US Army, then Chemical Officer of the Area, and on 9 Mar. 1940, before Professor Philip Cabot's Week End Conference of Business Executives at the Harvard Graduate School of Business Administration. On both occasions the speaker submitted to questions at considerable length. The substance of the important questions and answers is also incorporated in this paper, which was privately printed for the author in 1940 and was reprinted by permission in *Human Factors in Management,* ed. Schuyler Hoslett (Kansas City: Park College Press, 1946).

# 6 Leadership, Membership, Organization

R. M. Stogdill

The present paper is concerned with a point of view regarding the relation of leadership to group organization. It represents one attempt within the Ohio State Leadership Studies staff to clarify and systematize certain aspects of the leadership problem. Such clarification appears to be necessary as a preliminary step towards the development of an integrated programme of research on leadership problems in formal organizations.

The pioneering work of Lewin (1940), Moreno (1934), and their followers has resulted in marked progress in the development of methods for studying leadership as a phenomenon of *groups*. However, comparable progress remains to be made in the development of methods for the study of leadership as an aspect of *organization*. Several factors appear to have operated as barriers to the development of scientific theory and method in this area. One is the lack of an adequate definition of leadership. A second is the fact that, in much of the literature on leadership, the terms 'group' and 'organization' are used interchangeably or are defined in exactly the same terms. A third derives from two opposed theoretical approaches represented, on the one hand, by those theories of organization in which the leader is conceived as a symbol of authority or as an embodiment of superior personal traits, and, on the other hand, by a type of group-oriented theory in which leadership appears to be regarded as a manifestation of social pathology. A fourth, and related, obstacle results from a reaction of social scientists against the authoritarian principles advanced in many discussions of organization. Some social theorists appear to reject all concepts of organization as authoritarian; and some researchers appear reluctant to deal experimentally with such concepts as

R. M. Stogdill, 'Leadership, Membership, and Organization', *Psychological Bulletin*, 47 (1950), 1–14.

responsibility, authority, stratification, and similar phenomena related to organization. It is beyond the scope or purpose of this paper to portray the magnitude of the latter two difficulties. Nevertheless, it seems relevant to recognize the fact that they are present and act to the detriment of scientific work in the field.

The Ohio State Leadership Studies are being conducted on the basis of these assumptions: (1) that group organization is a recognizable social phenomenon in our culture; (2) that as such it is a legitimate subject for scientific study; and (3) that the variables of organization can be isolated and defined so as to permit their scientific study. It is the purpose of the present paper to examine various concepts relevant to leadership and organization, and to develop a formulation of the problem which will suggest hypotheses that can be subjected to experimental test.

## Groups and Organizations

Wilson (1945) has reviewed the important sociological literature relating to concepts of the social group. He reports that in 'current sociological literature one finds no consensus as to the meaning of the *group*', and concludes that much experimental work is yet to be done in order to delimit the group concept in any satisfactory manner. An important step in this direction has been made by Hemphill (1949), who has devised scales for the measurement of such group dimensions as size, permeability, stability, viscidity, homogeneity of membership, and the like.

The most satisfactory definition available at the present time appears to be that of Smith (1945), who defines a *social group* as 'a unit consisting of a plural number of organisms (agents) who have collective perception of their unity and who have the ability to act/or are acting in a unitary manner toward the environment'. Krech and Crutchfield (1948) present a similar view. They state that 'the criteria for establishing whether or not a given set of individuals constitutes a psychological group are mainly two: (1) all the members must exist as a group in the psychological field of each individual, i.e. be perceived and reacted to as a group; (2) the various members must be in dynamic interaction with one another'.

A special kind of group is the *organization*. An organization may be defined as a social group in which the members are differentiated as to their responsibilities for the task of achieving a common goal.

Znaniecki (1945) has reviewed the sociological literature relating to various concepts of organization. He stresses the fact that the terms *group* and *organization* are rather tenuous concepts, in that it is often difficult to determine whether a particular aggregate of persons constitutes a group, and that it may also be difficult at times to determine whether a particular group can be regarded as an organization. He points out that social organization . . .

> can be realized only in a lasting 'social group' or 'association'. Individuals belonging to such a group are aware that they will be regularly expected to perform certain actions, and some of them act as organizers, leaders, coordinators of the regular activities of others with reference to the common purpose. Not all of these individuals need be continuously active; indeed, in many groups a considerable proportion remain passive, acting only in reaction to the actions of others. The common purpose of the organized actions may be simple or complex.

Some of the consequences of distinguishing between the terms 'group' and 'organization' are the following. First, there is nothing in the term 'group' which gives any clue as to the nature of leadership. Secondly, there is nothing in the group definition which provides any foundation for integrating leadership with group phenomena, except at a superficial level of social perception or interaction. Thirdly, the group orientation can suggest research methods relating to leadership only in so far as the social group is defined in terms of organization. The concept of organization, however, with its implications for the differentiation of responsibility roles, does permit the study of leadership as an aspect of the relationships between members who are coordinating their efforts for the achievement of common goals.

A group may or may not have leaders. If it does have leaders, it is an organization, for at least some of the members are thereby differentiated from the others as to responsibility, or role expectation in relation to some common purpose. The members of a group may or may not have mutual responsibilities for a common task. If the members do have differentiated responsibilities in relation to common goals, then the group is an organization—a particular kind of group. The continued presence of leaders and of responsibility differentiations in relation to group goals are indicative of organization. It may not always be easy to determine the exact point at which a group emerges into an organization.

## Leadership as an Aspect of Organization

The following definition of leadership may serve as a starting-point for discussion. Leadership may be considered as the process (act) of influencing the activities of an organized group in its efforts towards goal-setting and goal achievement. The definition of leadership relates it directly to the organized group and its goal. It would appear that the minimal social conditions which permit the existence of leadership are the following:

1. a group (of two or more persons);
2. a common task (or goal-oriented activities);
3. differentiation of responsibility (some of the members have different duties).

There are innumerable other group and situational factors which may influence leadership in varying degrees, but these appear to be the minimal conditions which will permit the emergence of leadership. There must be a group with a common task or objective, and at least one member must have responsibilities which differ from those of the other members. If all members perform exactly the same duties in exactly the same way, there is no leadership. A leader then is a person who becomes differentiated from other members in terms of influence he exerts upon the goal-setting and goal-achievement activities of the organization.

The foregoing discussion suggests that leadership cannot emerge unless the members of a group assume different responsibilities. It has been suggested that group organization is also founded upon differentiation of responsibility. It would, then, appear that leadership and organization are derived from a common factor, or, viewed from a different fight, that leadership is an aspect of group organization. This view has been expressed in various forms by writers in the field of business organization. Davis (1940), for example, states that the

> . . . development of organization structure is largely a problem in the division of responsibility, and involves two important problems: (1) the grouping of similar functions to form the various organization elements in a manner that will promote effective cooperation, and (2) the determination of the paper relationships between functional groups and organization elements, with a view to promoting both cooperation and effective executive leadership.

The definition of leadership does not specify how many leaders an organization shall have, nor whether the leadership influence of an individual is continuous or intermittent, nor whether the influence of the leader shall be for the welfare or detriment of the organization and its members. It merely specifies that leaders may be differentiated from other members in terms of the extent to which they influence the activities of the organization in its efforts towards the achievement of goals. The definition of effective and ineffective leadership is an additional problem.

R. M. Stogdill

# Aspects of Responsibility

Brown (1947), in a challenging analysis of organization, maintains that 'an enterprise is a mosaic of its individual responsibilities. The sum of them must exactly equal the whole requirement of administration.' He continues, 'responsibility is that part in administration which is assigned to a particular member of an enterprise. Its definition is an act of organization.'

Responsibility cannot be regarded as a simple or uncomplicated variable. Jucius (1947) writes,

> By responsibility is meant, first, the obligation to do an assigned task, and, second, the obligation to someone for the assignment. But what is meant by obligation and how far does it extend? This implies a willingness to accept, for whatever rewards one may see in the situation, the burden of a given task and the risks which attend in the event of failure. Because of the rewards and penalties involved, it is highly essential to specify the limits of responsibility.

Formal organization can seldom define all the possible variations of responsibility and personal interaction to be expected of all members in all situations. Nevertheless, organization appears to be founded upon a basic system of stable expectations regarding differential responsibilities and relationships among the members. This is not a one-way process. That is, it is not the organization alone which sets up role expectations for its members. The members set up expectations for each other and for the organization as a whole. It is assumed for purposes of the present discussion that this principle applies not only to stratified organizations, such as military and industrial establishments. It applies as well to membership in any organized group, whether it be a business, political, educational, religious, fraternal, or social organization and regardless of size, stratification, purpose, or member characteristics. The essential relationship which makes possible the conduct of organized group activities is a differentiation of responsibility roles among the members. Without this there is no possibility of coordination or of leadership towards goal achievement. The very process of organization defines the responsibilities of the members and thereby the formal leadership of the group. It is true that in some organized groups, such as recreational groups, the responsibilities of members may appear to be vaguely defined. However, this is not equivalent to saying that no responsibilities exist.

Responsibility, in its broadest scope, defines not only the duties for which a member is accountable; it defines also the persons to whom and for whom he is accountable in the discharge of his duties. In doing so, it also defines a member's formal status, or location in the organization hierarchy. Authority and formal status systems in organization are but aspects of the division of responsibility.

Responsibilities in a systematic organization are determined by the assignment of persons to particular positions, the duties of which are outlined in an organization manual or organization chart. In less systematic organizations the responsibilities of a particular job or position may be determined by on-the-spot instructions, by general hints, or by unverbalized assumptions. In a systematic organization an individual's *work patterns* (the tasks he *actually* performs) will correspond fairly close with his *responsibility patterns* (the tasks he is *supposed* to perform). However, as the mission and activities of the organization change, there will be found in many instances an increasing discrepancy between the tasks being performed and the responsibilities originally outlined and defined.

## Attributes of Organization

The studies of Roethlisberger and Dickson (1939) and others have directed attention to the factor of informal groups within formal organization. Informal organization, as usually defined, refers to the friendship groups and cliques—based upon close association, mutual interests or antagonisms, and the like—which develop within formal organization. It has been pointed out by Homans (1947) that this conception is too narrow, since what is informal in a factory may be formal in a primitive society. Firey (1948), who defines informal organization in terms of schism, presents a more useful approach to the problem. He maintains that 'if we regard behavioral conformity, in which interactional processes are highly repetitive and synchronized, as the overt counterpart of a social system, then behavioral nonconformity may be taken as the overt counterpart of schism within a system'.

An organization in operation seldom corresponds exactly with the organization model as charted. The intervention of human social factors and other influences result in the emergence of informal organization that is, in the development of work patterns and interaction patterns which do not correspond with responsibility patterns.

It would appear then that there are two fundamental sets of variables which define the operations of an organized group. These are:

1. *Variables which define formal organization*
   (*a*) Responsibility variables (the work one is expected to do).
   (*b*) Formal interaction variables (the persons with whom one is expected to work).
2. *Variables which define informal organization*
   (*a*) Work performance variables (the tasks one actually performs).
   (*b*) Informal interaction variables (the persons with whom one actually works).

If we regard the variables listed above as basic variables of organization, we can also regard them as variables of membership and of leadership. In other words, an organization can be studied in terms of these four types of variables: responsibilities, work performances, formal interactions, and informal interactions. Leadership can also he studied in terms of the same variables.

*Responsibility variables* define the duties that the members are expected to perform. The responsibilities of a given position may remain the same, whether *A* or *B* occupies the position.

*Work performance variables* are defined by the tasks performed and by the methods of their performance. Individual *A* may accept a position previously occupied by *B*. The responsibilities as defined by organization charts and manuals may remain the same, but the tasks actually performed by *A* may differ somewhat from those performed by *B*, and the methods of performance may vary markedly.

*Formal interaction variables* define the persons to whom and for whom the members are accountable, as well as others with whom they are expected to cooperate, in the discharge of their responsibilities.

*Informal interaction variables* are defined by the persons with whom the members actually work and cooperate in the performance of their tasks.

Informal organization comes about as a result of the development of discrepancies (*a*) between work performance and responsibilities as defined and (*b*) between informal interactions and formally defined interactions. Thus leadership is ever confronted with the task of reconciling discrepancies—discrepancies between what ought to be done and what is being done, between goals and achievements, between organizational needs and available resources, between the needs of individuals members and the requirements of organization, between formal lines of cooperation and informal patterns of cooperation.

An organization in action comprises a complex of many variables in interaction. In making a pictorial representation of a business organization, the usual procedure is to plot the division of formal responsibility on a two-dimensional chart. The horizontal dimension of the chart shows the division of responsibility for various kinds of work. The vertical dimension of the chart shows the division of responsibility for different levels of decision-making, and indicates the persons to whom one is accountable and those for whose performance one is accountable in the discharge of duties. This dimension defines the formal authority and status systems of the organization. Level (position in the organization hierarchy) and function (kind of work performed) are not independent dimensions. Although functions tend to differ from level to level, there is considerable overlap. Results from the Ohio State Leadership Studies (Stogdill and Shartle 1948; Shartle 1949) have shown that the functions of top leadership tend to be supported at each lower level in the leadership structure by increasingly more detailed and routine work in the same functions.

Personal interaction can also be conceived as varying in both horizontal and vertical directions. The horizontal dimension is defined by the range (number) of members with whom an individual interacts. Some persons tend to work alone or with single individuals, while others are observed to work with large numbers of persons. The vertical aspect of personal interaction is defined by the number of strata (*echelons*) above and below his own in which a member works with others. Some persons may be observed to work only with others at the same level in the organization. Others tend to work only with subordinates, and still others tend to work only with superiors. These tendencies may or may not represent expression of individual differences in social interaction patterns. Results obtained thus far in the Ohio State Leadership Studies suggest that these patterns of interaction may be determined in part by the functions served by various types of positions. Technical consultants and staff aids tend to spend more time with superiors. Members in supervisory positions are observed, as would be expected, to spend more of their time with assistants, and subordinates. Members in coordinative positions tend to spend time with superiors and subordinates, as well as with associates at the same level in the organization. A member's function or duties may determine to a considerable degree which persons in the organization he may influence, as well as the nature of the influence that he can exert.

## Group Organization Defines and Delimits Leadership

The very process of defining responsibility serves to structure and delimit the role that the leader may play in the organization. He cannot perform all the duties of all the members. His own accomplishment is therefore dependent upon the performance of others. His responsibilities are circumscribed by the outlined procedures and delegated responsibilities necessary for the achievement of stated goals.

Each member must work within the organizational framework which defines the limits of his participation (how far he ought to go and beyond which he ought not to go) in performance of duties. It also sets the requirements for his cooperation with others and defines his relationships with his superiors and subordinates. This organizational structuring is not viewed alike by all persons. To some it appears as a barrier to participation or recognition. To others it appears as a prod and stimulus to greater effort and participation. For still others it provides a secure and comfortable sphere of activities and working relationships. Organization, therefore, in defining the responsibilities and working relationships of its members, sets up barriers to participation, as well as facilitating it.

Even as the organization sets boundaries by providing a framework within which members discharge their responsibilities, so the individual presents various barriers to the influence of the organization upon his own behaviour and reactions. Some members may be limited in capacity to discharge their responsibilities, while others who are highly skilled in the techniques of their responsibilities are limited in capacity to interact with others. Each member carries into the organization his past experiences, his needs, ideals, personal goals, and commitments to other organizations, which may modify and determine his capacity for participation. It would appear that the extent to which the behaviour of different members is determined by the characteristics of the group represents a continuum from little to great, and also that the extent to which the behaviour of the different individuals determines the behaviour of groups may be conceived as representing a similar continuum.

It becomes apparent that a study in leadership represents a study of relationships, of variables in interaction. According to Pigors (1935) a study of leadership must consider: (1) the leader, (2) the members as individuals, (3) the group as a functioning organization, and (4) the situation.

All organizations operate within a larger cultural and environmental framework. No organization can escape entirely the influence of the external situation. The organization may be influenced by the availability of resources, by changes in the social order of which it is a part, by competition of other organizations for the participation, resources, or loyalty of its members, and by innumerable other factors outside the control of the organization itself. These factors also influence the leadership of the group.

## Leadership and Effectiveness of Organization

According to Barnard (1938), the persistence of cooperation depends upon two conditions: (*a*) effectiveness, the accomplishment of cooperative purpose, and (*b*) efficiency, the satisfaction of individual motives. Thus, although in many situations it may appear desirable to effect a maximum of goal achievement with a minimum of organizational expenditure, such a procedure might jeopardize the welfare or morale of the members. It then becomes evident that there are many situations in which organization is confronted by a complex of contradictory factors which must be considered in arriving at a decision. It also becomes apparent that the effectiveness of an organization cannot always be evaluated in terms of the degree to which it has attained its objectives. It may be necessary first to evaluate the goals and objectives themselves or the cost of their attainment. A carefully thought-out discussion of factors to be considered in setting organizational goals, arriving at decisions, and evaluating the success of an organization has been presented by Simon (1947). He states: 'The accomplishment by an administrative program of its organizational goals can be measured in terms of *adequacy* (the degree to which its goals have been reached) or of *efficiency* (the degree to which the goals have been reached relative to the available resources).' Simon, in agreement with Barnard, maintains that the criterion of adequacy alone is not valid as a measure of group accomplishment. He observes that 'the fundamental criterion of administrative decision must be a criterion of *efficiency* rather than a criterion of *adequacy*. The task of administration is to maximize social values relative to limited resources.'

If organizational goals are employed as reference points in evaluating effectiveness, then the goals themselves must be subject to evaluation. In addition, the cost (human or material) of goal attainment must be considered as a factor in evaluation. Both Barnard and Simon imply that organization cannot be regarded as a unit in isolation—or as a law unto itself. The motive of organization is the creation of social value or goods for its members, and these values bear some significant relation to the values of society in general.

Since leadership is related to the determination of group goals, it becomes apparent that the leader is seldom a free agent. In influencing the activities of the organization in its striving towards goal achievement, he must consider certain social values, not only in relation to the members, but in relation to society as well. If he ignores the welfare of the members, he is likely to lose their following. If he ignores the welfare of society, he is likely to lead his group into difficulty. Thus leadership is subject to determination by factors which are external to the organization, as well as by internal group factors.

**R. M. Stogdill**

# The Definition of Leadership

The definition of leadership as a process of influencing the activities of an organized group in its task of goal-setting and goal achievement should perhaps be re-examined. Does it define leadership? What are its implications? Admittedly, it defines only at a high level of generality. Certainly it does not include all social acts and influences, but it is, nevertheless, an inclusive rather than a restrictive definition of leadership. Even so, it is more restrictive than most of those attempted in the recent literature. The definition restricts leadership to influence within the organized group. It does not imply domination or direction of others, nor any technique of influence; nor does it specify any particular member who should be regarded as a leader. The definition permits the study of any member of an organization to determine the extent of his leadership influence, and permits consideration of the possibility that every member may contribute towards determining the leadership of the organization.

The definition carries the implication that leadership may be not so much an attribute of individuals as an aspect of organization In this respect it parallels the concept of authority. It is generally recognized that an executive in a business concern has authority in relation to his employees only during the time they are working as members of the organization. His authority does not extend outwards into the direction of their personal or social lives. Nor does his position as an executive give him authority over other persons who are not members of his organization. In other words, authority is a relationship that exists between persons who are mutually participating as members of an organized enterprise. Authority is not an attribute of one or a few persons. Authority is an interactional process by means of which the organization defines for each individual the scope for action he has in making decisions, carrying out responsibilities, and enlisting the cooperation of others. The authority of any single individual will be largely circumscribed and defined by the authority of others, and, at the same time, his own degree of authority will in part determine the authority of others.

Leadership appears also to be determined by a system of interrelationships. As such it must be regarded as an aspect of organization, just as authority is a derivative of organization. If leadership is determined by a system of interacting variables, then each of the several dimensions of responsibility and personal interaction might be conceived as representing a gradient of influence. If so, then it should be possible to measure leadership influences in terms of these dimensions.

Some members may be regarded as rating higher than others in leadership by virtue of the fact that they have responsibility for making decisions which exert a marked influence upon the activities of the organization. Some members may influence the activities of the organization as a result of personal interaction with other members, even though they do not hold positions of high-level responsibility. Some members may rate high in both types of influence. It would not be expected that any organization could be found in which all influence is exerted by a single member. It would rather be expected that all the members of the organization could be ordered or ranked to some degree in terms of the influence they exert in various dimensions. The proposal to measure leadership in teams of the influence exerted by individuals may appear to contradict the statement that leadership is an aspect of organization rather than an attribute of individuals. But this is not a necessary conclusion. It was pointed out that authority is generally understood to be an aspect of organization. However, it can be observed that some members exercise more authority than others. The judgement can also be made that some persons have 'too much' or 'too little' authority. Such observations indicate an evaluation of conditions relative to various factors in the organization. In the same way it can be observed that member *A* exerts more leadership influence in some situations; while members *B*, *C*, and *D* exert more influence in determining activities of the organization in other instances. It may be that the leadership of *A* is circumscribed by the leadership of *B*, *C*, and *D*, who are in competition with him; or it may be that the leadership of *A* is dependent upon the supporting leadership of *B*, *C*, and *D*. In either event, the leadership influence of any one member is determined in part by the leadership exerted by others, and the balance may change from time to time.

## Summary

An organization is composed of individuals. Its existence is dependent upon the cooperation and performance of individuals who play different roles. Measures of authority, leadership, and the like, are but measures of aspects of organization, even though the measurements are made in terms of members and the relationships among members. Leadership exists only in so far as individuals, as members of organizations, are differentiated as to the influence they exert upon the organization; and the leadership influence of any one member will be determined to a large degree by the total leadership structure of the organization. It is for this reason that leadership has been here defined in terms of influence upon the activities of the organization, rather than in terms of influence upon persons.

The advantages of this formulation of the leadership problem are as follows. First, it removes leadership from the broad, vaguely defined realm of social interaction in general, and integrates it with the basic variables which describe an organized group. Second, and more important, is the fact that it suggests the development of methods for studying leadership as an aspect of work performance, work methods, and working relationships.

An attempt is being made to develop such methods for the Ohio State Leadership Studies. For example, the goals and structure of organization and the responsibility patterns of members are determined by examining organization charts and manuals and by interviews with members of the organization. Work patterns are determined by modified job-analysis procedures. Sociometric methods are employed to determine working relationships between the members and to chart the informal organization. The social values and role concepts of leaders and members are studied by means of attitude scales. These methods are supplemented by various checklists and rating scales.

In conclusion, a word of caution may be in order. The present paper has been concerned with a search for the minimal factors which will permit a functional integration of the concepts: leader, member, and organization. In attempting to isolate these minimal common elements, many other important factors associated with leadership and group functioning have been excluded as not contributing to this central purpose. The present formulation represents merely one segment of a set of hypotheses to be subjected to experimental test.

## References

Barnard, C. I. (1938), *The Functions of the Executive* (Cambridge, Mass.: Harvard University Press).

Brown, A. (1947), *Organization of Industry* (Englewood Cliffs, NJ: Prentice-Hall).

Davis, R. C. (1940), *Industrial Organization and Management* (New York: Harper).

Firey, W. (1948), 'Informal Organization and the Theory of Schism, *American Sociological Review*, 13: 15–24.

Hemphill, J. K. (1949), *Situational Factors in Leadership* (Columbus, Oh.: Bureau of Educational Research, Ohio State University).

Homans, G. C. (1947), 'A Conceptual Scheme for the Study of Social Organization', *American Sociological Review*, 12: 13–26.

Jucius, M. J. (1947), *Personnel Management* (Chicago: Irwin).

Krech, D., and Crutchfield, R. S.(1948), *Theory and Problems of Social Psychology* (New York: McGraw-Hill).

Lewin, K., Lippit, R., and Escalona, S. K. (1940), *'Studies in Topological* and *Vector Psychology, I', University of Iowa Studies on Child Welfare*, 16/3.

Moreno, J. L. (1934), *Who Shall Survive?*, (Beacon, NY: Beacon House).

Pigors, P. (1935), *Leadership or Domination* (Boston: Houghton-Mifflin).

Roethlisberger, F. J., and Dickson, W. J. (1939), *Management and the Worker* (Cambridge, Mass.: Harvard University Press).

Shartle, C. L. (1949), 'Leadership and executive performance', *Personnel*, 25: 370–88.

Simon, H. A. (1947), *Administrative Behaviour* (New York: Macmillan).

Smith, M. (1945), 'Social Situation, Social Behavior, Social Group, *Psychological Review* 52: 224–9.

Stogdill, R. M., and Shartle, C. L. (1948), 'Methods for Determining Patterns of Leadership Behavior in Relation to Organization Structure and Objectives', *Journal of Applied Psychology*, 32: 286–91.

Wilson, L. (1945), 'Sociography of groups', in G. Gurvitch and W. E. Moore (eds.), *Twentieth Century Sociology* (New York: Philosophical Library), 139–71.

Znaniecki, F. (1945), 'Social Organization and Institutions', in G. Gurvitch and W. E. Moore (eds.), *Twentieth Century Sociology*, (New York: Philosophical Library, 172–217.

# 7 Situational Control and a Dynamic Theory of Leadership

Fred E. Fiedler

Although empirical studies of leadership behaviour and performance became a serious concern of social scientists some fifty years ago, we are just now beginning to understand the structure of the leader–situation interaction and the dynamics of the leadership process. By dynamics, we mean here how the leader and organization interact, and how group performance is affected by a change in the leader's personality or experience, or by the changes in the organization which occur almost continuously in the course of time. An insight into these interactions is essential if we are more fully to understand and improve organizational performance. This study presents an integration of some key concepts which may enable us to develop a dynamic theory of leadership that takes into account the ever changing leader–organization interaction.

Traditionally, the main business of leadership research has been the relationship between personality attributes of the leader and the performance of his or her group or organization. At first, this search focused on finding the magic personality trait which might predict leadership performance. This enterprise finally received the *coup de grâce* from Stogdill's (1948) and Mann's (1959) now classical reviews of the literature.

The emphasis then shifted to the identification of specific types of leader behaviour which would determine the effectiveness of a group. While this effort did not succeed, it did result in the monumental factor analytic research by the Ohio State group under Carroll Shartle and his associates (Stogdill and Coons 1957), which identified the Consideration and Structuring dimensions

F. E. Fiedler, 'Situational Control and a Dynamic Theory of Leadership', in B. King, S. Streufert, and F. E. Fiedler (eds.), *Managerial Control and Organizational Democracy* (Washington: Winston & Sons, 1976), 107–31.

as the two major types of leadership behaviour which are seen by subordinates. Others (e.g. Bales 1951, Cattell 1951, and Likert 1961), identified similar types of behaviour on which leaders differed in their interactions with groups. The hope that these or similar behaviours would be directly related to leadership performance has not been realized, although a number of investigators still deal with this problem.

In particular, a number of leadership training programmes have been devoted to teaching managers how to be more considerate or more structuring. The well-known Fleishman, Harris, and Burt (1955) study showed that training of this type would not give lasting results unless the entire organization were to be changed. However, other types of training, working with the entire organization, have not been able to report much success in improving organizational performance. This applies to the orthodox approaches as well as such avant-garde programmes as T-group and sensitivity training. Stogdill (1974: 199), in his authoritative and comprehensive *Handbook of Leadership*, summarizes this type of research by censuring its 'failure to employ legitimate criteria of the effects of training'. And he goes on to say,

> It is necessary to demonstrate that change in leader behavior is related to change in group productivity, cohesiveness, esprit, or satisfaction in order to claim that leadership is improved or worsened by training. Only a few of the studies examined for this report satisfy the above requirements. The results of this small body of research suggest that group cohesiveness and esprit increase after sensitivity training of the leader but productivity declines. (Ibid. 199)

The acid test of leadership theory obviously must be its ability to improve organizational performance. For this reason, the ability to change and control and especially to train leaders is a very powerful test of our understanding of the process and theory. Our previous difficulties in this area may well derive from our inadequate understanding of the complex interaction which is inherent in leadership and even the way in which training itself affects the dynamics of the process. The simple notion that a particular type of behaviour, or a particular behaviour pattern, will result in effective leadership performance is no more viable than the earlier notion of a leadership trait. Leadership exists in the context of an organizational environment which determines, in large part, the specific kind of leadership behaviour which the situation requires.

Since the publication of the Contingency Model (Fiedler 1964, 1967), leadership theory has increasingly turned to formulations which consider not only the leader's personality or behaviour, but also critical situational factors. Such situational effects or contingencies also have been explicitly recognized by theorists such as House (1971), Vroom and Yetton (1973), and others. It seems fair to say that we are now beginning to predict the relationship between certain leader attributes and organizational performance at a given point in time with a reasonable degree of accuracy.

However, most of our predictions in this field tend to be cross-sectional. We cannot predict well for organizations which are undergoing change and we do not understand fully what factors are critical to leadership performance in this change process. Our major challenge in the area of leadership is to develop a theory which takes account of the changing organizational environment as well as the changes which occur in the leader.

The key concept, which is here proposed as a basis for developing a dynamic theory of leadership, is the leader's situational control. This is essentially the 'situational-favourableness' dimension of the Contingency Model. I hope to show that this concept gives us considerable understanding of the leadership process and also enables us to control the process—that is, to develop an effective leadership training programme which meets Stogdill's requirement that it affect organizational performance.

## The Contingency Model

Although the Contingency Model has been fully described in numerous publications, a brief summary provides the basis for the remainder of this study. This theory holds that the effectiveness of a group or an organization depends upon two interacting factors: (*a*) the personality of the leader (leadership style), and (*b*) the degree to which the situation gives the leader control and influence, or, in somewhat different terms, the degree to which the situation is free of uncertainty for the leader.

## The Personality of the Leader

The leader's personality, and, more specifically, his or her motivational structure, is identified by a measure which reflects the individual's primary goals in the leadership situation. One type of person, whom we call 'relationship-motivated', obtains self-esteem from good interpersonal relationships with groups members and accomplishes the task through these good relations. These basic goals are most apparent in uncertain and anxiety-provoking situations in which we try to assure that our most important needs are secured. Under these conditions, relationship-motivated individuals will seek the support of those who are most closely associated with them. In a leadership situation, we hypothesize that these are, of course, their immediate subordinates and co-workers. Once the support of co-workers and subordinates is assured and this basic goal is no longer in doubt, relationship-motivated leaders will seek support and esteem from others who are important. In a leadership situation in which esteem and approbation are given for good task performance, these individuals will devote themselves to the task in order to obtain the approval of their superiors, even if this means correspondingly less concern with the well-being and approval of subordinates. Thus, when relationship-motivated leaders enjoy a high degree of situational control, they tend to show task-relevant behaviour which is most likely to impress superiors.

The other major personality type is the 'task-motivated' leader who obtains satisfaction and self-esteem from the more tangible evidence of his or her competence. In a leadership situation which is uncertain and anxiety-provoking, this individual will focus primarily on the completion of the task. However, when task-accomplishment is assured, as would be the case whenever the leader enjoys a high degree of situational control, the leader will relax and devote more time to cementing the relationship with his or her subordinates. Thus, 'business before pleasure', but business with pleasure whenever this is possible.

These two motivational systems are measured by the Least Preferred Co-worker (or LPC) score which is obtained by asking the individual to think of all those with whom he or she has ever worked, and then to describe the one person with whom he or she has been able to work least well. This description is made on a short bipolar scale of the Semantic Differential format, shown below. We have used 16 or 18 eight-point scale items, e.g.

friendly:—:—:—:—:—:—:—:—:unfriendly
8 7 6 5 4 3 2 1

cooperative:—:—:—:—:—:—:—:—:uncooperative
8 7 6 5 4 3 2 1

The LPC score is simply the sum of the item scores. A task-motivated person describes the least preferred co-worker in very negative and rejecting terms. The person says, in effect, that the task is so important it is impossible to differentiate between others as co-workers and as individuals apart from the work relationship. That is, an individual who does not perform well must also have a very objectionable personality, i.e. unfriendly, uncooperative, unpleasant, and so on.

The relationship-motivated person is less dependent on esteem from task accomplishment and is, therefore, quite capable of seeing another as a poor co-worker but as otherwise quite pleasant, friendly, or helpful. Since this leader's emotional involvement in the task is comparatively less intense, a person who is difficult to work with is seen in a more positive manner.

Although the LPC score is normally distributed, there is a relatively small segment in the middle of the distribution which cannot be clearly identified as task- or relationship-motivated persons. For the purposes of this chapter, we shall be concerned primarily with the high and the low LPC leaders, who are much better understood.

A recent review of the literature by Rice (1977) shows that the LPC score reflects a relatively stable personality attribute. Rice located twenty-three test–retest correlations which ranged 'from 0.01 to 0.92 with a median of 0.67 and a mean (using Fisher's Z transformation) of 0.64 (standard deviation $= 0.36$, $n = 23$)'. He goes on to say, 'Somewhat surprisingly the test–retest reliability data . . . show only a moderate negative correlation between length of the test–retest interval and the magnitude of the stability coefficient ($r = -0.30$, $n = 23$, ns). This analysis suggests that the variance in stability coefficients is primarily due to factors other than the simple passing of time.' Exactly what other factors might affect the stability of the score is still not clear.

It is also of interest to note that the median retest reliability of LPC is well within the range of several other widely used personality measures. For example, Sax (1974) lists the stability of the Minnesota Multiphasic Personality Inventory (MMPI) for a period of only one week as 0.60, and the median stability coefficient of the Hartshorne and May honesty scales of a six-month interval as 0.50. Mehrens and Lehmann (1973) report the stability of the California Psychological Inventory for 13,000 subjects over a one-year period as 0.65 for males and 0.68 for females. While the retest correlations for such measures of cognitive abilities as intelligence are generally higher, relatively few stability coefficients of personality test scores fall above 0.70 for intervals of several months.

## *The Leadership Situation*

The other major variable of the Contingency Model is the leader's situational control or 'situational favourableness.' The method for operationally defining this concept is based on three subscales which indicate the degree to which (*a*) the leader is or feels accepted and supported by group members (leader–member relations); (*b*) the task is clear-cut, structured, and identifies the goals, procedures, and progress of the work (task structure); and (*c*) the leader has the ability to reward and punish, and thus to obtain compliance through organizational sanctions (position power).

Groups can be categorized as being high or low on each of these three dimensions by dividing them at the median or on the basis of normative scores. This leads to an eight-cell classification from high situational control (Octant I) to low control (Octant VIII) (shown in Fig. 7.1). Leaders will have high control if they enjoy the support of the group, have a clearly structured task, and high position power. They will have low control if the group does not support them, the task is vague and unstructured, and position power is weak. When measuring situational control, leader–member relations are given a weight of 4, task structure a weight of 2, and position power a weight of 1. This weighting system has been supported by several empirical studies (Beach *et al.* 1975; Nebeker, 1975).

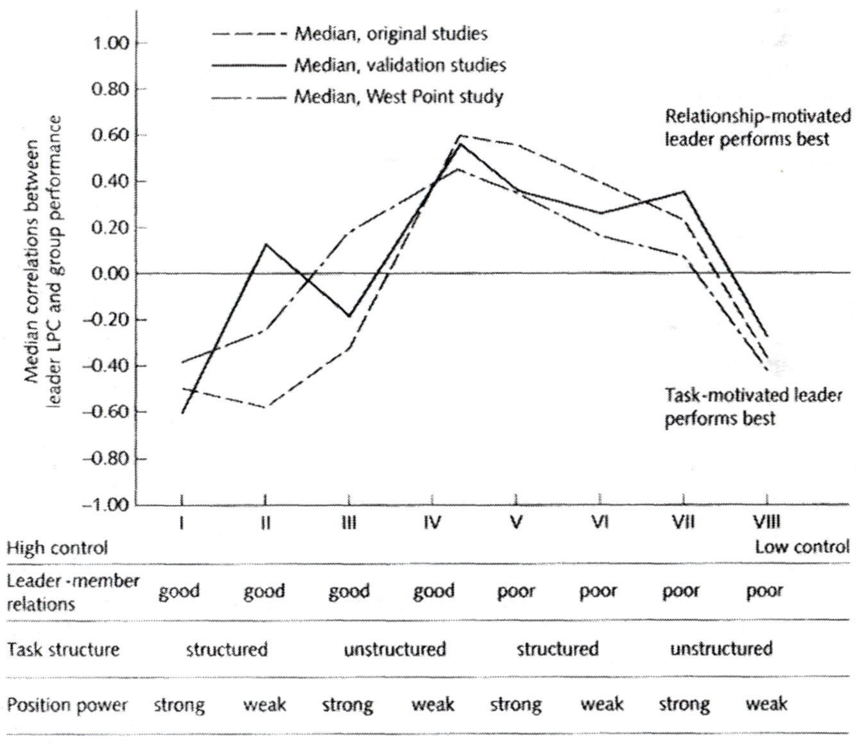


**Fig. 7.1.** Median correlations between leader LPC and group performance for studies conducted to test the Contingency Model.

Having high control implies that leaders will be assured that their particular goals and needs will be attained. Under these conditions, relationship-motivated leaders will worry less about interpersonal relations with the group and more about earning esteem from their boss or other important people in the organization. They accomplish this by showing concern for the job and exhibiting task-directive behaviour. Task-motivated leaders in a high-control situation are assured that the job will be accomplished and will devote themselves to improving and cementing relations with group members.

Low situational control will result in uncertainty and greater anxiety that the leader's goals will not be attained. Under these conditions, task-motivated leaders will concentrate on their goal of task accomplishment, while the relationship-motivated leaders will focus on achieving their goals of good interpersonal relations with the group.

## *The Personality–Situation Interaction*

The Contingency Model has shown that task-motivated leaders perform best when situational control is high as well as in situations where control is low. The relationship-motivated leaders tend to perform best in situations in which their control is moderate. These findings are summarized in Fig. 7.1. The horizontal axis indicates the eight cells of the situational-control dimension, with the high-control situations on the left of the graph and the low-control situations on the right. The vertical axis indicates the correlation coefficients between leader LPC scores and group performance. A high correlation in the positive direction (above the midline of the graph) indicates that the high LPC leaders performed better than did the low LPC leaders. A negative correlation indicates that the low LPC leaders performed better than the high LPC leaders.

The broken line in Fig. 7.1 connects the median correlation coefficients of studies conducted prior to 1963; the solid line connects the median correlations obtained in validation studies since 1964. The dotted line shows the results of a major validation experiment conducted by Chemers and Skrzypek (1972) and provides the most convincing support of the Contingency Model.

In this study, LPC scores as well as sociometric ratings to determine leader–member relations were obtained six weeks prior to the study. Eight groups were then experimentally assembled for each of the octants so that half the groups had high LPC leaders, half had low LPC leaders. Half of the groups consisted of men who had chosen each other sociometrically as preferred work companions while the other half had indicated a dislike for working with others who were placed on the same team. Half the groups, further, were given leaders with high position power and half the groups had leaders with low position power.

As can be seen, the results of the Chemers and Skrzypek study almost exactly replicated the findings of the original studies. The correlation points of the original studies and the West Point study correlated .086 ($p<0.01$) and a subsequent reanalysis of Shiflett (1973) showed that the West Point study accounted for 28 per cent of the variance in group performance.

As Fig. 7.1 clearly indicates, the effectiveness of the group or organization depends on leader personality (leadership style) as well as situational control. For this reason, we cannot really talk about a 'good' leader or a 'poor' leader. Rather, leaders may be good in situations which match their leadership style and poor in situations in which leadership style situational control are mismatched.

## Situational Control and the Dynamics of the Leadership Process

Let us now extend the Contingency Model to encompass the dynamic interactions in the leadership process. The integrating concept which allows us to do this is the leader's situational control and influence. Situational control will change partly in response to environmental and organizational events and partly as the leader's abilities to cope with the organizational environment change. Thus, leaders may be given different assignments, greater or lesser authority, more compliant or more 'difficult' subordinates, or a more or less supportive boss. Leaders may also learn through experience or training how to cope more effectively with the situation which confronts them, giving increased situational control or, in some cases, less control over their leadership situation.

As the Contingency Model has shown, leadership effectiveness depends on the proper match between situational control and leadership style as measured by the LPC score. A major change in the organization or in the leader will necessarily change this match and thus increase or decrease leadership performance. The nature of this relationship is schematically shown in Fig. 7.2. The horizontal axis indicates the degree to which the situation gives the leader control. The vertical axis indicates leadership performance. The solid line shows the performance of relationship-motivated (high LPC) leaders and the broken line the performance of task-motivated (low LPC) leaders. Again, of course, task-motivated leaders are shown as performing best in high- and low-control situations; relationship-motivated leaders are shown as performing best in moderate-control situations. Some of the major factors which would cause changes in the match to occur are presented below.

## *Experience*

The most obvious and inevitable change which generally takes place in the leader's control is the result of time on the job and the concomitant increase in experience. The first days and months on a new job are almost invariably bewildering to the point where it is difficult to cope with the many problems which arise. This feeling of being out of control and in need of help gradually gives way, over time, to increasing confidence that we know what is going on. This process of feeling in control may take no longer than a few days for simple jobs, or several years for the complex and difficult assignments.

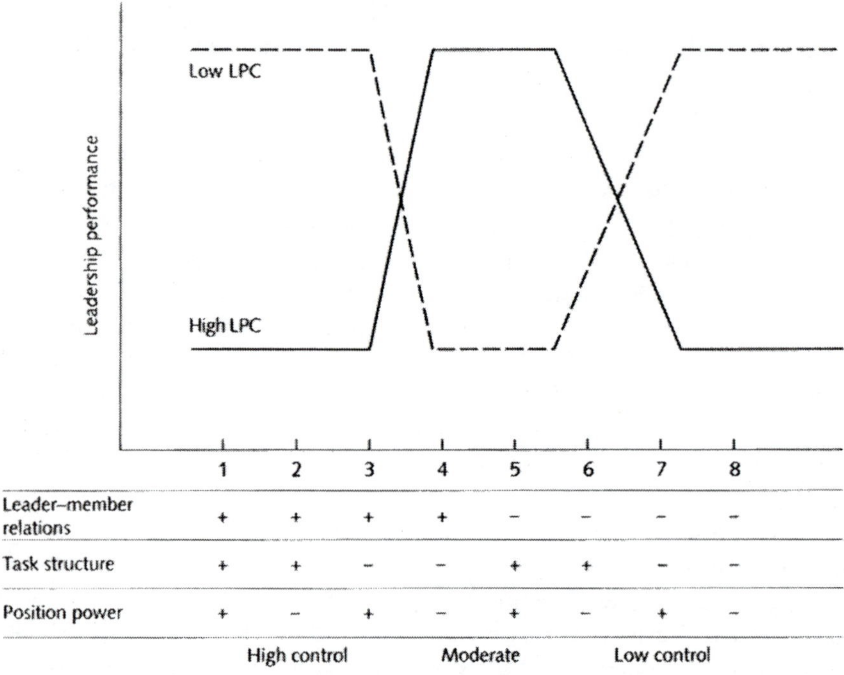


**Fig. 7.2.** Schematic representation of the Contingency Model.

Indeed, there are some jobs in which a leader may never really feel in control, no matter how long he or she has been in the position.

What does experience do for us? First of all, we learn the routines of the job. We know where things are, how we can get certain things done, and what the exact standards and requirements of the job are. In other words, the task, in our eyes, becomes more structured. Leaders will also become more familiar with subordinates. They learn what the group's idiosyncrasies are and how to handle them, and relations with them tend to become easier, more cordial, and mutually more supportive. Moreover, leaders will get to know their boss, what the superior's standards and expectations are, how to manage a relationship with him or her. Finally, with greater support from the boss and a better grasp of the informal and formal rules of the organization, leaders will know exactly how much power their position has, and how to use it.

By and large, then, we expect that the typical experience which comes with time on the job will correspondingly increase the leader's control over the leadership situation. This means that inexperienced leaders who come into low-control situations will perform well if they are task-motivated, but will gradually decrease performance as the gain in experience makes the situation one of moderate control. Under the same conditions, relationship-motivated leaders will perform poorly, initially, and gradually become better as experience increases.

Similarly, if we take a situation in which the leader has moderate control upon beginning the job, we should find that the relationship-motivated person performs well at first, but decreases in effectiveness as he or she gains in experience and the situation becomes high in control. The opposite will be true of task-motivated leaders.

A study by Fielder, Bons, and Hastings (1975), using squad leaders of an infantry division, supports this hypothesis. These are first-level supervisors who command a squad of between eight and twelve soldiers. The squad leaders were evaluated by two superiors shortly after the squads were formed—that is, while the division was still in a rather unsettled state; the leaders did not yet know their subordinates well, nor did they know their superiors well. A second performance evaluation was obtained from the same raters about five months later, after the unit had gone through training and completed their combat readiness tests.

An assessment of the leadership situation was obtained from outside judges and indicated that the situational control was moderate for the leaders at the time the division was established, but high after the leaders had gained experience and the division had shaken down. Fig. 7.3 shows the results when we compare the performance ratings of the same leaders by the same raters

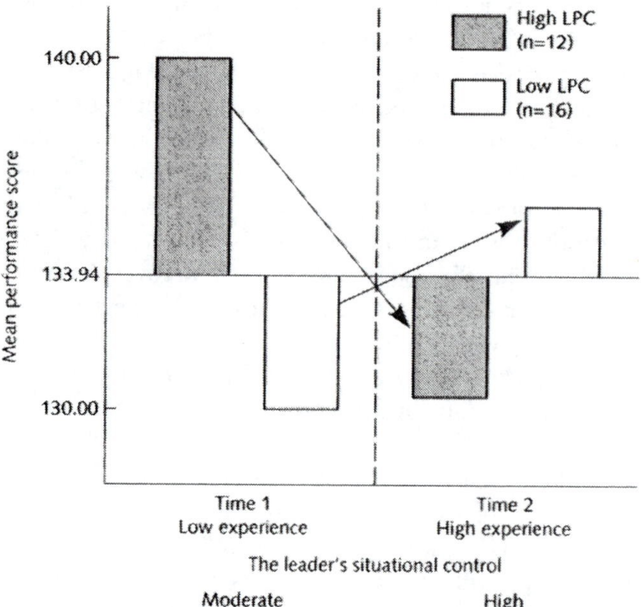


**Fig. 7.3.** Change in performance of high and low LPC leaders as a function of increased experience over five months (interaction significant.)

at the first and second time of evaluation. Similar results have been reported elsewhere (Fiedler and Chemers 1974).

## *Training*

We would expect, of course, that the effect of training will be quite similar to that of experience, provided that the training is relevant and reflects the experience of others who have been successful in the position. However, a considerable amount of leadership training has been devoted to participative and non-directive approaches which would, by and large, reduce the leader's control, since the leader must share information and decision-making functions with group members. It is, therefore, not always clear what effects training will have on leadership control. On the other hand, task training almost certainly will increase the perceived structure of the assignment and the leader's situational control.

A well-designed leadership training experiment, conducted by Chemers, Rice, Sundstrom, and Butler (1975), demonstrates the effects of this intervention. A sample of twenty Reserve Officer Training Corps (ROTC) cadets with high and twenty with low LPC scores were selected as leaders, while those with intermediate LPC scores along with students from a psychology class served as group members in this experiment. The three-man groups were further divided at random into those who received task training and those who were given no training. The assignment consisted of deciphering a series of coded messages. The training consisted of teaching the leaders some simple rules of decoding, e.g. that the most frequent letter in the English alphabet is 'e', that the most frequent three-letter word with 'e' at the end is 'the', that the only one-letter words are 'I' and 'a', etc.

The group climate scores were quite low, and the position power of the leaders was also low. Untrained leaders, who had an unstructured task, had low control, while trained leaders had a moderate degree of situational control. This means that the untrained low-LPC leaders should perform better than the untrained high-LPC leaders, while the trained high-LPC leaders should outperform the trained low-LPC leaders. The interaction between LPC and training is statistically highly significant (Fig. 7.4). The finding is especially startling, since the trained low-LPC leaders not only performed less well than high-LPC leaders, but they also performed less well than did the untrained low-LPC leaders.

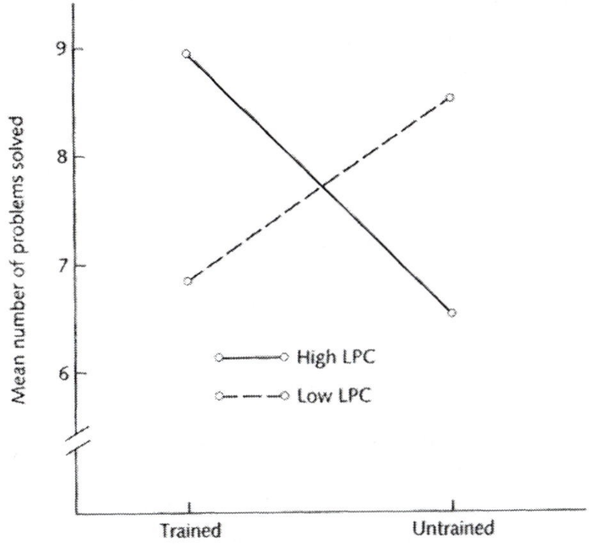


**Fig. 7.4.** The effect of training and LPC on group productivity.

### Organizational Turbulence

Changes in the organizational structure and function also affect the leader's situational control. These changes require the leader to adapt to new conditions and to learn how to cope with situations which are unfamiliar and which have less certain and less predictable outcomes. This is particularly true when the leader is given a new job, which typically also means that the boss is new, as are the leader's subordinates.

A study by Bons and Fiedler (1976) of squad leaders illustrates the effects of these changes on leader performance and behaviour. One additional point needed to be considered in this study. Some of the squad leaders were newly appointed to this first-level command position, while others had been squad leaders for several years—in fact, some for as much as ten years. For the latter, the situation obviously presented fewer new elements than it did for the newer, younger soldiers. For this reason, data for experienced and inexperienced squad leaders were analysed separately with the expectation that the situation would provide more control for the experienced than for the inexperienced leaders. Performance was assessed on the basis of ratings by two superiors.

In the sample of experienced leaders there was no evidence that task performance had been affected substantially by organizational turbulence. In the group of inexperienced leaders, however, a change in job was associated with a markedly lower-task performance on the part of high LPC leaders at time 2. Since we had made covariance adjustments for time 1 performance scores, these data imply that task performance of relationship-motivated leaders had decreased as a result of change in job, while that of task-motivated leaders had slightly increased (see Fig. 7.5; the broken line indicates the grand mean of task performance scores at time 1; the interaction of LPC × experience × change is significant at the 0.05 level).

## Leadership Selection and Placement

Current theory and practice in leadership selection best typify the non-dynamic nature of present thinking in this area. We try to select managers and leaders with the well-worn notion that the round pegs belong in round holes and square pegs in square holes. This is fine as long as the pegs and holes do not change their shape. In fact, however, as we have seen, changes in

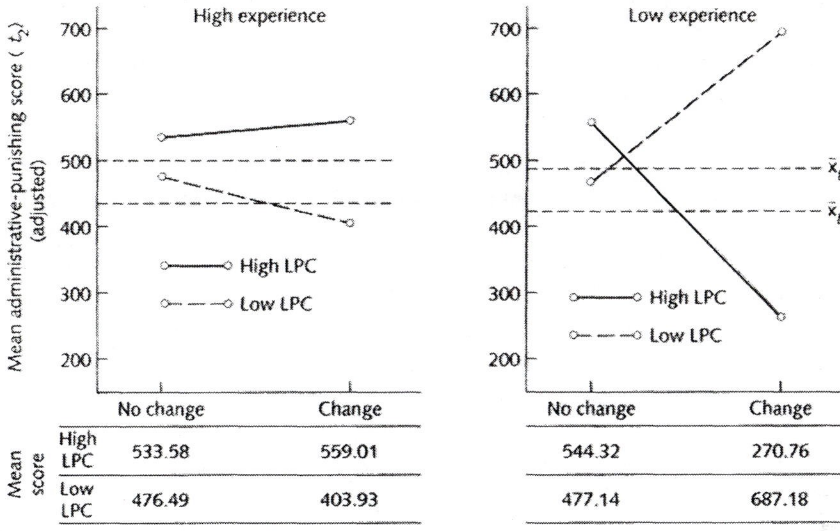


| Mean score | High experience: No change | High experience: Change | Low experience: No change | Low experience: Change |
|---|---|---|---|---|
| High LPC | 533.58 | 559.01 | 544.32 | 270.76 |
| Low LPC | 476.49 | 403.93 | 477.14 | 687.18 |

**Fig. 7.5.** Task-performance behaviour as a function of LPC and change in job for given levels of leader experience.

leaders' ability and job knowledge affect their situational control, and thus the match between leadership style and situational control.

This match may be excellent as the leader enters on a new job and he or she tends to perform well at first. However, leadership performance is likely to change as the leader gains greater control over the situation through experience and training. Thus, if the situation provides low control for the new leader, we would expect that the task-motivated individual will perform well and the relationship-motivated person will perform poorly. As experience and training increase situational control to 'moderate', the performance of the task-motivated leader will decrease and that of the relationship-motivated leader will increase. The opposite will be the case if the situational control is moderate in the beginning and high later on. Then, the relationship-motivated leader will perform well at first and poorly later on.

If selection and placement procedures are to be effective, they must take account of these dynamic changes. We must explicitly decide on the strategy which the organization should follow. As a rule, of course, selecting leaders to perform well when they are experienced will be best if the leadership job can be learned within a few weeks or months, even though the chosen leader may perform poorly at first.

A long-run strategy also will be more appropriate in very stable organizations in which the turnover of managerial personnel is very slow. However, in many organizations and especially in the military, it is rather unusual for a person to remain in the same job for more than one, two, or three years. This is also true in large organizations which have a policy of rotation as part of a managerial development programme. Rapid change in the leadership structure may also be the result of various economic and environmental forces which impinge on the organization. Examples are found in large manufacturing and research and development organizations which utilize matrix or programme management in order to accomplish special tasks or to develop specific product lines which are expected to discontinue after a given period of time.

Under these latter conditions, the requirements of the organization call for immediate top performance, and a short-run strategy is clearly indicated. The organization must then be prepared to accept the possibility that a particular leader, who has been assigned to the same job for an extended period of time, is likely to become less effective and must again be moved to a more challenging job.

The amount of time which will elapse before a leadership situation will change from low control to moderate control, or from moderate to high control, will depend on the degree of structure and complexity of the task, and the intellectual abilities of the personnel who are available for these positions. For such tasks as infantry squad leader, the time at which this occurs may be four or five months; for school principals, it appears to be between two and three years; and for community college presidents, between five and six years. Some management jobs may require even longer before the leader gains maximum control.

The important point is, of course, that a rational selection and placement strategy cannot assume that the match between leader and job will remain a good fit forever. Rather, we must consider the effects which increased or decreased situational control will have on the selection process.

## Situational Control and Leader Behaviour

Having shown that a change in situational control results in a change of leadership performance, we must now ask why a situational change should have this effect. Since we must eventually look to leader behaviour as the mainspring for leadership performance, we need to determine how situational control affects the behaviours of relationship- and task-motivated leaders.

As mentioned earlier, the behaviour of task- and relationship-motivated leaders differs in relaxed, high-control situations and in stressful, anxiety-arousing, low-control situations (Fiedler 1972). A study by Meuwese and Fiedler (cited in Fiedler 1967) will serve as an illustration. In this laboratory experiment, we compared the behaviour of task- and relationship-motivated leaders of ROTC teams which were engaged in creative tasks. In one condition, the cadets worked under low stress, assured that their performance would have no bearing on their future military career. In another condition, the cadets were asked to appear in uniform and were continuously evaluated by a high-ranking officer who was seated directly across the table from the team. This latter condition was rated as quite stressful.

The comments made by leaders were categorized as relevant to developing good interpersonal relationships in the team, specifically, involving group participation and democratic leadership behaviour, and as task-relevant (proposing new ideas and integrating ideas of others). The results are shown in Fig. 7.6 and support the interpretation that high- and low-LPC scores reflect different goals or motivational structures. That is, the behaviour of the leader in the stressful condition appears directed towards achieving the more basic goals—namely, task achievement for the low-LPC, and good interpersonal relations for the high-LPC leader. In the non-stressful condition in which the leader's control is high, and he can feel sure of achieving his basic goals, the leader's behaviour appears directed towards the attainment of secondary goals. These are a pleasant relationship for the low-LPC leader, and gaining approval of others by task-relevant behaviour on the part of the high-LPC leader.

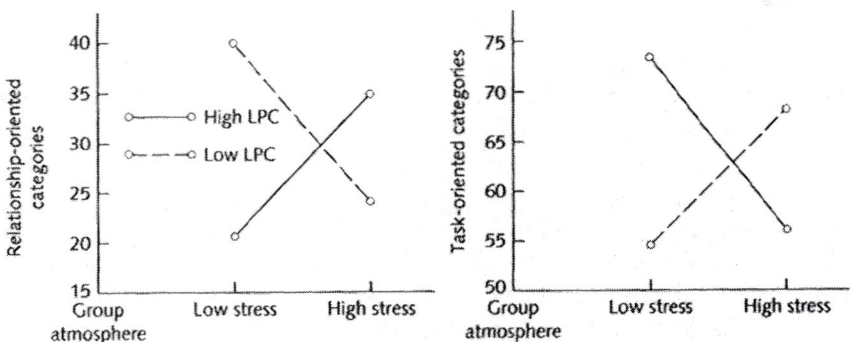


**Fig. 7.6.** The effect of stress on behaviour of relationship-motivated (high LPC) and task-motivated (low LPC) leaders.

It is also possible to ask whether the leader's behaviour will change as a result of a deliberate change in the leadership situation or one caused by organizational turbulence. According to the Contingency Model, an increase in the leader's control should make task-motivated individuals behave in a more considerate, social-emotional manner, while it should lessen the relationship-motivated leader's concern for group members. Lowering the leader's situational control should increase the relationship-motivated leader's concern for the group but decrease that of the task-motivated leader. Chemers (1969) tested this hypothesis using a culture-training programme which was designed to improve the American leader's ability to deal with Iranian co-workers in a more effective and more secure manner.

Chemer's experiment used three-person groups which were to make recommendations on two controversial issues in Iran at the time: (*a*) employment of women and (*b*) appropriate training for low-status supervisors. At the end of the task sessions, the two Iranian group members described the leader's consideration behaviour, the group climate, and their evaluation of the leader.

Half the leaders in the experiment were high- and the other half low-LPC persons. These were randomly assigned either to the culture-training condition or to a condition involving control training—that is, training in the physical geography of Iran. The culture training was, of course, expected to increase the leader's control, enabling more effective interaction with group members.

As can be seen from Fig. 7.7, the task-motivated leaders with culture training were seen as more considerate. They also were more esteemed and developed better group climate. The relationship-motivated leaders, on the other hand, were seen as less considerate, and as having developed a poorer group climate. (The interaction between LPC and training is significant.)

Let us now consider the effects which a stable leadership situation and an unstable, turbulent leadership environment will have on leader behaviour. A stable environment should increase the leader's control and thus cause the relationship-motivated leader to become less concerned with group member relations, while the task-motivated leader should become more concerned with interpersonal relations in the group. However, a leadership environment characterized by change and turbulence should cause anxiety and insecurity. Under these conditions, the relationship-motivated leader will seek the support of group members, while the task-motivated leader will become more controlling in order to assure that the job gets done. We assume, then, that a tendency to reward will improve interpersonal relations while a tendency to be punitive implies the desire for stronger control and concern for task accomplishment.

The study of infantry squad leaders, discussed earlier, provides data which

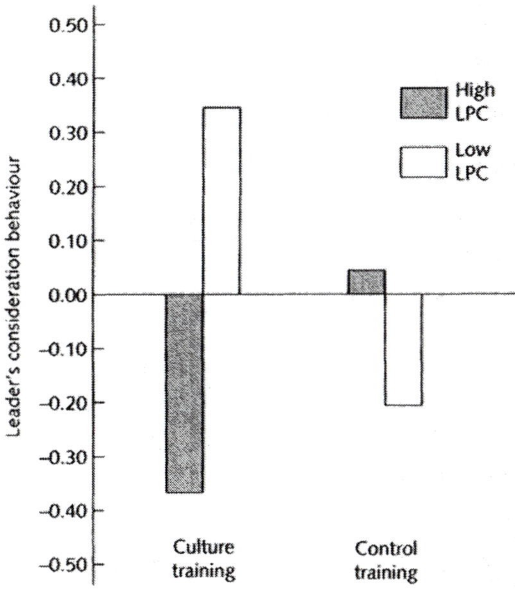


**Fig. 7.7.** The effect of culture training on considerate behaviour of high- and low-LPC leaders.

support this hypothesis. Fig. 7.8 shows the time 2 mean scores on rewarding behaviour as rated by subordinates and adjusted for time 1 scores. The broken line indicates the grand mean for time 1. As can be seen, there is little difference in rewarding behaviour for the group leaders who experienced no job change in the six to eight months which intervened between the first and second testing sessions. However, in the group which experienced a turbulent environment, the differences in time 2 rewarding behaviour are substantial and the LPC × change interaction is significant. We may thus infer that the high-LPC leaders became more rewarding, while the low-LPC leaders became less rewarding, as a consequence of the lower situational control which resulted from being assigned to a new job.

The opposite trend emerged from the analysis of administrative punishment behaviours (e.g. threatened or actual reduction or demotion or placement in the stockade). Fig. 7.9 indicates the effects on administrative punishment behaviour when both of the leader's superiors (platoon sergeant and platoon leader) are replaced in the time period $t_1 - t_2$. The LPC × experience × change interaction is significant. For the inexperienced leaders, the turbulent condition (new superiors) is associated with more punitive behaviour on the part of low-LPC leaders but less punitive behaviour on

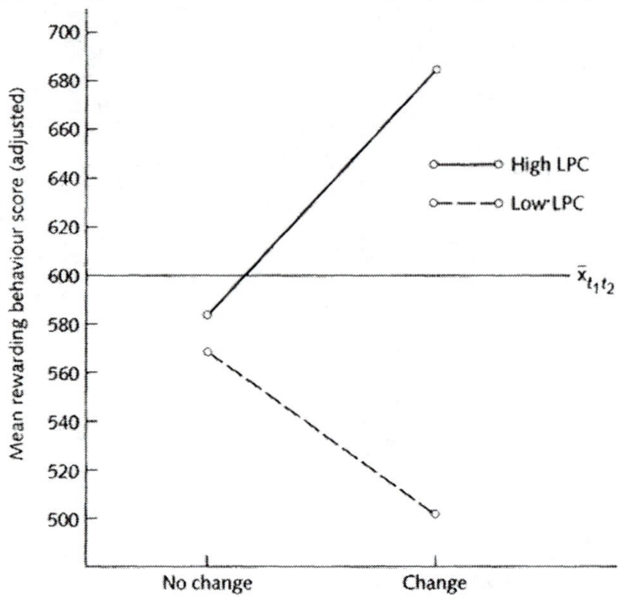


**Fig. 7.8.** Rewarding behaviour as a function of LPC and change in job.

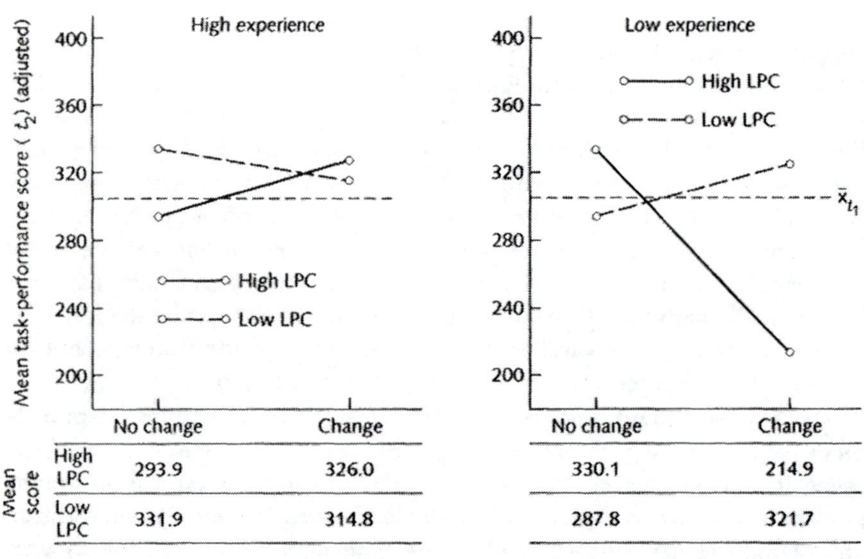


| Mean score | High experience: No change | High experience: Change | Low experience: No change | Low experience: Change |
|---|---|---|---|---|
| High LPC | 293.9 | 326.0 | 330.1 | 214.9 |
| Low LPC | 331.9 | 314.8 | 287.8 | 321.7 |

**Fig. 7.9.** Administrative-punishing behaviour as a function of LPC and change of boss for leaders with high and with low experience.

the part of high-LPC leaders. Among leaders with high experience who have considerable control over their situation, the high-LPC leaders are generally more punitive at time 2 than are low-LPC leaders.

The data described in this study make an important point. Situational control substantially influences leader behaviour, and, presumably, leader behaviour determines group performance. Behaviour and performance change, therefore, as the situational control of the leader changes.

## The Leader Match Program

One type of evidence that we understand a process is the ability to change the process in the desired manner. A demonstration that we know how to improve leadership performance, therefore, gives some hope that we are beginning to understand the dynamics of organizational leadership.

We recently developed a self-paced programmed instruction manual, entitled *Leader Match* (Fiedler *et al.* 1976), which incorporates the principles of the Contingency Model. Specifically, leaders are instructed to take the LPC scale and to interpret their score. They are given detailed instructions on how to measure leader–member relations, task structure, and position power, using various scales and appropriate exercises and feedback. Finally, the manual provides guidance on how to modify the leadership situation so that it will provide the appropriate degree of situational control.

As of this date, eight successive validation studies have yielded significant results which indicate that leaders who are trained with this programme tend to perform significantly more effectively than do those not so trained. Four of these studies were conducted in various civilian organizations and involved second-level leaders of a volunteer public health organization, middle managers of a county government, supervisors and managers of a public-works department, and police sergeants. In each of these studies, a list of eligible leaders was obtained from which a trained and a control group were randomly selected. While all studies yielded significant findings, attrition clouded the results.

Better control over the subject population was possible in a study of junior officers and petty officers of a navy air station and a study of junior officers and petty officers of a destroyer. Again trained and control subjects were selected at random, and performance ratings were obtained at the time of training and six months later from the same supervisors. There was no voluntary attrition in either study. As can be seen from Table 7.1, the trained

**Table 7.1.** Comparison of mean change scores for trained and control group leaders

| Change score for | Group | $N$ | $\bar{X}$ | $S.D.$ | $t$ | $P$[a] | $\omega^2$ |
|---|---|---|---|---|---|---|---|
| Overall performance | Trained | 27 | 0.5741 | 0.786 | | | |
| | | | | | 3.58 | <0.001 | 0.174 |
| | Control | 29 | −0.4595 | 1.257 | | | |
| Task performance | Trained | 27 | 0.5872 | 0.696 | | | |
| | | | | | 3.89 | <0.001 | 0.202 |
| | Control | 29 | −0.5158 | 1.283 | | | |
| Personnel performance | Trained | 27 | 0.5213 | 0.921 | | | |
| | | | | | 2.93 | <0.002 | 0.120 |
| | Control | 29 | −0.3659 | 1.246 | | | |

[a] Probability is one-tailed.

group significantly improved in performance when compared to the control group.

Two other studies were conducted by Csoka and Bons (personal communication). The first used officer trainees who were scheduled to become acting platoon leaders in operational units. One third of 154 men were randomly selected for training, while the others were used as controls. At the end of the test period, the unit officers' evaluations showed the *Leader Match*-trained leaders as performing better than untrained men within the same unit.

A second study involved training one randomly selected platoon leader of three in each of twenty-seven training companies. At the end of a four-month period, evaluation of all platoon leaders showed that the trained leaders were significantly more often chosen as the best of the three in their company.

Although the investigations are not yet complete, preliminary data show that the training with the *Leader Match* programme did enable leaders to modify their leadership so as to maintain the appropriate balance between their leadership style and situational control. Thus, using situational control as the key concept in a dynamic interpretation of the leadership process appears to be a highly promising and cost-effective approach.

# Conclusion

This study presents a dynamic interpretation of the Contingency Model in which the leader's situational control emerges as the critical variable for interpreting the complex processes of leadership performance in changing organizational environments. This interpretation accounts for the disappointing results which previous leadership training programmes have yielded, and the low correlations between years of leadership experience and leadership performance. Training and experience typically provide the leader with greater control while organizational turbulence, shake-ups in management, and similar events cause uncertainty and lessen the leader's control over the situation.

Recent research shows that we can improve organizational performance by teaching the leader how to diagnose and modify situational control in order to maintain an optimal match between leadership style and situation in a continuously changing organizational environment. These findings provide further important evidence that we are beginning to understand the dynamics of the leadership process.[1]

## Note

1. Keynote address, NATO International Conference on Coordination and Control of Group and Organizational Performance, 17 July 1976.

## References


Bales, R. F. (1951), *Interaction Process Analysis* (Cambridge, Mass.: Addison-Wesley).

Beach, B. H., Mitchell, T. R., and Beach, L. R. (1975), *Components of Situational Favorableness and Probability of Success* (Organizational Research Technical Report 75–66, Seattle: University of Washington).

Bons, P. M., and Fiedler, F. E. (1976), 'The Effect of Changes in Command on the Behavior of Subordinate Leaders in Military Units', *Administrative Science Quarterly*, 21: 433–72.

Cattell, R. B. (1951), 'New Concepts for Measuring Leadership in Terms of Group Syntality', *Human Relations*, 4: 161–84.

Chemers, M. M. (1969), Cross-Cultural Training as a Means for Improving Situational Favorableness', *Human Relations*, 22: 531–46.

—— Rice, R. W., Sundstrom, E., and Butler, W. (1975), 'Leader Esteem for the Least Preferred Coworker Score, Training, and Effectiveness: An Experimental Examination', *Journal of Personality and Social Psychology*, 31: 401–9.

—— and Skrzypek, G. J. (1972), 'An Experiment Test of the Contingency Model of Leadership Effectiveness', *Journal of Personality and Social Psychology*, 24: 172–7.

Fiedler, F. E. (1964), 'A Contingency Model of Leadership Effectiveness' in L. Berkowitz (ed.). *Advances in Experimental Social Psychology,* vol. i (New York: Academic Press).

—— (1967), *A Theory of Leadership Effectiveness,* (New York: McGraw-Hill).

—— (1972), 'Personality, Motivational Systems, and Behavior of High and Low LPC Persons', *Human Relations,* 25: 391–412.

—— Bons, P. M., and Hastings, L. L. (1975), 'The Utilization of Leadership Resources', in W. T. Singleton and P. Spurgeon (eds.), *Measurement of Human Resources,* (London: Taylor & Francis).

—— and Chemers, M. M. (1974), *Leadership and Effective Management* (Glenview, Ill.: Scott Foresman).

—— —— and Mahar, L. (1976), *Improving Leadership Effectiveness: The Leader Match Concept* (New York: John Wiley & Sons).

Fleishman, E. A., Harris, E. G., and Burt, H. E. (1955), *Leadership and Supervision in Industry* (Columbus, Oh.: Ohio State University).

House, R. J. (1971), 'A Path Goal Theory of Leader Effectiveness', *Administrative Science Quarterly,* 16: 321–38.

Likert, R. (1961), *New Patterns of Management* (New York: McGraw-Hill).

Mann, R. D. (1959), 'A Review of the Relationships between Personality and Performance in Small Groups', *Psychological Bulletin,* 56: 241–70.

Mehrens, W. A., and Lehmann, I. J. (1973), *Standardized Tests in Education* (New York: MacMillan).

Nebeker, D. M. (1975), 'Situational Favorability and Environmental Uncertainty: An Integrative Study', *Administrative Science Quarterly,* 20: 281–94.

Rice, R. W. (1978), 'Psychometric Properties of the Esteem for Least Preferred Coworker (LPC) Scale', *Academy of Management Review,* 3.1: 106–118.

Sax, G. (1974), *Principles of Education Measurement and Evaluation,* (Belmont, Calif.: Wadsworth).

Shiflett, S. C. (1973), 'The Contingency Model of Leadership Effectiveness: Some Implications of its Statistical and Methodological Properties', *Behavioral Science,* 18: 429–40.

Stogdill, R. (1948), 'Personal Factors Associated with Leadership: A Survey of the Literature', *Journal of Psychology,* 25: 35–71.

—— (1974), *Handbook of Leadership* (New York: The Free Press).

—— R. M., and Coons, A. E. (1957), *Leader Behavior: Its Description and Measurement* (Monograph No. 88; Columbus, Oh.: Ohio State University).

Vroom, V. H., and Yetton, P. W. (1973), *Leadership and Decision Making* (Pittsburgh: University of Pittsburgh Press).

# III. MODERN LEADERSHIP

The third, or Modern Leadership, wave extends the focus of the previous traditional forms of leadership but takes in three of the most significant new areas for research: democracy, cultural, and gender issues. Gastil tries to establish the parameters of democratic leadership and in particular when and where such leadership styles might be appropriate. Kakabadse *et al.* consider the case for another current theme, that of cross-cultural variations in leadership style, especially, in their case, with reference to the possible development of a European style. Bass and Avolio attempt to pick up the pieces of the allegedly shattered glass ceiling that has kept women out of leadership positions in business—and elsewhere—for so long. Finally, Rosener develops an explanation for why most women still remain trapped in non-leadership positions and argues for recognition of the value of differences at work.

One might regard democratic leadership as defined by Gastil as the opposite of the kind of leadership Fiedler was interested in. However, Gastil's claim is to suggest that undemocratic leaders carry with them a whole series of counter-productive edifices: they can generate dependent and apathetic followers; they may produce low-quality policies; they may result in inefficient implementation; they may mystify the decision-making procedure; they may instigate high levels of social conflict and they may undermine certain ethical ideals. Naturally, democratically elected leaders may do exactly the same—but then we can rid ourselves of such villains; we cannot do the same for undemocratic leaders. The possibility of having a 'good' undemocratic leader and a 'bad' democratic one impels Gastil to argue that the critical issue for democratic leadership is not the behaviour of the individual but the functions that the leader fulfils, and these functions are divided into three facets. First, the distribution of responsibility so that participation is maximized and becomes a required responsibility of all. We can hear an echo of Pericles' funeral oration here in which he denounces those who try to avoid taking responsibility for the decisions of the polity for: 'we do not say that a man who takes no interest in politics is a man who minds his own business; we say that he has no business here at all' (Thucydides 1972: 147). Secondly, a democratic leader should empower the membership to ensure that every member has a level of competence and leadership so that 'great leaders'—and their counter-productive effects—can be avoided. Thirdly, democratic leaders should facilitate the democratic process itself by keeping the group focused, by encouraging discussion, and by ensuring that the norms of behaviour and debate are followed. In this way the process by which a decision is made becomes the focus of the leader, rather than the particular content of the decision.

This raises the possibility, following Starhawk (1986), of constructing multiple leaders in a 'leaderful', rather than a leaderless, approach to organizational leadership, in which the leader's position is rotated so that all develop their skills and competencies in leadership, all are held accountable for their actions, all are held responsible for the group's well being, and all act to restrain any autocratic tendencies.

Gastil does not insist that democratic leadership is universally superior to all other variants but concedes that it works best when the interests of all are at stake, when all are suitably qualified to take decisions, and when it is at least as effective as any other mechanism. On the other hand, it is less suited for the resolution of technical problems with technical solutions, it ought not to be associated with the execution of policies, and it is ill-advised where the group is indifferent to the process. All this, of course, assumes that a consensus can be achieved as to the delineation of particular conditions where democratic leadership should be advanced or denied. As many democratic bodies have pondered since the days of Pericles, how do we vote on the need to vote? At this point Gastil refers to a Guardian, a non-member expert to whom the group may turn to for advice; a turn that even Plato—that great enemy of democracy—would no doubt approve of.

But whatever the merits of democratic leadership, its existence—at least in any pure form—is negligible, not just in business but in political life. Far too often those who find themselves elected to leadership positions seem to revert to an atavistic form of leadership that the democratic approach is intended to displace. Nevertheless, there are many issues within Gastil's chapter that resonate with current debates, not just about leadership styles but about motivating change, about empowerment of employees, and about securing commitment. Any mechanism of governance that can persist—albeit with large breaks—across almost three millennia has to have something to say for itself.

But to what extent is the leadership style of management dependent upon cultural background rather than embodying some kind of timeless and universal standard? Is there, for instance, a homogeneous European style currently developing and does it matter? These, amongst other things, are questions that Kakabadse *et al.* seek to answer in their chapter that assesses the results of a cross-cultural European study. The significance of culture in determining leadership, or at least management, style received a considerable boost from the work first of Hofstede (1980) and subsequently of Hampden-Turner and Trompenaars (1993). Of course, culture has been the bedrock of anthropology from the beginning and of much sociology for many years, but only recently have management academics turned towards it, as the Pacific Rim economies flex their muscles, as Europe becomes more (or less) integrated, and as the world of business has generally gone global.

Hofstede's research argued that cultures could be divided by the significance of individualism, power-distance, uncertainty avoidance, and masculinity, and through the reconstruction of these variables a four-part model results in which cultures are either: 'village markets', typified by Anglo-Saxon organizations; 'well-oiled machines', representing Germanic organizations; 'the family', as found in Asian organizations; and, finally, 'the pyramid of people', manifest in French organizations. As one might expect, since then a proliferation of models has erupted, with Hampden-Turner and Trompenaars's seven models leading the way and Gannon's (1994) country-specific metaphorical approach not far behind.

On the basis of their research, Kakabadse *et al.* surmise that no general European style exists but rather four different types exist. First there is the 'leading-from-the-front' approach beloved of the British, Irish, and Spanish. This combination immediately contradicts that of Hofstede and is rooted in the functioning of the leader and rests heavily on a form of pragmatic 'learn by doing' where rules and regulations are minimized and theoretical approaches are confined to the managerial dustbin.

The second form, Consensus, is a team-based approach with a distinctive Scandinavian flavour and a preference for open discussion and consensual decision-making. The third form, 'towards a common goal', has a similar end but a different means. In other words, the intention is to achieve the goal with everyone on board, but the process by which this is achieved is more classically authoritarian, with that authority premised upon the level of technical expertise of the leader. This is very much a systems and a systematic approach to management and appears to mirror the German and Austrian preferences.

The final form, representing French preferences, is labelled 'managing from a distance' and it has a similar authority system to the German/Austrian style but lacks the discipline of these. Here there may be an apparently open discussion and a consensus on the way forward but the execution of policy is likely to be both authoritarian and divisive.

But what can all this do to help those involved in managing multinational top teams? Kakabadse *et al.* argue that three areas need consideration. First, some system of disciplinary ground rules needs to be agreed and carried through, so that the diversity of styles does not disrupt meetings altogether. Secondly, these key managers must feel comfortable with the strategy if it is to have any chance of realization; that in itself may require rather longer than ordinarily planned for. Thirdly, the top team should be selected for congruent fit, rather than just selected by level in the hierarchy—a good idea but not one that is really addressed in any detail in the article. Indeed, this is yet another of those readings that ends up with more questions than it provides answers to—but perhaps that is all we can hope to do at this level of debate: make sure we are asking the right questions.

The question posed by Bass and Avolio is one that has been asked many times but with precious little consensus as to the answer: do men and women have different leadership styles? This question is particularly pertinent now, as it reflects the current state of play of the women's movement, which finds itself under increasing attack on several fronts, and not just in the form of a male backlash. The era of the 1980s and 1990s was, in theory, to be the point at which women began to move into management positions in large numbers as the demographic dip restructured the labour market in women's favour, and as the old staple industries in the West were gradually displaced by new industries that did not have the patriarchal traditions and hang-ups so common amongst manufacturing industry. That was the theory. In practice, while women have become an increasingly large proportion of the labour force in many countries, and as numbers of female students have grown disproportionately to male students, there has still to be any major restructuring of the higher echelons of business. The glass ceiling remains unshattered.

One consequence of the recognition that 'the men's club' remains the largest single block to the advance of women has been a funnelling of women into entrepreneurial and small-business activities. However, Bass and Avolio suggest that a more positive light can be cast on main—or male—stream organizations. A considerable amount of research has suggested that men and women adopt quite different leadership styles, and a similarly large amount suggests that they do not.

Following Bass's own work on the distinction between 'transformational' leadership (motivating followers to go beyond their own immediate self-interests) and 'transactional' leadership (just getting the job done), Bass and Avolio structure their research along the four elements or 'I's' of the Multifactor Leadership Questionnaire (MLQ) which involve some notion of idealized influence (charisma), inspirational motivation, intellectual stimulation, and individualized consideration. On three of these I's (the exception being an unreliable difference in intellectual stimulation) women score higher than men. Men, on the other hand, rate higher in terms of intervening to correct subordinate's mistakes and *laissez-faire* management.

As Bass and Avolio argue, one explanation for the better success rate of women on the transformational scale may be that women have to be better and work harder than their male colleagues for a similar position and reward level. On the opposite tack it may be that the reviewers of women managers are more lenient than they are on men, because they expect the latter to be better than the former. In the end Bass and Avolio opt for the explanation favoured by Rosener: that women may be more nurturing, caring, and sensitive than men—for whatever reason—and that these tendencies are more aligned with transformational leadership than transactional leadership. This may be because of the different socialization that aligns men and women with different role models or it may be because men and women are fundamentally different. Whether it's nature or nurture, the point is that the apparent model that is used by most women as a leadership blueprint appears closer to the style envisaged for the future organization than that used by men—which is much more closely aligned with organizational history. This does not mean that the glass ceiling is likely to be shattered in the near future, but it does suggest that more traditional organizations may not be around long enough to pick up the pieces.

Rosener's chapter is an attempt to hurry the shattering along. Her article in the *Harvard Business Review*, in 1990, argued that men and women were beginning to exhibit different forms of leadership. Originally, the only women who succeeded to the top were those who modelled themselves on men and led using command-and-control methods. Burns (1978) (and subsequently Bass 1985—see above) labelled the approach 'transactional leadership', since the relationships between leaders and led were rooted in exchange transactions: rewards and/or punishments. However, a second generation of women leaders were now emerging who adopted forms of leadership conventionally regarded as 'feminine' and subsequently relabelled as 'transformational leadership'. This form of leadership focused upon getting the subordinate to transform her or his interests into those of the group. While transactional leadership tended to derive from the significance of authority and positional status, transformational leadership owed its strength to the personal characteristics of the leader. Rosener's research suggested there was some support for a different form of leadership between men and women because, she argued, the 'interactive' style of women encouraged participation in power and information and sought to enhance the status of subordinates. The explanation for this difference Rosener related to the different patterns of socialization and the divergent career paths taken by men and women. In effect, the absence of formal authority over others required women to operate in a different leadership style from men, and in some circumstances (turbulent environments, rapid change, and professionally oriented organizations, for example) this style is allegedly more suited than traditional male forms of command and control.

As in so much research on gender, the criticisms of Rosener's approach and conclusion generated much heat: she had asked people to describe their styles—she should have observed them; the label 'interactive' was too universal, since all forms of leadership were axiomatically interactive; many men exhibited transformational styles and many women did not; and Japanese styles were very participative but simultaneously very masculine, and so on.

In her 1995 book, from which this chapter is drawn, Rosener extends the analysis and in this piece considers what she calls 'sexual static'—that is, the background noise or interference on TV or radio which disrupts the kind of messages women and men send to each other and which lead men in particular to feel uncomfortable besides women. This static builds from birth, as gender-based and differentiated socialization generates different expectations within children as to how they ought to behave and think. When traditional demarcations rooted in childhood are re-enacted at work, the situation appears calm, but as soon as individuals begin operating against their expected set of behaviours, confusion prevails. Rosener examines this, amongst other things, in the linguistic differences between men and women such that words associated with leadership are 'naturally' associated with men but not women. She continues this analysis by sketching the difference between the command-and-control and interactive leadership styles and asserts that: 'it is not only that men prefer the command-and-control style but that it *defines* leadership for them' (emphasis in original). In effect, women who lead interactively are not recognized as leaders, women who lead through command-and-control styles are not recognized as women. Moreover, where interactive styles appear to work better than command-and-control styles, the confused traditional males become ever-more bewildered.

The result, in Rosener's view, is that akin to two different tribes or cultures who cannot understand each other's language yet appear to speak the same words. Yet it is not just that the language is mutually incomprehensible, rather that the two tribes act in fundamentally different ways: 'Men talk about what they do. Women talk about how they feel', women appear to process information differently from men, they communicate differently and their culture is inclusive rather then the exclusive one associated with men. Hence, when women emerge in organizations as leaders, the sexual static increases and confusion rife. Unfortunately there is no easy answer for Rosener: 'Since men are the dominant group, they will have to remove the glass ceiling, and that will be difficult since for them it constitutes a floor—a feeling of security.' On the other hand, or perhaps floor, current research suggests that women may achieve a much greater level of leadership through their own businesses rather than through traditional organizations. For instance, women-owned businesses in the USA employ more people than the whole of the *Fortune 500* (Wilkinson 1996). In particular, Anita Roddick of the Bodyshop and Steve Shirley of F1 are just the tip of a growing proportion of women whose leadership has flowered beyond rather than underneath the glass ceiling. Of course, all this depends upon the prior assumption that men and women are essentially different—that is, that the differences lie within the minds of the genders observed rather than within the minds of the gendered observers (see Grint and Gill 1995, and Grint and Woolgar, forthcoming, for alternative accounts).

# 8 A Definition and Illustration of Democratic Leadership

John Gastil

Across the globe, the tumultuous political events of the past three years have raised hopes for the creation and revitalization of democratic institutions. In some countries, dictatorships have crumbled and new governments have crawled from the rubble. In others democratic opposition movements have gained strength, courage, and international recognition. Emboldened citizens in China, Czechoslovakia, Namibia, El Salvador, and elsewhere have organized to promote democratic social change, and new political parties and organizations in the West are striving to make their nations' political systems more democratic.[1]

Social scientists should respond to these international calls for democracy, because high-quality theory and research can aid those who seek to create democratic groups, communities, and nations. In fact, there already exists a substantial literature addressing the philosophical and empirical issues surrounding democratic governments, economics, and societies (e.g. Dahl 1989; Bellah *et al.* 1991).

The dynamics of democratic leadership, however, are not well understood. In fact, there is no clear and well-developed *definition* of the term within academia. In a classic review, Gibb (1969: 258) lamented the fact that 'the basic psychological meaning' of democratic leadership had 'nowhere been spelled out'. Twenty years later, Miriam Lewin (1987: 138) agreed, repeating Kurt Lewin's earlier 'call for a better understanding of the detailed nature of democratic leadership and followership through social science research'. A recent meta-analysis reached similar conclusions, finding that conceptual ambiguity and operational inconsistency has clouded the findings of the

J. Gastil, 'A Definition and Illustration of Democratic Leadership', *Human Relations*, 47/8 (1994), 953–75.

last four decades of research on democratic and autocratic leadership (Gastil, forthcoming).

Since leadership plays a vital role in democratic movements and democratic governance, it is essential that researchers address this issue. Ultimately, this entails empirical investigation of the practice of democratic leadership, but a necessary first step is creating a useful definition of the term itself.

## Previous Definitions of Democratic Leadership

In his comprehensive handbook on leadership, Bass (1990: 19–20) provides a general definition of leadership:

> Leadership is an interaction between two or more members of a group that often involves a structuring or restructuring of the situation and the perceptions and expectations of the members . . . Leadership occurs when one group member modifies the motivation or competencies of others in the group. Any member of the group can exhibit some amount of leadership . . .

This is essentially the definition of leadership adopted in this essay. The only exception is that, herein, leadership is viewed as constituting only *constructive* behaviours aimed at pursuing group goals. This defines leadership as 'an instrument of goal achievement' (Bass 1990: 15–16).

This definition gives 'leadership' a positive connotation. This normative aspect becomes greater still when one speaks of 'democratic' leadership. Literally hundreds of authors have not so much described as *advocated* democratic, participatory, and similar 'alternative' styles of leadership, contrasting them with authoritarian, supervisory, charismatic, and other conventional modes of leadership (for partial reviews, see Anderson 1959; Gibb 1969; Bass 1990; Hollander and Offerman 1990).

According to these advocates, undemocratic leadership styles result in a variety of undesirable outcomes: dependent and apathetic followers (White and Lippitt 1960; Barber 1984; Heifetz and Sinder 1987; Manz and Sims, 1989), low-quality policies coupled with inefficient implementation and constituent support (Maier 1952; Gibb 1969; Heifetz and Sinder 1987), the mystification of the decision-making process (Edelman 1988), and in some cases, social strife and aggression (Lewin *et al.* 1939; Starhawk 1986). In addition, undemocratic leadership undermines the pursuit of ethical ideals, such as self-determination, personal development, and democratic decision-making (Barber 1984; Sashkin 1984).

While criticizing existing leadership styles, authors have called for alternative styles of leadership, such as 'group or educational leadership' (Busch 1934), 'participative management' (Likert 1961), 'servant leadership' (Greenleaf 1977), 'nonconstitutive leadership' (Tucker 1981), 'transformative leadership' (Burns 1983), 'responsive leadership' (Starhawk 1986), 'public leadership' (Mathews 1988), 'superleadership' (Manz and Sims 1989), or 'values leadership' (Fairhorn 1991). The most common name for alternative leadership styles may be 'democratic leadership', which has appeared repeatedly during the last seventy years (e.g. Smith 1926; Tead 1935; Whitehead 1936; Lewin *et al.* 1939; Kutner 1950; Haiman 1951; Maier 1952; Abse and Jessner 1962; Gibb 1969; Lassey 1971; Barber 1984; NACLO 1984; Heifetz and Sinder 1987; Nagel 1987).

Kurt Lewin and his colleagues presented what has become the classic formulation of democratic leadership (Lewin and Lippitt 1938; Lewin *et al.* 1939; White and Lippitt 1960). They distinguished democratic leadership from autocratic and *laissez-faire* styles, arguing that democratic leaders relied upon group decision-making, active member involvement, honest praise and criticism, and a degree of comradeship. By contrast, leaders using the other styles were either domineering or uninvolved.

Unfortunately, Lewin and his colleagues never developed their definition beyond this rough sketch, leading some critics to find undemocratic implications in their ostensibly democratic model of leadership. Kariel (1956) argues that Lewin's notion of democracy is somewhat manipulative and élitist, and the exchange between Barlow (1981) and Freedman and Freedman (1982) suggests that Mao's 'mass-line leadership' in China used a model like Lewin's to mask coercion under the guise of participative group processes.

More directly, Graebner (1986) documents how the ideas and techniques of 'democratic engineers', such as Kurt Lewin himself, were used for undemocratic purposes in the first half of this century. For example, the Foremen's Clubs relied upon a 'democratic' style of discussion leadership to manipulate foremen. The meetings were supposed to appear participatory, yet they were 'designed to modify attitudes, and to convince foremen, a group increasingly tempted to unionize, that their natural allegiance was to capital rather than labor' (Graebner 1986: 139). Although such criticisms might overlook Lewin's obviously democratic intentions (K. Lewin 1950; Lippitt 1986; M. Lewin 1987), it is the ambiguity of his definition that made such interpretations plausible (Graebner 1987).

Despite the inadequacy of the Lewinian definition, the empirical research on democratic leadership conducted fifty years later continues to *employ* this model either explicitly (Wu-Tien and Hsiu-Jung 1978; Meade 1985) or implicitly (Kipnis *et al.* 1981; Kushell and Newton 1986). As a result, research on democratic leadership continues to base itself upon an unelaborated and potentially misleading definition. The absence of a clear definition may have also contributed to the decreased amount of research on democratic leadership in the last decade (see Bass 1990; Gastil, forthcoming).

## A Definition of Democratic Leadership

Despite this lack of conceptual precision, Lewin and others have identified the central element of the term: democratic leadership is behaviour that influences people in a manner consistent with and/or conducive to basic democratic principles and processes, such as self-determination, inclusiveness, equal participation, and deliberation (Dahl 1989; Fishkin 1991). What is missing is a systematic elaboration of this basic idea.

Integrating and supplementing existing theoretical writings on democracy and leadership will put flesh on the bones of this skeletal definition of democratic leadership. In turn, this section discusses the relationship between authority and leadership, the functions of democratic leadership, the distribution of leadership, the roles of democratic followers, and the settings in which the democratic model of leadership is appropriate.

### *Authority*

Leadership and authority are conceptually distinct (e.g. Gibb 1969; Heifetz and Sinder 1987; Hollander and Offerman 1990), so leadership 'should not be confused with the occupant of a formally established position in a hierarchical structure . . .' (Fisher 1986: 201). Democratic authorities do not necessarily serve as democratic leaders, and democratic leaders sometimes lack formal authority, as was the case with Mohandas Gandhi (Tucker 1981; Heifetz *et al.* 1991).

A given democratic group or body, called the *demos* (e.g. Dahl, 1989), confers administrative and, in some cases, legislative authority to specific individuals, all of whom are subject to removal by the membership. As Kutner (1950: 460) explains, 'Leaders need authority . . . but the delegation of authority in a democratic group is never a mandate for any leader to employ authority without the eventual approval of the group'.

To the extent that they have a measure of authority or power, democratic leaders must be accountable for the decisions they make as individuals and the roles they play in the demos (White and Lippitt 1960; Starhawk 1986).

tion of guilt by the usurpation of the individual conscience by the projected image of the leader, and of the wish for transformation' (Abse and Jessner 1962: 85). Democratic leaders show genuine care and concern for the members of the demos (Starhawk 1986; Desjardins and Brown 1991), but not in a way that makes them into a substitute parent or guardian. The democratic leader must never 'manipulate the masses through shrewd exploitation of their mentality. What is needed is the emancipation of consciousness rather than its further enslavement' (Adorno 1950: 421).

Most of all, democratic leaders must seek to make members into leaders (Theilen and Poole 1986). If a demos has few leaders, it is imperative that they seek to broaden the leadership base, distributing leadership responsibilities and making themselves replaceable. Good leaders 'can expand their ranks by becoming 'role models' to change novices from 'followers' to leaders' (Baker 1982: 325).

### *Aiding Deliberation*

Democratic leaders must distribute responsibility appropriately and empower other group members, but they must devote the bulk of their time and energy to ensuring productive and democratic decision-making. Deliberation is the heart of democracy (Barber 1984; Mathews 1988; Cohen 1989; Fishkin 1991; Yankelovich 1991; Gastil 1992*a*, *b*, 1993*a*), and high-quality deliberation requires effective democratic leadership (Busch 1934; Haiman 1951; Maier 1952; White and Lippitt 1960; Mathews 1988; Morse 1991). Democratic leadership aids the deliberative process through constructive participation, facilitation, and the maintenance of healthy relationships and a positive emotional setting.

Constructive participation means defining, analysing, and solving group problems through deliberation. Many authors have stressed this aspect of democratic leadership in its many forms. Political problems must be identified and defined or framed (Tucker 1981; Sheeran 1983; Heifetz and Sinder 1987). Problems must be carefully analysed, bringing out all relevant information and perspectives (Smith 1926; Maier 1952; White and Lippitt 1960). Possible solutions must be generated and assessed through creative reflection and critical evaluation (Lassey 1971; Tucker 1981; Heifetz and Sinder 1987), and careful listening and the respectful acknowledgement of others' views can help move discussion forward (Starhawk 1986; Morse 1991). A particularly important form of listening, sometimes called 'discernment' (Sheeran 1983), consists of carefully listening to group members' ideas and values, then tentatively attempting to identify the 'public voice' or the solution that best represents the group's collective interests (Busch 1934; Sheeran 1983; Nagel 1987; Mathews 1988). (For detailed discussions of constructive participation in small and large democratic groups, see Haiman 1951; Maier 1952; Barber 1984; Gastil 1992*b*, 1993*a*.)

Facilitation is conceptually distinct from constructive participation in that it is a form of meta-communication (i.e. communication *about* the group's deliberations). As Haiman (1951: 33) explains, 'The democratic leader . . . determines *how* the members of the group will think and decide, not *what* they will think and decide . . .'. The leader 'is the group's methodological agent' (emphasis in original). For example, a small group facilitator might point out that the group is running overtime. The comment is not so much part of the discussion of the problem at hand as it is a comment regarding the discussion.

Like constructive participation, there are many facets to facilitation, three of which deserve emphasis. First, effective facilitation involves keeping deliberation focused and on track (Maier 1952). In a small group discussion, this includes interrupting unnecessary digressions and untangling terminological difficulties that are unduly complicating an issue.

Secondly, facilitation involves the encouragement of free discussion and broad participation, which sometimes amounts to discouraging verbosity and drawing out shy or marginalized voices (Maier 1952; Sheeran 1983; Barber 1984). In a community, democratic leadership of this variety might mean reaching out to an isolated or ignored social group that belongs in an ongoing public debate. More generally, leaders can serve as a communicative link between different groups within a community (Rose 1968) or organization (Likert 1961). In a larger demos, leaders might use modern communications technology to set up televised public debate (Arterton 1987).

Thirdly, leaders can facilitate deliberation by encouraging members to observe the norms and laws that the demos has adopted. In the case of egregious or repeated violations of rules, this can amount to enforcement (Sheeran 1983; Starhawk 1986). In a large, parliamentary group, for instance, the chairperson might keep the group within the version of *Robett's Rules of Order* that the group has adopted. (For a more extensive discussion of facilitation, see Haiman 1951; Maier 1952; Lakey 1976; Center for Conflict Resolution 1977; Anderson and Robertson 1985; Kettering Foundation 1990; Arnold *et al.* 1991.)

Maintaining healthy emotional settings and member relationships is a similar and equally important function of democratic leadership. It may seem far afield from democracy, but democratic deliberation requires (or, at the very least, is greatly aided by) positive member relationships and a prevailing spirit of congeniality (Mansbridge 1983; Barber 1984; Barber and Watson, 1988; Mathews 1988; Gastil 1992*a*, 1993*a*).

Groups with good member relationships are replete with leaders who appreciate this often neglected dimension of deliberation. Some leaders may take the initiative to introduce and assimilate persons new to the group (Starhawk 1986). For example, a leader in a neighbourhood council might visit or send an invitation to a family that moves into the area. Leaders can also help strengthen or repair existing relationships among members of the demos (Desjardins and Brown 1991). In a small group, this could mean tactfully bringing up conflicts that are gradually building up group tension (Lakey 1976; Starhawk 1986) or mediating a conflict that has come to the surface (Sheeran 1983).

Democratic leaders can sustain the emotional health of a demos by trying to create a sense of excitement or vitality in the group (Tead 1935). On a national level, a leader might deliver a moving speech that sparks a public's willingness to deliberate upon and solve a pressing social problem. Democratic leaders can also contribute to the development of a warm, permissive setting conducive to open and honest communication (Haiman 1951; Maier 1952; White and Lippitt 1960; Desjardins, 1991). In the case of a newly formed small group, leaders could ask each group member to introduce themselves for a minute before beginning deliberation, relaxing more anxious group members by accustoming them to speaking in the group.

At this point, it should be apparent how these functions relate to the creation and development of democracy, but it may be helpful to review these connections. The distribution of responsibility relates to notions of a citizen's rights and duties. For instance, if a community takes responsibility for its own welfare, its members affirm their right to self-determination, and they simultaneously accept their duties as citizens to devote a portion of their energies to the governance of their community. Member empowerment makes citizens or group members stronger—more capable of participating as equals in politics and the other spheres of their lives. Finally, a strong demos requires collective deliberation, and democratic leadership plays a crucial role in ensuring productive discussion and open debate.

## *The Distribution of Leadership*

No single leader could possibly perform all of these functions, and since all functions must be served within a fully democratic group or organization, it is necessary to have multiple leaders (NACLO 1984). One might argue that diffusing leadership functions in this way would make a group leaderless, but, as Starhawk (1986: 270) explains, 'Such groups are not, in reality, leaderless.' Instead, they are '"leaderful'—everyone in the group feels empowered to start or stop things, to challenge others or meet challenges, to move out in front or to fall back' (see also Counselman 1991). In the ideal demos, more than one person serves every leadership function, no individual does an inordinate amount of the leading, and every group member performs leadership functions some of the time.

Sometimes, different leaders play different roles, with some inspiring the demos and others moderating its discussions and debates (Barber 1984). In most cases, it is possible to rotate leadership functions among the membership so that individual members become capable of serving a variety of leadership functions (Brown and Hosking 1986; Starhawk 1986). For example, in the housing cooperative where the author resided for two years, the responsibility of facilitator is rotated bi-weekly among all residents. By the end of a given year, almost every resident has developed the ability to facilitate a small democratic meeting.

## *Democratic Followers*

Even when leadership is widely distributed and roles are regularly reversed, some members lead while others follow at any given point in time. 'Leadership and followership are linked concepts, neither of which can be comprehended without understanding the other' (Heller and Van Till 1982: 405; see also Hollander 1992). Therefore, it is necessary to specify the responsibilities of democratic followers.

First, as a complement to the first function of democratic leadership, democratic followers must be willing to take responsibility for the well-being of the demos. Counterbalanced with freedom is an 'emphasis on the responsibility of the individual to cooperate with the group' and ensure its welfare (White and Lippitt 1960: 2). Democratic followers do not blindly accept burdens given them by leaders, but they remain open to leaders' requests that they take on greater responsibility.

Secondly, followers must be accountable for their actions and decisions (Mathews, 1988). For example, members of a democratic community might disagree with a collective decision. Although they might feel free to continue to speak out against the decision, only in the case of conscientious objection would they obstruct or violate a democratically established policy (White and Lippitt 1960; Barber 1984).

Thirdly, followers are ultimately responsible for maintaining their autonomy. Undemocratic leaders might remove followers' freedom against their will, but freedom can also be given away or taken for granted (Fromm 1965). Followers must regularly exercise their liberties and recognize, cherish, and guard their autonomy (Tead 1935; Lassey 1971; Barber 1984).

The fourth responsibility of followers is to recognize the ways in which they can function as leaders. They should strive to develop their leadership skills, viewing themselves as citizens capable of both leading and following others. In an ideal demos, follower and leader are roles that individuals constantly exchange by the minute, month, or year.

Finally, when playing the role of follower, members of the demos must be willing to work with those who are leading. Rejecting individual leaders because of their incompetence or undemocratic behaviour is justified, but entirely rejecting the notion of democratic leadership can undermine the democratic goals of a group (Freeman 1975; Baker 1982; Kowalewski 1983; Mansbridge 1983; Nagel 1987). At the same time, followers should avoid exploiting or adulating democratic leaders (Nagel 1987). The demos should be appreciative and supportive of leaders who make valuable contributions to the group (Smith 1926; Starhawk 1986), but 'to remain truly democratic' the demos must also be 'the watchdog of its own leadership' (Kutner 1950: 462).

## *Appropriate Settings*

Having defined democratic leadership and followership, it is necessary to state more precisely when and where this model is appropriate. When is this form of leadership appropriate for an international association, a nation, a corporation, a public university, a neighbourhood, or a social group? As Verba (1961: 243) argues, 'There is no one best leadership structure. What structure is best must depend upon the group setting, task, and membership—in short, upon the total situation.'

This notion parallels contingency theories of leadership effectiveness. Contingency or situational theorists seek to identify the variables that determine which of a variety of leadership modes is most appropriate in a given situation (Fiedler 1967; Hersey and Blanchard 1975; Fiedler and Garcia 1987; Vroom and Jago 1988; Field *et al.* 1990). This section does not propose a rigid contingency theory, but it does presume that certain moral and pragmatic issues are relevant to deciding whether or not to pursue democracy and democratic leadership.

As for the ethics of democracy, Dahl (1989: 85, 97–8, 100) argues that the democratic process is morally justified if one presumes that 'the good or interests of each person must be given equal consideration' and 'all members are sufficiently well qualified' to make collective decisions on their behalf (or, at least, none is definitely more qualified to do so). Focusing on democratic management in business, Sashkin (1984) suggests that participatory decision-making process is an ethical imperative when it is at least as efficient and productive as more autocratic methods and workers desire a participatory process. It is justified over equally efficient processes because it uniquely satisfies basic human needs—power, achievement, and affiliation—that are essential for the physical and psychological health of workers.

Some situations, however, do not call for democratic methods of decision-making and leadership. Heifetz and Sinder (1987: 185) acknowledge that the democratic process is inappropriate when a problem is clearly defined and has a straightforward technical solution. The authors use a medical analogy to illustrate their point. In the case of a broken wrist, 'the patient's expectations that the doctor can provide a solution are realistic and the problem situation can be defined, treated, and cured using the doctor's expertise and requiring very little work on the part of the patient'.

Nevertheless, Heifetz and Sinder demonstrate that few large-scale public problems are so straightforward and technical.

Haiman (1951: 66) also identifies types of problems that make a democratic process unnecessary, The author explains that there are times the demos should turn to an executive or a judge. 'The function of the executive-leader, or administrator, is to translate verbal policies into action.' This may mean implementing a policy or enforcing a law enacted by the demos. Of course, the demos has ultimate authority over the actions of the executive, but even a small, direct democracy will frequently assign the implementation of a task to a particular member or committee, giving them a measure of executive power. Judges serve the demos by interpreting the details of the decisions of the demos. Like executives, they must remain accountable, but just as individual citizens sometimes agree to binding arbitration, so might a democratic society give provisional power to judges and juries.

Finally, Maier (1952: 198) points out that the democratic process is not appropriate 'if the group is indifferent to a problem or its solution'. Also, the problem under consideration must be within the jurisdiction of the demos. This latter consideration is more complicated than it appears on first glance. It asks whether the existing democratic unit is more justified than any other possible unit. This is a thorny question in almost any setting, for a group's decisions almost always affect people outside the group, revealing the interconnection of all existing (and hypothetical) political units. (For a straightforward attempt to address this issue, see Dahl 1989.)

Fig. 8.1 integrates these considerations into a decision tree, listing and ordering the questions one must ask in determining the appropriateness of democracy and democratic leadership. Starting at the trunk of the decision tree, one first assesses the nature of the problem. If the problem involves only one person, an autonomous decision can be reached. While one might wish to consult others, a collective decision-making process is not necessary.

If the problem involves merely implementing or working out the details of a previous decision, an executive (or judicial) decision-making process is in order. If the problem is of no concern to group members, an executive decision might be in order.

However, note the question within the first oval, 'Might the problem matter to them if they discussed it?' This question asks one to consider the possibility that members of a group would care about a problem if they had the information or insight required to understand it. This question (like the other two questions within ovals) views the decision-making process as a means for changing the mindset or character of the membership. It asks one to take into account the dynamic quality of the discussion process (see Barber 1984; Fishkin 1991; Yankelovich 1991).

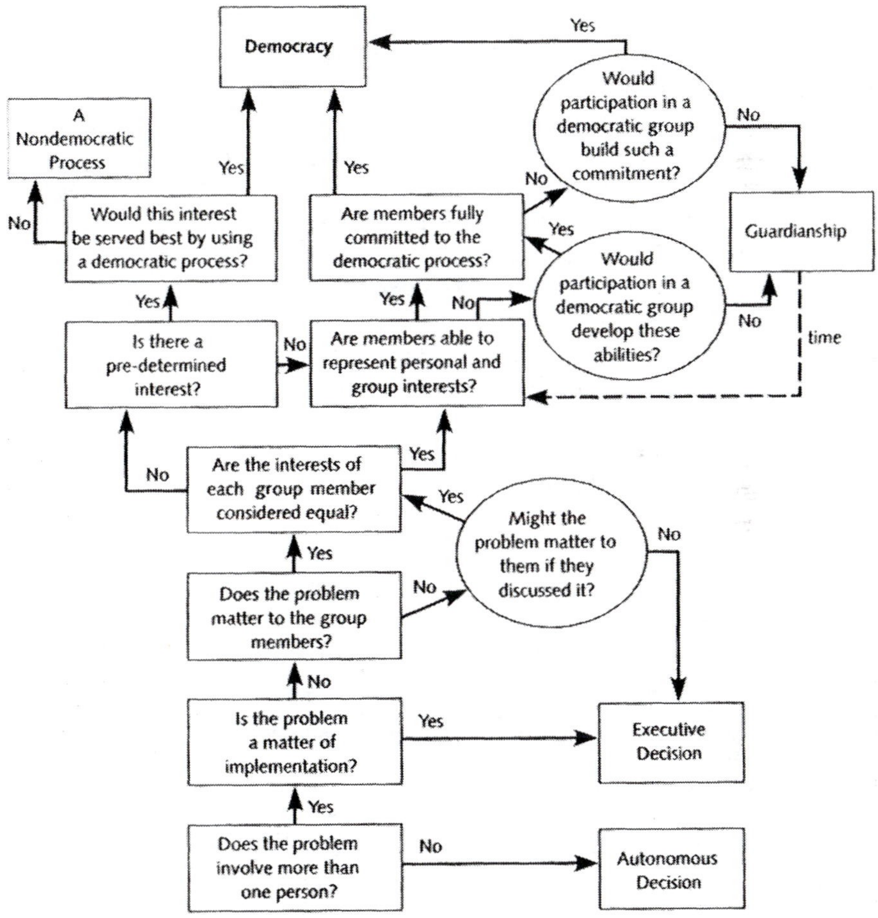


**Fig. 8.1.** Decision tree for democracy and democratic leadership.

If one determines that the problem is a serious matter of concern to the group as a whole, the decision tree then poses the most difficult question: 'Are the interests of each group member considered equal?' This is not a factual question, but a moral or ethical one. A *no* answer to this question implies that, for some reason, certain members' interests should be favoured over others'. A yes means that each member's interests should be weighed equally in making a decision. Does a factory worker have the right to play a role in management or earn a share of company profits? What rights do students and parents have to shape public school curriculums? Are the interests of family members considered equal for all family decisions? Questions such as these are often difficult to answer, but they must be addressed (e.g. Pateman 1970, 1983; Cohen 1988; Dahl 1989).

If the interests of group members are considered unequal, the individual with exclusive authority might still have no predetermined interest. If a predetermined goal does exist, one simply employs the decision-making process that best realizes that goal (on the productivity and satisfaction of democratic leadership, see Bass 1990; Gastil, forthcoming).

When the interests of all group members are considered equal, different questions arise. If group members are not, at present, the best representatives of their own interests or incapable of effectively participating in democratic deliberations, one must consider whether participation in democratic decision-making might develop the requisite deliberative competencies (Pateman 1970; Barber 1984; Warren 1992).

If group members cannot 'learn by doing', guardianship may be the best form of decision-making (see Dahl 1989). The term 'guardian' is more commonly used in the case of minors or mentally incapacitated individuals—people who may require an adult to take responsibility for seeing that their best interests are served (for a critical view, see Iris 1990).

More generally, groups have goals other than democracy, such as member satisfaction, cohesion, and productivity at some group task. If a group holds one of these goals above democracy, it might choose to appoint a group member or hire a non-member to make a particular decision for them. In effect, the group decides that a provisional guardian will better serve their interests than they would if they acted as a democratic group.

In the event that guardianship is considered optimal, it important to note the broken line on the decision tree that moves away from guardianship. This line suggests that, with the passage of time, one needs to re-examine the characteristics of the membership. Ideally, a system of guardianship develops the skills and character of its members. This idea underlies the guardian authority of teachers and mentors, many of whom strive to make their students or apprentices fully capable and independent.

If group members are capable of democratic activity but do not value democracy, there is still the danger that they might subvert the democratic process, wilfully or carelessly using it to pursue undemocratic ends. Again, one needs to ask if democratic values might emerge through participation in democracy. If one decides that such values could emerge, it is important to gauge whether they would develop *in time*—before the process was subverted. If the danger of subversion remains too high, guardianship may be more appropriate.

If these questions lead one to conclude that democracy and democratic leadership are appropriate, the last question is whether or not time permits deliberation. If time pressure requires an immediate decision, the group can quickly vote, but such a situation is far from optimal (Gastil 1993*a*). If time permits deliberation, then the group can go through a fully democratic decision-making process, eventually arriving at a decision.

## An Illustration: The National Issues Forums

At this point, it may be useful to illustrate the above model of democratic leadership. This is done through a description of the National Issues Forums (NIF), an excellent case study in democratic leadership. NIF is a programme developed by the Kettering Foundation that aims to revitalize the political system in the USA, making it more democratic through improving the quality of public deliberation. A summary of qualitative research on the Forums suggests that they have proven somewhat effective at changing both individuals and communities (Dedrick 1991).

Across the country, hundreds of convenors (individuals and private or public organizations) use 'issue books' created by the Kettering Foundation that present three or four policy directions or 'choices' on current national issues. Convenors distribute these booklets and other materials to organizations or community members, then hold large forums or small study circles to discuss the issues. NIF provides citizens an opportunity to engage in national policy debates, often changing the way they view their role in politics, their relationship with other citizens, and their views on national issues (McAfee *et al.* 1991).

A number of individuals and organizations involved in the NIF programme have served as democratic leaders at various times. At a national level, the Kettering Foundation has encouraged citizens to take responsibility for setting the direction of national policies on issues such as health care, drugs, and affirmative action. The foundation has told citizens (and policy-makers) that only the citizenry can provide 'public knowledge', only 'the people' can tell us 'whether issues have been framed so as to engage what really concerns the public', and '*why* the public thinks what it does' (McAfee *et al.* 1991: 30).

NIF convenors, and those who assist them, are also serving an empowerment function by encouraging citizens to develop their political abilities and take on leadership roles. Those attending forums are expected to participate constructively, providing ideas, information, critical thinking, and moral insight. Participants are asked to facilitate themselves, discussing challenging and emotionally charged issues in a thoughtful and respectful manner. After forums, enthusiastic participants are sometimes encouraged to go a step further, leading other forums or conveying the fruits of forums to policymakers (Kettering Foundation 1990; McAfee *et al.* 1991).

The convenors and forum moderators also serve the facultative function of democratic leadership. They serve as community-wide facilitators by bringing people together and setting up a framework for public discussion, and the one or two individuals who moderate each forum facilitate the face-to-face discussions themselves. These moderators also attempt to maintain a healthy relational and emotional atmosphere, for one of the purposes of NIF is to improve the relationships that exist among citizens (Kettering Foundation 1990).

The democratic leadership involved in NIF is widely distributed among organizations and individuals, and efforts are made to increase the number of leaders. The leadership that makes NIF successful often originates in people who are already strong leaders in various capacities, but the Kettering Foundation and regional NIF convenors hold a series of Public Policy Institutes designed to develop the knowledge and abilities of potential NIF convenors and moderators. Locally, former NIF participants are sometimes trained to become moderators of future forums. Within the forums and study circles themselves, all participants are encouraged to play brief but essential leadership roles by encouraging one another and actively participating in discussions (Kettering Foundation 1990).

Those who follow these leaders do so in a democratic manner. The relationship between the Kettering Foundation and the NIF convenors is one of respect; it is not characterized by rejection, exploitation, or adulation. Convenors take responsibility for conducting the forums themselves, cherish their autonomy, and take on leadership roles. Convenors generally appreciate the work of the foundation, but they assess its materials and ideas critically and usually adapt them to suit their own purposes.

Taken all around, the different levels of the NIF programme illustrate the different facets of democratic leadership and show the model's applicability to a wide range of social scales.

## Questions for Future Enquiry

The definition presented in this essay is useful by itself, as it suggests a clear model of leadership for both theorists and practitioners. Nevertheless, important questions regarding democratic leadership remain: What is an adequate *operational* definition of democratic leadership? What are the effects of democratic leadership? What are the obstacles to democratic leadership? And how do we overcome or confront these barriers?

The first question acknowledges that the definition outlined in this essay is a 'nominal' definition, as opposed to an 'empirical' or 'operational' definition (Chaffee 1991). This essay has taken an essential first step, but it does not provide the level of detail necessary for making reliable observations regarding the presence/absence of democratic leadership or the amount present in a given setting at a given time.

As for the second question, a large body of experimental and field research exists on the effects of various definitions and operationalizations of democratic vs. autocratic leadership (Anderson 1959; Gibb 1969; Bass 1990; Gastil forthcoming). Based on these studies, one might guess that the model of democratic leadership presented in this essay will prove both satisfying and productive, but these conclusions are speculative because of conceptual and methodological inconsistencies in past research. What previous studies unambiguously demonstrate is that investigators should carefully select their operations, measures, and study settings. Doing so will make their conclusions more persuasive and, ultimately, facilitate the integration of their findings.

The third and fourth research questions also correspond to a set of suggestive data. Since democratic leadership and democracy go hand in hand, obstacles to the latter are obstacles to the former. Previous writings on democracy suggest that the democratic model of leadership surely faces political, economic, and social barriers that exist in the status quo (e.g. Pateman 1970; Mansbridge 1973; Rothschild-Whitt 1979; Cohen and Rogers 1983; Barber 1984; Schwartz 1986; Herman and Chomsky 1988; Dahl 1989; Gastil 1992*b*, 1993*a*, *b*).

Previous writings on democracy and democratic leadership suggest that people often reject this form of leadership for at least four reasons. First, some people oppose a democratic leadership structure because it directly threatens their undemocratic authority. Moving towards democracy would strip them of some of their status, power, and, in some cases, wealth (Slater and Bennis 1990). Secondly, some people have authoritarian values and are not easily swayed from a strong belief in the justness and efficiency of powerful, directive authorities (Tead 1935; Bell 1950; Lassey 1971). Thirdly, most people have, to some degree, an unconscious or conscious desire for a hero, a charismatic figure capable of solving our problems and sweeping away our confusion (Smith 1926; Abse and Jessner, 1962). Finally, some reject the notion of democratic leadership for the opposite reason, having no faith whatsoever in leaders of any kind and no belief in their necessity (Tead 1935; Nagel 1987).

Overcoming these barriers to democratic leadership requires changing the way people think about themselves and leadership. It is difficult to cause people to change their undemocratic attitudes and behaviour patterns (Smith 1926). Changing views and habits requires nurturing the sense of self-responsibility and self-confidence that gives rise to a desire for, or acceptance of, democratic procedures (Lassey 1971; Heifetz and Sinder 1987; Gastil 1992*c*). People must develop a greater sense of trust in themselves and others (Lassey 1971) and come to believe that all people are potential leaders (Tead 1935). Respect for critical enquiry must flourish, with citizens seeking the better argument rather than the better orator (Smith 1926; Slater and Bennis 1990).

Structural changes might also lead to the development of more democratic values and behaviours. Democratic leadership, like democracy itself, grows better in some social, economic, and political environments than in others. Democratic leadership may flourish where there exists a free press, a relatively egalitarian family structure, a relatively prosperous economy, and a wealth of personal freedoms (Tucker 1981; Dahl 1989; Slater and Bennis 1990).

In conclusion, there is reason to believe that the democratic style of leadership may become more widely understood and practised. In the last quarter century, democracy has witnessed both progress and regression (Slater and Bennis 1990), and democratic leadership may experience similar cycles. More directly, Lippitt (1982) identifies a number of promising trends in the 1970s and early 1980s that are probably still present today: expectations of shared power and responsibility are increasing; there is a greater degree of collaboration and communication; and people have an increasing awareness of the need for organizational openness and flexibility.

Although other trends may go against democratic leadership, the prevailing winds are favourable. Moreover, if democratic leadership spreads through economic, political, and cultural networks, it may make people even more prepared for democratic social change, making democratic leadership increasingly viable. Of course, this will not come to pass without the efforts of the millions who believe in the value of democratic leadership. It is the hope of the author that this essay might inspire some readers to become one among those millions.

## Notes

The first draft of this essay was made possible by a research assistantship at the Kettering Foundation, and I would like to thank the Foundation staff for its assistance.

1. The successes and failures of democratic movements are discussed in several periodicals, including recent issues of the *Journal of Democracy and Current History.* For general overviews of the prospects for democratization around the globe, see Barber and Watson (1988); for a more academic review, see Dahl (1989). There also exist many regional reviews, such as Decalo's (1992) appraisal of the potential for democratic change in Africa, and there are numerous writings on new democratic organizations, such as the Greens (Dobson 1990, 1991) and the New Party in the USA (Pope and Rogers 1992).
2. 'Each of these functions applies to both large and small social groups. When an example is provided that pertains to a particular social scale, the reader should not infer that this is the only relevant scale. For instance, 'aiding deliberation' may sound relevant to only smaller groups, and some authors have discussed it solely in terms of such groups (e.g. Busch 1934; Haiman 1951; Maier 1952; Starhawk 1986). Nevertheless, those who focus on larger social scales argue that democratic leadership plays a role in community-wide and nationwide policy debates and deliberation (e.g. Barber 1984; NACLO 1984; Heifetz and Sinder 1987). There will be differences in the actual behaviours of those guiding a small group discussion and those facilitating a nationwide debate, but these different behaviours serve a similar function.

## References

Abse, D. W., and Jessner, L., (1962), 'The Psychodynamic Aspects Of Leadership' in S. Graubard and G. Holton (eds.), *Excellence and Leadership in a Democracy* (New York: Columbia University Press), 76–93.

Adorno, T. (1950), 'Democratic Leadership and Mass Manipulation', in A. W. Gouldner (ed.), *Studies in Leadership* (New York: Harper & Bros.), 418–35.

Anderson, L. F., and Robertson, S. E. (1985), 'Group Facilitation: Functions and Skills', *Small Group Behavior* 16: 139–56.

Anderson, R. C. (1959), 'Learning in Discussions: A Resumé of the Authoritarian-Democratic Studies', *Harvard Educational Review,* 29: 201–15.

Arnold, R., Burke, B., James, C., Martin, D., and Thomas, B. (1991), *Educating for a Change* (Toronto: Doris Marshall Institute for Education and Action and Between The Lines).

Arterton, F. C. (1987), *Teledemocracy* (Newbury Park, Calif.: Sage).

Baker, A. (1982), 'The Problem of Authority in Radical Movement Groups: A Case

Study of a Lesbian–Feminist Organization', *Journal of Applied Behavioural Science* 18: 323–41.

Barber, B. (1984), *Strong Democracy* (Berkeley and Los Angeles: University of California Press).

—— and Watson, P. (1988), *The Struggle for Democracy* (Boston: Little, Brown & Co.)

Barlow, J. A. (1981), Mass Line Leadership and Thought Reform in China, *American Psychologist*, 36: 300–9.

Bass, B. (1990), *Bass & Stogdill's Handbook of Leadership* (New York: The Free Press).

Bell, D. (1950), 'Notes on Authoritarian and Democratic Leadership', in A. W. Gouldner (ed.), *Studies in Leadership* (New York: Harper & Row), 395–408.

Bellah, R. N., Madsen, R., Sullivan, W. M., Swidler, A., and Tipton, S. M. (1991), *The Good Polity* (New York: Alfred A. Knopf).

Brown, M. H., and Hosking, D. M. (1986), 'Distributed Leadership and Skilled Performance as Successful Organization in Social Movements', *Human Relations*, 39: 65–79.

Burns, J. M. (1983), *Leadership* (New York: Harper & Row).

Busch, H. M. (1934), *Leadership in Group Work* (New York: Association Press).

Cartwright, D., and Zander, A. (1968), 'Leadership and Performance of Group Functions: Introduction', in D. Cartwright and A. Zander (eds.), *Group Dynamics: Research and Theory* (3rd edn., New York: Harper & Row), 301–17.

Center for Conflict Resolution (1977), *A Manual for Group Facilitators* (Santa Cruz, Calif.: New Society Publishers).

Chaffee, S. H. (1991), *Communication Concepts 1: Explication* (Newbury Park, Calif.: Sage).

Cohen, J. (1988), 'The Economic Basis of Deliberative Democracy, *Social Philosophy and Policy* 6: 25–50.

—— (1989), 'Deliberation and Democratic Legitimacy', in A. Hamlin and P. Pettit (eds.), *The Good Polity* (New York: Basil Blackwell), 17–34.

—— and Rogers, J. (1983), *On Democracy* (New York: Penguin Books).

Counselman, E. F. (1991), 'Leadership in a Long-Term Leaderless Women's Group, *Small Group Research*, 22: 240–57.

Dahl, R. A. (1989), *Democracy and its Critics* (New Haven: Yale University Press).

Decalo, S. (1992), The Process, Prospects and Constraints of Democratization in Africa', *African Affairs*, 91: 7–35.

Dedrick, J. (1991) 'The Results of National Issues Forums: A Review of Selected Documents, 1981–1991, unpublished manuscript (Kettering Foundation, Dayton, Oh.).

Desjardins, C., and Brown, C. O. (1991), 'A New Look at Leadership Styles', *Phi Kappa Phi Journal* (Winter), 18–20.

Dobson, A. (1990), *Green Political Thought* (London: Unwin Hyman).

—— (1991) (ed.), *The Green Reader: Essays toward a Sustainable Society* (San Francisco: Mercury House).

Edelman, M. (1988), *Constructing the Political Spectacle* (Chicago: University of Chicago Press).

Evans, S., and Boyte, H. (1986), *Free Spaces* (New York: Harper & Row).

Fairhorn, G. W. (1991), *Values Leadership: Toward a New Philosophy of Leadership* (New York: Praeger).

Fiedler, F. E. (1967), *A Theory of Leadership Effectiveness* (New York: McGraw-Hill).

—— and Garcia, J. E. (1987), *New Approaches to Effective Leadership: Cognitive Resources and Organizational Performance* (New York: John Wiley & Sons).

Field, R. H. G., Read, P. C., and Louviere, J. J. (1990), 'The Effect of Situation Attributes on Decision Method Choice in the Vroom-Jago Model of Participation in Decision-Making', *Leadership Quarterly*, 1: 165–76.

Fisher, B. A. (1986), 'Leadership: When Does the Difference Make a Difference?', in R. Y. Hirokawa and M. S. Poole (eds.), *Communication and Group Decision-Making* (Beverly Hills: Sage), 197–215.

Fishkin, J. (1991), *Democracy and Deliberation* (New Haven: Yale University Press).

Freedman, A., and Freedman, P. E. (1982), 'Mass Line Leadership: Another View of Mao's China', *American Psychologist*, 37: 103–5.

Freeman, J. (1975), *The Politics of Women's Liberation* (New York: David Mckay Co.).

Fromm, E. (1965), *Escape from Freedom* (New York: Avon).

Gastil, J. (1992*a*), 'A Definition of Small Group Democracy', *Small Group Research*, 278–301.

—— (1992*b*), 'Democratic Deliberation: A Redefinition of the Democratic Process and a Study of Staff Meetings at a Co-operative Workplace', Masters Abstracts, 30-04m, 1114 (University Microfilms No. 1348177).

—— (1992*c*), 'Why We Believe in Democracy: Testing Theories of Attitude Functions and Democracy', *Journal of Applied Social Psychology*, 22: 423–50.

—— (1993*a*), *Democracy in Small Groups* (Philadelphia: New Society Publishers).

—— (1993*b*), Obstacles to Small Group Democracy', *Small Group Research*, 24: 5–27.

—— (forthcoming), A Meta-Analytic Review of the Productivity and Satisfaction of Democratic and Autocratic Leadership', *Small Group Research*.

Gibb, C. A. (1969), 'Leadership', in G. Lindzey and E. Aronson (eds.), *Handbook of Social Psychology* (Reading, Mass.: Addison-Wesley), 205–82.

—— (1971), 'Dynamics of Leadership and Communication', in W. R. Lassey (ed.), *Leadership and Social Change* (Iowa City, Ia.: University Associates Press), 85–99.

Graebner, W. (1986), 'The Small Group in Democratic Social Engineering, 1900–1950', *Journal Of Social Issues*, 42: 137–54.

—— (1987), 'Confronting the Democratic Paradox: The Ambivalent Vision of Kurt Lewin', *Journal of Social Issues*, 43: 141–6.

Greenleaf, R. K. (1977), *Servant Leadership* (New York: Paulist Press).

Haiman, F. S. (1951), *Group Leadership and Democratic Action* (Boston: Houghton-Mifflin).

Heifetz, R. A., and Sinder, R. M. (1987), 'Political Leadership: Managing the Public's

Problem Solving', in R. Reich (ed.), *The Power of Public Ideas* (Cambridge, Mass.: Ballinger), 179–203.

Heifetz, R. A., Sinder, R., Jones, A., Hodge, L., and Rowley, K. (1991), 'Teaching and Assessing Leadership Courses: Part One', *Phi Kappa Phi Journal* (Winter), 21–5.

Heller, T., and Van Til, J. (1982), 'Leadership and Followership: Some Summary Propositions', *Journal of Applied Behavioral Science*, 18: 405–14.

Herman, E. S., and Chomsky, N. (1988), *Manufacturing Consent* (New York: Pantheon).

Hersey, P., and Blanchard, K. (1975), 'A Situational Framework for Determining Appropriate Leader Behavior', in R. N. Cassel and F. L. Heichberger (eds.), *Leadership Development: Theory and Practice* (North Quincy, Mass: Christopher Publishing House), 126–155.

Hollander, E. P. (1992), 'Leadership, Followership, Self, and Others', *Leadership Quarterly*, 3: 43–54.

—— and Offerman, L. R. (1990), 'Power and Leadership in Organizations', *American Psychologist*, 45: 179–189.

Iris, M. A. (1990), 'Threats to Autonomy in Guardianship Decision Making', *Generations*, 14: 39–41.

Kariel, H. S. (1956), 'Democracy Unlimited: Kurt Lewin's Field Theory', *American Journal of Sociology*, 62: 280–9.

Kettering Foundation (1990), *National Issues Forums Leadership Handbook* (Dayton, Oh.: Kettering Foundation).

Kipnis, D., Schmidt, S., Price, K. and Stitt, C. (1981), 'Why Do I Like Thee: Is it your Performance or my Orders?', *Journal of Applied Psychology*, 3: 324–8.

Kowalewski, D., (1983), 'New Leftist Leaders and Followers: The Authority Gap in Participatory-Democratic Groups', *International Journal of Group Tensions*, 13: 3–17.

Krech, D., Crutchfield, R. S., and Ballanchey, E. L. (1962), *Individual in Society* (2nd edn, New York: McGraw-Hill).

Kushell, E., and Newton, R. (1986), 'Gender, Leadership Style, and Subordinate Satisfaction: An Experiment', *Sex Roles*, 14: 203–8.

Kutner, B. (1950), 'Elements and Problems of Democratic Leadership', in A. W. Gouldner (ed.), *Studies in Leadership* (New York: Harper & Row, 459–67.

Lakey, B. (1976), *Meeting Facilitation* (Santa Cruz, Calif.: New Society Publishers).

Lassey, W. R. (1971), 'Dimensions of Leadership, in W. R. Lassey (ed.), *Leadership and Social Change* (Iowa City, Ia.: University Associates Press), 4–11.

Lewin, K. (1950), 'The Consequences of an Authoritarian and Democratic Leadership', in A. W. Gouldner (ed.), *Studies in Leadership* (New York: Harper & Row), 409–17.

—— and Lippitt, R. (1938), 'An Experimental Approach to the Study of Autocracy and Democracy: A Preliminary Note', *Sociometry*, 1: 292–300.

—— —— and White, R. K. (1939), 'Patterns of Aggressive Behavior in Experimentally Created "Social Climates"', *Journal of Social Psychology*, 10: 271–9.

Lewin, M. (1987), 'Kurt Lewin and the Invisible Bird on the Flagpole: A Reply to Graebner', *Journal of Social Issues*, 43: 123–39.

Likert, R. (1961), *New Patterns of Management* (New York: McGraw-Hill).

Lippitt, R. (1982), 'The Changing Leader–Follower Relationships of the 1980s', *Journal of Applied Behavioral Science*, 18: 395–403.

—— (1986), 'The Small Group and Participatory Democracy: Comment on Graebner', *Journal Of Social Issues*, 42: 155–6.

McAfee, N., Mckenzie, R., and Mathews, D. (1991), *Hard Choices* (Dayton, Oh.: Kettering Foundation).

Maier, G. (1952), *Principles of Human Relations* (New York: John Wiley & Sons).

Mansbridge, J. J. (1973), 'Time, Emotion, and Inequality: Three Problems of Participatory Groups', *Journal of Applied Behavioral Science*, 9: 351–68.

—— (1983), *Beyond Adversary Democracy* (Chicago: University of Chicago Press).

—— Feminism and Democracy', *The American Prospect*, 1/2: 126–39.

Manz, C. C., and Sims, H. P. (1989), *Superleadership* (New York: Prentice Hall).

Mathews, D. (1988), *The Promise of Democracy* (Dayton, Oh.: Kettering Foundation).

Meade, R. D. (1985), 'Experimental Studies of Authoritarian and Democratic Leadership in Four Cultures: American, Indian, Chinese and Chinese-American', *High School Journal*, 68: 293–5.

Morse, S. (1991), 'Leadership for an Uncertain Century', *Phi Kappa Phi Journal*, (Winter), 2–4.

NACLO (1984): National Association of Community Leadership Organizations, *Exploring Leadership* (Alexandria, Va.: Naclo).

Nagel, J. H. (1987), *Participation* (Englewood Cliffs, NJ: Prentice Hall).

Pateman, C. (1970), *Participation and Democratic Theory* (Cambridge: Cambridge University Press).

—— (1983), 'Feminism and Democracy', in G. Duncan (ed.), *Democratic Theory and Practice* (Cambridge: Cambridge University Press), 204–17.

Pope, S., and Rogers, J. (1992), 'Out with the Old Politics, In with the New Party', *The Nation*, 255: 102–5.

Rose, A. M. (1968), 'The Ecological Influential: A Leadership Type', *Sociology and Social Research*, 52: 185–92.

Rothschild-Whitt, J. (1979), 'Conditions for Democracy: Making Participatory Organizations Work', in J. Case and R. C. R. Taylor (eds.), *Co-Ops, Communes, and Collectives: Experiments in Social Change in the 1960s and 1970s* (New York: Pantheon Books), 215–44.

Sashkin, M. (1984), 'Participative Management is an Ethical Imperative', *Organizational Dynamics*, 12/4: 5–22.

Schwartz, B. (1986), *The Battle for Human Nature* (New York: W. W. Norton).

Sheeran, M. J. (1983), *Beyond Majority Rule* (Philadelphia: Philadelphia Yearly Meeting).

Slater, P., and Bennis, W. G. (1990), 'Democracy is Inevitable', *Harvard Business Review*, 68/5: 167–76.

Smith, T. V. (1926), *The Democratic Way of Life* (Chicago: University of Chicago Press).

Sniderman, P. (1976), *Personality and Democratic Politics* (Berkeley and Los Angeles: University of California Press).

Starhawk, (1986), *Truth or Dare* (New York: Harper & Row).

Tead, O. (1935), *The Art of Leadership* (New York: McGraw-Hill).

Theilen, G. L., and Poole, D. L. (1986), 'Educating Leadership for Effecting Community Change through Voluntary Associations', *Journal of Social Work Education*, 19/2: 19–29.

Tucker, R. (1981), *Politics as Leadership* (Columbia, Mo.: University of Missouri Press).

Verba, S. (1961), *Small Groups and Political Behavior* (Princeton: Princeton University Press).

Vroom, V. H., and Jago, A. O. (1988), *The New Leadership* (Englewood Cliffs, NJ: Prentice Hall).

Warren, M. (1992), 'Democratic Theory and Self-Transformation', *American Political Science Review* 86: 8–23.

White, R. K., and Lippitt, R. (1960), *Autocracy and Democracy* (New York: Harper & Bros.).

Whitehead, T. N. (1936), *Leadership in a Free Society* (Cambridge, Mass.: Harvard University Press).

Wilkins, L. (1986), 'Leadership as Political Mentorship: The Example of Wayne Morse', *Political Psychology*, 7: 53–65.

Wu-Tien, W., and Hsiu-Jung, C. (1978), 'Teacher Leadership Behavior as Related to Students' Expectation, Achievement, and Adjustment', *Bulletin of Educational Psychology*, 11: 87–104.

Yankelovich, D. (1991), *Coming to Public Judgement* (New York: Syracuse University Press).

# 9 Top Management Styles in Europe: Implications for Business and Cross-National Teams

A. Kakabadse, A. Myers, T. McMahon, and G. Spony

At an individual level, *Eurobarometer* (CEC 1991), which assesses public opinion in the European Community (now the European Union), posed the question in its survey 'how frequently does one feel European?' In the European Community only 15 per cent of citizens said they thought of themselves as not only their nationality but also European 'often', 33 per cent 'sometimes', and 49 per cent 'never'. A positive shift in opinion is likely to take time, perhaps a number of years.

At an organizational level, based on the number of mergers and acquisitions that have taken place in recent times, a large number of multinationals are now operating inside the European Community: for example, Sumitomo's acquisition of Dunlop's European operation, Rhône-Poulenc's full integration with May and Baker, Tryghansa's expansion throughout Europe. As a result, some commentators believe that the emergence of a European management style is a distinct possibility. As Europeanization is well under way, with the removal of technical and regulatory barriers, are we really any closer to defining a European style of management?

According to some authors, when comparing European and US organizations, Europe's largest corporations are beginning to develop their own distinctive management style, which is moving away from US practices. These commentators argue that, whereas the tried-and-tested US model of management concentrates on finance and marketing and the Japanese one

A. Kakabadse, A. Myers, T. McMahon, and G. Spony, 'Top Management Styles in Europe: Implications for Business and Cross-National Teams', *European Business Journal*, 7/1 (1995), 17–27.

on quality and just-in-time production, Europe's version emphasizes softer people skills. These include the ability to form a common vision in culturally diverse organizations and to help to promote collaboration across borders.

It could be argued that to succeed in the Europe of 1993 and beyond, managers must react quickly to changing market conditions and must start 'acting like Europeans' (Guterl 1989). By using the term Europeans a population group is being defined that is the direct result of Europeanization.

This article provides evidence as to why the concept of a European management style has still not emerged as a reality, but may provide some indications as to how it could be happening at a cross-national team level. It draws on the work of two key authors: Hofstede and, more recently, the cross-cultural research of Trompenaars. It also looks in some detail at a recent cross-cultural survey of top managers undertaken by Professor Kakabadse at the Cranfield School of Management in the UK. The Cranfield study takes the argument further by explaining how differing European management styles can impact on the business and on managers operating in cross-national teams.

## Europeanization: Challenges to Overcome

It is argued by certain authors that Europeanization is the first step towards global integration. This would involve coordination at a European level rather than a national level 'to serve a common cause in culturally, historically, economically, socially, ideologically, and politically heterogeneous environments' (Caproni *et al.*, 1991). The Single European Act attempts to facilitate such coordination, by working towards a fundamentally homogeneous environment. The Single Market is open for 'big business'. It has been perceived as a process towards deregulation by creating a freer market through the breaking-down of fiscal and physical barriers.

As the Single Market takes shape, management styles of European and international managers will become increasingly important, as decisions among members of cross-national teams will need to be undertaken and effectively implemented at a pan-European level.

The extent to which individuals will be responsive to working in groups composed of people of different national backgrounds will be dependent partly on the individuals themselves but also on their background and upbringing. In terms of national culture Hofstede believed that there were mechanisms which allowed for the maintenance of stability in culture patterns across many generations (see Fig. 9.1). In each national culture a different value system is likely to exist which can potentially produce divergent ways of thinking.

In the centre of Fig. 9.1 there is a system of what are defined as societal norms, which are shared by major groups of the population. Their origins are in a variety of ecological factors, in other words, factors affecting the physical environment. The societal norms have led to the development and pattern maintenance of institutions in society with a particular structure and way of functioning. These include the family, education systems, politics, and legislation. These institutions, once they have become facts, reinforce the societal norms and the ecological conditions that led to them. Hofstede continues by saying that any change in these norms will come mainly from the outside, through forces of man or forces of nature.

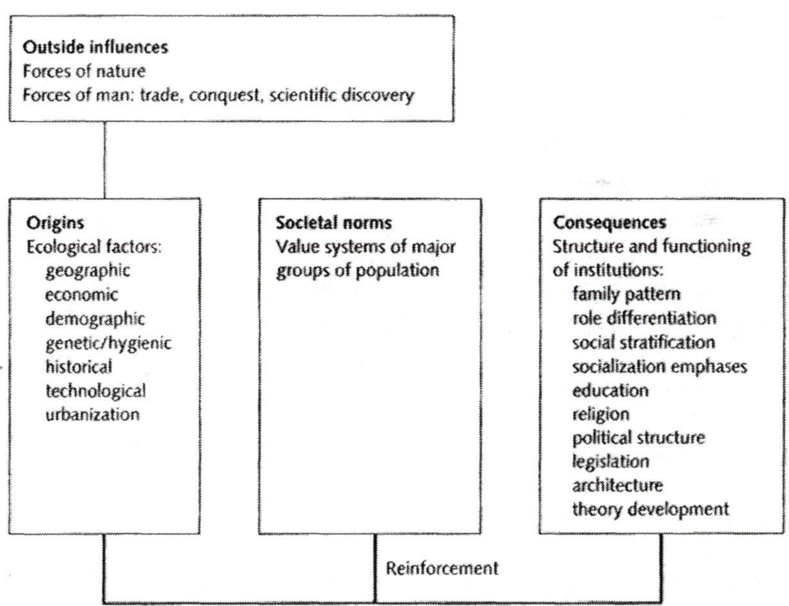


**Fig. 9.1.** The stabilizing of culture patterns.
***Source:*** Hofstede (1980).

## Europeanization as an Outside Influence

To manage effectively on a European-wide basis can be described as a recent 'outside influence, as depicted in Hofstede's diagram (see Fig. 9.1). The likely implication in the future is that Europeanization will act as a reinforcement to 'origins' and 'societal norms'. One of the consequences of Europeanization has been the legislation that has accompanied it, not just at an economic level, but at a social level as well. The right to free movement of labour throughout the European Community is one example, as it acts as a good indicator to how reinforcement could work in the future. It could be argued that Europeanization will rationalize the decision-making process within cross-national teams in an increasingly homogeneous environment, thus creating convergent patterns as opposed to divergent ones.

Relating the issues back to Hofstede's model (Fig. 9.1), over a period of time one could argue that the free movement of labour across boundaries is likely to have an effect on the demographic characteristics within a region and whether people consider themselves to be European or not. This in turn will lead to the population becoming increasingly 'multicultural'. Gradually, over a number of generations, we are likely to see populations represented through increasingly greater 'similarities' rather than differences and thus a more consistent cultural pattern will emerge. More recently, however, Hofstede, observing evidence from a number of researchers, indicates that cultural diversity and diverse ways of thinking will remain with us for a very long time to come.

However, through the processes of Europeanization, one could argue that management styles within European organization cultures, which are different from national culture and their corresponding societal norms, could be expected to become more convergent than divergent over a shorter period of time. It is perhaps then that we can truly define ourselves as having a European style of management.

## Organizational Cultures

In terms of cross-cultural research there are numerous references to Hofstede's work of 1980 and more recently 1991. In 1980 Hofstede identified four different cultural dimensions, that is individualism, power distance, uncertainty avoidance, and masculinity. Through the integration of the power distance and uncertainty avoidance dimensions four different models of organizational culture were elicited, namely:

- 'Village market'—no hierarchy or rules, but the demands of the situation determine the outcomes (low power distance and low uncertainty avoidance, characteristic of Anglo-Saxon organizations).
- 'Well-oiled machine'—interference by management is minimal as appropriate rules are in place (low power distance and high uncertainty avoidance, a characteristic of Germanic organizations).
- 'Family'—where the owner-manager is the grandfather (high power distance and low uncertainty avoidance, typical of Asian countries—for example, China and Malaysia).
- 'Pyramid of people'—the general manager at the top of the pyramid and each successive level in its appropriate place below (high power distance and high uncertainty avoidance, characterized by French organizations) .

More recently, Trompenaars talks about corporate culture and how national culture can influence the development of distinct values and norms within organizations. In his cross-cultural work he also identifies four different types of corporate culture, namely the 'family', the 'Eiffel Tower', the 'guided missile', and the 'incubator'. In practice, the types are overlapping but with one culture dominating. He shows how national culture differences can assist in the determination of a corporate culture type.

Trompenaars regards the *family* culture as power-oriented where the leader is regarded as a 'caring father' who knows, better than the subordinates, what should be done and what is beneficial for them. Here, Latin countries are predominant.

German and Austrian managers are identified as being typical of the *Eiffel Tower* culture. Such a culture stands for a formal depersonalized organization, where a rational-legal system exists in which everyone is subordinate to rules made locally. These rules demand a hierarchy to uphold and enforce them (an affinity with Hofstede's model).

The *guided missile* culture is a task-oriented culture, more often than not undertaken by teams or project groups. The ultimate value of the performance of an individual in this culture is to what extent that individual is contributing with other members towards achieving the desired result. The UK and the USA are said to be part of this culture (again comparable with Hofstede's model).

The *incubator* culture is based on the assumption that the fulfilment of individuals is more than the organization. The culture acts as a 'sounding board' for innovative ideas and tries to respond intellectually to new initiatives.

Sweden fits into this category (Hofstede's description of low masculinity and low power distance).

## Top-Management Cultures

A number of similarities can be identified between a cross-cultural study undertaken at the Cranfield School of Management, and Hofstede's and Trompenaars's work—with four management cultural styles merging. However, whereas the work of Hofstede and Trompenaars focused predominantly on middle managers, this article focuses on those at a senior level working within the organization's top management team—that is, directors, managing directors, and chief executives. In effect a top management culture is being observed, which may differ from the organizational culture yet may influence it.

This part of the article focuses on how these differing styles at a senior level have an impact on the business and also the impact that they can have on cross-national teams.

## Cranfield Research Programme

The Cranfield Research Programme has been ongoing for the last six years. The research was initiated out of concern, based on extensive consultancy experience with top managers and top management teams, that existing competency and management development research had put too much emphasis on individual rather than top management team performance and competence.

The initial phase of the research was based on intensive, in-depth observation, which involved consulting and counselling with over 500 executives, observing top management teams, working in thirty-five companies in the UK, other parts of Europe and the USA, in public and private, service, and manufacturing sectors. From this experience, it became apparent that high-performance and low-performance top management teams had clearly identifiable success and failure factors. Success or failure of the top management team had clear corresponding identifiable influences on the team itself, on the wider organization, and on business performance.

With the data gathered from the first stage, a questionnaire was developed for the second stage which examined areas of competence, management orientations, management style, and performance and correlated them with effects on people, the organization, and the business. The questionnaire also included an extensive demographic and organizational background section allowing for the examination of the effect of these factors on performance. The questionnaire was piloted for reliability and face validity. The questionnaire, in its final format, was distributed to chairmen, CEOs, managing directors, and senior managers/directors in the UK. In total 600 responses were received.

The third stage of the research programme was to use adapted versions of the questionnaire at a cross-cultural level, identifying not only the level of competence in different countries, but, further, the added value to the business if these competencies are effectively applied together with the opportunity costs should these be applied badly. Based on the data gathered from the third stage, we attempted to examine leadership styles across a number of European countries. The definitions of these styles are based on how top executives responded to certain behavioural and attitude statements (measured on a 1 to 5 scale, where 1 = strongly disagree through to 5 = strongly agree) from the survey questionnaire. These behaviours and attitudes statements related mainly to how managers responded to issues such as the ability to manage change, job satisfaction, general management experience and qualities, and the ability to work with organization processes and people.

Executives from Austria, Finland, France, Germany, Ireland, Spain, Sweden, and the UK participated in the research. Back translations were employed to assure for consistency in the interpretation. In total the database now numbers over 2,500 top executives.

## Research Questions

Two research questions are currently being investigated:

1. Is there a homogeneous top-management style that currently exists within Europe?
2. If styles vary, do these differing management styles in a cross-national team have a positive or negative effect on the way the organization operates?

## Top-Management Styles: The Cranfield Study

Within the framework of the study, it is considered that the predominant management style that top managers display within the organization has repercussions on the people in the organization, the organization itself, and the business as a whole. First, styles can impact on the performance of the organization. For the purposes of this study, organizational performance has been assessed in terms of: profitability through sales/marketing; focusing on key customer groups; discussions concerning competitor impact; following-through on commitments made to clients/customers; positive responses to new initiatives; an understanding of the organization structure and how it operates; issues affecting the long term—for example, cost management and control; the future of the organization in the market in which it operates; and the quality of dialogue within the top team. Secondly, internal relationships are also likely to have an impact on the functioning of the organization, for example, between functions or departments and members of the top team.

The results indicate that there is no general European management style at a senior level, providing evidence that to 'act European' is, at present, an unrealistic expectation. Distinct cultural differences in management do appear, and exploratory analysis of the data has resulted in the identification of four basic types (Fig. 9.2). (The analysis used here was a rigorous factor analysis of the scaled data. The new scales created were then discriminated by country.) These have been defined as: 'consensus' (executives mainly from Sweden and Finland); 'working towards a common goal' (typified by

**Leading from the front**

Charisma
Reliance on individual's leadership ability
Rules and procedures hinder performance
Self-motivation
Dominance

**Consensus**

Team spirit
Effective communication
Attention to organizational detail
Open dialogue
Consensual decision-making

**Managing from a distance**

Lack of discipline
Pursuit of personal agendas
Strategic/conceptual thinkers
Ineffective communication
Ambiguity

**Towards a common goal**

Valuing functional expertise
Authority-based leadership style
Clear roles of responsibility
Discipline oriented
Identity with systems and controls

**Fig. 9.2.** Four types of management style.

executives from Germany and Austria); 'managing from a distance' (French executives only); and 'leading from the front' (predominantly, executives from the UK, Ireland, and Spain). So, as with Hofstede's and Trompenaars' work, the Cranfield team have identified, not just one type of management style or culture but four—but all within Europe. Each of these styles can have significant implications for the people in the organization and the business itself. The characteristics of these different styles, based on responses to attitudinal and behavioural statements in the questionnaire, are discussed below, together with their implications.

## *Consensus*

Team spirit is a key feature for this group. Top managers from Sweden (50 per cent) and Finland (49 per cent) are more likely to fall into this category. Such managers tend to place emphasis on people moving forward together through effective communication and stability; attention to organizational detail—for example, such executives are more likely to agree with the questionnaire statement: 'A well-disciplined organization is fundamental to success'; and the motivation of individuals through open dialogue and consensus decision-making.

Consensus is arrived at through open discussion at team meetings so that everyone knows where the organization is going and is kept informed by way of developments. The greater the perceived level of consensus the greater the degree of job satisfaction, and where this is the case then this is likely to have a positive effect on internal relationships, the performance of the company, dealing with future issues, and the process of change management. It is to be highlighted that the clustering of top managers who tend to prefer a consensual approach all belong to Western countries scoring very low on Hofstede's masculinity scale.

## *Towards a Common Goal*

This grouping consists of executives who strongly value functional/technical expertise—agreeing with the statement: 'I enjoy getting others to understand some of the more technical aspects of my job', and who strongly display an authority-based style of leadership when it comes to managing subordinates and projects. The assumption is that, having identified a common goal, then the expert contribution of each individual should equally be clear. The need for someone to take authoritative command in order to promote the necessary focus is equally acceptable. Such executives are likely to display discipline when carrying out their duties. They also identify with systems and controls—disagreeing with the statement: 'The systems and controls in this organization are a hindrance to me'—as mechanisms for the achievement of the common task. The majority of German (84 per cent) and Austrian executives (79 per cent) fit into this classification.

The systems, controls, and procedures that are in place are seen as an effective vehicle for promoting success. This being understood by those within the organization leads to effective internal relationships and team performance. Managing change, however, can be problematic if individuals in the organization cannot identify with or find disconcerting the new systems that are introduced. Discordant change can be perceived as a considerably threatening experience as the lack of systems and routines can generate substantial confusion. Again this classification can be associated with the 'well-oiled machine' defined by Hofstede and the 'guided missile' as described by Trompenaars.

## *Managing from a Distance*

The only classification that contains the top managers from one nation is that of the French. The majority of French managers (83 per cent) in the sample display a passion for discussion but tend to desire independence—they agree with the statement: 'I like to be left alone to do my work as I see fit' and tend to pursue their own agendas after meetings. A command rather than a consensus model of decision-making predominates. They are identified as being strategic/conceptual thinkers and understand a need for procedures, but seem to lack discipline in implementation. Considerable resentment seems to be generated among subordinates as their managers are perceived as inconsistently communicating key strategies and messages. Attention to conversation does not mean effectiveness of communication in terms of appropriateness of behaviour.

Peer-level discussion at meetings may be quite open. However, despite whatever decisions are made inconsistency of implementation of decisions has a profound impact on the management of change. A management culture whereby pursuing one's own agenda plays a key part in the behaviour of managers is negatively associated with managing change. Respect for discipline in this type of management culture is minimal, which further negatively impacts on team performance. In interview, considerable numbers of middle management and staff experienced high levels of uncertainty within their organization leading to a high degree of ambiguity. Internal relationships were seen as strained, with even top managers expressing little faith in the leadership capacity of management positively to address issues affecting the future of the company.

The uniqueness of the French organization in Europe was first highlighted as far back as the early 1960s; Hofstede's research supported this. This is the only Western country that displays a paradoxical feature of having both a high level of individualism and a high score on the power-distance index. Consequently, it is not surprising that this particular configuration leads to the isolation of the French sample from the other top managers in the Cranfield study.

## *Leading from the Front*

This group is typified by countries from a different background, showing that, sometimes, very different cultural backgrounds can elicit similarities in behaviour and attitudes. The previous classifications fit Hofstede's and Trompenaars' model quite well but this one does not.

Here, there are two cultures that produce similarities: a Latin culture (74 per cent of Spanish top managers); and an Anglo-Saxon culture (73 per cent of British and 62 per cent of Irish top managers respectively). Top managers belonging to these countries can be described as having a leadership style that is centred primarily on an individual's performance. That is to say, both types of culture rely on the belief that the charisma and skills of some particular individuals will lead to either the success or the failure of their organizations. This is often seen as a positive challenge: 'I enjoy the challenge of my role in the company.'

This classification is to be contrasted with cultures which primarily favour the functioning of rules, procedures, and forecasting as an essential condition for success (as described above in the 'towards-a-common-goal' and to a lesser extent 'managing-from-a-distance' classifications).

Relying above all on an individual's ability (the myth of the idealized father figure for the Latin culture and the efficient successful achiever for the Anglo-Saxon culture), both types of top manager are reluctant to move towards any kind of functioning which may impede the freedom of these idealized cultural figures. Spanish top managers may perceive any form of rules or forecasting as restricting their status and putting into question their natural intuitive ability and adaptability. On the other hand, British top managers are pragmatic, result oriented, and believe in the process of learning by doing as the best way to succeed. Rules and forecasting are perceived as theoretical and futile exercises which are far away from the complex reality which calls for a firm pragmatic approach.

## Discussion

As with Hofstede's and Trompenaars' results, differences of behaviour and style are identified. Certain differences are consistent and comparable across the three studies—that is, the styles, behaviours, and exhibited attributes of the German and French managers—whilst other results do not neatly match—namely, the similarity in the Cranfield study between the British and Spanish senior managers, which did not emerge in the other studies. The question is whether such differences are due to issues of demography—differences of sample shape and size; differences in seniority of managers, company size, range of industrial sectors covered, age and experience of the respondents—or overlaps in national and organizational culture. The question remains of what significance are such differences in terms of managerial behaviour and organizational performance.

Case 1 highlights how these differing top management styles described above become apparent within an organization.

The sales and marketing issue, identified in Case 1, is fundamental to understanding the deterioration that ensued. The Cranfield study indicates that sales and marketing are contextual/regional concepts. What sales and marketing means is dependent on the requirements of the particular circumstances and the interpretation provided by the top manager involved. Hence, reaching a shared understanding as to the shape and identity of the sales and marketing contribution in a multinational group setting requires that respect and attention be given to dialogue. That quality of dialogue did not take place in the European board of the US multinational. Once the General Managers (GMs) recognized that the European board was not addressing their needs, national differences seriously influenced patterns of communication.

Case 1. An American in Europe

A US based multinational invested heavily in developing its European business. The UK and Ireland became the centres for R&D and manufacturing with sales and marketing teams placed locally in each of the European countries. An American, with a long track record of success as head of different functions in the organization, was appointed as European President, located in London.

After initial success in terms of improved sales, to varying degrees in each of the European countries, there followed a plateauing and then a slow decline of sales for the next two years. The manufacturing capacity was not reduced, with the net result that there was an excessive volume of customized European products that it was difficult to sell in the market place.

The European President interpreted these events as the challenge that needs to be overcome in gaining a presence in new markets. The General Managers (GMs) of the countries disagreed, highlighting that the sales and marketing requirments of each country of Europe were not understood and this was reflected in the poor quality dialogue (their perception) that was taking place at European board level. In effect this was not a phase that was going to go away, but a problem that needed airing.

As time passed, relationships on the board deteriorated. The British and Spanish GMs became fairly vociferous in their condemnation of the current situation stating that the mismatch of styles on the board was now inhibiting the necessary dialogue required both fully to understand the business and to gain the commitment of the management in order to implement consistently the strategies being pursued. The German cluster GM, responsible for Germany, Austria, and Switzerland, complained that the meetings were becoming increasingly unproductive as there was little follow-through on any of the key decisions made in the meeting. The Scandinavian and French contingents contributed less and less to board meetings, but discussed their frustrations in private to each other and with the European President. The Swedes made some attempt to implement whatever decisions were made on the board. The French tended to turn up to meetings, with, as they admitted in private, little intent to put into practice the policies and strategies to which they verbally agreed.

In the third year of operation, the American board took control of the situation. The two key manufacturing sites in Britain were shut down. The R&D activity in Europe was considerably reduced, with a number of projects being merged with their American counterparts. The European President was transferred back to the USA and retired with the year. Reporting relationships were changed. The European GMs now reported directly to the USA.

Unfortunately, the situation has not improved as, in the opinion of the European GMs, reporting directly to the USA does not allow for a more sensitive understanding of local conditions and hence for sensible targeting of both costs and revenues. Further redundancies are expected.

The British and Spanish GMs, more personally independent and vociferous, voiced their grievances. The German GM was more focused in terms of his complaints. The Swedish and French GMs, experiencing considerable discomfort with the dynamics they witnessed on the board, contributed less at meetings, but behaved quite differently on return to their work locality. The Swede attempted to implement the decisions made at board meetings, even though he did not believe in them. The French GM had lost faith in the European structure and the management proceedings, took little notice of what was happening at meetings, and pursued his own course of action.

Interestingly, the Cranfield study showed that different outcomes are likely to be dependent on the behaviour of the top managers within a team rather than necessarily the organizational culture itself. A British manager who resists group interaction and avoids entering into a shared, meaningful dialogue with colleagues in essence displays a need for independence, is likely to disrupt team relations, and, to varying degrees, demotivates those around him/her. A French manager displaying similar inclinations is more likely to induce business harm as the individual's influence can seriously disrupt discussion, the understanding others should have of current business circumstances, and hence the insight necessary to address those issues that impact on the organization's future. Seemingly, the British are more likely to accommodate a more 'difficult' superior, whereas the French are less likely to question but more likely to pursue the direction provided, which in turn will affect business performance, either positively or negatively. For the Americans in Case 1, not having appreciated the importance of the sales and marketing issue nor the different style of the European GMs, little improved with the departure of the European President and the change of reporting relationships. Business opportunities continued to be lost. To date the deterioration has led to further reorganization, further downsizing, and a concentration by the Americans on their home market.

## Managing Differences of Styles in Cross-National Teams

Developing a European management framework is only likely to be important when an organization is building a top management team of cross-national members over a long period of time. This is highly relevant as the implications of the different styles identified above in the Cranfield study become much more profound within a cross-national team. The Cranfield research highlights how differences of style can have a significant impact on both team and organizational performance. Differences are identified in terms of approach to dialogue, trust within the team and of top management by staff and lower level management, and levels of cohesion and consistency in terms of implementation of decisions.

Three important considerations in terms of managing differences of style are identified, namely, promoting discipline at meetings, managing the key interfaces, and selection for executive fit and development within the team.

## *Promoting Discipline at Meetings*

The way a team operates within the context of the different styles of management is likely to vary greatly, especially when it comes to agenda discipline in team meetings. For example, a 'leading-from-the-front' team-meeting style is likely to be one where there is considerable discussion on various issues which may go beyond the agenda, particularly for the Spanish. For the British, this would be tolerable as long as a conclusion is reached. A 'consensus' team-meeting style is one where everyone needs to show that they are pulling in the same direction. This is likely to involve detailed discussion—issues debated in a cross-national team which are not on the agenda may be tolerated to a certain extent, but if deviation occurred frequently then it is likely that new meetings would be organized to discuss new issues. The 'working-towards-a-common-goal' team-meeting style is likely to be one where an agenda has been set with the sole purpose of making decisions—deviation from that agenda is not likely to be tolerated. The 'managing-from-a-distance' team style again is likely to consist of considerable debate across a broad range of issues. Such discussion is likely to be based on each individual's pursuit of his or her own agenda. Whatever decisions are reached verbally, effective implementation is unlikely to occur unless considerable one-to-one discussion has taken place after the meeting.

Bringing together each of these team styles in the business arena will be a difficult task. It will need effective control and experience from the chairperson of cross-national member team meetings. The establishment and acceptance of ground rules to performance and contribution at meetings is desired. The ground rules would need to address the basics—for example, start and finish times, attendance, the location of the meeting, involvement in the setting of agendas, the right to challenge during the debate but with the necessity for 'cabinet responsibility' in jointly implementing decisions reached in the meeting. In addition, attention would also need to be paid to differences of culture at a personal level. With principally a German audience, time on three key points could adequately be worked on in two hours. However, meetings in southern Italy to address the same points may take all day. Getting to know each other—for example, enquiring about each other's backgrounds, and generally creating the space and time for more general discourse—may be necessary. The chairperson should accept the responsibility of promoting effective discipline at meetings, by paying attention to the evolving quality of relationships amongst the members of the meeting, which may be driven by personalities and/or local cultural differences, in order successfully to promote a high quality of dialogue.

## *Managing the Key Interfaces*

In the implementation of strategy, the management of the key interfaces within the structure of the organization is of crucial concern. The managers at the key interface points may or may not be members of the executive of the organization but they are likely to be vital opinion leaders, interpreting strategy to fit with their internal and external circumstances. In order to achieve an acceptable level of cohesion and consistency, the key interface managers would need to identify with the strategy, feel comfortable to share information with top management and with each other, and trust the decisions and actions of their bosses and colleagues. Hence, attention to the needs and requirements of the interface managers is important in order for them to pursue the strategic direction identified by top management.

Issues of substance—that is, business developments within regional/national situations or within particular functions, need to be considered as seriously as issues of style—that is, regional/national differences in terms of behaviour and communication. Towards this end, the development of an accepted 'company way of working' is important. What issues of substance need to be discussed? What, if at all, inhibits dialogue from taking place? Who is not but should be fully involved in key conversations? What are the opportunity costs for individuals, teams, and the organization of not having an openness to discuss pertinent issues of business and internal interfacing? The more senior managers concentrate on issues of substance and are less distracted by issues of style, the more likely a greater understanding of and tackling of the problems that face the organization will take place in a coherent manner throughout the key interfaces of the structure. If, however, issues of style are the key determinant of their behaviour, then more time is likely to be spent on internal relationship and trust issues and less time on the business. In terms of improving managerial performance, the aim would be to acknowledge that national/regional style differences exist, but such differences need not be a major problem. Helping managers to address their shared business challenges maturely, whilst recognizing the style differences of their pan-European colleagues, is best achieved through understanding which issues require openness of conversation.

## *Selecting for Executive Fit and Contribution*

A paradoxical demand is likely to be made on multifunctional/cross-national teams—namely, that the members 'fit' in with each other and jointly contribute to the success of the organization. Attaining a level of workable fit is unlikely to occur by accident. Apart from the fact that each of the team members may have his or her own agenda to pursue, personal and regional differences could disrupt the quality of dialogue necessary for enhancing commitment to the concept of the team and its purpose and to the making and enacting of decisions. Hence, attention to details such as executive fit and contribution is required to develop a workable blend of management styles within the team.

The integration of human-resource policy with the strategy of cross-national team development is a precondition to effectively creating and managing complex teams. Hence, the practice of executive selection and development requires careful consideration to ensure that the desired qualities are being identified and that management development is conducted in a manner that is perceived to be supportive to those involved in the process. For example, attendance at a selection/development centre may be an acceptable northern European experience, but undertaking off-site tests and exercises may be viewed as too artificial a setting to others of a different culture. An inability to identify with simulation may result in the individual emerging from the development centre being labelled as a 'poor performer'. Similarly people's capacity to respond effectively to feedback, group discussion, formal presentations, in fact, simulations of different sorts, needs to be seriously taken into account so that managers feel supported by the organization as opposed to marginalized and prejudiced. Sensitivity needs to be applied equally into each individual's behaviour within the team. If 'poor behaviour' is witnessed, is that due to cultural differences, poor quality dialogue, or more the personality and attitudinal make-up of the person? To make an error of judgement could considerably demotivate people in such potentially sensitive circumstances.

By effectively attending to team selection, and by sensitively managing the key interfaces, a company language is likely to develop which in turn is likely to offshoot into a series of team languages. In this way, communication in the company is likely to have a common basis that is strictly oriented to the business of the company. It is from here that trust, respect, and a willingness to adapt to a common purpose becomes a self-enforcing code of everyday working life.

The following case (Case 2) is a good example of the problems that a multinational faces in attempting to make cross-national teams work across Europe.

The data show that one style of management could have a serious influence on the way another style performs. This can have negative effects on business performance. The formation of the cross-national team will therefore require careful attention to allow for a blend of management styles to be represented on cross-national teams.

Both leaders and members of any cross-national team need to be aware of the differing individual and team styles that exist to enable the identification of potential areas of conflict and to anticipate and deal with them as and when they arise. The success of a cross-national team depends on it.

Case 2. Pulling together—making teams work

A French semi-state but nevertheless, multinational organization promoted a mission of customer care and quality of service to customers. In order to implement the mission, a matrix structure was devised whereby key product/service areas, termed lines of business, had to interface with the country teams whose prime task was to sell to and positively respond to the requirements of clients within that locality. Through lines of business, the high potential revenue-earning products and services would provide key focus whilst the country teams would attempt to promote customer satisfaction, thereby hopefully enhancing customer loyalty. Not surprisingly, a great deal depended on the quality of interfacing at the crucial points in the structure between the line of business managers and the key managers within the countries.

The matrix structure, in principle, was bought into by line management. In practice tensions and difficulties became the norm. For example, in attempting to promote a particular line of service or product range, the line of business managers argued that different pricing structures for the same product or service would not be a sound proposition as customers from different regions talked to each other. In the long term, a differential pricing policy would generate an unwelcome image for the company in the market place. The regional managers championed the need for flexibility in order to adjust to the local culture, customer needs, and local competition—for example, Sweden being a customer-aware, highly competitive, and mature market, unlike Spain, Portugal, and Greece.

Awareness of the issues and the forcefulness of argument were not the concern. What required attention was the manner in which the debate was conducted. The handling of meetings was a problem. Senior managers from France would invite the key regional and line-of-business managers to address particular problems. The expectation of the Germans would be to reach a decision. The French treated the meeting as a talking shop, seemingly reaching agreement but, at times, announcing an alternative decision, after the meeting. The British, often in frustration, would take control of their area(s) and responsibility and pursue a particular course of action which suited them, at times in direct contradiction to the direction given from above. The Scandinavians expressed considerable discontent with the whole situation, in that the lack of meaningful discussion prevented any real commitment emerging to addressing this somewhat complex and sensitive issue of pulling teams together in trying circumstances.

The issue, to date, has not been resolved, with both sets of managers complaining that lack of positive progress is undermining growth of the revenue streams.

## Summary

A number of commentators have identified the potential emergence of a European management style. However, we have provided evidence from three sources of cross-cultural research at different management levels as to why this is not yet the case in the national context. In Hofstede's, Trompenaars's, and the Cranfield studies four basic 'types' emerge, whereby certain European countries may portray a more dominant management style.

We have highlighted two important implications from the Cranfield survey. First, differing top-management styles can have an impact on the business and the way an organization is run—in terms of managing change, dealing with issues affecting the future, internal relationships, and the performance of the company. Secondly, differing styles can have an effect on the way a cross-national team operates.

However, it can be envisaged that an emerging European style of management could develop for particular cross-national teams after experience of working together. Such a possibility is likely to be a slow but inevitable process.

## References

Caproni, P. J., Lenway, S. A., and Murtha, T. P. (1991), 'Multinational Mind Set: Sense Making Processes in Multinational Corporations', Paper presented at the Academy of International Business Annual Meeting, Miami, October.

CEC (1991): Commission of the European Communities, 'Public Opinion in the European Community', *Eurobarometer*, 36, (June) (Brussels).

Guterl, F. V. (1989), 'Europe's Secret Weapon', *Business Month*, 134/4 (October).

Hofstede, G. (1980), *Culture's Consequences—International Differences in Work-Related Values* (Beverly Hill, Calif. Sage).

—— (1991), *Culture and Organizations: Software of the Mind* (London: McGraw-Hill).

Kakabadse, A. P. (1993), 'The Success Levers for Europe: The Cranfield Executive Competencies Survey,' *Journal of Management Development*, 12/8.

Trompenaars, F. (1993), *Riding the Waves of Culture* (Avon: The Economist Books, The Bath Press).

# 10 Shatter the Glass Ceiling: Women May Make Better Managers

Bernard M. Bass and Bruce J. Avolio

On '60 Minutes' (21 October 1991) former Italian Foreign Minister Giovanni Michalis, who preferred to employ women on his staff, argued that women might dominate the positions of power in the near future as men do today. Far-fetched for a culture comprised of organizations currently dominated by males? So far, despite decades of affirmative action in the USA, and the full emergence of women in the workplace, top management remains mainly a men's club, and management in general is still seen as a man's job, despite the many women who have attained supervisory and management positions (Van Velsor 1987).

Ironically, some women advocates have argued that females have actually lost ground over the last decade rather than gained ground (Eagly and Crowley 1986). In a recent survey of 400 female managers reported in *Business Week* (1992), over half the managers polled indicated that progress was slowing with regard to the hiring and promotion of women in US organizations. Seventy per cent saw the male-dominated corporate culture as a significant block to their success. Perhaps most disturbing was that nearly one-third of the sample believed that the number of female managers being promoted into executive ranks will either stay the same or drop over the next five years. Supporting their high degree of pessimism is the fact that 95 per cent of senior management is still male. It seems obvious that women simply have not advanced to the top ranks in direct proportion to their participation in the workforce.

Perhaps women have shattered a glass ceiling of a different sort. Specifically,

B. M. Bass and B. M. Avolio, 'Shatter the Glass Ceiling: Women May Make Better Managers', *Human Resource Management*, 33/4 (1994), 549–60.

there are now 4 million female entrepreneurs who have started their own corporations in the USA. The enormous growth of female entrepreneurs may be partially attributed to the corporate ceiling remaining rigid to advancing women into the upper ranks (Segal and Zelner 1992).

The current percentage of women in top corporate positions may be unlikely to detect a possibly oncoming sharp break with the past. We foresee a potential shattering of the glass ceiling based on results summarized later in this article. These results indicate that females display behaviours and characteristics that have been related to higher levels of effort, performance, and advancement across organizations. Conventional wisdom would have it otherwise, and it may be that it is this conventional wisdom that holds women back from promotion into senior management.

## Looking Back in Time

The same conventional wisdom that may inhibit female managers from ascending to senior management ranks in organizations today may also account for the following outcome noted at NASA back in the 1960s. In 1962 NASA tested twenty-five female pilots along with male applicants for the astronaut programme.

> I was painfully aware of the absence on screen of 25 female pilots who had been given the same tests as John Glenn and Alan Shepard and had passed them with flying colors. Indeed, one of them, Jerrie Cobb, had entered the program with twice as many air miles as John Glenn, and also emerged lucid from hours in a sensory deprivation tank that had left a male astronaut crying and imagining he heard dogs barking. By its end, this first Mercury Program had found that women in general were more resistant to radiation, less subject to heart attacks, and better able to endure extremes of heat, cold, pains, noise, and loneliness. Since they weighed less than the men and required less food and oxygen, they would also have saved money in the expensive per-pound business of capsule launching. Nonetheless, their success seemed to come as such a shock that NASA simply decreed: No women. (Steinem 1992).

## In a more Current Setting

An unusual setting perhaps to examine the ascendance of women into executive policy-making roles occurred at the 1992 Earth Summit. A coalition called the 'World Congress of Women for a Healthy Planet' argued that an integral problem in nations worldwide is the subordination of women. Frank Allen, the author of the article, noted that the summit itself reflected the state of the world regarding women in executive decision-making roles: 'Men dominated delegation rosters, plenary sessions and high level treaty negotiations, while women answered phones, made photo copies and served coffee' (Allen 1992).

## How Different are Men and Women Leaders?

A perennial question that continues to guide research which compares men and women managers headed an article appearing in the December 1990 issue of *Fortune* magazine. Jaclyn Fiermani (1990) wrote: 'Do women manage differently?' Similarly, Sharon Nelton (1991), in *Nation's Business,* wrote: 'Are women's leadership styles different from men's?' Ms Fiermani's response (1990: 115) was 'Yes . . . and they're far better suited than men to run companies in the nineties.' However, there are exceptions to this conclusion. For example, Donnell and Hall compared 2,000 matched pairs of male and female managers and concluded that, 'the disproportionately low numbers of women in management can no longer be explained away by the contention that women practice a different brand of management from that practiced by men' (Donnell and Hall 1980: 76). Gary Powell suggested that 'Those who choose managerial careers, like firefighters, have a lot in common. The best embody stereotypes of both genders' (Powell 1993: 116).

Returning to Ms Nelton, after posing the question of whether men manage differently from women, she goes on to say that the new generation of women managers are characterized as being more open with colleagues and are consensus builders who encourage wider participation in decision-making. She contrasts this style with the old command-and-control style that has dominated US corporations, not coincidentally led by male managers. Ms Nelton, however, supports the importance of men and women learning the strengths of each others' styles, as opposed to one approach being necessarily better than the other. What has been missing in these discussions is the inclusion of a broader range of leadership styles that directly impact on motivation, effort, and performance. Most of the prior research comparing male and female leaders has been restricted to a very narrow range of leadership styles.

## The Changing Face of Organizations

The traditional top-down hierarchical organization that favoured dictation by authority seems to be giving way to a call for more caring and concern about relationships and collaboration across levels. Indeed, in the list of the 100 best organizations for which to work, many of the organizational characteristics differentiating the best firms from the total represent traditional feminine qualities such as concern for the individual, devotion to others, family orientation, sharing, being helpful, and promoting collaboration (Levering, Moskowitz, and Katz 1985). Writing in the *Harvard Business Review,* Judith Rosener (1990) concluded that women leaders are more likely to structure flatter organizations and to emphasize frequent contact and sharing of information in webs of inclusion.

In comparing men and women managers, it should be asked: (1) whether women are different as managers, (2) why they are different, and (3) whether they are better than their male counterparts, as Helgesen (1990) claimed. This approach leads to an obvious question: What is leadership? Work in the leadership field prior to 1980 defined a good leader as someone who integrated getting the work done (task-orientation) with concern (consideration) for those doing the work. In the frequent transactions that occur between leaders and followers, followers were commended if they complied or disciplined if they failed. These transactions formed the basis of highly popular training programmes such as Blake and Mouton's (Blake and Mouton 1964) Managerial Grid, and Hersey and Blanchard's (Hersey and Blanchard 1977) Situational Leadership Theory.

Recent research (Bass and Avolio 1993) shows that followers are *more* motivated, productive, and satisfied when their leaders add transformational leadership to these base transactional styles. As argued by Bass (1985), leaders evaluated as transformational move followers to go beyond their self-interests to concerns for their group or organization. They help followers develop to higher levels of potential. Such leaders diagnose the needs of their followers and then elevate those needs to initiate and promote development. They align followers around a common purpose, mission, or vision. They provide a sense of purpose and future orientation; they are role models followers want to emulate. They encourage followers to question basic assumptions underlying problems, to consider problems from new and unique perspectives, and to accept challenges as opportunities. They work with followers to elevate expectations, needs, abilities, and moral character.

Evidence (that we and our colleagues have gathered from several thousand executives, managers, supervisors, and administrators in industrial, military, educational, health care, and not-for-profit organizations) confirms that leaders rated higher by followers on transformational leadership behaviours generate greater effort, performance, and satisfaction (Bass and Avolio 1990*b*). A partial summary of the results of this work is presented below:

- Unit cohesion and morale were higher among Marine helicopter squadrons led by officers rated higher by their direct reports on transformational leadership (Salter 1987).
- Business units led by senior Canadian executives who were rated higher on transformational leadership were evaluated a year later as more effective and satisfying units to work in. Those units were also more productive (Howell & Avolio 1993).
- Membership growth and Sunday attendance were greater for Methodist ministers rated higher on transformational leadership (Onnen 1987).
- School principals of middle schools in New York State that were recognized by awards for their highly innovative programmes were evaluated by their staff as displaying more transformational leadership behaviour (Gorham 1991).
- Executive champions of innovation were rated higher in transformational leadership than non-champions in Canadian firms (Howell and Higgins, 1990). Industrial research and development teams were more effective if headed by transformational project leaders (Keller, 1990).

A primary measure of transformational leadership has been the Multifactor Leadership Questionnaire (MLQ), developed by Bass and Avolio (1990*a*). The MLQ is comprised of *four* distinct transformational leadership factors: idealized influence or charisma, inspirational motivation, intellectual stimulation, and individualized consideration (Avolio *et al.* 1991). For ease of recall, these factors are referred to as the '4 I's' of transformational leadership. A brief definition of each factor is presented below:

- *Idealized influence or charisma.* Generally defined with respect to follower reactions to the leader as well as the leaders' behaviour.

Followers identify with and emulate these leaders; the leaders are trusted and viewed as having articulated an attainable mission and vision. Such leaders are thoroughly respected, have much referent power, maintain high standards, and set challenging goals for their followers. Sample item: has my trust in his or her ability to overcome any obstacle.

- *Inspirational motivation.* May or may not overlap with idealized influence or charismatic leadership, depending on how much followers seek to identify with the leader. The leader provides symbols and simplified emotional appeals to increase awareness and understanding of mutually desired goals. He/she elevates follower expectations. Sample item: uses symbols and images to focus our efforts.
- *Intellectual stimulation.* Followers are encouraged to question their old way of doing things or to break with the past. Followers are supported for questioning their own values, beliefs, and expectations, as well as those of the leader and organization. Followers are also supported for thinking on their own, addressing challenges, and considering creative ways to develop themselves. Sample item: enables me to think about old problems in new ways.
- *Individualized consideration.* Followers are treated differently but equitably on a one-to-one basis. Not only are their needs recognized and perspectives raised, but their means of more effectively addressing goals and challenges are dealt with. With individualized consideration, assignments are delegated to followers to provide learning opportunities. Sample item: coaches me if I need it.

Thus, the behaviours and actions that represent each of these characteristics comprise what has been referred to as transformational leadership.

## Comparing Male and Female Managers with a Broader Range of Leadership Styles

To our knowledge, there has been relatively little discussion comparing men and women managers on transformational leadership. Apart from the occasional anecdotal account (e.g. Women tend to be more empathetic and therefore *should be* more individually considerate in the transformational sense), there have been no direct comparisons between male and female managers on leadership characteristics that seem to have the greatest impact on individual, group, and organizational performance.

The results reported below which compare men and women managers come from an investigation in which the MLQ survey was used. The MLQ made it possible to gather data using behavioural items such as 'He or she presents a vision to spur us on.' This item represented inspirational motivation. Eighty items were rated by 582 male and 219 female direct reports, each of whom evaluated one of 150 male or 79 female managers. The target managers came from six Fortune 500 firms and were drawn mainly from the top three levels of management. Each manager distributed the MLQ to three to five of his or her direct reports. The managers were also told that they would receive feedback on the MLQ at an upcoming training workshop. All respondents were assured that their responses would remain anonymous.

Contrary to the shibboleths that women dislike working for women or the converse, that each sex will favour its own kind, results were the same whether the followers rating their respective managers were men or women. Women managers, on average, were judged more effective and satisfying to work for as well as more likely to generate *extra effort* from their people. Women were also rated higher than men on three of the '4 I's' comprising transformational leadership. Such female leaders were rated as having more idealized influence or charisma, being inspirational and individually considerate than were their male counterparts. Although rated higher on intellectual stimulation, this difference was not large enough to be considered reliable. There were no significant differences for ratings of male and female leaders on scales representing transactional contingent reward nor *laissez-faire* styles of leadership. The contingent reward scale in the MLQ represents leadership behaviours that focus on clarifying expectations and agreements with followers, as well as recognizing successful performance. As seen in Fig. 10.1, the women managers were higher in all the transformational leadership scales (statistically significant for idealized influence [charisma] and individualized consideration), and in the outcomes of extra effort, effectiveness, and satisfaction with the leaders. Men were rated higher in management-by-exception (intervening to correct followers' mistakes) and *laissez-faire* leadership, both less proactive styles linked to less effective outcomes.

The profile that emerges here is of a female manager who is seen as a more proactive role model by followers, who is trusted and respected, and who shows greater concern for the individual needs of her followers.

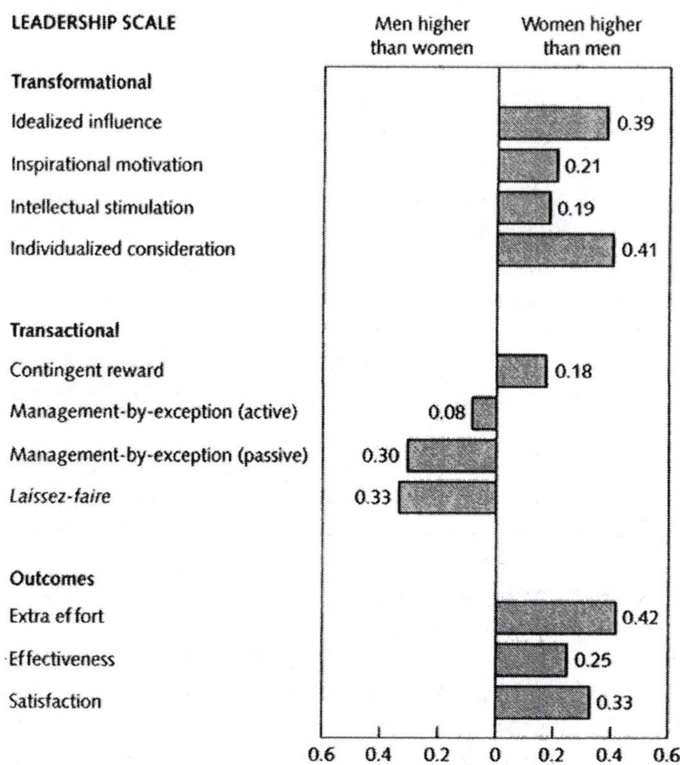


**Fig. 10.1.** Mean differences among men and women managers in MLQ scores when rated by subordinates.

## Some Alternative Explanations

Paradoxically, male chauvinism could also be an explanation of our results, with the argument that women have to be that much better leaders than their male counterparts to attain the same positions of responsibility and levels of success as men. The opposite can also be argued by suggesting that affirmative action has pushed women faster and higher than justified by their competencies. Further, the range of organizations included in this study suggests that there may be other factors in operation to help explain these results.

One explanation may lie in the expectations or stereotypes maintained by followers that male leaders have to live up to higher standards than do female leaders. Women leaders may have been judged more leniently by their followers as they were expected to do poorly because of negative stereotypes, but actually did better than expected. Stereotypes may still persist that women are less suited for management than men. Consciously or not, women may be seen as being deficient for managerial roles (Epstein 1991). Conversely, male leaders were seen as not living up to their followers' expectations and were judged more severely. This may also have occurred and would require a systematic examination of the expectations that followers have of male versus female leaders. Since most managers are typically required to get their work units to perform at acceptable levels, it is our opinion that it is unlikely that such differences in expectations could be maintained over time. Before drawing any firm conclusion, however, this alternative explanation should be examined more closely.

We think a better and more plausible explanation for the observed differences regarding transformational leadership ratings may lie in the tendencies of women to be more nurturing, interested in others, and more socially sensitive. This position is consistent with that of Judith Rosener (1990), who argued that women leaders are more likely than men to encourage participation, to enhance the self-worth of others, and to get followers to trade off their self-interests for the overall good of the organization. Women leaders may simply display qualities more in line with transformational leadership, which in turn makes them more effective in the eyes of their followers. Again, and as we stated at the outset, these are the same qualities that organizations appear to be validating as being essential to effective leadership.

Among the particular strengths Jean Baker Miller (1986) attributes to women which might explain our results are the ability of women to *accept* their vulnerability while men are more likely to react in anger when confronted by their weaknesses. According to Miller's psychoanalytic views, women are also allowed to accept their feelings of fear; men develop tendencies to reject such feelings. Women are more often encouraged not to discount emotions, feelings, and intuition; to help others to develop; and to assume greater responsibility for cooperation. Caring for others enhances women's self-esteem. Much effort is being made by women to break out of earlier limiting roles to become a new kind of person. They are becoming the best proponents of human potential according to Miller. Our results may also reflect how much leaders as seen by Block (1993) should be the servants of followers, providing them with the resources and autonomy to do their work.

According to Kuhnert and Lewis (1987), there is also a strong component of moral values in the behaviour typically exhibited by transformational leaders. And Powell, Posner, and Schmidt (1984) have shown that it is women managers who tend to show more concern for others than do men when dealing with ethical and moral considerations. When it comes to moral reasoning, women focus on care and responsibility, men on rights and justice. Again, women in our sample may have been seen as more transformational to the degree that they are less self-serving in their leadership style.

Finally, the differences observed between male and female managers may be due to the notion that men and women generally perceive the world differently and therefore communicate differently (Gilligan 1982). For women, the world is a network of connections in which support and consensus are sought and confirmed. For men, the world is made up of individuals in a hierarchical social order in which life is a competitive struggle for success, the gaining of independence and advantage over others, and avoiding the loss of power (Tannen 1990). Male leaders are more inclined to pay more attention to fairness and rules and are more attuned to focusing on failings of their followers, rather than caring about them as individuals, as women leaders appear to be more likely to do (Brockner and Adsit 1986).

## Conclusions

In sum, we must add to Alice Eagly's and B. T. Johnson's (1990: 248) dictum that 'the view . . . that women and men lead in the same way should be very substantially revised'. It must also be noted that women managers, on average, tend to be more transformational and more proactive in addressing problems. As a consequence, they are likely to be seen as more effective and satisfying as leaders by both their male and female followers. Unfortunately, the glass ceiling may keep organizations from the best use of their management potential, and perhaps it is time the glass ceiling was shattered. Equally important, women may need to revise their own views of what leads to successful advancement in organizations. 'Tom Peters reminded us that the days of women succeeding by learning to play men's games are gone. Instead men now have to learn to play women's games' (Peters and Waterman 1982). The move toward flattening organizations with authority less concentrated at the top will require a different strategy of leadership than has dominated organizations in the past. This strategy should not be recognized for being more feminine but rather for the fact that it comprises the most appropriate leadership behaviours to develop followers to achieve their highest levels of potential.

## References


Allen, F. W. (1992), 'Coalition Links Issues of Women and Environment', *Wall Street Journal* (30 June), B4.

Avolio, B. J., Waldman, D. A, and Yammarino, F. J. (1991), 'Leading in 1990's: Towards Understanding the Four I's of Transformational Leadership', *Journal of European Industrial Training,* 154: 9–16.

Bass, B. M. (1985), *Leadership and Performance Beyond Expectations* (New York: Free Press).

—— and Avolio, B. J. (1990*a*), *Multifactor Leadership Questionnaire* (Palo Alto, Calif.: Consulting Psychologists Press).

—— —— (1990*b*), 'The Implications of Transactional and Transformational Leadership for Individual, Team, and Organizational Development', in W. W. Woodman and R. Passmore (eds.), *Research in Organizational Change and Development* (Greenwich: JAI Press), iv. 231–72.

—— —— (1993), 'Transformational Leadership: A Response to Critiques', in M. M. Chemers (ed.), *Leadership Theory and Research: Perspectives and Directions* New York: Academic Press.

Blake, R. R., and Mouton, J. S. (1964), *The Managerial Grid* (Houston, Tex.: Gulf).

Block, P. (1993), *Stewardship* (San Francisco: Berrett-Koehler).

Brockner, J., and Adsit, L. (1986), 'The Moderating Impact of Sex on the Equity-Satisfaction Relationship: A Field Study', *Journal of Applied Psychology,* 71: 585–90.

*Business Week* (1992), 'Corporate Women' (8 June), 74–83.

Donnell, S. M., and Hall, J. (1980), 'Men and Women as Managers: A Significant Case of No Significance', *Organizational Dynamics,* 8: 60–76.

Eagly, A. H., and Crowley, M. (1986), 'Gender and Helping Behavior: A Meta-Analytic Review of the Social Psychological Literature', *Psychological Bulletin,* 100: 283–308.

—— and Johnson, B. T. (1990), 'Gender and Leadership Style: A Meta-Analysis', *Psychological Bulletin,* 108: 233–56.

Epstein, C. F. (1991), 'Ways Men and Women Lead', *Harvard Business Review,* 68: 150–60.

Fiermani, J. (1990), 'Do Women Manage Differently? *Fortune* (December), 115–18.

Gilligan, C. (1982), *In a Different Voice* (Cambridge, Mass: Harvard University Press).

Gorham, R. D. (1991), 'Transformational Leadership of Middle Grade Level Principals Involved in Policy Implementation', unpublished manuscript (University of Rochester, Rochester, New York).

Helgesen, S. (1990), *The Female Advantage: Women's Ways of Leading* (New York: Doubleday Currency).

Hersey, P., and Blanchard, K. H. (1977), *Management of Organizational Behavior: Utilizing Human Resources* (Englewood Cliffs, NJ: Prentice Hall).

Howell, J. M., and Avolio, B. J. (1993), 'Predicting Consolidated Unit Performance:

Leadership Ratings, Locus of Control and Support for Innovation', *Journal of Applied Psychology*, 78: 891–902.

Howell, J. M., and Higgins, C. A. (1990), 'Leadership Behaviors, Influence Tactics, and Career Experiences of Champions of Technological Innovation', *Leadership Quarterly*, 1: 249–64.

Keller, R. T. (1990), *Toward a Contingency Theory of Leader Behavior and Creative versus Incremental Innovative Outcomes in Research and Development Project Groups* (Center for Innovation Management Studies, Lehigh University, Bethlehem, Pa.).

Kuhnert, K. W., and Lewis, P. (1987), 'Transactional and Transformational Leadership: A Constructive/Developmental Analysis', *Academy of Management Review*, 12: 648–57.

Levering, R., Moskowitz, M., and Katz, M. (1985), *The 100 Best Companies to Work for in America* (New York: Addison-Wesley).

Miller, J. B. (1986), *Toward a New Psychology of Women* (2nd end.), Boston: Beacon Press).

Nelton, S. (1991), 'Men, Women and Leadership', *Nation's Business* (May), 6–22.

Onnen, M. K. (1987), *'The Relationship of Clergy Leadership Characteristics to Growing or Declining Churches'*, (Doctoral Dissertation, University of Louisville, Ky.).

Peters, T. J., and Waterman, R. (1982), *In Search of Excellence* (New York: Harper & Row).

Powell, G. N. (1993), *Women and Men in Management* (Newbury Park, Calif.: Sage).

—— Posner, B. Z., and Schmidt, W. H. (1984), Sex Effects on Managerial Value Systems', *Human Relations*, 37: 909–21.

Rosener, J. (1990), 'Ways Women Lead', *Harvard Business Review*, 68: 119–25.

Salter, D. I. (1987), 'Leadership Style in United States Marine Corps Transport Helicopter Squadrons (Masters thesis, Naval Postgraduate School).

Segal, A. T., and Zelner, W. (1992), 'Corporate Women' *Business Week* (8 June) 71–7.

Steinem, G. (1992), 'Seeking out the Invisible Woman', *New York Times*, 13 March, Cl–1.

Tannen, D. (1990), *You just* Don't *Understand: Women and Men in Conversation* (New York: William Morrow).

Van Velsor, E. (1987), *Breaking the Glass Ceiling: Can Women Make it to the Top in America's Largest Corporations?* (Reading, Mass.: Addison-Wesley).

# 11 Sexual Static

Judy B. Rosener

Whatever their fundamental origin, gender differences give rise to a subtle phenomenon seldom taken into account in discussions of women in the workplace. I call this phenomenon 'sexual static'.[1]

Sexual static is like snow on the television set or noise on the radio—it causes interference with messages being communicated. In the workplace, messages sent between men and women are difficult to understand because of sexual static in the air. Both men and women experience sexual static. It causes frustration for women and discomfort for men. Women are frustrated because they feel the static could be minimized if men understood gender differences. Men just want the static to go away. They feel working with women means walking on eggshells, and although they're not sure what causes the static, they know it's associated with the presence of women. For this reason, men subconsciously find excuses for excluding women from the executive suite. As the *Wall Street Journal* report on the glass ceiling put it, 'The biggest obstacle women face is also the most intangible; men at the top feel uncomfortable beside them.'[2]

It's difficult to measure sexual static, because men don't like to admit they're confused or uncomfortable working with women, and even if they did, discomfort is very subjective. Nor do women want to admit they're the cause of male discomfort. But, since sexual static leads to the underutilization of women, it cannot be ignored. First it is necessary to understand the sources of sexual static and its relationship to the underutilization of women. Apart from office romance and sexual harassment—obvious sources of sexual static that are discussed only in passing since so much has been written about them and their impact on work interactions[3]—these sources

J. B. Rosener, 'Sexual Static', in *America's Competitive Secret: Utilizing Women as a Management Strategy* (Oxford: Oxford University Press, 1995), 67–83.

can be categorized as follows: (1) *role confusion*, or confusion about the changing roles of men and women at work; (2) *garbled communication*, or differences in the way men and women communicate; and (3) *culture clash*, or the conflict between male and female cultural values. Individually and collectively, these generate sexual static.

## Role Confusion

Most of us grew up with specific expectations about how we were supposed to behave as girls and boys, women and men. This socialization process begins at birth, but as Jean Lipman-Blumen says, 'Pink and blue blankets are only the symbolic tip of the socialization iceberg.'[4]

It is no secret that parents, doctors, nurses, and others who interact with new-borns treat girl babies and boy babies differently. In an experiment recounted by Lipman-Blumen, nurses were handed male new-borns wrapped in pink blankets and female new-borns wrapped in blue blankets. In almost all cases, the nurses handled the infants in the blue blankets, assumed to be boys, much less carefully than those in the pink blankets, assumed to be girls.[5] The differential treatment continues as babies grow. Parents buy dolls for girls and cars for boys. Boys are allowed to be boisterous and noisy. Girls are expected to be quiet and cooperative. Boys pick up sticks that soon become guns. Girls pick up sticks that become magic wands. No one knows if heredity or environment accounts for these differences. Sociologists point to environmental factors, but mothers who have tried to raise children in a non-sexist way might be tempted to vote for heredity.

The socialization of males and females takes place both within and outside the home. As children grow up, they see that nurses are women and doctors are men, teachers are women and principals are men, secretaries are women and CEO's are men, and so on. Thus, sex role expectations are reinforced by everyday experience. Girls learn that their role in life is to provide service and support, and boys learn that their role in life is to command and control.[6] It should therefore be no surprise that, when girls and boys become adults and enter the workforce, they experience 'sex-role spillover'.[7] That is, the sex-role expectations of early childhood spill over into the work environment, where men are clearly expected to be in control and women are clearly expected to provide service and support. This explains why the first wave of women executives tended to be in staff positions—in human resources, public relations, and legal departments, for example—rather than line positions. A staff position is consistent with female role expectations. Men feel comfortable with women managers in support functions.

Today these expectations have changed, and there is a great deal of role confusion. Men and women are constantly bombarded with a blurring of role expectations. On the one hand, they hear that men and women alike are free to make any career choice they wish; on the other hand, they hear that traditional values need to be reinstated and that women should stay at home because families are suffering from the absence of mothers.

A friend of mine owns a large mergers and acquisitions firm that buys and sells companies. She was on her way from Los Angeles to New York for a business meeting when her plane was delayed. While she was waiting in an airport bar, a man approached her. 'Hello, would you like a little company?' he asked. 'Sure,' she said. 'Do you have one for sale?' She was thinking business, he was thinking female. This sort of misunderstanding is common today, now that women are in professions and managerial positions that have historically been all male. It's no wonder men are confused.

For many years I have been collecting data from professional men and women about their perceptions of gender differences. As I visit organizations across the country, I ask people to list the words that first come to mind when they hear the word 'leader'. The words that appear most often are these.

Words Associated with 'Leader'

- strong
- rational
- independent
- linear thinker
- aggressive
- competitive

When I ask women to list the words that come to mind when they hear the word 'male', these are the words they mention.

Words Women Associate with 'Male'

- strong
- in control/domineering
- husband/father/brother
- macho
- power
- rational

When I give talks to male and female managers, I show these responses on a slide. A woman attending one talk raised her hand and said she didn't think men were rational. 'If they were,' she said, 'they would ride horses side-saddle!' The women in the audience laughed. But however rationality or any other attribute is defined, when we look at the two lists of free associations, it is obvious that in general the attributes associated with leaders are similar to the attributes associated with men. This simple exercise shows why women are not seen in terms of leadership potential: they don't exhibit male attributes.

When I ask men to list the words that come to mind when they hear the word 'woman', it's clear they aren't thinking of leaders. The words they most often list are these.

Words Men Associate with 'Female'

- sex
- mother/wife
- beauty
- soft/curves
- sensitive

'Sex' is usually the first or second word on the list when men are asked to think about women. It is usually sixth or seventh on the list when women are asked to think about men. This is not to say that women don't enjoy sex but that sex is not the first thing they think about when they think about men. The importance of this word-association exercise is that it reveals men's tendency to view women in terms of their sexuality rather than in terms of their leadership potential. Since words structure thought, the lists provide a clue to a source of sexual static for men when they interact with women at work: they view them initially in a sexual rather than a work context.

Notice that none of the words men use to describe women is similar to the words associated with leaders. This suggests why men are so confused about whether women can lead. If men see women in terms of their sexuality, or as they see their wives and mothers, then they are forced to change gears when they encounter women as peers, competitors, or leaders. This sense of having to shift gears is a major source of sexual static for men. (In my talks I do not ask women to list the attributes they associate with women, although the responses would be interesting. But because it is men who are in a position to recruit and promote women, I focus on male perceptions of women as key to understanding the underutilization issue.)

When I ask professional women what they would like men at work to change, this is what they say.

What Women Want Men to Change

- Be honest about the fact that they are uncomfortable working with women.
- Stop being so patronizing.

- Take women seriously and treat us like professionals.
- Stop sexist remarks and jokes.

These responses suggest that women know how confused men feel about changing female roles, and that they want men to talk about their discomfort. Women hope that in the process of talking about their own feelings, men will begin to understand why women feel devalued.

When I ask men what they would like women at work to change, these are their responses.

What Men Want Women to Change

- Stop being so defensive.
- Don't try to be masculine.
- Be more assertive.
- Don't be so emotional.
- Be more self-confident.

This list says it all. It shows sex and role spillover in action. It reveals the confusion men experience in working with professional women. The responses are full of contradictions, what psychologists call 'cognitive dissonance',[8] or conflicting thoughts. Men want women to act like men—that is, be more confident, unemotional, and assertive—but at the same time they want them to be feminine. They want women to stop being defensive, yet they make them feel defensive by treating them as sex objects. The list seems to echo Henry Higgins in *My Fair Lady,* who asked, 'Why can't a woman be more like a man?' at the same time that he was thinking 'Vive la difference'.

A similar dynamic is at work in the different leadership styles men and women prefer, as we can see if we look again at the behaviours associated with each.

Command-and-Control Leadership Style

- top-down decision-making
- use of structural power
- focus on self-interest of followers
- control by reward for specific tasks
- stress on individual contribution
- emphasis on 'rational' decision-making

Interactive Leadership Style

- shared decision-making
- use of personal power
- focus on achievement of organizational goals
- control by generating empowerment

- stress on shared power and information
- emphasis on non-traditional forms of decision–making

Like the word lists, these lists reflect very different ways of looking at the world. It's not only that men prefer the command-and-control style but that it *defines* leadership for them. Thus, when men encounter women who use the interactive leadership style, they may have difficulty recognizing them as leaders at all. Conversely, when they encounter women leaders who have adopted the command-and-control style, they may have difficulty relating to them as women. I suspect that this role confusion is exacerbated for men by the new interest in the interactive leadership style in many organizations. The possibility that interactive leadership may sometimes be more effective than command-and-control leadership in today's organizational environment creates sexual static for men because it makes them realize that their style may not be the only one that works.

The role confusion illustrated by the lists also shows up in work-related social gatherings in which it is still assumed that the men are the invitees and the women are their spouses. Both women and men tell stories of how confusing this can be. In the case of a high-ranking male official at a White House gathering in 1992, it turned out to be a disaster. Kathryn Thompson, CEO of a major development company in California, made a $100,000 contribution to George Bush's presidential campaign and thus became a member of what was called Team 100. She and the other Team 100 members were invited to a party in their honour. Of the twelve attendees she was the only woman present. The official approached her and said, 'And little lady, to whom do you belong?' After controlling her anger, she looked him in the eye and said, 'I used to belong to Team 100!'

## Garbled Communication

It's not surprising that Deborah Tannen's *You Just Don't Understand* topped the best-seller lists for a number of years.[9] Its popularity attests to the fact that garbled communication between men and women is common. Tannen says that men and women live in different worlds; thus, conversation between them is like cross-cultural communication. John Gray believes that it's not just a matter of different worlds but different planets; hence the title of his best-seller, *Men are from Mars, Women are from Venus.*[10] Both authors believe that women speak and hear a language of connection and intimacy, and men speak and hear a language of status and independence. Men communicate to obtain information, establish their status, and show independence. Women communicate to create relationships, encourage interaction, and exchange feelings. This difference creates sexual static.

Just as Tannen's book alerts men and women to their own respective communication styles, the movie *Thelma and Louise* shows how men and women selectively perceive messages communicated to them. I have asked many mixed audiences to talk about the message *Thelma and Louise* conveys. Almost always, men describe the movie as a female *Sundance Kid*. They talk about what the gun-toting women did in the movie—got angry, swore, frequented bars, left their mates. Women, on the other hand, talk about how *Thelma and Louise* felt, how they were controlled by the men in their lives and would rather be dead than oppressed. Both messages are communicated. However, the fact that men and women interpret the movie so differently says something about how men and women think and view the world.

Men talk about what they do. Women talk about how they feel. This gender difference is important because men think that talking about feelings at work is unprofessional but talking about doing is OK. Men are confused and uncomfortable listening to women at work. Women don't understand why men are so hesitant to talk about feelings, and men don't understand why women spend so much time talking about feelings. The point is that neither talking about feelings nor talking about doing is necessarily related to work. None the less, women's tendency to talk about personal feelings is a source of irritation to men, and that frustrates women, who don't see why it's not acceptable.

Men and women not only communicate about different things but their manner of communicating differs. Men tend to speak declaratively, as in 'I want the report by Friday.' Women are likely to ask, 'Will the report be done by Friday?' The declarative statement seems more leaderlike because it is consistent with the traditional command-and-control leadership style.

In addition to being more declarative than women, men also tend to express themselves in fewer words. Women frequently leave their sentences dangling. They surround their statements with 'I'm not sure, but. . .' or 'You may not agree, but. . .' Sometimes this is because of low self-esteem, but often it is because women tend to think while they speak. Thus, what seems to men like female babbling or excessive verbiage is normal talk to women. Men's irritation with this stylistic difference comes across in comments like 'Get to the point,' 'Spit it out,' or 'What are you trying to say?' It's clear that the way women tend to talk is another source of sexual static for men.

Men and women also seem to differ in the way they think, an idea that captured the public's fancy some years ago when there was a spate of books and articles about 'right-brained' (female) versus 'left-brained' (male) cognition.[11] Dr Joe E. Bogen, a renowned neurosurgeon who has spent his life studying the brain, says, 'It is clear that there are, on average, gender differences in the brain.'[12] The early work of Jerre Levy and the work of Professor Doreen Kimura at the University of Western Ontario supports Bogen's view. 'It would be amazing if men's and women's brains were not different, given the gross morphological and often striking behavioral differences between men and women which are not restricted to their different roles in parenting and reproductive behavior,' Kimura writes.[13] The discovery by Professor Christine de Lacoste-Utamsing that the corpus callosum—a mass of nerve fibres that connect the brain hemispheres—is larger in women than in men suggests that women may process information differently because there is more communication between the right and left halves of the brain.[14]

The cognitive differences most often identified by researchers are the 'better' performance of men on certain spatial tasks and in mathematical reasoning, and the 'better' performance of women on verbal fluency tasks and tests of perceptual speed.[15] These differences are thought to be associated with the way the brain is organized. Notice that the word 'better' is used to characterize the differences. It is this that causes sparks, ignites debate, and provides fuel for the one-best-model assumption, since the mental processes women are 'better' at are often devalued outside the laboratory.

Women seem to order the information housed in their brains in a mysterious way and to arrive at answers by putting the information together in a holistic fashion. This is what is meant by 'women's intuition'. The word 'scatterbrained', also associated with women, describes a way of thinking in which there is no apparent cohesive organization of data. It suggests that information is floating around in disconnected pieces and that the thought process is not linear or logical. Because processing information in a linear manner has been labelled 'rational' and 'logical', the judgements of women who think intuitively are often seen as untrustworthy. As long as the linear processing of information is considered 'better', women who communicate in a non-linear fashion are apt to be misunderstood and devalued.

Garbled communication can also be related to the way in which words are used. For example, many men can't understand why their wives, but not their female colleagues, like to be called girls. It doesn't occur to men that professional women don't want to be treated like wives. Nor do they realize why this is so. The word 'girl' is defined in the dictionary as 'a young person' or 'a female servant or employee'. 'Girl' connotes youth, which women like, but it also implies low status. 'Lady' is another troublesome word for some women. The word has many meanings, most of them having to do with good breeding, propriety, domestic management, or 'receiving the homage or devotion of a knight or lover'. That is, 'lady' connotes a woman of social position. Like 'girl', it is value-laden. The word 'woman', however, simply describes an adult human being, and is an analogue for the word 'man'. That is why most professional women prefer to be called women.

Granted, not all women are equally concerned about the words used to address or describe them. Nevertheless, words communicate status and tell a great deal about the way people think. While word usage may seem inconsequential to men, it is often a source of distress for women. When the issue is raised, men frequently say to women, 'Why do you have a chip on your shoulder?' or 'You're being oversensitive.' In reality women are only trying to make communication gender-neutral and to reduce the amount of garbled communication.

Touching is another area fraught with potential misunderstandings. Touching is not only a way of showing affection, it is also a way of exercising power. People 'touch down', they don't 'touch up'. People in positions of power tend to touch subordinates, but subordinates generally don't touch bosses. Since men have historically been the bosses and women the subordinates, women have accepted touching as part of their jobs. Until recently, most women didn't complain much about being touched, though today many women speak up when touched in ways they consider inappropriate. They have also discovered the need to be careful about touching male colleagues, so that their own behaviour will not be viewed as inappropriate. Men worry much more today that touching in the wrong place, at the wrong time, or in the wrong way will be construed as sexual harassment. They find themselves being very careful about touching. Since individuals react to touching differently, it is difficult to develop workplace guidelines for touching behaviour. For this reason, touching remains a major source of garbled communication.

Men and women communicate in non-verbal ways other than touching. The way they look, sit, walk, and carry themselves sends messages. In general women tend to be more sensitive to body language than men because as organizational outsiders they use non-verbal cues as a survival tool.[16] Being insiders, men don't need to pay attention to body language because they know the rules. Men and women don't interpret body language in the same way. A man may give a female colleague the familiar 'up and down look' and think he's paying her a compliment, whereas the woman may see it as an insult. She may feel she is being viewed as a sex object rather than a professional peer. Thus, non-verbal communication can also become garbled and contribute to sexual static.

Judy B. Rosener

## Culture Clash

The sexual static generated by the combination of role confusion and garbled communication would seem to be reason enough for men to feel confused and uncomfortable working with women. Yet there is still another source of sexual static: culture clash.

What is meant by this term? First, what is meant by the word 'culture'? It has been defined in a variety of ways. For our purposes, it is 'a system of shared meaning'.[7] We have already seen that because of their different experiences men and women have different systems of shared knowledge and meaning. In other words, then, they live in different cultures, as John Gray and Deborah Tannen argue. This is not to say that men and women don't have a common culture based on experiences they share as human beings. Rather, in addition to their common culture, men and women have unique cultural characteristics by virtue of their sex. This is no secret. Boys and girls play different kinds of games, read different kinds of books, shoulder different kinds of family responsibilities, and talk about different kinds of things. So do men and women. When male and female cultures come into conflict, culture clash occurs.

The definition of culture as a system of shared meaning helps explain the power of men in the workplace, where the dominant culture is male. Few would disagree that men hold most positions of authority in American institutions. Because of their shared experiences as men, they have an advantage when it comes to learning the rules of the organizational game and playing by them. That's because the rules are based on the male experience. Given the pervasiveness of the assimilation model, those in subcultures, e.g. women and people of colour, have to learn the rules of the dominant culture in order to succeed.[18] Granted, women and men may share the belief that employees should be rewarded on performance, that honesty is the best policy, that 'quality is job one', that it's important to pay attention to customers or constituents, and so on. But men and women would probably differ on how to reward performance, what is meant by honesty, what is meant by quality, and even what constitutes a customer. Because male culture is the dominant culture of the workplace, it is men's shared meanings that prevail.

Historically, there have been so few women in upper or even upper middle management that there was little questioning of the dominant culture. It was assumed that the behaviours and attitudes of those in the dominant group should be emulated. However, in the late 1970s and 1980s, when women began to join the workforce in large numbers looking for careers, not jobs, they found themselves at a disadvantage because they did not share the dominant culture. They started asking questions, and the clash of cultures began. Their questions were prompted by their inability or unwillingness to assimilate to the one best model. They wondered why working long hours, as men could do because they had wives at home, was better than working shorter hours, as women wanted to do, if the same amount of work was accomplished. They wondered why companies offered paid time off for drug and alcohol rehabilitation but not for parental leave. They wondered why golf or drinking after work was considered an important part of bringing in business but women's social activities were not. They wondered why life insurance for a spouse was considered a major benefit when many women were single or had spouses with their own insurance.

Today, women continue to question some of the basic assumptions implicit in the dominant culture. They question the command-and-control leadership style, the hiding of emotions, the criteria used to measure performance, and the importance of golf. They are not asking that the dominant male culture be replaced but that it be expanded in a way that values the female culture. Women are asking that the dominant culture be *inclusive* rather than *exclusive.* They want performance criteria that reflect the worth of the female way of doing things, and benefits and perks that reflect women's concerns. And they want the freedom to behave differently from men.

The reason culture clash generates sexual static is that it challenges male values and behaviours. Until recently, those in the dominant culture did not have to think about the values of those in subcultures. Thus, men find the static created by the clash of cultures particularly irritating. They see the conflict as a zero-sum game. If women win, men lose. However, there is reason to believe that, when competency wins, everyone wins, irrespective of gender. The clash of cultures, while confusing and troublesome, can lead to positive change if understood.

When you add culture clash to role confusion and garbled communication, it's easy to see why men feel bewildered and irritated working with women. It's no one's fault that sexual static permeates the air. It's not men's fault that they feel confused and annoyed, or women's that they feel frustrated. However, sexual static exists and is directly related to the underutilization of women. In order to avoid sexual static, men often find subconscious reasons to devalue women, which in turn serves as a justification for excluding them. It's that simple.

Talking about sexual static points us in the direction of change that can bring men and women together rather than tearing them apart. If we can learn more about how role confusion, garbled communication, and culture clash cause uncertainty and discomfort, perhaps we can minimize the amount of sexual static in the air. It may be emotionally satisfying to think that sexual static will disappear on its own as time passes and men and women get used to working with each other, but that isn't likely without the active participation of men.

Since men are the dominant group, they will have to remove the glass ceiling, and that will be difficult, since for them it constitutes a floor—a feeling of security. But women cannot be expected to break the ceiling from below. Think of what happens when a pane of glass is hit from below—those beneath the glass get cut and bloody. That's why women are looking for new answers. One answer may be to reduce sexual static. When men recognize that the static they're experiencing can be minimized, they will be more comfortable working with women, and more likely to value and utilize their talents. For this reason, it is important to learn more about how men feel and how their feelings relate to the underutilization of women.

## Notes

1. J. B. Rosener, 'Coping with Sexual Static', Business World, *New York Times Magazine*, 7 Dec. 1986.
2. C. Hymowitz and T. D. Schellhardt, 'The Glass Ceiling', *Wall Street Journal*, 24 Mar. 1986.
3. For just a few examples, excluding numberless articles in newspapers and magazines, see B. A. Gutek, *Sex in the Workplace* (San Francisco: Jossey-Bass, 1985); L. A. Maniero, *Office Romance: Love, Power, and Sex in the Workplace* (New York: Rawson Associates, 1989); P. D. and J. C. Horn, *Sex in the Office* (Reading, Mass.: Addison Wesley, 1982); and R. E. Quinn, 'Coping with Cupid: The Formation, Impact, and Management of Romantic Relationships in Organizations', *Administrative Science Quarterly*, 22 (Mar. 1977), 30–45.
4. J. Lipman-Blumen, *Gender Roles and Power* (Englewood Cliffs, NJ: Prentice Hall, 1984), 54.
5. Ibid. 59.
6. S. Harter and C. Chao, 'The Role of Competence in Children's Creation of Imaginary Friends', *Merrill-Palmer Quarterly*, 39: 3 (June 1992), 350–63.
7. Gutek, *Sex in the Workplace*, 15–16.
8. See R. A. Wicklund and J. W. Brehm, *Perspectives on Cognitive Dissonance* (Hillsdale, NJ: Erlbaum, 1976).
9. D. Tannen, *You Just Don't Understand* (New York: William Morrow, 1990).
10. J. Gray, *Men are from Mars, Women are from Venus* (New York: Harper Collins, 1992).
11. See, e.g. J. Durden Smith and D. Desimone, *Sex and the Brain* (New York: Arbor House, 1983); A. Moir and D. Jessel, *Brain Sex* (New York: Carol Publishing

Group, 1991); E. Weiner and A. Brown, *Office Biology* (New York: Master Media, 1993).

12. Dr J. E. Bogen, conversation with author, 30 Jan. 1993.
13. J. Levy, 'Lateral Specialization of the Human Brain: Behavioral Manifestations and Possible Evolutionary Basis', in J. A. Kiger (ed.), *The Biology of Behavior* (Eugene: University of Oregon Press, 1972); D. Kimura, 'Are Men's and Women's Brains Really Different?' *Canadian Psychology*, 28: 2 (1987), 133.
14. Smith and Desimone, *Sex and the Brain*, 76; A. Fausto-Sterling, *Myths of Gender* (New York: Basic Books, 1985), 38, 'Sizing the Sexes', *Time*, 20 Jan. 1992, 42.
15. D. Kimura, 'How Different are Male and Female Brains?' *Orbit* (Ontario Institute for Studies in Education), 17: 3 (Oct. 1986), 13–14.
16. Lipman-Blumen, *Gender Roles and Power*, 91–6.
17. C. R. Geertz, *The Interpretation of Cultures* (New York: Basic Books, 1973).
18. 'Subculture implies that the group shares some of the larger national culture, but has some values or customs that differ from the larger culture' (W. B. Gudykunst, *Bridging Differences* (Newbury Park, Calif.: Sage, 1991), 44).

# IV. MYTHICAL LEADERSHIP

The penultimate wave takes an equally modern but substantively different direction by reconsidering the significance of myth amongst leadership studies. In their diverse ways all three chapters take radical swipes at traditional 'myths' of leadership and suggest either that it is virtually impossible to separate myth from reality in terms of what leaders are 'really' like (Pears), or that a substantial proportion of our leaders are there for reasons that the rest of us should worry about (Kets de Vries), or, finally, that leadership in and of itself is a myth propagated to keep the rest of us quiet (Gemmill and Oakley).

Pears's account concerns two of the greatest mythical leaders of all times in the Western world: Wellington and Napoleon. We have great difficulty in disentangling the myth from the reality because their characters are so tightly woven into the construction of national cultures. Colley (1992) has argued that the notion of a British identity was constructed in and through the wars with France in the eighteenth and early nineteenth century as each country came to construct itself against an imagined 'other', and Pears takes a similar line but routes the construction through the contradictions of the two military and political leaders of the nations. Wellington died in 1852 at the apotheosis of the British Empire and Pears argues that history was rewritten at the time to demonstrate the inexorable rise of the Empire and the personification of all things British by Wellington. Even the funeral of Wellington is caricatured as the product of the inevitability of progress as the 'bronze and oak' of Wellington's coffin is compared to the 'pine and papier mâché' of Napoleon's. In effect the history of the world appears to be rewritten as the clash between two nations and then reduced to the fight between the two generals: one effortlessly British, the other patently French.

That their respective reputations should project such polarized characters is perhaps not coincidental; like so many other military leaders before them

(Julius Ceasar, Alexandra the Great, and Nelson to name a few), they both wrote extensive autobiographies, and many of their compatriots read into their characters the quintessential essence of Britishness and Frenchness. Indeed, it is remarkable how the risk-soaked 'strategic genius' of Napoleon—obviously French: watch their rugby—became counterpoised to the pragmatic doggedness of Wellington—obviously British: watch their rugby. Thus Napoleon, the commoner, succeeded by natural flair, by passion, and by engendering high levels of emotional commitment from his troops. Wellington, in contrast, succeeded by hard work to ensure the logistics worked, by determination, and by engendering respect from his troops—but never emotional commitment. The result was that the heroic nature of the two leaders was read quite differently: 'The hero is the man who upsets the status quo. Wellington's impact was less dramatic; Napoleon tore the world to pieces, and Wellington's task was merely to put it back together again.' Wellington, therefore, came to be seen as embodying the archetypal British leader: distanced from his followers by status, pragmatic, amateur, a gentleman, conservative, long lasting, and generally invisible. Napoleon, on the other hand, was archetypically French: close to his followers, outrageously talented, a commoner, a professional, a human meteor that necessarily failed in the end, and a visible destabilizer.

What are we to make of Pears's argument? It is important to remember that a foundation stone of this kind of approach is that leaders, as most other things, live in our imaginations not in 'reality'. This is not the same as suggesting, as Napoleon himself did, that 'History is a set of lies agreed upon' (quoted in Peter 1978: 246). But it is to suggest that we can never be certain of the real truth, since so much of what we know has to go through a sifting mechanism that prevents us from drowning in all the possible knowledge available. That sifting is itself premised upon an interpretative process that subsequently generates an account of the truth about a leader—but not 'the' truth about a leader. In short, we can only ever know a minimal amount about any leader, so the question becomes whose account is the most persuasive and why?

Secondly, we should be aware of the context within which leaders operate. They may be free-floating organisms driven by volition, but our accounts of them are inevitably constructed through a context that itself changes through time. As Wellington himself suggested: 'I am the Duke of Wellington and must do as the Duke of Wellington doth.' It should not be surprising, then, when our accounts of previous 'heroic leaders' change over time. This is not a contingent issue: that leaders may be appropriate for one condition but not another (e.g. Churchill was an appropriate leader in war but not in peace), but rather concerns whether our assumptions about what makes a good leader change radically across time (was Churchill an appropriate leader at all?).

Kets de Vries continues the cautionary note against leadership studies that study more and more about less and less. He accepts that leaders do make a difference and that leaders must fulfil two roles if they are to be successful:

first, they must fulfil a charismatic role—they must develop the three 'E's: envision, energize, and empower; secondly, they must develop an instrumental role which involves organizational design and the control and reward of behaviour.

The charismatic role—which is clearly different from the notion of charisma adopted by Bryman following Weber—is ultimately concerned with managing a high degree of cognitive complexity and managing to turn this complexity into a manageable picture. But the picture of where the company is going is inadequate in itself, for it needs to be associated with a high level of dissatisfaction with the status quo, and it often helps to focus the minds of employees if an external 'enemy' or competitor can be 'discovered'. As Pears argued above, organizational identity is much easier to shape *against* something which is held to embody the opposite characteristics. It is also better to aim high, since to aim low and hit low seems to be a favourite pastime of risk-averse organizations entering periods of rapid change (Grint and Willcocks 1995).

But whereas conventional notions of charismatic leadership may well lead to disempowering of subordinates, Kets de Vries is keen to suggest that the opposite is a prerequisite for success: only where leaders empower their followers is there any chance of enacting the vision. Since there are many leaders who have achieved substantial parts of their vision by disempowering their subordinates (Stalin and Hitler will do for two), there must be a question mark over this, and the same goes for Kets de Vries's claim that empathy is a fundamental building block of successful leaders. Indeed, the listing of common traits for leaders is itself a testament both to an earlier view on leadership and to a model that involves a considerable degree of romantic configuring of the leader. To assume that all leaders must be conscientious (Nero?), agreeable (Stalin?), extrovert (John Major?), dominant (ditto), self-confident (ditto), energetic (Reagan?), lacking in ethnocentrism (Hitler?), and emotionally stable (ditto) is to stretch the term too far. Nor are these problems associated only with political leaders.

On the other hand, Kets de Vries's exploration of the role of the unconscious and the irrational is more fruitful, especially in the assumption that a leadership position almost inevitably leads to the reconstitution of one's social networks as the politics of greed, envy, and fear begin to muscle in. Yet more dangers lie in store for those organizations that manage to secure leaders who are not what he calls 'constructively narcissistic' (leaders who are satisfied with themselves), but 'reactive narcissist'—those leaders whose leadership role is used to achieve revenge upon what is perceived by the leader in childhood as an apparently uncaring and destructive world.

Whatever the significance of the narcissistic perspective on leadership, it does offer us an explanation for a leader's aberrant behaviour. What it does not do is link the issue of charismatic leadership strongly enough to the aberrant behaviour. In short, if, as Napoleon said: 'Glory is fleeting but obscurity is forever', then we must beware the glory seekers whose intent is not to advance the wheel of progress but to mark their own existence in the wheel with a knife.

## Mythical Leadership

That leadership is a necessary element of all organizations tends to be taken as read far too easily, and the piece by Gemmill and Oakley sets about reminding us that there are alternative perspectives that have to be taken seriously, especially if we want to avoid the kind of potential problem outlined by Kets de Vries. The reification of leadership is the starting-point for their analysis and it begins by considering the way in which disempowered and helpless people strive to take control of their surroundings by attributing another individual with powers of control that diminish their own anxiety. The consequences of this 'myth' are self-perpetuating, because once the 'leader' has been recognized, all responsibility is projected onto him or her. Thus the 'learned social helplessness' generates yet further expectations that the leader will resolve all the problems—and the problems mount as the population withdraws from responsible proactive action. Eventually the result is their search not for any old leader but for a Messiah, a charismatic figure who can bring forth salvation—and can do it within the existing social order; charismatics are OK but charismatic revolutionaries need not apply. The result of this multiple and open-myth construction is to offer support to the existing élite and to provide the followers with a rationale for their own apparent failure.

The value to the follower of this apparent self-deception is to control, channel, and therefore rationalize the very strong sense of anarchy, or randomness, that pervades the world. Since we cannot know what will happen next, and since there is no one to blame for what happens next, we prefer to concentrate responsibility on one person. Whether that person, the leader, can resolve our problem is secondary to the point that at last and at least someone now appears to be in control. In short, we now appear to be going somewhere rather than wandering around in the desert, and, even if the direction is wrong, at least it is a definite direction. Leadership as a 'ghost dance', a native American Indian dance used at the end of the nineteenth century to restore collapsing fortunes, appears an accurate metaphor for this misplaced faith in leadership. For those readers dubious about the utility of Gemmill and Oakley's article, I suggest they ponder this last point and see just how many organizations it appears to fit.

On the other hand, we might consider whether the significance of the leader is indeed unrelated to the actual utility he or she brings to the party. That is, it may be that a leader is practically useless in and of himself or herself, but if he or she manages to facilitate his or her followers into cohesive action then he or she has indeed provided a necessary catalyst. This, of course, is different from Gemmill and Oakley's point where followers are disempowered rather than empowered by their leader.

Indeed, when leaders are called upon to enact their actions, it becomes a critical test for their followers as much as for themselves. Where followers attribute their leaders with hopelessly unrealistic expectations, the leader must inevitably fail. This does not mean that followers then question their own beliefs about leadership; rather, they search for another Messiah who will just as surely fail them. One has only to look at the turnover of professional football managers to see this in action. Having been unsuccessful for many years, a team replaces its manager, who also and inevitably fails to win every match, so, rather than reconceptualize their thoughts about football managers, the supporters seek out another Messiah.

Nor should we think that such learned helplessness relates only to other people or to specific kinds of crisis. As Gemmill and Oakley note, the Milgram experiments and the mass suicides of several cults in recent years are evidence enough that many people succumb to authoritarian tendencies. Furthermore, this issue of learned helplessness may well help explain the general failure of the moves towards empowerment: since empowerment embodies the opposite direction to that still displayed by most leaders, we should not be surprised to see so many cases fail. Worse, the consequence of such failures is merely to confirm that reality could not be otherwise, that there is no alternative, and that we must once again turn to our leaders for salvation—knowing that it will probably never come and, if it does, it will further disempower us.

# 12 The Gentleman and the Hero: Wellington and Napoleon in the Nineteenth Century

Iain Pears

Since the earliest guidebooks in the sixteenth century, the English view of the foreigner has changed remarkably little. Despite the rise and fall of several empires, the alliances with and wars against virtually every country on the Eurasian continent, the English have been able to comfort themselves with the view that foreign character is pretty much stable. From the Tudors if not earlier, Germans have been seen as obedient but unimaginative gluttons; Italians as greasy and dishonest; Spaniards as cold and sinister; the French as dandies and egotists; the Dutch as worthy but dull. All, it went without saying, were untrustworthy, most were dishonest, and none could match an Englishman.

The constancy of these stereotypes is strange, considering that Englishmen's views of themselves—and hence of the qualities which they considered worthy—have undergone remarkable transformations in the same period. In the sixteenth century, Erasmus commented on their openness, and proneness to kissing everyone. In the seventeenth century, they went through a dour and serious phase before national frivolity broke out once more. While supposedly possessing Bottom, that great ability to endure suffering without complaint, the eighteenth-century English were very much proud of their emotions, which supposedly led them to burst into tears on any occasion, commit suicide with frequency, become melancholy, get drunk, and fall in love with noisy panache.

I. Pears, 'The Gentleman and the Hero: Wellington and Napoleon in the Nineteenth Century', in R. Porter (ed.), *Myths of the English* (Cambridge: Polity Press, 1992), 216–36.

The arrival of the Victorian worship of self-discipline—again in myth if not necessarily in reality—represented an enormous swing of self-perception that was accompanied by the rise of the Great Man cult. The nineteenth century saw the production of innumerable biographies, portraits, and statues to give examples of true merit. This was not, of course, an entirely new phenomenon; a 'temple of British Worthies' had been constructed at Stowe in the 1740s, and in the early eighteenth century 'heads of eminent men' were displayed to inspire the owners with thoughts of greatness. The difference was that the eighteenth-century hero tended to be long dead, the representative of abstract ideals—courage, patriotism, learning, and so on; the nineteenth century revered more recent heroes, frequently ones who were still alive, presenting their lives in close detail through the medium of the well-researched, authoritative, and often polemical biography, and stressing the qualities of their personality as much as their deeds.

The visions of the foreigner and the Englishman were embedded in stereotypical characters for simplicity's sake, with the creation of a gallery of stock characters—the mynheer, the burgomeister, the courtly fop, the bravo, the inquisitorial priest—which served to encapsulate each nation and was contrasted with an equally stereotypical Englishman—the squire, John Bull, or whoever. Such characters popped up in cartoons, on the stage, and in literature from the sixteenth century to the nineteenth.[1] At the same time, and on a slightly more intellectual level, real characters from history or the recent past could be brought into close proximity, one of the classic combinations being the trio of Henry VIII, Francis I, and Charles V: bluff and hearty, frivolous and artistic, serious and pious. Other conjunctions—Elizabeth and Philip, Marlborough and Louis XIV, Buckingham and Richelieu—could all be compressed through the medium of history or biography in a way which illuminated, reinforced, and, in some measure, created differences in national character.

Of all the nineteenth century's modern heroes, the Duke of Wellington was by far the most eminent, and the contrast between him and Napoleon Bonaparte was an enduring element in contemporary literature. The importance of this conjunction is no longer obvious; Napoleon is still a perennial topic for biography and continues to exert a fascination, but the reputation of Wellington has faded somewhat. Children are no longer taught about Vittoria, Salamanca, or the Talavera, let alone Assaye; his tomb draws only a fraction of the visitors who go to the Invalides. This personal eclipse, however, partly masks the permanent impact Wellington exercised in the way his character, and the qualities he came to symbolize, became built into the national consciousness as part of the essential fabric of Englishness. This is not to assert that Wellington created a new image of what it was to be English; rather, he encapsulated a newly-forming vision of national type which, through his personal success and the way he could be opposed to the personification of foreign threat, provided a form of shorthand by which this notion could be disseminated.

In this essay I will try to lay out the salient elements of Wellingtonian Englishness, and to argue that he represented the prototype of a new model gentleman, fine-tuned to suit the requirements of an industrial but hierarchic society still deeply alarmed at the implications of France's revolutionary legacy. Particularly after his withdrawal from active politics and especially after his death, Wellington-worship was a curious amalgam of diverse elements—xenophobia, modernism, chivalry, patriotism, individualism, classicism. Equally, it was a reasonable reflection of the Duke himself, for he imprinted his character on the English self-image at the same time as he was a vehicle for national aspiration and moulded himself to fit the requirements of others. As he himself said: 'I am the Duke of Wellington, and must do as the Duke of Wellington doth.'[2]

For several hundred years the English had, against all contrary evidence, loudly asserted their superiority over—and to—all comers. It was disconcerting when Waterloo suggested this boasting might be true after all. Being the richest and most powerful nation in Europe was dangerous unless reasons could be found to explain it; unless the sources of superiority could be isolated, they could not be reproduced, and if they were not reproduced England's dominance would prove illegitimate and perhaps also short lived. Modern scholarship would maintain that the explanation which found favour—one based essentially on an account of character—was entirely erroneous. None the less, it was still strongly held and found its most perfect embodiment in the victor of Waterloo. 'In all that has singled out England from the nations, and given her the front place in the history of the world, the Duke of Wellington was emphatically an Englishman.'[3]

Perhaps one of the highest points of extreme 'Wellingtonism' came on 18 November 1852, when he was given the last heraldic funeral in England.[4] The emphasis on elements of chivalry was unusual; as a writer to the *Gentleman's Magazine* noted, heraldic devices were now rare: 'In the ordinary modern funeral, even of persons of the highest rank, all these various modes of heraldic display are now obsolete.'[5] However much the code of chivalry was attracting renewed attention, Wellington's funeral was unique in being awash with Pennons, Guidons, and Banners, Trophies, Achievements, and Bannerols. Similarly, enormous play was made in almost every newspaper and magazine which wrote on the event (and they all did) of the extraordinary list of honours the Duke racked up over his long life, this being read out in full by a herald over his coffin and reprinted almost obsessively by biographers for the next two decades.

Alongside this clear reference to English hierarchy and tradition, however, the funeral also stressed classical parallels and more modern elements of British history. The funeral car itself was a direct allusion to the long line of British worthies who had been similarly honoured—including Cromwell (1658), Marlborough (1722), and Nelson (1806)—but also to the common ancestor of them all, the wagon which had borne Alexander the Great to Alexandria.[6] At the same time, and showing the distinct footprints of Prince Albert, instructions were issued that the car 'should . . . do credit to the taste of the artists of England'.[7] More than this, it was to 'afford an instance of the remarkable rapidity with which the most elaborate works can be manufactured in the gigantic establishments of Sheffield and Birmingham'.[8]

The funeral ceremony itself was also an exemplar of modernism, a state affair which built on the experience of the Great Exhibition the previous year, and had some of the same objects in view. For contemporary commentators, the significance of both was proven by the sheer quantity of people who attended, the mobilization of a mass audience serving as a demonstration of national solidarity and unity. At both, the huge numbers were brought in by rail, with the rail companies organizing special funeral excursions for the latter occasion.[9] Equally, recent practice in handling large numbers of people—the police were organized by the man who had directed crowd control at the Exhibition—enabled the authorities to ensure a dignified ceremony by concentrating forces in the places where experience suggested they might most be needed.[10]

But why was such an enormous effort made to honour Wellington? He was, certainly, England's most distinguished military commander since Marlborough, but it was none the less the case that no general had ever been praised, in life or in death, with the extraordinary generosity he received. Part of the explanation lay not merely in his role in recent events but also in the way in which much of the history of Europe was reconstructed by English writers around the middle of the century. Just as the Whig historians had tended to present a spectacle of progress towards the triumph of constitutional liberty, so now the international past was recast as an inexorable rise towards national hegemony. Sir Edward Creasy's *Fifteen Decisive Battles of the World*, for example, presented a logical progression from Marathon to Waterloo, with the last campaign ushering in an era of universal peace, freedom, and prosperity.[11] Wellington was portrayed, therefore, not merely as a successful general, but rather as the culmination of two millennia of strife, and as the man who finally produced the peace of nations under the benevolence of English supremacy. A further stimulus, of course, was the more immediate fear that this happy state might prove short lived without the sturdy resistance which he represented; his funeral took place less than a year after the *coup d'état* which brought Napoleon III to the French throne, and authors of all stripes linked the death of the English hero and the resurrection of the French one through his nephew as a possibly ominous sign for the future.

More overtly, however, the event was also shaped as an answer to a similar funeral which took place in Paris some twelve years previously, with the 'retour des cendres' and the ceremonial burying of Napoleon Bonaparte's mortal remains under the dome of Les Invalides. From the beginning, comparisons were made with this earlier ceremony. While the French funeral had been sneered at for the gimcrack nature of its decorations, and the flimsy, temporary style of its furniture, the organizers of the Duke's farewell set out to ensure that it contained 'nothing mean, tawdry, theatrical, inappropriate'.[12] While Napoleon's funeral car was of 'pine and papier-mâché', Wellington's was of bronze and oak.[13] The funeral was to emphasize substance rather than style, and provide a material contrast between English solidity and the French preference for flashy but empty display.

None the less, caution was required. The English liked to see themselves as a nation pre-eminently able to produce heroes, but peculiarly resistant to the fawning displays of devotion to them that was so dangerous an element of the French character. As the *Illustrated London News* explained, 'The English are said to be a people who do not understand shows and celebrations . . . unlike the French and other nations of the continent, they have no real taste for ceremonial. There is, doubtless, some truth in this. We are a practical people.' The funeral of the Duke was thus not an adulatory farewell for a Great Man, but rather a demonstration that the English could excel even at things for which they had no natural affinity: 'What Englishmen resolve to do, they always do well . . . this event shall be solemnized as becomes the mightiest nation in the world.'[14] Equally, the Wellington who was entombed in St Paul's had not aroused such emotions when he was prime minister in the 1830s; his direct political involvement rather tended to be written off as something of an aberration by authors more concerned with delineating the greatness of his character and concentrating on the magnitude of his military achievements.

Just as Wellington's funeral took place in the shadow of Napoleon's and was in a sense an answer to it, so the depiction of the Duke's character was marked throughout all the biographies by the presence of his great adversary. This was inevitable; Wellington's entire career depended on Napoleon, and the parallels between the two men—born in the same year, educated in French military academies, rising through their abilities, leading their countries' armies, and meeting once in a final showdown—were too obvious and appealing to be resisted. 'There does not exist an epic, the foundations of which are better suited for artistic purposes than the story of Wellington's struggle with Napoleon's power.'[15]

Carefully interpreted, the quarter century of fighting involving the whole of Europe could be reduced to a more simple collision between two countries and two sets of ideas as represented by two men. That they were portrayed in highly different fashions goes without saying, but nothing could be further from the truth than the comment of a French journalist that 'France and England will never agree on the manner of judging Napoleon and the Duke of Wellington'.[16] In fact, French and English commentators agreed almost entirely; it was the meaning read into the judgements which often differed radically.

From the beginning, the biographical approaches to the two men have differed markedly. It is, for example, remarkable how Wellington's personal reputation is jealously guarded. While Napoleon's memory has been subjected to innumerable accounts of his somewhat dull love life, the state of his haemorrhoids examined in medical treatises, his relationship with his mother and his marshals scrutinized for the slightest sign of homosexuality, his death analysed for evidence of murder, the personal activities of Wellington—who had as many, if not more, affairs and whose attitude to such matters was much more open than the somewhat prim Bonaparte's—have been treated with the most extreme delicacy.[17]

To a considerable extent, the pair were responsible for their later reputations; certainly few men in the period devoted as much time to the attempt to fine tune their images. Napoleon laboured away on St Helena writing his memoirs to boost the idea of the peaceful lawgiver; Wellington carefully had others edit vast volumes of his dispatches to strengthen the image of 'a chief, distant, Olympian, severe'. Thus, he was described as being disdainful of honours and titles, despite the enormous collection he acquired, some of which he had solicited; mindful only of his duty, despite the vast financial rewards he accumulated; too direct and honest to be a politician, despite three years as prime minister and nearly two decades of dominance in the back rooms of power. His military reputation was scarcely touched by the fact that his role in baulking reforms led to disaster in Crimea, his reputation as a defender of liberty unmarked by his willingness to turn out the troops to block reform movements in England.

To list these factors is not to say that Wellington was in fact reprehensible; rather, I merely wish to note that abundant material existed for an unfavourable portrait at the time of his death or afterwards, had anyone wanted to make use of it.[18] It is similarly notable that, however much his memory might have faded in recent decades, his reputation has not changed a great deal. On most important points, the portrait painted in Elizabeth Longford's biography of 1969 is the same as that offered by Brialmont in 1852, or Guedalla in 1931.[19] Biographers create their subjects through the material they choose to use; with Wellington the concern was to present a picture of almost unalloyed virtue embodied in a particular character and outlook. As with many other heroes, too, memorialists were not always content to stay firmly with the record, but were often happy to invent anecdotes to fit the point being made. Some at least of the Duke's reputation for the terse but pungent *bon mot* depends on statements he never actually made or which were improved on afterwards.

For all that many admired him, most French commentators assigned Wellington a very secondary place in the universal pantheon of Great Men. John Lemoinne maintained that 'it will not be said that Wellington was of the true race of Heroes'.[20] Biographies of Napoleon habitually compare the Emperor with the likes of Alexander, Caesar, and Charlemagne, that is, with soldier-rulers, rather than with mere generals. Rarely do his admirers even bother to mention the man who beat him at Waterloo. Indeed, they implied that Wellington did not defeat Napoleon. Only God was mighty enough to bring him down: 'To the question, was it possible for Napoleon to win this battle, our answer is, No. Because of Wellington? Because of Blucher? No. Because of God . . . Napoleon had been impeached in heaven and his fall decreed; he was troublesome to God.'[21] For admirers of Napoleon, French or English, the Emperor bestrode the continent like a colossus, while Wellington was a mere theatre commander. Any comparison between the two could only reduce the Emperor and, according to one French author, the Duke was almost unknown in France by the time of his death.[22] In contrast, writers on Wellington rarely adopted the tactic of trying to diminish Napoleon's ability—'Let him be exalted, on the contrary, for it suffices to have conquered and dethroned him'[23]—rather laying out a series of parallel but opposite qualities possessed by their chosen champion. Waterloo was sufficient demonstration of their superiority.

So what lessons did admirers of Wellington draw from the perusal of the two careers? In the stampede of biographies that followed his death, the contest between the two men was elevated to a battle of giants, a personalized clash in which two opposing forces—good and bad, Frenchness and Englishness struggled against each other. Generally speaking, there was agreement that, if seen in strictly personal terms, Napoleon was infinitely superior as both man and hero: 'It may be conceded that the schemes of the French emperor were more comprehensive, his genius more dazzling, and his imagination more vivid . . .'[24] In comparison, his opponent was a plodder: most commentators were willing to agree, more or less, with Hugo's statement that 'Wellington was the technician of war, Napoleon was its Michelangelo.'[25] This, of course, meant that Waterloo needed to be explained. None of the constituent elements of Wellington's success was flashy, none would ever excite any but the most diligently patriotic poets to launch into verse. But, demonstrably, they won, and it was in Wellington's very mundaneness, the almost dull doggedness that eschewed personal extravagance, that the source of true greatness was found.

So, in contrast to his opponent's fire and brilliance, Wellington possessed 'patience in action'[26] or 'simplicity sublime'.[27] As *The Times* obituary put it, allying his achievements with the fundamental nature of the nation, 'the chief characteristic of Wellington's mind was that sterling good sense which is said to distinguish the capacities of his countrymen in general'.[28] Common sense was not important merely as a personal quality, but could be seen to have had profound political overtones. Napoleon was the upstart, the man gifted with talents so enormous that they could not be contained and which ended up being perverted and used for personal gain; Wellington forever the loyal servant, was, acting for the best of his King and country at all times.

> 'From the instant I gained a superiority, I have recognized neither master nor laws'—was the confession of Napoleon.
>
> 'I am the Prince Regent's servant, and will do whatever he and his government pleases' was the language of Wellington.[29]

Napoleon was the creation of the revolution, and ended by bringing his country and cause to ruin and defeat. Wellington, the product of Burkean conservatism, boosted his to world dominance and utter security. In the political and social turmoil of the period of reform and Chartism, their careers were also a lesson in the virtues of English political stability:

> With a nation like the French, fond of glory, enamoured more of equality than of liberty, a General like Bonaparte must of necessity arrive at dictatorial power, and next, at the crown. But with a nation like the English, a man of Wellington's mould could aspire but to constitutional and regular greatness. On both sides, men and countries were admirably adapted to each other.[30]

The self-characterization of Wellington as 'nimmukwallah', a man who had 'eaten the King's salt'[31] and was bound to obey him forever, was perhaps the most constant theme referred to throughout biographies, and was again a characteristic accepted as perfectly English by domestic and foreign commentators.

Allied to this theme of service to the state was a contest to gain the moral high ground of classical precedent. On both sides of the channel, Roman memory was important; Napoleon's eagles, legion of honour, and triumphal arches are an easy demonstration of French awareness. But, whereas admirers of Napoleon preferred to concentrate on the soldier, laying stress on the period before the Imperial adventure, supporters of Wellington concentrated on Napoleon as Emperor: for them, the Englishman was the representative of Roman republican values, with Napoleonic egotism and self-aggrandizement embodying the excesses of Roman decline. Wellington is compared to the likes of Fabius, Scipio, and other loyal servants of the ancient Republic—'In all he seemed the Roman of old, save in pomp.'[32] Equally, ever more stress is laid on Spartan simplicity, again in a fashion which erases something of the true picture. Thus the youthful dandy, or the Wellington of Apsley House and Stratfleld Saye, vanishes in favour of the 'abstemious, active, self-denying man' who never tasted wine or spirits, rose at dawn, and slept on a couch with a pillow stuffed with horsehair. Moreover, there were few who omitted to draw the appropriate moral lesson that the revolutionary who grabbed for personal supremacy brought the world down on his head, while the loyal servant ended up as prime minister, loaded with riches and honours, and died universally admired and loved.

The emperor fell, the scaffolding crumbled away and he who raised it with heroic temerity only survived his irreparable shipwreck for a few years in exile. His fortunate rival . . . saw open before him another career . . . is not such a lesson a striking proof of the final ascendancy of reason and of good sense over all the boldness and all the flights of imagination and of genius?[33]

In military ability also, biographers almost deliberately stressed different aspects of the two men's respective abilities, so that Napoleon appeared a more exciting leader and Wellington a less. While the Emperor's strategic skills and vision in command were constantly referred to—the lightening dashes across half a continent, the tactical flair and imaginative grasp of strategic possibilities—Wellington was singled out for his logistical skills, his caution, and his humanity. Such an opposition is forced; Napoleon's success lay above all in his organizational abilities and Wellington was capable of rapid and imaginative moves. The way such a contrast was built up through selection of evidence again illuminates the method by which the Englishman was shown to be superior. Wellington relied little on providence and more on forward planning. Napoleon, beloved of fate, was supported by fortune in the manner of a Greek hero, and when fortune abandoned him he fell. Much of his success, therefore, was owed less to his inherent abilities than to plain good luck:

Napoleon might be said to have been one of those brilliant, but wild batsmen who with luck in their favour can hit up a century in record time. In his first innings sixes and boundaries flowed from his bat, but with catches dropped all over the field . . . His luck held for a long time . . . but he never attempted to play for his side and in other features of his game he was quite useless. His second innings was short and ignominious, though the bowling against him was easy and his opponents an unpractised and hastily got together team.[34]

English accounts refer frequently to the rapacity of French troops but stress Wellington's attempts to keep his under control. Once again, the contrast is forced. The sack of Badajoz was as violent as anything performed by the Grand Army, and the death of more than 100,000 Portuguese as a result of the Torres Vedras campaign generally fails to be mentioned even in a footnote.[35] Such omissions were virtually compelled by the idealized opposition created between Napoleon the egotist and destroyer, and Wellington the selfless protector:

[Napoleon] marshalled on his side licence, cupidity and expediency and transfigured them with a bright haze of glory. Wellington headed the protest of law against licence, of conscience against cupidity, of justice against expediency, and walked in the plain light of duty . . . In Napoleon's case, living men became dead corpses merely to prop his throne; in Wellington's they were sacrificed that mankind might be delivered from an intolerable yoke.[36]

Thus, the juxtaposition of the two men, and the aspects of their careers singled out for emphasis, were essential for the task of transforming Wellington—the man who restored the Bourbons in Spain and France, who opposed the Reform Act and deployed thousands of troops to protect London against the Chartists—into the champion of liberty: 'The sword of Wellington was never drawn to enslave, but to liberate. He was never the oppressor, but always the friend of the nations among whom he appeared.'[37]

For all that Wellington was presented as a saviour, however, the picture presented was not one of a typical hero; rather, biographers were at pains to leave such characteristics to the Emperor and define their subject almost in deliberate opposition to them.[38] However electric and fascinating, heroes were dangerous people to have around in a quiet, peaceful, law-abiding country. Heroes, especially romantic ones, had particular qualities that enabled them to be recognized. Above all there was the notion of destiny, of being touched by God and preordained for great things. While biographers of Napoleon successfully isolated incidents from his youth which presage the actions of the man—for example, his leading a snowball fight at school—writers on Wellington gave up and confessed that he was not a 'heaven-born general'.[39] Quite the opposite, in fact; in his youth, even his mother remarked that 'anyone can see he has not the cut of a soldier'. Wellington's achievements came from hard work, study, and practice. While he earned greatness, Napoleon did not, in the sense that the Frenchman had no option but to be great—the implication being that Wellington was in some way more meritorious and industrious.

A second aspect of heroes is that they leave everything changed after them, their presence in the world pushing it in a new direction. The hero is a man who upsets the status quo.[40] Wellington's impact was less dramatic; Napoleon tore the world to pieces, and Wellington's task was merely to put it back together again.

Having battled for the established order as a soldier, he fought a rear-guard action against change as a politician. Calculating and grudging retreat was scarcely the stuff of the hero; Wellington and his ilk were not creators, inventors, parents of ideas. The world cannot live upon negations; it requires faith, as lungs require air. Man must love liberty as an absolute good, not submit to it as a necessary evil.[41]

A third characteristic is that heroes have, to use the modern term, charisma; their uniqueness is instantly sensible to those who come into contact with them. Again, Napoleon, portrayed as Jove, the man who struck like a thunderbolt, had this quality and he 'dazzled the world'. Wellington's personality never dazzled anyone; Nelson took him for some junior officer until told who he was. At the opposite end of his life he was accosted in the street by someone who thought he was 'Mr Smith'. The anecdotes themselves would be trivial, but for the fact that they were repeated countless times by biographers who sensed in them something characteristic of a man who, although inordinately vain about his position, liked to present himself as ordinary. The image also comes through in art: Ingres showed Napoleon as Jupiter or touching soldiers for scrofula; David's portrayal of Napoleon crossing the Alps shows an elemental hero. The parallel depiction of Wellington crossing the Pyrenees looks more like an English gentleman out for an afternoon's exercise in Kent. In his life and in the way he was represented, Wellington was portrayed in a consciously unheroic fashion.[42]

Similarly, heroes inspire enormous love and loyalty in those who will pick themselves up and follow. Napoleon was said to have generated enormous passion among his army and among the French, driving his hungry and ill-equipped soldiers in Italy on to ever greater deeds through his personality, oratory, and example. The image of the *petit caporal* was carefully preserved throughout the period of Empire, as one of the few remnants of revolutionary fraternalism. Wellington inspired little devotion in those who served him. While Napoleon talked to his soldiers in the familiar *tu*, Wellington pointed at his with a cane and called them scum.[43] Napoleon liked to give his troops a fraternal embrace, Wellington recommended flogging them. 'He was not a lovable character,' said one historian, while another noted that he acquired a reputation for being unsympathetic, ungenerous, and ungrateful to his subordinates.[44] He never spoke of glory to his army, and took no interest in soldiers once his task was done; the army was packed up 'like a machine', and unlike other generals Wellington associated afterwards only with his old officers.[45] Again this was taken as a reflection of national character:

The English soldier does not like to feed upon imagination, and with empty stomach he would not care much about being contemplated by forty centuries. But with such high-sounding words as those you will make the French soldier go on to the end of the world . . . it is quite enough to talk to him of victory and glory; he will readily die for the sake of a rhyme.[46]

A further element of nineteenth-century heroism was individualism, and the way biographers treated both men in this respect presents one of the most intricate tinkerings with conventions in the portraits. Napoleon's genius marked him as an individual *par excellence*; Wellington's contentment with serving militated against such isolation. But from another perspective there was an attempt to reverse the picture—Napoleon's achievement was seen as the result of the mass mobilization of an entire country, and indeed an entire continent; his victories were ascribed to the vast resources he had at his disposal and represented as the ultimate expression of French centralism. Wellington, on the other hand, was presented as the lone voice in the wilderness, fighting almost forgotten in the Peninsula, the only person who could see that victory was possible and having to defeat not only the French but also the British government in order to achieve his ends. His triumph was the embodiment of the confused and ramshackle approach in which the English have always taken such inordinate pride.[47] Again this point was raised almost to a key tenet of military theory to explain his victory. Wellington's professionalism was downplayed in favour of pragmatic improvisation so that it could be contrasted with the rigidities of a Cartesian devotion to grand plans: 'They planned their campaigns just as you might make a splendid piece of harness. It looks very well; and answers very well; until it gets broken; and then you are done for. Now I made my campaigns of ropes. If anything went wrong, I tied a knot; and went on.'[48] Wellington himself stressed his indispensability: 'I am obliged to be everywhere and if absent from any operation something goes wrong.'[49] Later authors also concentrated on the idea that the British government was more of an obstacle than a help to his progress. 'Napoleon was never . . . so harassed by the French, as Wellington was by the English, Spanish and Portuguese governments.'[50] The point was of some importance, and it was the only one in which French and English biographers differed, each trying to demonstrate that their hero was the more personally responsible for his achievements. Hugo maintained that the victory of Waterloo was the victory of the army, not of the general, while also implying that Napoleon's triumphs were his own. An obituary in the legitimist *L'Union* maintained that, far from the government impeding Wellington, he was merely 'the instrument of British policy'.[51]

Finally, the true hero resembled a human meteor; such people 'burn quickly and die young'.[52] Alexander, the greatest of them, conquered the world and died by his mid-thirties; more recently the likes of Shelley, Byron, and Schubert, romantic artists all, died before middle age. Nelson, the opposite of Wellington in many ways, and Wolfe, died at the point of ultimate victory.[53] Wellington neither burned himself out nor ended his career in exile, poverty, or misunderstood disgrace. He 'had none of that compulsive anxiety, or of that theatrical melancholy, which often leads heroes to private asylums'.[54] Or, it could be added, leads them to exile. While Napoleon ended as Prometheus, chained to the rock of St Helena, Wellington's iron control of his talents and passions enabled him to outlive his rival by thirty years and end his days strolling in Hyde Park surrounded by grandchildren and universal adulation. Napoleon in death was shown in apotheosis, the heavens rent by an enormous thunderstorm; the illustration of Wellington dying showed him comfortably asleep in his armchair, surrounded by friends and family, to the accompaniment of typically English drizzle.[55] In all, one was depicted through allegory, the other was shown in comfortable affluent domesticity.

The post-mortem contest and contrast of Napoleon and Wellington was given many meanings by those who used it. It typified the contest of order against revolution (or freedom against feudalism for the Napoleonists); of method against madness (or caution against genius); of modesty against ambition, of civilization against anarchy and even of gentlemen against players. It is notable, for example, that, while English writers stressed Napoleon's professionalism to the point of describing him virtually as a mercenary, Wellington's equally professional outlook on soldiering was played down. In the context of the English tradition that very much distrusted the narrowing effects of specialization, preferring the generalist as the more appropriate embodiment of gentility, this is not, perhaps, altogether surprising, especially when combined with a long-standing suspicion of standing armies and a preference for local militias too incompetent to pose a constitutional threat. However inappropriate, the notion that Waterloo represented the triumph of the gentleman over the professional was another major element in Wellington's Englishness.

While Napoleon's genius made him an aberration who could be admired but not imitated, the qualities of a Wellington—acquired rather than innate, human rather then godlike—could serve as a useful example for others. Biographers were at pains to point out that the abilities of Wellington were such that he would have been successful at any task to which he turned his hand, great or small. The qualities of a Napoleon, in contrast, could come through only in the deeds he performed: without an entire continent at his disposal and an empire to run, he rapidly became absurd. For Wellington's biographers it was a note of praise to assert that he had many of the qualities of a good book-keeper, and to mention that his post-Waterloo career was longer than his time as a serving soldier. Napoleon could not do anything but be himself; he withered and died after power was taken from him, and his efforts to drill a couple of hundred troops on Elba, or cultivate his garden on St Helena, became a symbol of personal decline.

The elaborate construction of the two men had the strange effect of making the defender of hierarchy more of a 'man of the people' than was the son of revolution. As servant of the Crown he acted more in the interests of the people than Bonaparte as the self-appointed protector of 1789. However high his achievements raised him, Wellington was merely a man and a subject, and so others could follow the path he took without endangering everyone else. His career and success were moral object lessons for those who came after him, the main point being that staying within the system was both more honourable and more rewarding than trying to change it. 'Children of England, great and noble as Wellington was, here are qualities you can all imitate. This is the stuff of which heroes are made . . . This path of duty is the *Queen's* highway open to both sexes and to all ranks and conditions . . .'[56] The difficulty was, of course, that it could have been reasonably pointed out that relatively few women, hand-loom weavers or coal miners had much of a chance of being elevated to the peerage, let alone being placed in command of an army or made prime minister. To counter such arguments Wellington was recast in such a way that he became both the epitome of hierarchy and an example of the new meritocracy, a mingling of two conceptions of personal value that had been effectively opposed for at least a century. In this respect his origins as a member of the somewhat lowly Irish aristocracy was useful. While his aristocratic forebears enabled genealogists to stretch his lineage back to the English warrior King Edward I,[57] and enormous stress was placed on his place in the social hierarchy,[58] he was also presented—indeed he developed the impression himself—as a form of self-made man, who rose through talent rather than connection: 'He possessed interest enough to make merit available, but not enough to dispense with it. On a remarkable occasion in after times he spoke, in the House of Peers, of having "raised himself" by his own exertions to the position he then filled.'[59]

Since the sixteenth century, gentility in England has been described in terms of both birth and merit. While Wellington was more than aware of the former—his tendency to prefer members of the aristocracy for officers has been widely noted—the public presentation emphasized the latter. He became the ultimate definition of gentility, of social and political position justified by merit rather than as a right, and thus helped modify the concept which, throughout the nineteenth century, was the English ideological answer to the revolutionary notion of equality. As a response to the Citizen, the English placed greater stress on the Gentleman, and found its most perfect embodiment in the man who was 'far prouder of being an English gentleman than of all his honours and titles'.[60]

While in the context of English politics Wellington could be presented as a self-made man, in that of international competition, his aristocratic birth was stressed. Wellington had the balance, modesty, and moderation of the true gentleman by birth; Napoleon the vulgarity, coarseness, and excitability of the Mediterranean *parvenu*. Wellington's measured tone was contrasted with the egotistical propaganda of France, with authors particularly fixing on Waterloo as the ultimate example; very few fail to mention that, whereas Napoleon issued a triumphant dispatch announcing victory before the battle had started, Wellington's own account was so underplayed that many thought he was announcing a defeat. Again, the evidence was stretched to make it fit the contrast between English understatement and French bombast. Wellington's army frequently complained that his dispatches failed to mention meritorious conduct and gave the impression that he alone was responsible for victory; where these complaints are referred to, his actions are explained away as arising from his belief that all had acted as a team.

National myths grow out of circumstance and survive even when a substantial body of evidence exists to suggest that they may, in fact, be erroneous. The association of character and power embodied by Wellington not only survived throughout the heyday of Empire; the type he represented may be said to have reached its apotheosis in the Second World War. Once again, the image was of an England standing alone, threatened by a foreign tyrant and nearly defeated by a larger, more aggressive foe. None the less it overcame its civilized distaste for fighting, and won through by sheer persistence when all others had given up. The public-school fighter pilots were the descendants of Wellington's aristocratic officers, just as Montgomery's logistical skills and caution were considered sounder than Rommel's dash and flair. Churchill took on the previously Wellingtonian role of the lone outsider convinced that victory was possible and getting on with producing one. As with the Napoleonic wars, the verdict tends to be that England should not have won; that Germany had the greater resources and the better generals and was better able to mobilize an ideologically inspired society, while all Britain had was a dogged determination to defend freedom and civilization. Ultimately, defects of character brought Hitler low, just as they had undermined Napoleon, and British moral superiority enabled the nation to keep its nerve until the foreigner made the fatal mistake which reified his faulty personality. The fact that the crucial error in both cases was to invade Russia made the parallel even more convincing.

Each age needs its myths, and the Victorian age in particular needed its great men. Where the Victorian heroes did not exist, they were invented or, as in the case of Wellington, reconstructed and modified. The picture presented to the public was not false; merely selected, simplified, and overladen with authorial comment to stress comparisons and make points. Wellington was a far more complex, contradictory, and interesting character than he ever admitted or Victorian adulation allowed him to be.

On his death nearly a quarter of a million people filed before his coffin, and more than that number lined the route to St Paul's on the day of the funeral. Most came from precisely those classes of people he had worked so hard to keep out of political power, and yet they came none the less and gave every indication of genuine sadness on his death. Popular admiration for Wellington existed because he represented a national self-image which was valid even for those who disagreed absolutely with the politics he espoused. For all his innumerable faults, his reputation as the man of honour, the embodiment of power without ambition, courage without ostentation, loyalty without greed, care without distasteful public shows of emotion, had become and remained the essence of how the English liked to see themselves—'In him England admires her own likeness.'[61] Rather than concentrating on diplomatic negotiations, industrial and economic resources, his victory became a triumph of national and individual personality, and established the pattern for the popular interpretation of later conflicts as well: 'Wellington may have been less gifted in scope and vision than Napoleon, but he was far superior in character, and it is usually character that wins in the long run.'[62]

## Notes

1. Other nations also had their own collections; in France the *milord* has only recently been challenged by the football hooligan as the abbreviated quintessence of Englishness.
2. Quoted by N. Thompson, 'The Uses of Adversity', in N. Gash (ed.), *Wellington: Studies in the Military and Political Career of the First Duke of Wellington* (Manchester, 1990), 9.
3. *Gentleman's Magazine* (Oct. 1852), 423.
4. A good account of the ceremony can be found in M. Greenhalgh, 'The Funeral of the Duke of Wellington', *Apollo*, (Sept. 1973), 220–6.
5. *Gentleman's Magazine* (Dec. 1852), 592.
6. L. Ettlinger, 'Wellington's Funeral Car', *Journal of the Warburg and Courtauld Institutes*, 3 (1939–40), 254.
7. Ibid.
8. *Illustrated London News (hereafter ILN)*, 30 Oct. 1852, p. 354.
9. Account in *Independence Belge*, reprinted in *ILN*, 27 Nov. 1852, p. 467: 'More than a million and a half men, women and children assembled from the extremities of the kingdom . . . The railways had organised *funeral trains*, which, during all the previous afternoon and night, brought thousands of spectators.'
10. *ILN*, 23 Oct. 1852, p. 335.
11. First published in 1851, the year before Wellington's death.
12. *ILN*, 25 Sept. 1852, p. 242.
13. M. Marrinan, *Painting Politics for Louis-Philippe: Art and Ideology in Orleanist France, 1830–48* (New Haven, 1988), 193. Napoleon's funeral car was destroyed; the Duke's was for years in the crypt of St Paul's and is now at Stratfield Saye.

Not everybody approved; Charles Greville called the Duke's wagon 'tawdry, cumbrous and vulgar', and the reputation for technical expertise it was meant to bolster was damaged when the mechanism for getting the coffin off at St Paul's stuck solid, delaying proceedings for an hour. See Neville Thompson, *Wellington after Waterloo* (London, 1986), 263.

14. *ILN,* 25 Sept. 1852, pp. 241–2.
15. E. B. Hamley, *Wellington's Career: A Military and Political Summary* (Edinburgh, 1860), 66. Macaulay, of course, at one stage sketched out a spoof Wellingtoniad.
16. Extract from the *Assemblée Nationale,* repr. in *ILN,* 25 Sept. 1852, p. 266.
17. See, e.g., H. Fleischmann, *Napoleon adultère* (Paris, 1908); L. A. F. de Bourrienne, *La Jeunesse de Bonaparte* (Oxford, 1907); and, for more modern works, D. Carrington, *Napoleon and his Parents* (London, 1988), and F. M. Richardson, *Napoleon, Bisexual Emperor* (London, 1972). With Wellington, even in 1987 the prospect of a film suggesting he had had an affair with the Duchess of Richmond (which he probably had) drew protests from his descendants and press comment (*Daily Mail,* 27 Oct. 1987).
18. Wellington's heroic reputation settled into orthodoxy more or less with his retirement from politics. During the 1820s, especially, he was more closely identified with current government policies and hence more of a target for factional abuse. Thus, during the passage of the 1829 Catholic Reform Act, opponents blotted out streets named after him, while in the early 1820s radicals like William Cobbett drew strong parallels between the size of the pension given to him and the falling wages of agricultural labourers. See W. Cobbett, *Rural Rides, ed.* G. D. H. and M. Cole (London, 1930), vol. i. 114.
19. E. Longford, *Wellington: The Years of the Sword* (London, 1969); A. H. Brialmont, *Histoire du duc de Wellington,* 3 vols. (Paris, 1852–3); trans. and amended by G. R. Gleig, 4 vols. (London, 1858–60); P. Guedalla, *The Duke* (London, 1931).
20. J. Lemoinne, *Wellington from a French Point of View* (London, 1852), 6.
21. Victor Hugo, *Les Misérables* (London, 1982), 302–3.
22. J. Maurel, *The Duke of Wellington: His Character, his Actions and his Writings* (London, 1853), 10.
23. Ibid. 102.
24. Lord Roberts, quoted in the *Dictionary of National Biography,* xx (Oxford, 1921–2), 1081–94.
25. Hugo, *Les Misérables,* 314. While the attitudes of many commentators are coloured by their responses to Napoleon III, it is clear that in many cases the Emperor's reputation survived his nephew; Hugo (whose father was one of Napoleon's marshals) wrote his rhapsodies on the Emperor while in exile on Jersey.
26. J. W. Fortescue, *A History of the British Army* (London, 1920), x. 222.
27. Arthur Griffith, *The Wellington Memorial* (London, 1897), 255.
28. *The Times,* 15–16 Sept. 1852 (repr. (London, 1852), 124).
29. *The Military Achievements of Field Marshall the Duke of Wellington, by a Peninsular and Waterloo Officer* (London, 1854), ii. 279.
30. Lemoinne, *Wellington,* 20.

31. Wellington's phrase, quoted in Griffith, *Wellington Memorial*, 107, and elsewhere.
32. R. Blakeney, *A Boy in the Peninsula War* (London, 1899), 338; quoted in Longford, *Wellington, 426*.
33. *ILN*, 25 September 1852, p. 266.
34. C. O. Head, *Napoleon and Wellington* (London, 1939), 130. It may be noted how Wellington received renewed attention around the time of the Second World War. One of the most notable contributors to this revival of interest was Jacques Chastenet, who, writing from Paris in 1944, produced a French-language biography that aimed at 'characterizing British methods and temperament' which, he concluded, had neither 'degenerated nor lost their virtue' (*Wellington* (repr. Paris, 1979)).
35. It is notable that French accounts (such as Georges Lefebvre's *Napoleon, 2* vols. (Paris, 1935–6)) contrast the barbarism of English soldiers and Napoleon's attempts to control his men.
36. Hamley, *Wellington's Career*, 20, 41.
37. *ILN*, 18 Sept. 1852, p. 225.
38. For a good summary of Victorian heroism, see W. E. Houghton, The *Victorian Frame of Mind, 1830–1870* (New Haven, 1957), 305–40. For heroism in general, see J. Campbell, *The Hero with a Thousand Faces* (London, 1988), esp. 334–64.
39. *The Times* (1852).
40. Campbell, *The Hero*, 337.
41. Lemoinne, *Wellington*, 34–5.
42. It is notable that one of the few attempts to portray Wellington in the grand allegorical fashion—by James Ward—was a lamentable fiasco. See J. W. M. Hichberger, *Images of the Army: The Military in British Art, 1815–1914* (Manchester, 1988), 14–30.
43. See Marrinan, *Painting Politics*, esp. pp. 158 ff.
44. Fortescue, *History of the British Army*, x. 219; Griffith, *Wellington Memorial*, 225.
45. Socially speaking this was important in the days before pensions and disability allowances. Large numbers of officers in the army spent time and money before and after actions aiding their old troops. Wellington did little, which is one reason that, while London abounds in pubs called the Marquis of Granby or the Raglan—generally because they helped the original proprietors set them up—there are few named after Wellington. In contrast, he did throw the annual Waterloo banquet for officers—still continued—which helped perpetuate the memory of how much the country owed him.
46. Lemoinne, *Wellington*, 17–18.
47. For which see C. Barnett, *Britain and her Army, 1509–1970: A Military, Political and Social Survey* (London, 1970).
48. Sir W. Fraser, *Words on Wellington* (London, 1899), 37.
49. 15 May 1811, quoted in Longford, *Wellington*, 318.
50. Sir W. Napier, quoted in *The Life, Military and Civil, of the Duke of Wellington. Digested from the Materials of W. H. Maxwell and in Part Re-written by an old Soldier* (London, 1852), 420. The English hold the idea of the lone hero saving the nation from the consequences of its own folly very dear. The Second World War,

in which nearly all the fondest notions of Englishness reached their highest point, produced a particularly fine crop of the type.

51. Quoted in *The People's Life of the Duke of Wellington* (London, 1852), introduction.
52. Lemoinne, *Wellington*, 7.
53. Unfortunately there is not enough space here to dwell on the character of Nelson in English myth. He had some of the attributes of Wellington—above all the notion of duty—and much of the more charismatic personality of Napoleon. Although he was a more popular figure, Victorian biographers spent less time on the quality of his personality, not least because of the unfortunate existence of Emma Hamilton. Another figure frequently contrasted with Wellington was the Duke of Marlborough, who similarly led allied armies to victory over the French. While some commentators tended to conclude that Marlborough was the superior soldier, most stressed that Wellington's victory was the more complete.
54. Maurel, *The Duke of Wellington*, 109. The popular myth of the lunatic who thinks he is Napoleon may be noted here; I have never come across any example, in fiction or reality, of someone mad enough to think he was the Duke of Wellington. In England, at least, wanting to be the Emperor was crazy, wanting to be the Duke was wholly understandable and even to be encouraged.
55. H. R. Evans, *The Napoleon Myth* (Chicago, 1905), 36.
56. *The Patriot Warrior*, 277–8.
57. *ILN*, 25 Sept. 1852, p. 267.
58. Even his charger, Copenhagen—an important motif again implicitly linking him with Alexander the Great—was described as being of 'distinguished pedigree'; see *The Life, Military and Civil*, 449–50.
59. *The Times*, 1852.
60. Fortescue, *History of the British Army*, x. 224–5.
61. Lemoinne, *Wellington*, 35.
62. Head, *Napoleon and Wellington*, preface, p. x.

# 13 The Leadership Mystique

Manfred F. R. Kets de Vries

> Leadership is the ability to get men to do what they don't like to do and like it.
>
> (Harry Truman)
>
> Better to reign in hell than serve in heaven
>
> (John Milton)
>
> We are all worms, but I think that I am a glow worm
>
> (Winston Churchill)

When we plunge into the organizational literature on leadership we quickly become lost in a labyrinth: there are endless definitions, countless articles, and never-ending polemics. As far as leadership studies go, it seems that more and more has been studied about less and less, to end up ironically with a group of researchers studying everything about nothing. It prompted one wit to say recently that reading the current world literature on leadership is rather like going through the Parisian telephone directory while trying to read it in Chinese!

The proliferation of literature on effective leadership is amply reflected by the increase in the number of articles in its bible, *Stogdill's Handbook of Leadership.*[1] While the old handbook, published in 1974, listed only 3,000 studies, that number increased to 5,000 within seven years, a pace of publication that has accelerated ever since. It is unfortunate, however, that the popularity of leadership research has not been equated by its relevance. One of the problems has been that too many theories about organizations seem to have had their gestation in the ivory towers of academia. The titles of the theories—new and old—reveal the nature of their contents, plodding and

M. F. R. Kets de Vries, 'The Leadership Mystique', *Academy of Management Executive*, 8/3 (1994), 73–92.

detached, often far removed from the reality of day-to-day life. These kinds of papers continue to appear; fortunately, however, some changes can be noted. An increasing number of scholars have become interested in going beyond the confinement of social science laboratory experiments to observe real leaders in action.

## Why Follow the Leader?

What do leaders really do? What makes people follow leaders? Why are certain types of leaders more effective than others? Do effective leaders have certain characteristics in common?

Although effective leadership strongly depends on a complex pattern of interaction among leader, follower, and situation, in general successful leaders fulfil two roles. One can be called the *charismatic* role, the other the more *instrumental* role. The first role encompasses the way in which leaders *envision*, *empower*, and *energize* in order to motivate their followers. At the same time, every effective leader has to fulfil the *instrumental* role and be an *organizational* designer, and control and *reward* behaviour appropriately.

Coming back to the first dimension of the charismatic role, we all know that a primary part of the leadership role is to determine where a company needs to go and to build commitment to go in that direction. There can be no leadership without vision. Hopefully, everyone who comes within the leader's sphere of influence will align themselves behind this vision. It represents the leader's core values and beliefs, and enables him or her to define the guiding philosophy of the organization: the mission.

Furthermore, in order to arrive at some kind of vision, leaders need to have the knack of perceiving salient trends in the environment. They must be able to process many different kinds of information, and use their perceptions as a basis for judging the direction in which environmental forces are going. And, in studying leaders closely, it becomes clear that they are much better than other people at *managing cognitive complexity*. They are good at searching out and structuring the kind of information they need; their strength lies in making sense of an increasingly complex environment and then in using the data obtained in problem-solving. This talent manifests itself in their knack for simplification, of making highly complex issues very palatable. Carlo De Benedetti of Olivetti, and Percy Barnevik of ABB, are examples of individuals who have used this talent to good effect.

Moreover, if people are to be motivated, if they are to commit themselves to the prevalent vision, the mission statement derived from the vision also needs to be inspirational. To talk merely about increasing the shareholders' wealth, or to stress the company's style ('We want to be fast followers'), is not good enough. It is much more effective to find a niche in the market where one can be the best and say so. The mission statement should be simple, yet it should stretch the minds of all the company's executives.

People in the political arena are particularly good at developing visions and they often excel at articulating them. Such people are inspirational because, when there is dissatisfaction with the existing status quo, they recognize it, are able to present an acceptable alternative, and rally others around them to make it happen. For example, Mahatma Gandhi had a vision of an independent India where Muslims and Hindus would live together in peace. Martin Luther King had a vision of harmony between blacks and whites. John F. Kennedy, when he was president, had a very specific vision of wanting a man on the moon by the end of the Sixties. Gorbachev had a vision of a more open Soviet society. Then there were the darker visions of Adolf Hitler's thousand-year Reich. In the domain of business, we find Ingmar Kamprad of IKEA who wanted to make affordable furniture for the common man, while Mads Øvlisen, the president of the Danish pharmaceutical company Novo-Nordisk, emphasizes his company's desire to improve human life by preventing and treating diseases.

It also helps to have an enemy to focus on while enacting a mission. Doing so gets the competitive juices flowing. Moreover, it provides a focus, concentrating the mind. 'Enemies' help in shaping the organizational identity. And successful companies watch their competitors very closely. They want to know everything about a competitor so that they can build a base of attack. Think about the Pepsi and Coca-Cola wars. Remember Nike, Adidas, and Reebok? Compaq and Dell seem to take pleasure out of destroying each other in their advertisements. And what about Honda, which once used the slogan: 'We will crush, squash, and slaughter Yamaha.' If something like that doesn't get you going, nothing will!

Another factor that differentiates leaders from ordinary mortals is their ability to get people involved. They know how to take advantage of the Pygmalion effect in management. Effective leaders are very good at building alliances and creating commitment so that others will share their vision. They possess great *team-building skills*. They know how to get the best out of their people.

The term empowerment is often used in this context. Leaders make the empowerment of followers seem deceptively simple. The trick is to express high performance expectations. This shows employees that their leader has confidence in their ability to reach certain predetermined goals. Given the needed resources and a facilitating structure (the instrumental part of the leadership role), in most instances empowered employees will do their utmost to oblige. This is the obvious way to build commitment. By empowering people one enhances their self-esteem and feelings of self-confidence, often motivating them to perform beyond expectations. Catherine the Great already seemed to be familiar with the Pygmalion effect in business. Wasn't it she who said, 'Praise loudly, blame softly'? And Napoleon declared that every French soldier carried a marshal's baton in his knapsack. This process of empowering may also work the other way: if you tell a person regularly that he is an idiot, he may start behaving like one. Unfortunately, however, empowerment is difficult for some leaders, given their addiction to power. It is hard for them to let go and push power down in the organization. They lack the perspective to realize that, by empowering their followers in a positive way, they are in fact strengthening their organization and thus their own hold on power. In the domain of the psychology of power, the desire for short-term gains tends to dominate the consideration of long-term benefits.

Truly great leaders realize, however, that envisioning without empowerment leads to a poor enactment of the vision. They recognize that the art of leadership is to create the kind of environment where people have peak experiences, where in their excitement they become completely involved in what they are doing and lose their sense of time. Here, the empowerment process plays a major role, and this should be reflected in the design of the organization. Organizational structures have to be created in which people have a sense of control, a feeling of ownership in what they are doing. As General Patton used to say: 'If you tell people where to go, but not how to get there, you will be amazed at the results.'

Another key word in describing successful leaders is energizing. In every organization there is an enormous amount of free-floating aggressive and affectionate energy. Leaders know how to channel this energy in the right direction. Well-channelled energy will positively influence the enactment process. One should never forget that a vision without action is a form of hallucination.

Here it is important for aggressive energy to be directed externally. People in the organization should not fight each other but fight the competition. As Jack Welch of General Electric used to say, 'I don't want you to fight your neighbour at the next desk. If you are in plastics, I want you to fight Du Pont; if in electronics, I want you to fight Westinghouse.'

The other part of the energy management process is to use affectionate energy appropriately. Every leader, at whatever level, is to some extent a kind of psychiatric social worker, a container of the emotions of his or her subordinates.

The way he or she goes about creating this kind of holding environment distinguishes effective from ineffective leaders. Remember, the derailment of the CEO is seldom caused by his or her being insufficiently informed about the latest techniques in marketing, finance, or production, but rather by a lack of interpersonal skills, a failure to get the best out of the people who may possess this information.

In managing energy in organizations, empathy becomes critical. Interpersonal and intrapersonal sensitivity is a *sine qua non* for leaders. Closely linked to these qualities are the willingness to trust others and the ability to convince them that one is trustworthy. In this context, it is also essential to possess a sense of *generativity*, which basically means obtaining pleasure from helping the next generation. When leaders lack this quality and are envious of others, organizational learning will be stifled and the future of the organization will be endangered.

The envisioning, empowering, and energizing facets of the charismatic role rest on the solid foundation of the instrumental role. The elements of the instrumental role—organizational design, control, and reward—have been amply described in the leadership literature and so I will not expand on them here. I do want to emphasize, however, that the combination of the charismatic role with the instrumental role can be very powerful: the charismatic part of leadership becomes more concrete and focused, and the instrumental part becomes more flexible and human.

Obviously implicit in a number of the dimensions of the two main leadership roles are characterological issues.[2] Certain aspects of character make some leaders more suitable than others to taking on these roles. The singularities in a person's cognitive, affective, and behavioural functioning affect the way a person adapts to the external environment.

Looking at the current literature on leadership traits, we find that, although the quantity of this literature is overwhelming and often confusing, there is a certain amount of commonality among the findings.[3] Among the traits that have been discerned regularly among effective leaders (confirmed by my own observations) are *conscientiousness* (which includes dependability, achievement orientation, and perseverance), *extroversion, dominance, self-confidence, energy, agreeableness* (meaning flexibility and sense of trust), *intelligence, openness to experience* (including a lack of ethnocentricism), and *emotional stability*. A closer look at many of these traits, however, makes it clear that each of them can be the subject of a heated polemic about its true meaning and its applicability to specific character types.[4] In addition, particularly in the clinical literature, labels such as agreeableness and emotional stability may open an enormous can of worms. It can be argued that leaders will be more or less effective depending on the specific combination of these traits. To understand these building blocks of character, we have to go to the roots of leaders' developmental histories. (For an overview of the various aspects of effective leadership mentioned in the first section of this paper, see Fig. 13.1.)

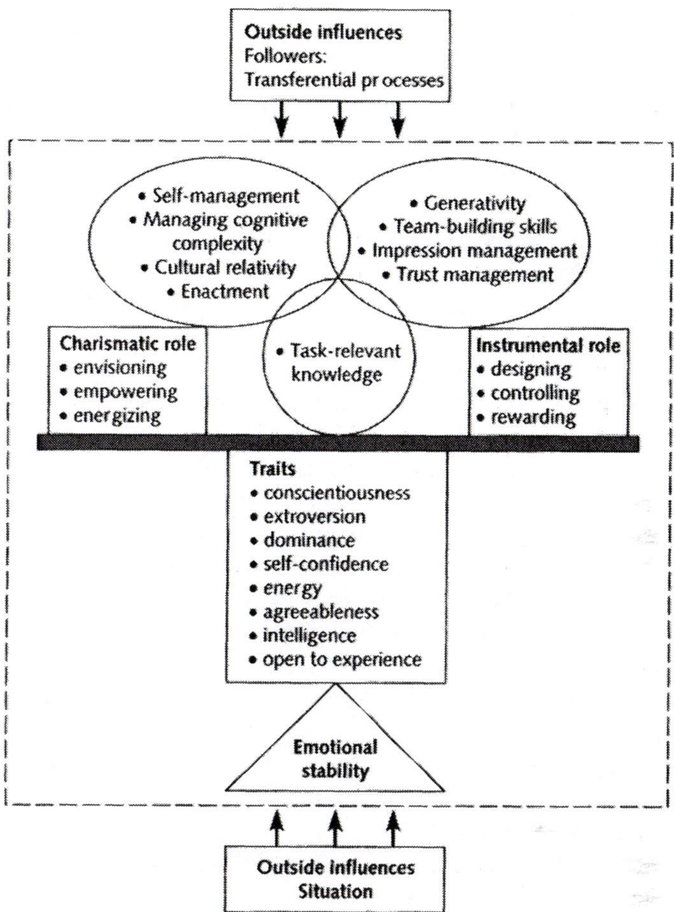


**Fig. 13.1.** Leadership in a global context.

## Deciphering the Roots of Leadership

Describing some of the behavioural patterns and traits that make for effective leadership is one thing, but to explain how they evolve we have to go beyond the obvious and ask deeper questions. Where does this vision and sense of mission come from? What is the source of charisma? How do these various traits develop?

And more pragmatically, what differentiates two powerful and visionary leaders such as Jack Welch and Robert Maxwell? Why should one succeed while the other derails? How much of the credit or blame for their company's situation lies with them personally? My clinical work with executives has shown that the personality of a top executive influences the strategy, corporate culture, and even structure of his or her organization to a much greater extent than most people, in particular executives themselves, are likely or willing to admit.

In organizations, people tend to seek the holy grail of the perfect business model managed by a logical, rational leader. There seems to be an obstinate survival of the myth of rationality. Many people cling to the reassuring notion that humans are logical decision-makers, that irrational forces do not play a role in organizational life.

Of course there is a rational element to actions of senior executives. Leaders process large amounts of information; they look for strategic niches; they define the parameters of the corporate culture; they create the structures and set strategy. In spite of this preoccupation with rational data-processing, however, even the best of leaders may be driven by motives that are less sensible and obvious than they seem. For example, was Henry Ford's introduction of the assembly line based on a rational analysis of the economic benefits of division of labour? Did he do an in-depth quantitative analysis of all the relevant economic factors? Or were there irrational elements that pushed him in that direction? Could one of his motivations for wanting to make cheap cars for farmers have been to redeem himself in the eyes of his own father, who was a farmer? Similar speculations can be made about the behaviour of Walt Disney. How much had Disney's extraordinary vision to do with his own unhappiness as a child?

In the best of all worlds, a leader's vision is compatible with external forces in the environment. But in many instances that is not the case. As many of us have learned the hard way, a CEO can be completely derailed by his or her hidden motives, and not only make life miserable for his or her staff but disrupt the organization's equilibrium enough to contribute significantly to its decline. As clinical investigation shows, the reasons why leaders have a particular outlook tend to be deeply rooted. All of them are driven and influenced by a very strong, vivid inner theatre—a specific script that determines a person's character. This inner theatre is what drives them to externalize private motives and present them on a public stage. Consequently, transcending the model of the economic man and looking closely at the inner theatre of the top executive will give us a unique perspective on the dynamics of an organization.

But how do we go about it? How do we arrive at insights about this inner theatre? How do we decipher a person's character? What I have found is that putting executives on the couch (metaphorically speaking) proves to be a good way of analysing the conflicts and motivations that occur within their organizations. It adds an additional dimension to understanding organizational dynamics.

I should explain here the basis of my clinical approach to management. The clinical paradigm, which takes concepts from psychoanalysis, dynamic psychiatry, family systems theory, and cognition, rests on a number of premisses. The first is that all behaviour is somehow determined. What at first glance may seem completely irrational may on closer inspection have an explanation and a deeper rationale. Secondly, there is such a thing as the unconscious. We are not always aware of many of our wishes and fantasies; a considerable amount of our actions and behaviour appears to be beyond conscious awareness. Furthermore, in order to understand behaviour patterns it is important to realize that intrapsychic and interpersonal processes determine the way we act and make decisions. Patterns of behaviour acquired in the past strongly influence present and future behaviour.

All of us possess some kind of inner theatre and are motivated by a specific inner script. Over time, through interactions with caretakers, teachers, and other influential people, this inner theatre develops. The internalized core conflictual relationship themes which make up this inner theatre form the core of an individual's personality and are the matrix on which behaviour and actions are based.[5] Our internal theatre, in which the patterns that underlie our character come into play, influences our behaviour throughout our lives and plays an essential role in the moulding of leaders.

## Setting the Stage

Clinical observation confirms that even the most successful organizational leaders are not exactly rational, logical, sensible, and dependable human beings, but are in fact prone to irrational behaviour. That being the case, the application of the clinical paradigm will be helpful in providing insight into the underlying reasons for their behaviour and action. Organizations cannot perform successfully if the quirks and irrational processes that are part and parcel of the leader's inner theatre are ignored. This dimension of human action needs attention if one wants to engage in preventive maintenance and successful intervention.

In my teaching and consulting work, I push executives to open the curtains of their inner theatre, to find the deeper meaning behind their actions. I want them to understand that they, and sometimes their organization, get into trouble because of unconscious processes they neither see, understand, nor accept. I have learned from bitter experience, however, that it is very difficult for most executives to delve into the dark corners of their own psyche. In many cases they cannot do it alone; they need help. And it can be even harder for them to understand how strongly something as personal as their inner theatre can affect their company.

To facilitate the sometimes painful process of self-examination, in my MBA and executive classes I ask participants to become organizational detectives by studying well-known business leaders and their companies, to try to make sense out of their behaviour and actions. Leaders such as Jack Welch, Percy Barnevik, Richard Branson, Carlo de Benedetti, and Ernest Saunders are the subjects of key case studies used in my classes. To set the investigative process in motion, I ask participants leading questions. For example, why did Henry Ford of the Ford Motor Company stick to the Model T for nineteen years in spite of changing market conditions and an enormous drop in market share? Why did he behave so strangely and erratically? When his engineers presented him with a slightly modified version of the Model T, he flew into a tantrum and kicked the car apart. Why? What made him so unwilling to change the car? What did the car symbolize to him? Why did he unleash a reign of terror in the company, employing henchmen like Harry Bennett, a person with close connections to the Detroit underworld? What lay behind his strange political activities, his isolationism, and his anti-Semitism? Why did he consistently undermine his son Edsel's efforts to steer the company back on course? And what was it, despite all these quirks, that made him such a visionary? He was the first person to recognize the value of using the assembly line to make a mass-produced car at a time when consumer trends were pointing in the opposite direction. What were his anxieties, his defences, his conflicts? What were his strengths and his weaknesses? What differentiated him from other people? What could be said about his character? What made him such an innovator?

Ford's personal history gives us insight into many of his seemingly bizarre actions. He was extremely close to his mother, whom he felt loved him unconditionally. Unfortunately, she died when Ford was 13. Ford's relationship with his father was very difficult. According to Ford, his father disapproved of Ford's mechanical bent, his wish to leave the farm, and his vision of the future of the automobile, although Ford's sister felt that their father was not nearly as opposed to his son's ideas as Ford led people to believe. In any case, Ford's relationships with other men were never intimate, and he had few real friends. A quotation from the man who Ford hired to run the personnel department is very revealing:

A judge of national repute once said to me, 'I have a great admiration for Henry Ford, but there is one thing about him that I regret and can't understand, and that is his inability to keep his executives and old time friends around him. The answer is that it is not a matter of inability, but disability. He can't help it. He is built that way.'[6]

Observing that 'he is built that way' is not enough, however. The challenge of organizational detective work is to find the underlying reasons for his peculiar leadership style; to understand better the critical dimensions that made up his inner script. To arrive at deeper insight in our discussions, theories are introduced, and inferences are made, shot down, and replaced by others. And, while struggling with their confusion, participants gradually arrive at a better idea of what kind of person Ford really was, the nature of his interpersonal relationships, his defensive patterns, and how his style affected the organization. They begin to realize the extent to which his behaviour in the Ford Motor Company was coloured by his personal history. They realize how much Ford was a prisoner of his past.[7]

Interestingly enough, class participants occasionally begin to see the symptoms of similar patterns of behaviour and character traits in themselves. At times this may be frightening, but this process of recognition generally makes them think. My experience is that this process triggers self-reflection and growing insight. Fledgling and experienced consultants, entrepreneurs, investment bankers, or industrialists all profit from this new way of looking at organizational dynamics. It gives them a better idea of how to master processes such as power, authority, influence, and control. It makes them realize how easily they themselves could get stuck in vicious circles and become prisoners of their own past. Furthermore, they may become aware of the kind of organizations they should avoid, realizing the extent to which certain types of organization may adversely affect them mentally or even physically.

A play like Arthur Miller's *Death of a Salesman* or films such as Orson Welles's *Citizen Kane* or Ingmar Bergman's *Wild Strawberries* can provide further insight into these elusive phenomena. The right side of the brain, the part responsible for more intuitive processes, is not exactly nurtured in the daily routine of an organization. But that is even more reason to become sensitized to what makes a person or an organization really tick.

During this process of mutual exploration, many questions come up in my classes which I cannot answer immediately and which lead to further investigation. Eventually, these deliberations lead to a kind of closure. My work with my patients has also been an important contributing factor to the understanding of executive behaviour: many of their initially puzzling remarks have helped me greatly with the process of discovery and self-discovery.

In addition, an executive seminar which I have been teaching for a number of years at INSEAD has also helped me in clarifying issues associated with leadership. This very unusual programme, different from all the others I participate in, focuses on the life case study. Spending three intensive weeks (spread out over a period of six months) working with twenty senior executives, discussing their lives, their major concerns, their fears, and their efforts to change their lives, is an emotionally draining experience. This exercise of mutual problem-solving, combined with a mirroring process in which participants are brought firmly up against the image others have of them, can be dramatically powerful. The discovery that people are not alone in facing a particular type of problem, that they are not that different from other people, can counteract frequently intense feelings of isolation and give a sense of reintegration with the human race.

Of course, helping executives understand how their behaviour affects their companies is not the same as psychoanalysing a company. What I try to do in my seminars, in consultation, and in therapy, is to bring out the underlying dynamics of an individual executive's problems—these core conflictual relationship themes or inner scripts that make up character—and look at how they affect his or her organization. I want executives to face those themes and become aware that certain problems are deeply rooted, and cannot be resolved by merely introducing a new planning system, changing appraisal and reward systems, writing up new job descriptions, or tinkering with the organization's design. I want executives to face their weaker points, obtain deeper insights about their ways of functioning, understand their defensive structure and character traits, and recognize how their behaviour affects their organization. I want them to recognize the psychological pressures leaders are particularly subjected to. And I want executives to become self-confident enough to create a culture of trust and fair play in their organization, in which one doesn't kill the messenger of bad news and one allows people to engage in contrarian thinking.

Creating this kind of company culture is much more easily said than done. Neutralizing the darker side of leadership can be quite difficult. Many leaders are not up to the challenge. Many of them prefer to remain blind and deaf to what is happening around them. Executives have to look beyond the superficial, however, and realize that in organizational change and development there is no such thing as a quick fix. They need to understand the extent to which they, and ultimately their organizations, are influenced by their own inner theatre; they need to realize the deeper meaning of their actions.

## Psychological Pressures on Leadership

What are some of the psychological themes that emerge when talking to leaders? What preoccupies them? What are the pressures that trouble them? Dealing with their inner world, we quickly recognize that making it to a top position is not necessarily a bed of roses. Along with the perks comes a great deal of pressure. First, there is the problem of the loneliness of command. The moment one becomes top dog, old relationships are going to be disturbed. The original support network changes. Every move leaders make has a great deal of symbolism attached to it. If they have to make critical decisions about people's future, they cannot be as close to old colleagues as they once were. Whether the new leader likes it or not, some distance has to be kept. This is not always easy. After all, leaders still have their own dependency needs, and who is going to take care of them? This can cause a considerable amount of stress and frustration.

Then there is the troublesome problem of envy. Many people look at the power and trappings of leadership and become envious. To some senior executives, the envy of others can be extremely disturbing and may cause a great deal of anxiety.

There is the fear—not always unreasonable—that others will try to take away what has cost the leader so much to gain. The fear of losing the power of office, being the subject of envy, can put a debilitating strain on leaders. They become, ironically, afraid of success. Some may act accordingly and behave in a dysfunctional manner, snatching defeat out of the jaws of victory, through self-destructive behaviour. Others may become depressed, and seemingly paralysed by the demands of decision-making. In certain instances, clinical investigation demonstrates that this dysfunctional behaviour is based on the irrational, originally unconscious, fear of surpassing parents' accomplishments. Unconsciously, the person may believe that such a victory could have terrible consequences. They fear (correctly, in some cases) that it will cause an envious parent to withdraw affection, or even provoke a hostile reaction.[8]

Another cause of depression for an executive who has finally made it to the top may be the sense of 'what now?' The goals that the leader has worked for all his or her life have been accomplished; there is nothing else to strive for. One can call this sense of unease 'the Faust Syndrome', the melancholia of having completed everything. Again, if these feelings are not dealt with, they may lead to irresponsible action as the individual tries to fight emerging depression.

A frequent problem is what Freud described as the phenomenon of a 'false connection', meaning that followers may not perceive and respond to their leader according to the reality of the situation, but as if the leader is a significant figure from the past, such as a parent or other authoritative person.[9] This misplaced attachment, known as transference in clinical terminology, is an ubiquitous element of the human condition, a way in which we process information and organize experience. It is a strange but nevertheless a very real process: the emotional legacy of the past pushes followers into displacing many of their historic hopes and fantasies onto the present leader. A frequent result of this process of displacement of person and time is that followers will try to do anything they can to please their leader.

In many instances, this need to idealize authority figures (a universal need that is part and parcel of our early developmental processes) is likely to meet with a very receptive response, particularly from leaders with strong narcissistic dispositions. Leaders of this type welcome the outpouring of applause and admiration. Even worse, they may arrive at the stage where they cannot function without this kind of emotional fix. Of course, it is possible for this kind of mutual admiration society to create a lot of energy in the system. It can be useful in aligning and energizing subordinates in order to enact a common vision. The leader's ability to transform what were once only fantasies into reality adds to the heady experience of being on top.

However, the danger of this form of interaction is that some leaders may find themselves in a hall of mirrors, hearing and seeing only what they want to hear or see. And, even worse, if people do not oblige—if followers are unwilling to share these leaders' distorted view of the world—they may throw an adult version of a tantrum, re-enacting patterns of childhood behaviour. Such leaders will perceive non-compliance as a direct attack on the very essence of their personality, given their fragile sense of self-esteem. Past feelings of helplessness and humiliation may be revived, leading to blind rage. However, this time, given the power they wield, their tantrums make a great difference. The impact of their rage on their immediate environment can be devastating.

Predictably, such outbursts of rage will intimidate people and can lead to regressive, childlike behaviour and a climate of dependency among followers. The dynamics of such leaders' lives are very simple: people are either for them or against them in a world of black and white. There is no room for nuances. Independent thinkers cannot survive; those who do not collaborate immediately become the new villains; deviants from these leaders' ideals are assigned an inferior, sub-human status and are targets for their anger

Most people quickly fall in line and collude, either passively or actively, with the leader's victimization of those who are not prepared to conform. This is self-protective in two ways. First of all, it limits the possibility that one will become a victim of the leader oneself. Secondly, 'identifying with the aggressor' is a way of resolving one's sense of helplessness and powerlessness in the face of totalitarianism. Feeling close to the leader—becoming part of the system—creates the illusion of being more powerful oneself.[10]

Thus the individual, in this special form of identification with the aggressor (which does not necessarily happen on a conscious level), assumes the latter's attributes and thus transforms himself or herself from threatened to threatening. It is basically a defensive manœuvre, a way of controlling the severe anxiety caused by the perceived aggressor. The person in the one-down position hopes to acquire some of the power that the other person possesses. The wish to obtain some of the dominant person's power can explain why people hang in there, in spite of the abrasive behaviour of the aggressor. For example, this process may explain to some extent the kind of group dynamics which prevailed in the companies run by the late Robert Maxwell.

This process of 'identification with the aggressor', the inducement to participate in a form of group think, is accompanied by certain rites of passage, the least subtle of which is the pressure to participate in the violence directed towards the aggressor's designated enemies. Sharing the guilt in this way becomes a sign of commitment which the leader can feed with an endless supply of people to be made into villains. The majority of followers, torn between love and fear of their leader, will submit to the demands put upon them. They are presented with many handy scapegoats on which to enact group revenge when things do not go the way the leader wants—tangible entities on which to project everything of which they are afraid, everything that is perceived as evil and threatening to the system. This kind of development can have terrifying results. It can lead to the complete self-destruction of an organization or, in the case of a national leader, the end of an entire nation.

These negative personality traits are present to a lesser degree in many individuals, but, as far as leaders are concerned, the pressure of their exposed position can encourage extreme manifestations of their emotional disability. The question is how do these traits develop, and why are some leaders more affected than others?

## The Inner Theatre of Leaders

The shaping of an individual's personality begins early in life. Child psychologists have pointed out that the first three years of life are particularly critical to development. These are the years during which the core patterns of personality are shaped; it is the period when we emerge as a person with a sense of our own body, gender identity, name, mind, and personal history. The foundations are laid for the kind of person we are going to be, and are likely to remain, for the rest of our life. Of course, this does not mean that later life experiences are of no importance, but these tend not to have the same impact as the ones we encounter early in life.

The clinical term for the changes that take place during these early years of life is narcissistic development. Narcissism is the engine that drives people. And narcissism and leadership are intricately connected.

A healthy dose of narcissism is essential for human functioning. It is the danger of excess, particularly in the case of leaders, which gives narcissism its often derogatory connotation. We may be amused by Oscar Wilde's statement that 'to love oneself is the beginning of a life-long romance', but, when we consider how the word is generally used, narcissism evokes associations of egotism, self-centredness, and exaggerated self-love. After all, who wants to be compared to that unfortunate young man, the Narcissus of Greek myth, who fell in love with his own reflection and pined to death?

Narcissism is a strange thing, a double-edged sword. Having either too much or too little of it can throw a person off balance, and when that equilibrium is lost, instability may develop in the core of an individual's personality. We must remember that narcissistic elements help constitute the basis of self-esteem and identity.

Narcissism (when we go beyond the everyday usage of the word) refers to a stage of infantile development we all have to pass through, a stage during which the growing child derives pleasure from his own body and its functions. And this early stage is a very delicate time in the child's life. The kind of treatment received during this critical period of development will very much colour his or her view of the world right through to adulthood.

The role of parents or caretakers in the development of narcissism is obviously very important. Have they been supportive or inconsistent? Have family circumstances meant that the child has experienced a series of deprivations? The key question is whether the child received a large enough narcissistic supply. Was a solid foundation laid for positive self-regard and initiative in establishing stable relationships? Did the child have the opportunity to acquire a healthy dose of self-esteem? Unfortunately, of course, no parent is perfect. Becoming a person is not at all like that comfortable period of intra-uterine existence when everything was automatically taken care of. In most instances, growing up implies a certain amount of inevitable frustration. For normal development, however, frustration should occur in tolerable doses.

In an attempt to deal with this sense of frustration, the child tries to retain the original impression of the perfection and bliss of her or his early years by creating both a grandiose, exhibitionistic image of his or her self and an all-powerful, idealized image of her or his parents (the latter taking on the roles of saviours and protectors). Psychoanalysts call these two narcissistic configurations the 'grandiose self' and the 'idealized parent image'.[11] Over time, if the child receives what we call 'good enough' care, these two configurations which make up the bipolar self will be tamed by the forces of reality. Parents, siblings, and other important figures in the child's life will modify his or her exhibitionistic displays, channelling grandiose fantasies of power and glory in proper directions, thus laying the foundation for realistic ambitions, stable values, well-defined career interests, and a secure sense of self-esteem and identity.

But not everyone is lucky enough to have a special bond, or to receive age-appropriate frustration. Many things can go wrong in the process of growing up. In some situations, prolonged disappointment due to parental overstimulation, understimulation, or highly inconsistent, arbitrary behaviour can lead to problems of a narcissistic nature. And if violence and abuse are part and parcel of the package, the stage is set for an inner theatre complete with malevolent imagery.

The cartoonist Matt Groening once drew an illuminating but very disturbing cartoon. In the drawing is an extremely unhappy, monstrous-looking little child who has been tied up and locked in a cell. Two pairs of eyes are looking through the cell-door windows, and the caption reads, 'I hope you realize you're breaking our hearts.' This cartoon, which portrays the alarmingly mixed signals given by some parents, is a good illustration of the kind of child-rearing which contributes to one's *not* becoming a healthy individual.

Children who have been exposed to these types of parenting may come to believe that they cannot reliably depend on anyone's love or loyalty. As adults, they will act according to these convictions. These are people who, despite their claims to self-sufficiency, are troubled in the depth of their being by a sense of deprivation, anger, and emptiness. In order to cope with these feelings, and perhaps as a cover for their insecurity, their narcissistic needs will turn into obsessions. Such individuals become fixated on issues of power, beauty, status, prestige, and superiority. They try continually to manœuvre others into strengthening their shaky sense of self-esteem. They are also preoccupied with thoughts of getting even for the hurts (real or imagined) they experienced during childhood. And, in the case of public figures, these scenes may be acted out on a world stage later in life.

## Reactive and Constructive Narcissism

From many in-depth studies of leaders I have concluded that a considerable percentage of them have become what they are for negative reasons. On many occasions I have found that, due to hardships encountered in childhood, they are driven to prove the world wrong. After having been belittled and maltreated when young, they are determined to show everyone that they amount to something as adults. Some may even suffer from what may be called (after Alexander Dumas's novel) the 'Monte Cristo Complex': they have a very strong need to get even for the wrongs done to them at earlier periods in their lives.

Pierre Cardin, the French couturier, may be an example of the 'Monte Cristo Complex'. Growing up as an Italian youngster in France, Cardin was teased by other children and called names like 'macaroni', all of which hurt. Second-class status is not easy to take. Cardin's family had lost most of their possessions during the war, and this had affected his father very badly.[12] As a result his father drifted from job to job, adding to the sense of upheaval in the family. The young Cardin was kept going, in spite of all the turmoil around him, by the strong support of his mother. (This brings to mind Freud's famous statement that the child who has been the 'mother's undisputed darling [will] retain throughout life the triumphant feeling, the confidence in success, which not seldom brings actual success with it'.) We can speculate, however, that this whole experience left Cardin with a sense of having to get back at his tormentors, to show them that he amounted to something, to become the redeemer of the family. And he certainly did. Perhaps because once people had looked down at him and his family, he became a specialist in levelling. He democratized fashion and brought *haute couture* to the common man. At present, sales under his name amount to over a billion dollars. Almost 200,000 people work for his label through more than 840 licensing arrangements in 125 countries. He has put his name on everything. He even thumbed his nose at the French upper classes by buying the famous restaurant Maxim, once their favourite watering hole. But no longer: Maxim has been democratized. You can now eat there with salesmen from Cleveland!

Pierre Cardin's example illustrates that it is entirely possible for a person with a narcissistic disposition to be very successful. In some of my earlier writings, I made a distinction between people guided by this kind of reactive narcissism driven by a need to get even and somehow to come to grips with their past, and a type of constructive narcissism (individuals who are well-balanced, have a positive self-regard, and a secure sense of self-esteem).[13] Thus, to summarize these two ways of dealing with the world, constructive narcissists have the capacity for introspection; they radiate a sense of positive vitality and are capable of empathic feelings. Narcissists of this type can become the kind of excellent leader that I described at the beginning of this article. This contrasts with the reactive narcissists, who are continually trying to boost a defective sense of self-esteem and are preoccupied with emotions such as envy, spite, revenge, or vindictive triumph over others. (Some reactive narcissists, however, eventually overcome their original feelings of bitterness and are motivated by reparation—that is, trying to prevent others from suffering as they have.)

True reactive narcissists tend to have a grandiose sense of self-importance. They habitually take advantage of others in order to achieve their own ends. They also live under the illusion that their problems are unique. Then there is a sense of entitlement, the feeling that they deserve especially favourable treatment and that the rules set for others do not apply to them. Furthermore, they are addicted to compliments—they can never get enough. They lack empathy, being unable to experience how others feel. Last, but certainly not least, their envy of others, and their rage when prevented from getting their own way, can be formidable.[14]

Reactive narcissism is probably the most salient indicator of defective leadership. It is at the centre of a host of characterological problems such as paranoid, schizoid, passive-aggressive, histrionic, and compulsive behaviour patterns or 'neurotic styles'.[15] What is already bad enough in an individual can, in an organizational context, lead to serious repercussions. The observation of senior executives shows that parallels can be drawn between individual pathology—excessive use of one neurotic style, such as reactive narcissism—and organizational pathology, the latter resulting in poorly functioning organizations, or what I have called elsewhere 'neurotic' organizations.'[16] In these earlier writings, I illustrate how the 'irrational' personality characteristics of principal decision-makers can seriously affect the overall management process. At the head of a 'neurotic' organization (especially one in which power is highly centralized) one is likely to find a top executive whose rigid neurotic style is strongly mirrored in the nature of inappropriate strategies, structures, and organizational cultures of his or her firm. If this situation continues for too long, the organization may self-destruct. A comparison of the most recent Fortune 500 list with the same list of twenty years ago is very revealing. A large number of the firms listed in the early 1970s are no longer in existence.

In classifying these various neurotic types, I have made a distinction among the dramatic, suspicious, detached, depressive and compulsive organizations, each with its unique, salient features.'[17] For a description of how—among these various neurotic types—inner scripts, personal styles, organizational types, culture, and strategy interrelate, see the summary in Table 13.1.

Table 13.1. The characteristics of 'neurotic' organizations

| Type | Organization | Executive | Culture | Strategy | Guiding Theme |
|---|---|---|---|---|---|
| Dramatic | Too primitive for its many products and broad market: over-centralization obstructs the development of effective information systems; second-tier executives retain too little influence in policy-making. | Needs attention, excitement activity, and stimulation; feels a sense of entitlement, has a tendency towards extremes. | Dependency needs of subordinates complement 'strong-leader' tendencies of chief executive; leader is idealized by 'mirroring' subordinates; leader is catalyst for subordinates' initiative and morale. | Hyperactive, impulsive, venturesome, dangerously uninhibited; executive prerogative to initiate bold ventures; diversifications and growth rarely consistent or integrated; action for action's sake; non-participative decision-making. | Grandiosity: 'I want to get attention from and impress the people who count in my life.' |
| Suspicious | Elaborate information-processing; abundant analysis of external trends; centralization of power. | Vigilantly prepared to counter any and all attacks and personal threats; hypersensitive; cold and lacks emotional expression; suspicious, distrustful, and insists on loyalty; overinvolved in rules and details to secure complete control; craves information; sometimes vindictive. | 'Fight-or-flight' culture, including dependency, fear of attack, emphasis on the power of information, intimidation, uniformity, lack of trust. | Reactive, conservative; overly analytical; diversified; secretive. | 'Some menacing force is out to get me; I had better be on my guard. I cannot really trust anybody.' |
| Detached | Internal focus, insufficient scanning of external environment, self-imposed barriers to free flow of information. | Withdrawn and not involved; lacks interest in present or future; sometimes indifferent to praise or criticism. | Lack of warmth or emotions; conflicts, jockeying for power; insecurity. | Vacillating, indecisive, inconsistent; the product of narrow, parochial perspectives. | 'Reality does not offer satisfaction; interactions with other will fail; it is safer to remain distant.' |

| | | | | | |
|---|---|---|---|---|---|
| Depressive | Ritualistic; bureaucratic; inflexible; hierarchical; poor internal communications; resistant to change; impersonal. | Lacks self-confidence, self-esteem, or initiative; fears success and tolerates mediocrity or failure; depends on messiahs. | Lack of initiative; passivity; negativity; lack of motivation; ignorance of markets; leadership vacuum. | 'Decidiphobia'; attention focused inward; lack of vigilance over changing market conditions; drifting with no sense of direction; confinement to antiquated 'mature' markets. | 'It is hopeless to change the course of events; I am just not good enough.' |
| Compulsive | Rigid formal codes; elaborate information systems; ritualized evaluation procedures; thoroughness; exactness; a hierarchy in which individual managers' status derives directly from specific positions. | Tends to dominate organization from top to bottom; insists that others conform to tightly prescribed procedures and rules; dogmatic or obstinate personality; perfectionist or is obsessed with detail, routine, rituals, efficiency, and lockstep organization. | Rigid, inward-directed, insular; subordinates are submissive, uncreative, insecure. | Tightly calculated and focused, exhaustive evaluation; slow, unadaptive; reliance on a narrow established theme; obsession with a single aspect of strategy; e.g. cost-cutting or quality, the exclusion of other factors. | 'I don't want to be at the mercy of events; I have to master and control all the things affecting me.' |

**Manfred R. F. Kets de Vries**

# Struggling with the Demon

For leaders who are caught up in a web of irrationality at the head of a neurotic organization, escape is not easy. In most cases, they cannot break out of their self-constructed prison alone. They are the captives of their character and they will need some kind of professional help to break the chains that restrict their behaviour and lead to dysfunctional organizations. Leaders must recognize the potential destructiveness of their actions, and understand the extent to which past experiences can influence their present and future behaviour. In talking to leaders, however, I am often struck by the number of them who fail to realize the continuity in their past, present, and future. These people make the same mistakes over and over again because they are unable to recognize certain repetitive patterns in their behaviour which have become dysfunctional. They are stuck in a vicious circle, and do not know how to get out. It makes one realize that mental health really comes down to having choices in life. The Danish philosopher Kierkegaard expressed the sadness and poignancy of this when he said that the tragedy of life is that we can only understand it backwards, but we have to live it forwards.

Freud once told the novelist Stefan Zweig that all his life he had been 'struggling with the demon'—the demon of irrationality. Wise leaders do the same. They realize the extent to which unconscious, irrational processes affect their behaviour. They recognize the limits of rationality and become more aware of their own character traits. Leaders who fail to take their irrational side into account, however, are like captains who blindly plough their ships into a field of icebergs; the greatest danger is hidden below the surface.

Whatever happens to leaders, however enlightened they may be, it is important that they keep a check on their narcissism. The hubris of leaders is all too familiar, and narcissism and hubris go hand in hand. Glory is a great temptress and the pursuit of glory can be surprisingly self-destructive. All too often, insufficient heed is paid to its dangers. For leaders, the narcissistic pull is frequently too strong. As Napoleon (an expert on the topic) once said: 'Glory is fleeting but obscurity lasts forever.' In pursuing glory, many leaders end up as victims of hubris. Such an ending could be avoided, however, if they paid attention to their intrapsychic life, and found help in exploring their blind spots.

In their interpersonal relationships, leaders who are wary of the dangers of hubris should bear in mind what I term the three H's of leadership: humility, humanity, and a good sense of humour. Such qualities help to prevent excessive organizational neurosis, and may contribute to emotional stability. As someone who obviously had some knowledge of leadership once said to me, 'Any time you think you possess power as a leader, try ordering around someone else's dog!'

## Notes

1. B. M. Bass, *Stodgill's Handbook of Leadership* (New York: Free Press, 1981).
2. M. F. R. Kets de Vries and S. Perzow, *Handbook of Character Studies* (Madison, Conn. International Universities Press, 1991).
3. Bass, *Stodgill's Handbook*; M. R. Barrick and M. K. Mount, 'The Big Five Personality Dimensions and Job Performance: A Meta-Analysis', *Personnel Psychology*, 44 (1991), 1–26.
4. T. Millon, *Disorders of Personality* (New York: John Wiley & Sons, 1981).
5. L. Luborsky, P. Crits-Chrisoph, J. Minz, and A. Auerbach, *Who Will Benefit from Psychotherapy?* (New York: Basic Books, 1988).
6. S. S. Marquis, *Henry Ford: An Interpretation* (Boston: Little Brown, 1923).
7. A. Jardim, *Henry Ford and the Ford Motor Company* (Cambridge, Mass.: MIT Press, 1969).
8. M. F. R. Kets de Vries, *Leaders, Fools and Impostors* (San Francisco, Calif.: Josey-Bass, 1993).
9. J. Breuer and S. Freud, 'Studies on Hysteria', *The Standard Edition of the Complete Psychological Works of Sigmund Freud*, (London: Hogarth Press, 1956), ii.
10. A. Freud, *The Ego and the Mechanisms of Defense* (New York: International Universities Press, 1936).
11. H. Kohut, *The Analysis of the Self* (Madison, Conn.: International Universities Press, 1971); H. Kohut and E. S. Wolf, 'The Disorders of the Self and their Treatment: An Outline', *International Journal of Psychoanalysis*, 58 (1978), 413–26.
12. R. Morais, *Pierre Cardin: The Man Who Became a Label* (New York: Bantam Press, 1991).
13. M. F. R. Kets de Vries and Danny Miller, 'Narcissism and Leadership: An Object Relations Perspective', *Human Relations*, (1985), 583–601; M. F. R. Kets de Vries, *Prisoners of Leadership* (New York: Wiley, 1989); Kets de Vries, *Leaders, Fools and Impostors*.
14. O. Kernberg, *Borderline Conditions and Pathological Narcissism* (New York: Jason Aronson, 1975).
15. Kets de Vries and Perzow, *Handbook of Character Studies*.
16. See above.
17. M. F. R. Kets de Vries and D. Miller, *Unstable at the Top* (New York: New American Library, 1987).

# 14 Leadership: An Alienating Social Myth?

Gary Gemmill and Judith Oakley

As a result of deeply ingrained cultural assumptions, approaches to the study of leadership usually start with the idea that leaders are unquestionably necessary for the functioning of an organization. Belief in hierarchy and the necessity of leaders represents an unrecognized ideology which takes its power chiefly from the fact that it is an undiscussable aspect of reality based upon epistemological and ontological beliefs outside conscious awareness (Anthony 1977; Gemmill 1986; Neumann 1989). Campbell (1977) is quite accurate in pointing out that discussion of the purposes and problems for which leadership concepts and data are to be used is notably absent from studies in the field. Why is a leader really necessary? What problems or issues in an organization indicate a real need for a leader? Exactly what underlying existential needs or problems the concept of a leader is meant to address has not been clearly articulated.

Some of the confusion around the concept of leadership seems to stem from the process of reification. Reification is a social process which converts an abstraction or mental construct into a supposed real entity. Through reification the social construction of leadership is mystified and accorded an objective existence. It is a social fiction that represents a form of what Fromm labels 'false consciousness' which refers to the content of the conscious mind that is fictitious and has been introjected or assimilated without awareness through cultural programming. With reification, social progress is viewed as 'caused' by or 'determined' by a leader, a cadre of leaders, or 'leadership.' It is assumed by researchers and practitioners that, because there is a word ('leader' or 'leadership'), there must be an independent objective reality it describes or denotes. Reification functions to trap such labelled individuals within a mode of existence that serves to meet

G. Gemmill and J. Oakley. 'Leadership: An Alienating Social Myth?', *Human Relations*, 45/2 (1992), 113–29.

various unconscious emotional needs of members of an organization and of a society.

The leadership myth functions as a social defence whose central aim is to repress uncomfortable needs, emotions, and wishes that emerge when people attempt to work together (Jacques 1955; Gemmill 1986). Stated somewhat differently, when members of a group are faced with uncertainty and ambiguity regarding direction, they often report experiencing feelings of anxiety, helplessness, discomfort, disappointment, hostility, and fear of failure. Frightened by these emerging emotions and impulses, which are ordinarily held in check by absorption into the prevailing social system, they collude, largely unconsciously, to dispel them by projecting them onto 'leadership' or the 'leader' role. The projection allows organizational members to avoid directly confronting the emerging emotions and regress to a form of social order with which we are familiar. As Hirschhorn (1988: 2) states, social defences are rituals that induce mindlessness and, 'by not thinking, people avoid feeling anxious'. The undiscussability of the myth is rooted in the lack of questioning of the alienating consequences and resultant reification of the social forces that position 'leadership' as a healthy concept.

The tendency of social groupings and individuals to create social defences and mindlessly act out rituals results in a flawed process of reality construction. Morgan (1986) points out that while individuals create their reality, they often do so in confiding and alienating ways. People create worlds out of mental constructs, or psychic prisons, in which they become trapped by their own ideas. The thesis examined here is that the concepts of 'leader' and 'leadership' have become psychic prisons. While leadership is viewed as having a positive connotation, we suggest that contrariwise it is a serious sign of social pathology, that it is a special case of an iatrogenic social myth that induces massive learned helplessness among members of a social system. Learned helplessness is characterized by an experienced inability to imagine or perceive viable options, along with accompanying feelings of despair and a resistance to initiating any form of action (Seligman 1977). It is our thesis that much of the current writing and theorizing on leadership stems from a deepening sense of social despair and massive learned helplessness. As social despair and helplessness deepen, the search and wish for a messiah (leader) or magical rescue (leadership) also begins to accelerate. We argue that the current popular writings and theories of leadership clearly reflect this social trend. When pain is coupled with an inordinate, widespread, and pervasive sense of helplessness, social myths about the need for great leaders and magical leadership emerge from the primarily unconscious collective feeling that it would take a miracle or messiah to alleviate or ameliorate this painful form of existence.

We further argue that the major significance of most recent studies on leadership is not to be found in their scientific validity but in their function in offering ideological support for the existing social order. The idea of a leadership élite explains in a Social Darwinistic manner why only certain members of a social system are at the apex of power and entitled to a proportionably greater share of the social wealth. So-called leader traits are woven into a powerful social myth, which, while serving to maintain the status quo, also paradoxically sows the seeds of its own destruction by accentuating helplessness, mindlessness, emotionlessness, and meaninglessness. The social myth around leaders serves to programme life out of people (non-leaders) who, with the social lobotomization, appear as cheerful robots (Mills 1956). It is our contention that the myth making around the concept of leadership is, as Bennis (1989) asserts, an unconscious conspiracy, or social hoax, aimed at maintaining the status quo.

## Leadership and Alienation

The radical humanist perspective on leadership incorporates a deconstructionist approach (Parker and Shotter 1990). Deconstructionism is an approach to the philosophy of knowledge that aims to demonstrate how a discourse (leadership) is undermined by the very philosophy on which it is based (Culler 1982). To deconstruct a discourse is to unravel hidden assumptions, internal contradictions, and repressed meanings. For example, by uncovering the underlying assumption that a leader or leadership is necessary in discourses on leadership, hidden presuppositions are identified, examined, and made visible in order to reveal the hidden political and social beliefs implied in the text.

Within the radical humanist paradigm alienation is viewed as a central concept, a concept Burrell and Morgan (1979: 298) define as: 'The state in which . . . a cognitive wedge is driven between man's consciousness and the objectified social world, so that man sees what are essentially the creations of his own consciousness in the form of a hard, dominating, external reality.' Controversy exists concerning the nature of the relationship between reification and alienation (Marx 1973). The radical structuralist viewpoint, represented by theorists such as Karl Marx, views forms of social structure as primary in the formation of alienation. From a Marxist viewpoint, changes in social structures result in changes in personal alienation and awareness. Radical humanists, on the other hand, view alienation as primary in forming social structure and social consciousness. Changing personal awareness, social structure, and social consciousness concurrently can result in lessening alienation.

Max Pages articulated the radical humanist viewpoint on alienation in his view of organizational change where change is seen as 'a different kind of relationship with people. They [organization members] want to have the opportunity to express their needs and be able to pursue them. They want not to be bossed; they want to enter into relationships that will not be possessive. This is what I wish to mobilize when I work with people . . . I believe I can be more useful if I help people destroy the organizational forms in which they are imprisoned' (Tichy 1974: 9–10). Our viewpoint of this epistemological issue is that alienation and reification are codeterminant and that changes in personal awareness of the process of reification is a necessary but not a sufficient condition for changes in experienced alienation, social structure, and social consciousness.

Erich Fromm (1955) and R. D. Laing (1967) have cogently argued that a statistical concept of 'normal' can be pathological since it reflects only false consciousness. Alienation is seen as the dominant reality of modern man—unauthentic existence resulting from the false consciousness of ideologies and norms imposed from outside the individual and resulting in social and organizational behaviours that are characteristically pathological and neurotic (Fromm 1955). Laing (1967: 27–8) has pointedly stated, 'What we call "normal" is a product of repression, denial, splitting, projection, introjection, and other forms of destructive action or experience . . . the condition of alienation, of being asleep, of being unconscious, of being out of one's mind, is the condition of the normal man.' Fromm (1955: 312–13) expressed a similar diagnosis when he stated: 'the danger of the future is that man may become robots. True enough, robots do not rebel. But given man's nature, robots cannot live and remain sane . . . they will destroy themselves because they cannot stand any longer the boredom of a meaningless life.'

Erich Fromm (1955) approaches alienation as a social as well as an individual issue. Alienation in organizations and society as a whole is viewed by Fromm (1955) as caused by the powerlessness and paralysis experienced by individuals as a result of their experiences in industrial societies which make in difficult to lead meaningful, self-directed lives. In Fromm's view, the socialization process in industrial societies has stripped us of our ability to take initiative due to the false belief that happiness comes as a result of material comfort and high levels of consumption. The false belief is reinforced by reified institutions, lifestyles, and ideologies that necessitate social organizations with a high degree of centralized control. In this alienated state, individuals disclaim responsibility for their lives by believing that their fate is not under their own personal control. In a similar vein, Steiner (1975) elaborates on the social factors operating in alienation. He views alienation as a form of social deception, in which the majority of people are mystified into believing that society is not depleting them of their humanity and vitality, and, even if it were, there are good reasons for it. The net effect is that the average person, instead of sensing his oppression and being angry by it, decides that her feelings of emptiness and despair are her own fault and own responsibility. When this happens, the person feels alienated, since she is unaware of the social deception.

## The Social Myth of Leadership

According to Fromm (1960), each society becomes caught up in its own need to survive in the particular form in which it has developed. This is accomplished by fabricating a repertoire of fictions and illusions. The effect of society acting to preserve itself is not only to funnel fictions into consciousness, but also to prevent the awareness of reality that might threaten the existing 'natural order'. Because the social fiction of the leader is inculcated outside awareness, reality-testing is blocked and the development of genuine insight into social issues is threatened, as is any experimentation that might lead to more vital ways of relating in a work setting.

There exists a strong tendency to explain organization outcomes by attributing causality to 'leadership' (Calder 1977; Pfeffer 1977). This attributional social bias creates the illusion that 'leaders' are in control of events. The use of leadership as a cause or social myth seems to stem, in part, from the natural uncertainty and ambiguity embedded in reality which most persons experience as terrifying, overwhelming, complex, and chaotic (Pedigo and Singer 1982). The terror of facing feelings of helplessness and powerlessness can lead a society, as Becker (1973) speculated, to focus emotions on one person who is imagined to be all powerful ('the leader'). The attribution of omnipotence and omniscience allows the terror to be focused in one place instead of it being experienced as diffused in a seemingly random universe.

The major function of the leader myth is to preserve the existing social system and structure by attributing dysfunctions and difficulties within the system to the lack, or absence, of 'leadership.' The dysfunctional and destructive aspects of the social system itself and the corresponding personal behaviour of the members go unexamined, as does the collusion among members in creating and maintaining the social myth of leadership. Because the myth is undiscussable by members, self-sealing non-learning about the dynamics of the myth is constantly reinforced. As long as faults, imperfections, and hopes can be attributed to leadership, the social system itself remains unexamined and unchanged.

## The Resurgence of the Great Leader Myth

The recent fascination with leadership characteristics and traits in the management literature is reminiscent of a ghost dance, an attempt to resurrect and revive the spirit of a time gone by. Ghost dances were a predominant expression of religious movement that gained popularity among native American tribes in the latter half of the nineteenth century in reaction to the impending destruction of their way of life (Hultkrantz 1987). The ghost dance was performed to receive the spirits of the ancestors in the hope that this would lead to a restoration of the past and prevent further disintegration of their dying civilization. Similarly, the revival of the 'traitist' approach to leadership seems a 'ghost dance' aimed at restoring and preventing disintegration of our own civilization. Increasing alarm and concern with the defection or total absence of leadership is a sign of increasing social despair and massive learned helplessness.

The current re-emergence of the 'traitist' approach to leaders and 'charisma' is embodied in recent books by Bennis and Nanus (1985), Zaleznik (1989), and Tichy and Devanna (1987). The traits they attempt to identify are in a sense a different form of abstracted traits than the earlier studies done on leadership traits. For example, Zaleznik (1990: 12) writes: 'For a leader to secure commitment from subordinates he or she has to demonstrate extraordinary competence or other qualities subordinates admire.' In the same vein, Bennis and Nanus (1985: 218) impute almost magical qualities to leaders: 'leadership can move followers to higher degrees of consciousness, such as liberty, freedom, justice, and self-actualization.'

'Charisma' is the leadership trait most often examined by members of the 'leadership mafia'. Charisma is a social phenomenon similar to the illusionary aspects of the reported UFO phenomenon in the sense that it is viewed as of divine origin beyond our material world. Weber's (1968: 48) most frequently cited definition is: 'Charisma is a quality of an individual personality by virtue of which he is set apart from ordinary men and treated as endowed with supernatural, superhuman, or at least specifically exceptional qualities'. The mistake in theory-building and research on 'charismatic' leaders is the belief that 'charisma' is a measurable attribute of the person to whom it is attributed that is entirely independent from the perceptual distortions of those attributing the 'charisma'. While leadership studies on charisma have largely been oriented towards identifying individual traits, Wasielewski (1985) has recently proposed it be considered an interactional relationship that is the product of an emotional interaction between charismatic leaders and followers. We argue along similar lines that the importance of 'charisma' is to be found in its meaning as a social fiction or social delusion that allows 'followers' to escape responsibility for their own actions and inactions. The label 'charisma' is like the term leader itself—a 'black hole' in social space that serves as a container for the alienating consequences of the social myth resulting from intellectual and emotional deskilling by organization members.

## Unconscious Aspects of Leadership

The meaning of leadership in contemporary organizations can be discovered by examining the socially constructed meanings and behaviour patterns that emerge from perceptions and reactions to the concept of leadership. In many organizations, a stable dichotomy exists between the leaders and the followers, with the leaders being viewed by their followers as performing both protective and nurturance functions, much as parents are viewed by their children. In this relationship, leaders are unconsciously perceived by their followers as providing protection against external threats and preventing internal infighting and destructive acts within the organization. By projecting their anxiety and aggression onto the leaders, followers perceive themselves as freed from the anxiety and responsibility of taking initiative, seeking autonomy, taking risks, or expressing their own fears and feelings of aggression and destructiveness. When organization members accept and act these feelings unreflectively, they adapt the authoritarian personality as described by Erich Fromm in *Escape from Freedom* (1941), and in much of the classical sociology literature, such as Whyte's 'organization man', C. Wright Mill's 'cheerful robot', or David Riesman's 'lonely crowd' (Whyte 1956; Mills 1956; Riesman 1961). In contrast, those attracted to a leader role have an exaggerated narcissistic need to project their fears of inferiority and inadequacy onto persons of inferior social status and to gain satisfaction from the enhanced power, superior status, and material rewards that accompany leadership positions (Schwartz 1987).

A more complete understanding of the meaning of leadership in organizations can be gained by examining the collective unconscious assumptions about leadership and authority. Collective unconscious assumptions (basic assumptions) are formed concerning leadership and authority which affect both individual and group behaviour (Bion 1961). As Bion points out, under the influence of the pairing basic assumption in groups, members become preoccupied with the thought that sometime in the future a person (leader) or idea (leadership) will surface that will eventually solve all their problems without any effort on their part. There is a messianic hope that in the future everything will finally work and members will be delivered from their anxieties, fears, and struggles. The predominant emotions are manic-like forms of hope, faith, and utopianism. According to Bion (1961), these emotions can persist only as long as the leader or idea remains 'unborn' and unmaterialized. Because of the unreality of the omnipotent and magical idealization, it is impossible for a person or idea ever to live up to the expectations. Eventually, the faith and hope of members are shattered, opening the door to despair, disappointment, and disillusionment, the emotions lurking behind the more manic ones such as hope. The manic emotions constitute a defence against depression (Winnicott 1987). It is when the group is caught in a manic defence that members are least likely to feel they are defending against depression. At such times, they are most likely to feel elated, happy, busy, excited, humorous, omniscient, zestful, and are less inclined to look at the seriousness of life with its heaviness and sadness.

Bion (1961) describes another basic assumption that occurs in groups, the dependency basic assumption, as a social fiction that impairs work on the real issues in a group or organization. The dependency basic assumption group comes into operation when members act as if they were joining together in order to be sustained by a single leader on whom they depend for nourishment and protection. The essential aim of the dependency assumption group is covertly to attain security through establishing a fantasy that members of a group are coming together to be nurtured and protected by 'a leader'. Members act as if they know nothing, as if they are inadequate and helpless. Their behaviour in this regard implies that the leader by comparison is omnipotent and omniscient. In over-idealizing the leader, members deskill themselves from their own critical thinking, visions, inspirations, and emotions.

In the emotional state of dependency, the members want extremely simple explanations and act as if no one can do anything that is difficult. A person in a leader role functions as an emotional container for other members that results in an alienating intellectual and emotional deskilling in them. The person designated as the leader can function as a central figure for containing both positive and negative projections of followers. As Muktananada (1980: 34) states: 'there is a great mirror in the Guru's eyes in which everything is reflected.' There is similarly a great mirror in the eyes of the leader in which the intrapsychic conflicts of the group members at large are reflected. However, in projecting their own senses of completeness and incompleteness onto a leader, people become alienated and caught in an illusion of helplessness and failure without realizing that they limit the leader's power as well as their own by their denial, projection, and passivity.

Looking towards people in authority to define what is meaningful work activity occurs without much conscious thought and reflection. The childlike dependency basis of the leader myth is seen clearly in the writing of Smircich and Morgan (1982) who view leadership as a process whereby 'followers' give up their mindfulness to a 'leader' or 'leadership'. As they state: 'Leadership is realized in the process whereby one or more individuals succeeds in attempting to frame and define the reality of others' (Smircich and Morgan 1982: 257). Milgram's (1974) classic studies on obedience to authority as well as studies on cult groups such as Jim Jones's 'People's Temple' (Ulman and Abse 1983) attest to the primitive unreflected acceptance and unconscious compliance with an authority figure's definition of what aspects of reality are to be given conscious attention. The unreflected acceptance of the authority figure's or power élite's definition of how the world of work is to be enacted is the infrastructure of false consciousness.

In addition to providing a focus for dependency issues, the person assigned a leader role often represents and acts as a voice for the intrapsychic conflicts of followers and is unconsciously used to act out a shared collective issue. For example, repressed anger is often projected onto someone in a leader role, who then acts it out for the group in such a way that group members become vicariously satisfied. Projecting violent, aggressive, and hostile feelings onto a leader allows people to reduce the discomfort of having openly to confront these feelings either in themselves or with each other. From the standpoint of projecting away positive attributes and emotions, people engage in a deskilling process that leaves them feeling empty, helpless, and powerless. Maslow (1971) seems to capture well the underlying dynamics of the deskilling process that accompanies alienation with what he termed the 'Jonah Complex'. He used the term in reference to an individual evading and running away from his or her undeveloped potential for creativity and greatness. He believed that people paradoxically fear not only their worst qualities but also their best qualities. With the projective numbing and relinquishing of their abilities to create and nourish themselves, they experience confusion, feel overwhelmed, and feel helpless. When this happens, alienated members of an organization willingly submit themselves to spoon feeding, preferring safe and easy security to the possible pains and uncertainty of learning by their own effort and mistakes. In this respect, Freud (1960) believed that members of a group desperately seek illusions to protect themselves from emotional truths and avoid reality.

## The Contemporary Ideology of Leadership

Leadership theories espousing 'traits' or 'great-person' explanations reinforce and reflect the widespread tendency of people to deskill themselves and idealize leaders by implying that only a select few are good enough to exercise initiative. This view of leadership must be questioned in the light of the dysfunctional and alienating consequences perpetrated by this social myth. The deconstruction of leadership and the creation of alternative definitions necessitate placing a value on inverting and debunking cultural assumptions that hold in place the current leader myth. Proposing alternative realities in organizations is often viewed as taking a dangerous risk, since it challenges prevailing perceptions of reality held by the current leadership. Throughout history, successful challenges have been made by persons acting in the role of the sage-fool (Kets de Vries 1990). Traditionally, the sage-fool's role has been institutionalized in the roles of court jester, clown, and anti-hero. In these roles, sage-fools balance the hubris of the kings or other powerful persons by parodying the foolishness and stupidity of the leader's false consciousness and misuse of power by using humour to cushion the impact of uncovering unspeakable truths and other information considered to be socially destructive (Kets de Vries 1990). In contemporary organizations, this role is often taken up by outsiders such as organizational development (OD) consultants. From the radical humanist perspective, however, an OD consultant cannot succeed just by presenting his or her version of the alternative reality to the organization's members and their leaders. Real change occurs only when members can learn to liberate themselves through expanded awareness and self-created programmes of action (Tichy 1974). As noted psychoanalyst Alan Wheelis (1975: 15) so poignantly expresses it: 'Freedom is the awareness of alternatives and the ability to choose.'

Increasing awareness of alienation and reification in work settings means finding ways to examine consciously the beliefs about existing structures and attitudes concerning power authority. Neumann (1989) proposes that many people automatically adopt a traditional 'work ideology' and subsequently feel uncomfortable with organizational interventions designed to increase participation in decision-making. This commonly occurs because of the widespread acceptance of organizational norms that promote abdication of decision-making authority to those above. In recent years, empowerment has emerged as an idea designed to increase involvement and participation in decision-making by those perceived as working in environments where taking orders and being told what to do is the norm and self-management is not practised. The idea of empowerment has gained popularity in corporate and academic circles due to the widespread perception that, by delegating more decision-making authority to organization members, productivity and performance will be enhanced (Kanter 1979; Manz and Sims 1980; Peters and Austin 1985; Lawler 1986; Bennis 1989).

To some, the idea of empowerment has become another magic solution designed to promote widespread changes in organizational perceptions and practices. Without an examination of deeply held beliefs about leadership constructs and power and authority relationships, however, it is unlikely that fundamental change will occur. Encouraging subordinates to take increased responsibility for outcomes and managing themselves may have little impact if intellectual and emotional deskilling and other problems arising from constructs around leadership are not directly addressed. Under present conditions in organizations, many of the changes involving empowerment may be seen as an attempt to shift blame and responsibility for organizational problems from the top management to other organization members without a corresponding change in actual power relationships. Alternatively, implementing empowerment programmes may also be viewed by other organization members as an attempt to co-opt them by creating the illusion that a decrease in top management control and an increase in self-monitoring is equivalent to equal participation in decision-making processes (illusionary power equalization). Focusing attention on the leader myth and its role in shaping individually—and collectively—held beliefs can create awareness of choices and the predisposition for risk and experimentation necessary for changing behaviours and creating new paradigms.

## Experimenting with New Paradigms

Chris Argyris (1969) points out that one danger in conducting only 'naturalistic' and 'descriptive' research on behaviour within organizations is a tendency to view what exists at the present time as inevitable or immutable. Truly, if only the prevailing human conditions in organizations were studied, the risk would be one of reinforcing a concept of a person whose 'natural' behaviour is concealing feelings, playing games, mistrusting, being bored with work, being passive, feeling powerless, and not taking risks (Argyris 1990). The basic danger of descriptive research is failing to consider alternative systems in which meaninglessness and powerlessness are minimized or eliminated. With limited awareness and lack of experimentation with alternative realities, resignation in accepting as human nature the pathological status quo evidence in the descriptive data is likely.

Acceptance of the leader myth promotes alienation, deskilling, reification of organizational forms, and dysfunctional organizational structures. Contrariwise, the dynamics of leadership, when viewed as a social process, are quite different from the idea of a leadership élite, where acceptance of a leader requires abdicating authority to a power outside the self. Leadership as a social process can be defined as a process of dynamic collaboration, where individuals and organization members authorize themselves and others to interact in ways that experiment with new forms of intellectual and emotional meaning. Experimenting in this sense is similar to Weick's (1977) concept of enactment, where proactive behaviour occurs and is not necessarily linked to specific goals. The presence of well-defined leaders often decreases the ability of a group to experiment, whereas a revolt against leaders and efforts to work without them may give rise to new, more amorphous forms of leadership where organization members work at their boundaries through a process of dynamic collaboration (Smith and Gemmill 1991). Working in dynamic collaboration requires individuals to change their perceptions and develop new norms and structures which create a variety of new options and increases the possibility that new structures will be found which are better suited to the current environment (Ashby 1970; Bronowski 1970).

An alternative view of leadership has emerged in recent decades from the expanding body of feminist theory on the nature of power and authority. Radical feminists view power as exercised in contemporary society as 'power over', representative of a masculine, or patriarchal world-view in which social relationships originate from primary relationships defined by male 'power over' women and children (Rich 1976). Alternatively, a feminist conception of leadership redefines power as the ability to influence people to act in their own interests, rather than induce them to act according to the goals and desires of the leader (Carroll 1984). Feminists envision new paradigms that reconceptualize leadership and power relationships based on supportive and cooperative behaviours. Feminist theory, therefore, points to the need for new forms of leadership by re-defining the meanings attached to leadership behaviour, as in Bunch and Fisher's (1976: 3) definition of leadership as 'people taking the initiative, carrying things through, having ideas and the imagination to get something started, and exhibiting particular skills in different areas'. Unawareness of viable alternatives to present behaviour associated with leadership, and limited experimentation, have been, perhaps, the greatest impediments to creation of less alienating work relationships.

Michels' (1915) iron law of oligarchy could easily be recast into the iron law of non-learning in organizations or social systems. According to Michels, organizations that start out with egalitarian or anarchistic political values tend to become as, or perhaps more, authoritarian and alienating than the organizations they were designed to reform or replace. The issue seems to be that people cannot simply will themselves into a new way of operating. They inevitably end up enacting and reacting the prior structures because experientially and behaviourally they are unable to transcend them. Awareness of alienation, social defences, and false consciousness are a necessary but not sufficient condition for changes in a social system or organization (Hirschhorn 1988). For example, Argyris (1990) suggests that executives are often aware of ineffectual interpersonal behaviour in other executives they perceive as ineffectual, yet they themselves exhibit the same ineffectual behaviour. Even when they become aware of their own ineffectual behaviour, however, it is not enough to effect change in their behaviour. For change to occur, it is necessary to experiment with new paradigms and new behaviours to find more meaningful and constructive ways of relating and working together. While such social experimentation is a process marked by uncertainty, difficulties, awkwardness, disappointment, and tentativeness of actions, it is indispensable if people are to experience a non-alienated mode of existence in a work environment or in society as a whole.

## Conclusion

Jung (1958), in writing on the phenomena of reported flying saucers, seems accurately to describe how illusionary social processes perpetuate such social myths and reflect the pervasive sense of helplessness. He hypothesizes that the reports of UFOs, flying saucers, and alien beings represent an intrapsychic longing for wholeness and unity which seems impossible to accomplish in our existing world. In a Sartre-like drama (Sartre 1955), people become alienated from their true creative and vital life force and project it outward so that they see it coming to them in an alien form. The longing or wish is projected via a quasi-hallucinatory process where it is perceived as alien to the self, or extraterrestrial. Jung (1958) contended that, apart from whether the UFOs objectively exist, it seems clear that they psychologically exist in the experience of many humans in a wide variety of cultures.

Similarly, we speculate that leadership as a social myth symbolically represents a regressive wish to return to the symbiotic environment of the womb: to be absolved of consciousness, mindfulness, and responsibility for initiating responses to our environment to attain what we need and want. The womb represents a protected environment that we have all experienced where we did not have to take risk, experience angst and pain, feel frightened, and expose our inadequacy or incompetence. To become completely infantilized is the ultimate form of deskilling and learned helplessness. Jung (1957: 70–1) may have had this in mind when he wrote:

> Where there are many, there is security; what the many believe must of course be true; what the many want must be worth striving for, and necessary, and therefore good. In the clamor of the many there lies the power to snatch wish-fulfillments by force; sweetest of all, however, is that gentle and painless slipping back into the kingdom of childhood, into the paradise of parental care, into happy-go-luckiness and irresponsibility. All the thinking and looking after are done from the top; to all questions there is an answer, and for all needs the necessary provision is made. The infantile dream state of the mass man is so unrealistic that he never thinks to ask who is paying for this paradise.

It is a fact of existence that everyone has had a unitive experience of being completely taken care of without any conscious effort on their part. Hence, the regressive wish is not just something spun out of thin air but is borne of an actual experience with a symbiotic environment, albeit pre-linguistic and pre-verbal. The unitive experience of a symbiotic environment is the basis for the regressive wish.

Members of a social system often behave as alienated robots in work relationships. They often seem paralysed by their fears and cannot bear to experience their work relationships as a changing process in which nothing is ever really fixed. The work process is imbued with meaning by every individual; therefore it has no objective meaning of its own. At times, the creative possibilities of events and experiences carry us in directions and towards goals of which at the time we are only dimly aware. This process can be fraught with both fascination and fright, since there is no fixed end point or closed system of behaviour, actions, or unchanging set of principles by which work relationships develop creatively and constructively. In reality, there are multiple ways of being together in the work process. Members of an organization can be free to relate to each other in the work process any way they choose. They are limited only by their fears, imagination, cultural programming, and psychohistories. Admittedly, these are significant limitations, but not necessarily insurmountable.

Hopefully, we have provided a foundation, a beginning, in our analysis that can serve both to encourage and to guide much needed future research on leadership and alienation. Interventions designed to demythologize leadership and lessen alienating consequences need to be more precisely developed and tested in the crucible of experience. At present, the Tavistock group relations-type conference can be used as a powerful intervention for demythologizing leadership as well as a research methodology for investigating unconscious behaviour associated with leadership. Making discussable what is typically undiscussable about leadership and alienation is a step toward demythologizing and personal 'reskilling'. Amplifying personal awareness of the leadership myth and its social function allows one to examine one's own projective identification and ways of deskilling oneself unnecessarily. It is our contention that only disenchantment and detachment from the central social myth and ritual of dependency on leadership can promote the change necessary for opening up new possibilities for creativity and change in the ways we structure life at work so that it loses the toxicity associated with alienation.

## References

Anthony, P. D. (1977), *The Ideology of Work* (London: Tavistock Publications).

Argyris, C. (1969), 'The Incompleteness of the Social Psychological Theory', *American Psychologist*, 24: 893–908.

—— (1990), *Overcoming Organizational Defenses* (Boston: Allyn & Bacon).

Ashby, W. R. (1970), *Design for a Brain* (3rd edn., London: Methuen).

Becker, E. (1973), *The Denial of Death* (New York: Free Press).

Bennis, W., (1989), *Why Leaders Can't Lead: The Unconscious Conspiracy Continues* (San Francisco, Calif.: Jossey-Bass).

—— and Nanus, B. (1985), *Leaders: The Strategies for Taking Charge* (New York: Harper & Row).

Bion, W. R. (1961), *Experiences in Groups* (New York: Basic Books).

Bronowski, J. (1970), 'New Concepts in the Evolution of Complexity', *Synthèse,* 21: 228–46.

Bunch, C., and Fisher, B. (1976), 'What Future for Leadership', *Qest*, 2 (Spring) 2–13.

Burrell, G., and Morgan, G. (1979), *Sociological Paradigms and Organizational Analysis* (Portsmouth, NH: Heinemann).

Calder, B. (1977), 'An Attribution Theory of Leadership', in B. Staw and B. Salanck (eds.), *New Directions in Organizational Behavior* (Chicago: St Clair).

Campbell, J. P. (1977), 'The Cutting Edge of Leadership: An Overview', in J. C. Hunt and L. Larson (eds.), *Leadership: The Cutting Edge* (Carbondale, Ill.: Southern Illinois University Press).

Carroll, S. J. (1984), 'Feminist Scholarship on Political Leadership', in B. Kellerman (ed.), *Leadership: Multidisciplinary Perspectives (*Englewood Cliffs, NJ: Prentice-Hall).

Culler, J. (1982), *On Deconstruction: Theory and Criticism after Structuralism* (Ithaca, NY: Cornell University Press).

Freud, S. (1960), *Group Psychology—The Awareness of The Ego* (New York: Bantam).

Fromm, E. (1941), *Escape from Freedom* (New York: Rinehart & Co.).

—— (1955), *The Sane Society* (New York: Fawcett Premier Books).

—— (1960), 'Psychoanalysis and Zen Buddhism', In D. Suzuki, E. Fromm, and R. Demartino, *Zen Buddhism and Psychoanalysis* (New York: Harper & Row).

Gemmill, G. (1986), 'The Mythology of the Leader Role in Small Groups', *Small Group Behavior*, 17/1: 41–50.

Hirschhorn, L. (1988), *The Workplace Within: The Psychodynamics of Organizational Life* (Cambridge, Mass.: MIT Press).

Hultkrantz, A. (1987), *Native Religions of North America: The Power of Visions and Fertility* (San Francisco: Harper & Row).

Jacques, E. (1955), 'Social Systems as a Defense against Persecutory and Depressive Anxiety', in M. Klein, P. Heiman, and R. Mohey-Kyrle (eds.), *New Directions in Psychoanalysis* (London: Tavistock), 478–98.

Jung, C. G. (1957), *The Undiscovered Self* (New York: Mentor).

—— (1958), 'Flying Saucers: A Modern Myth of Things Seen in the Sky', in *The Collected Works of C. G. Jung*, ed. G. Adler, M. Fordham, W. Mcguire, and H. Read, (Princeton: Princeton University Press).

Kanter, R. M. (1979), 'Power Failure in Management Circuits', *Harvard Business Review*, 57/4: 65–75.

Kets de Vries, M. F. R. (1990), 'The Organizational Fool: Balancing a Leader's Hubris', *Human Relations*, 43/8: 751–70.

Laing, R. D. (1967), *The Politics of Experience* (Baltimore, Md: Ballantine Books).

Lawler, E. (1986), *High-Involvement Management: Strategies for Improved Organizational Performance* (San Francisco, Calif.: Jossey-Bass).

Manz, C., and Sims, H. (1980), 'Self-Management as a Substitute for Leadership: A Social Learning Perspective', *Academy of Management Review*, 5: 361–7.

Marx, K. (1973), *Grundisse: Foundations of the Critique of Political Economy*, transl. M. Nicolaus, (New York: Vintage).

Maslow, A. (1971), *The Further Reaches of Human Nature* (New York: Viking Press).

Masterson, J. F. (1988), *The Search for the Real Self. Unmasking the Personality Disorders of our Age* (New York: Free Press).

Michels, R. (1915), *Political Parties: A Sociological Study of Oligarchical Tendencies of Modern Democracy* (London: Jarrold & Sons).

Milgram, S. (1974), *Obedience to Authority (*New York: Harper & Row).

Mills, C. W. (1956), *The Power Élite* (Oxford: Oxford University Press).

Morgan, G. (1986), *Images of Organizations* (Beverly Hills, Calif.: Sage).

Muktananada, S. (1980), *The Perfect Relationship* (Geneshpuri, India: Gurudeu Siddha Peeth).

Neumann, J. E. (1989), 'Why People Don't Participate in Organizational Change', in R. W. Woodinan and W. A. Pasmore (eds.), *Research in Organizational Change and Development*, iii (Greenwich, Conn.: Jai Press).

Parker, I., and Shotter, J. (1990), 'Introduction', in Parker and Shotter (eds.), *Deconstructing Social Psychology* (New York: Routledge), 1–14.

Pedigo, J., and Singer, B. (1982), 'Group Process Development: A Psychoanalytic View', *Small Group Behavior*, 13: 496–517.

Peters, T., and Austin, N. (1985), *A Passion for Excellence: The Leadership Difference* (New York: Random House).

Pfeffer, J. (1977), 'The Ambiguity of Leadership', *Academy of Management Review* (Jan.), 104–12.

Rich, A. (1976), *Of Woman Born* (New York: W. W. Norton & Co.).

Riesman, D. (1961), *The Lonely Crowd: A Study of the Changing American Character* (New Haven: Yale University Press).

Sartre, J. P. (1955), *No Exit, and Three Other Plays* (New York: Vintage).

Schwartz, H. (1987), 'The Psychodynamics of Organizational Totalitarianism', *Journal of General Management*, 13/1: 41–54.

Seligman, M. E. P. (1977), *Helplessness: On Depression, Development, and Death* (San Francisco: W. H. Freeman & Co.).

Smircich, L., and Morgan, G. (1982), 'Leadership: The Management of Meaning', *Journal of Applied Behavioral Science*, 18/3: 257–73.

Smith, C., and Gemmill, G. (1991), 'Change in the Small Group: A Dissipative Structure Perspective', *Human Relations*: 44: 697–716.

Steiner, C., *et al.* (1975), *Readings in Radical Psychiatry* (New York: Grove Press).

Tichy, N. (1974), 'An Interview with Max Pages', *Journal of Applied Behavioral Science*, 10/1: 8–26.

—— and Devanna, M. (1987), *The Transformational Leader* (New York: John Wiley & Sons).

Ulman, R., and Abse, D. (1983), 'The Group Psychology of Mass Madness: Jonestown', *Political Psychology*, 4/4: 637–61.

Wasielewski, P. (1985), 'The Emotional Basis of Charisma', *Symbolic Interaction*, 8/2: 207–22.

Weber, M. (1968), *Economy and Society: An Outline of Interpretive Sociology*, ed. G., Roth, and C. Wittich (New York: Bedminister Press).

Weick, K. E. (1977), 'Organizational Design: Organizations as Self-Designing Systems', *Organizational Dynamics*, 6: 31–46.

Wheelis, A. (1975), *How People Change* (New York: Harper & Row).

Whyte, W. (1956), *The Organization Man* (New York: Simon & Schuster).

Winnicott, D. W. (1987), *Through Paediatrics to Psychoanalysis* (London: Hogarth).

Zaleznik, A. (1989), *The Managerial Mystique: Restoring Leadership in Business* (New York: Harper & Row).

—— (1990), 'The Leadership Gap', *Academy of Management Executive*, 4/1: 7–22.

# V. ALTERNATIVE LEADERSHIP

The final approach, the Alternative Leadership wave, combines three recent developments in theoretical understandings of leadership that pose a rigorous challenge to much of what has gone before. Hosking challenges us to consider whether our accounts of leadership are too static and assume an existence beyond us that reifies leaders and organizations. Lilley and Platt's account of Martin Luther King proceeds in a related direction by noting the diversity rather than the solidity of King's character and the role of followers in constructing such an unstable and variegated leadership image. Finally, and probably the most challenging of the readings, Calás and Smircich suggest that leadership embodies no definitive meanings and that multiple readings are potentially possible. The one that appears to prevail is a strongly masculinized account that lends itself to a quite different reading and one that returns us to the problem we started with: what is leadership?

Hosking goes some way to help us reconsider the points raised by Gemmill and Oakley in the previous chapter by displacing leadership as an issue of 'people' with leadership as an issue of 'process', and replacing 'organization' as a noun with 'organizing' as a verb. The consequence is that leadership becomes read as a skill involving social relationships, and organization becomes an entity not a condition.

Hosking supports this claim by juxtaposing the traditional top-down idea of organization as an entity which exists independently of its members, with a bottom-up idea of organizing as an achievement of its members. The point of this reversal is not to reduce the role of leadership but to secure its significance—for leaders must 'bring off' the organization by organizing—that is, they must make it happen rather than just assuming its existence is secured in and through the organization chart which implies it exists independently of any member. In particular, leaders try to secure a consensus upon the nature of the organization by the members but, unlike traditional forms of analysis, the process-oriented approach implies that this is unlikely to occur as participants negotiate with leaders and each other to define the organization. This leads Hosking to suggest that organiz*ing* is a unit of analysis not a concrete organiz*ation*.

The problem with regarding things as definitive and concrete entities, rather than as interpretative and tentative constructions, also pervades Hosking's approach to leaders and leadership. Disputing the case that leadership is a personal attribute and an entity, she argues that the arena is more one akin to a social process where leaders are expected, and perceived, to make salient contributions to what is a negotiated social order. The implication of order being negotiated is that it is essentially a political process and not something that can exist within a unitary framework, in which the accounts of leaders are sufficient to ensure a high degree of compliance by the subordinates.

This means that an effective leader is not someone who sits in a leadership position but someone who is skilled at leading—it is an active not a passive affair but it is not one restricted to face-to-face interpersonal skill nor is it restricted to a single actor's behaviour. On the contrary, a crucial skill for leaders is social networking in which leaders act to persuade others about the nature of the subject under discussion but do not impede the free flow of information, since this may be important for the resolution of any problem. In fact, the networking issue is also relevant to ensure that the group becomes committed to whatever the project is, such that the project is 'owned' by the group rather than 'given' to them by the leader. It is also a means by which organizational learning can occur so that a subsequent iteration of the problem does not require a return to reinventing the wheel.

The consequences of this kind of approach to leadership should be clear. If it is assumed that the individual leader, and the organization, are entities outside the conceptual apparatus of the participants then traditional top-down autocratic leadership should be sufficient to secure the compliance of the subordinates in the achievement of what should be a consensual hierarchy of goals. On the other hand, if leaders cannot operate on their own, if organizations appear more indeterminate than determinate, and if the goals of an organization appear to be the result of much political infighting, then perhaps we should abandon the entitative approach to organizations and adopt the processual approach to organizing. After all, if it really was that easy to lead organizations, we would only need to read *the* leadership book to know how to do it. (Then all we have to do is find out which book it is.)

That our leaders are less solid than we think, and that we followers are significant in their construction, is the essence of Lilley and Platt's account of Martin Luther King. Their analysis of the Civil Rights Movement, and the leadership of Martin Luther King, suggests that he represented a markedly heterogeneous figure to the followers of the movement. For instance, using 621 letters sent by correspondents to King, Lilley and Platt claim that writers regarded him as one of (at least) four different characters—as a black leader, as a Christian leader, as a non-violent leader, or as a democratic leader. Nor does this division map 'naturally' onto the background of the writer—for example, not all black writers regarded him as first and foremost a black leader. As Lilley and Platt argue:

> he bore several meanings simultaneously for both black and white participants in the movement. . . . Correspondents saw in King and his efforts multiple conceptions of his leadership and performances. . . . King seems aware of his multiple public meanings for he once confided, 'I am conscious of two Martin Luther Kings. . . . The Martin Luther King that the people talk about seems to be somebody foreign to me.'

One critical implication of this is that a social movement need not be rooted in a consensus to achieve an effective solidarity—there was no consensus about what King represented, but there did appear to be an effective solidarity within the Civil Rights Movement. In Kertzer's (1988) words, rituals can construct 'solidarity without consensus . . . since what often underlies people's political allegiances is their social identification with a group rather than their sharing of beliefs with other members'.

One need not assume that leaders are merely the prisoners of the webs spun by their followers here. On the contrary, it may well be that intentional ambiguity on the part of leaders is precisely what facilitates the incorporation of a large body of followers who are freely able to interpret the meaning of leadership, courtesy of ambiguous leadership. One might usefully borrow here from Barthes's (1990) distinction between 'writerly' and 'readerly' texts with the former facilitating a more ambiguous reading than the latter. The point here is twofold. First, one might argue that, the more ambiguous the text (speech, action, practice, and so on), the more likely leaders are to facilitate the multiple interpretation (reading) that encourages heterogeneous followers to combine. Secondly, this still denotes an 'author-itarian' model in which it is the writer/leader rather than the reader/follower who denotes what counts as an ambiguous text/speech/practice. In effect, the ambiguous readings by followers may well serve to corral or coerce a heterogeneous body of followers, but what counts as an ambiguous text/speech/practice does not essentially lie in the hands of the writer/leader.

Finally, we take one more step in the radical epistemology direction with what is probably the most challenging piece of the collection, both in terms of the writing and the message. Calás and Smircich adopt different postmodern approaches to several key leadership texts to demonstrate the significance of multiple meanings being derived from the 'same' text when 'read' differently. Through this process they attempt to demonstrate that the meaning of the term 'leadership' is not simply ambiguous but can be read as necessarily masculine in origin and effect. In particular, they suggest a profound link between leadership and seduction in that, while leadership appears to 'suppress' desire, it can be read as embodying the very thing it claims to suppress.

From Foucault's genealogical approach, Calás and Smircich suggest a way of understanding texts that claim to overturn traditional theories of leadership while actually reconstituting them. From Derrida's deconstructionist approach they suggest a greater focus on the linguistic constitution of 'reality', since the latter only makes an appearance through the former. From feminist poststructuralism they orient the discussion around gender by considering the way some forms of knowledge are regarded as acceptable and others are not (the article itself is an interesting test case for this). In particular, they consider the way leadership appears to construct a form of understanding in which only replicating forms are admissible: in effect, only what counts as masculine is recognized as leadership, to the extent that leadership appears as 'homosocial seduction'.

They begin by adopting a conventional postmodernist approach in which meanings are necessarily polysemous—that is, multiple. They then suggest that 'seduction'—a term frequently used in opposition to the term 'leadership'—is actually just as important yet, ultimately, just one more possible interpretation of the idea traditionally located within the term 'leadership'. Thus 'to seduce' appears to be the opposite of 'to lead' and the former is associated with women while the latter is restricted to men.

In the first example, Calás and Smircich use Chester Barnard's *Functions of the Executive* to map out the way Barnard's original text can be read in a curiously configured tension between the sexual catalyst of the leader and 'his' priest-like abstinence. The end result sees Barnard's leader as a cult figurehead who must seduce 'his' followers into obedience.

In the second example, McGregor's *The Human Side of Enterprise,* Calás and Smircich reconstruct the way the 'logic of supplementarity' implies that opposites embody weaknesses that can be transcended only by combination. Hence men need women and vice versa to the extent that not only do leaders need followers but followers need leaders. In short, the legitimation for the action of leaders is derived through the absence of actions on the part of the followers in a form of different but (un)equal organizational apartheid.

The third reading comes from Mintzberg's *The Nature of Managerial Work* and, following Horney's 'lead', posits leaders as narcissistic. Here male leaders maintain their own superiority by devaluing women, and women promote a form of submissive identity to avoid (male) aggression. The only route for women leaders, therefore, is to clone their male counterparts—to be more masculine than men.

The final reading is of Peters and Waterman's *In Search of Excellence,* in which the original attempts to adopt specifically non-sexist language are reinterpreted by Calás and Smircich in an effort to reveal a reading that appears essentially masculine, not neutral.

Calás and Smircich conclude that leadership texts are possible only because of what they avoid saying explicitly but which none the less can be read into them. Leadership is concerned with organizational discipline achieved through the seduction of others in a homosocial order of domination and servitude. How 'leadership'—whatever this means—might be imagined in other worlds forms the last part of the article, and this may be taken as the final point of the reader: that leadership can be otherwise, but only if we permit ourselves to break free of the dead grip of tradition.

# 15 Organizing, Leadership, and Skilful Process

Dian Marie Hosking

The terms 'leader' and 'leadership' are much used, but poorly understood; there is little agreement on their proper meaning, whilst at the same time, many—if not most—expect leadership to be of significance in relation to group and organizational performance. In the pages that follow, definitions of these terms will be developed in ways which permit a truly social-psychological perspective. A model is outlined in which the concepts of leadership and organization are integrated using the concept of skill. The model is intended to be sensitizing, to facilitate the appreciation and analysis of leadership and organization whenever, wherever, and however they appear.

Three general arguments will be expressed. The first is for a change in research strategy, switching attention from leaders, as persons, to *leadership* as process. It will be argued that we need to understand leadership, and, for this, it is not enough to understand what leaders do. Rather, it is essential to focus on leadership processes: processes in which influential acts of organizing contribute to the structuring of interactions and relationships, activities and sentiments; processes in which definitions of social order are negotiated, found acceptable, implemented and renegotiated; processes in which interdependencies are organized in ways which, to a greater or lesser degree, promote the values and interests of the social order.

In sum, leadership can be seen as a certain kind of organizing activity: for this reason, leadership is central to the dynamics of organization (Hosking 1983; Hosking and Morley 1985). The concept of 'organization' is here being used as a verb, not a noun, as is more usual. This leads to the second general

D. M. Hosking, 'Organizing, Leadership, and Skilful Process', *Journal of Management Studies*, 25/2 (1988), 147–66.

argument: there is need for more attention to 'organizing'. Few have adopted an organizing perspective in theory development, and even fewer to guide their research. Further, little effort has gone into developing the concept of organizing as a substitute for the concept of organization. Work of this kind has much to recommend it.

In addition, it will be argued that the skills of leadership are the skills of organizing: the concept of skill will be offered as a way of integrating the analysis of leadership and organization. The skills involved are claimed to be those implicated in the processes of complex, social, political decision-making. Processes of this kind are viewed as fundamental to the creation and maintenance of social order within and between groups. Broadly speaking, a perspective is adopted in which leadership processes are understood to define and implement understandings concerning the status quo, or, rather, potential changes which imply either losses or gains for a given group.

These arguments will be developed through separate and sequential examination of the literature on organization, leadership, and social skill. In each case, the dominant perspectives will be outlined, and an alternative argued for. The discussion is intended to show what kind of approach facilitates the appreciation of leadership and organization; how it differs from that which already exists; and why such an approach is needed.

Lastly, these arguments will be applied through articulation of a general model of social skill. This model was developed from theories in fields such as organization studies, broadly construed, along with diverse literature concerning cognitive, social, and political processes. The model also reflects research findings concerning, for example, the activities, interactions, and sentiments of officials such as politicians, government officers, negotiators, managers, and trade unionists. The model has been applied to original case material (Brown and Hosking 1986; Grieco and Hosking 1987), from which selected illustrations will be drawn.

## Definitions and Perspectives on Organization

Writers on organization have typically been reluctant to offer formal definitions. Further, on the rare occasions on which they have done so, the definition has seldom been implemented. It has been common practice to move directly to the discussion of 'organization characteristics', rather than first say what 'organization' is. This situation is changing: more attempts are being made to conceptualize organization (e.g. Meyer *et al.* 1985), and 'paradigms' are being hotly contested (Zey-Ferrell and Aiken 1981; Donaldson 1985).

It is perhaps relatively uncontroversial to suggest that the concept of organization implies the following three elements. First, there is a fundamentally social reference: people, or some subset of their values, identities, and behavioural repertoires are 'included' (Lewin 1947). Secondly, there is implied some minimal level of activity, interaction, and cooperation by and between actors: organization implies relationships having cognitive (broadly speaking), social, and—as will later be argued—political aspects. Thirdly, these activities and relationships will show a degree of stability and order such that actions and interactions can be grounded in 'explanations' of the past, and anticipation of the future.

The many writings on organization can broadly be distinguished into two traditions. These emphasize, on the one hand, organization as a noun, as a state, entity, or 'condition', and, on the other hand, organization as a verb, as activity and process (see Hosking and Morley 1985). A more precise description of these traditions can be achieved through examination of four issues: issues where proponents of an 'organizing' perspective typically take one position, whilst those who focus on the 'organized condition' take another.

Of course, distinctions are rarely so neat in practice, and published work often can be seen to combine some elements of both perspectives (e.g. Meyer, Stevenson, and Webster 1985). Distinctions are further complicated by the fact that the concept of the 'organized condition' has largely been induced from research practices—as was noted earlier; definitions have seldom been made explicit. This has a drawback in that research is guided not just by theory, but also by the need to make pragmatic decisions.

With these *caveats* in mind, one final clarification is required concerning comparisons between these two perspectives. The argument here is not that those who focus on organization have no interest in processes, nor that those who stress processes reject the use of ordinary language descriptions of organization to locate and circumscribe their investigations. Such an argument would trivialize both perspectives; further, examples of both types are not hard to find (e.g. Blau 1964; Weick 1979; Manning 1982; Meyer *et al.* 1985). The existence of such examples has been taken to mean that the two perspectives (taken as wholes) are compatible (Meyer *et al.* 1985). However, the view taken here is that the concept of organization intrinsic to each directly conflicts with the other.

Differences in perspective are here understood to reflect different research interests, and /or contrasting views on what is important, and/or varying beliefs about the advantages of particular methodologies. They may reflect fundamental disagreements over issues of epistemology and ontology—indeed, this is generally held to be the case (e.g. Burrell and Morgan

1979). However, the view taken here is that questions of ontology are beyond the scope of social science. In addition, the coupling of methodologies and perspectives, on the one hand, and epistemological assumptions, on the other, is too loose to justify such conclusions.

The two perspectives will next be discussed in relation to the four key issues mentioned earlier. They are: 'top-down' or 'bottom-up' approaches; emphasis on 'physical' or 'social realities'; 'unitary' or 'pluralist' views of values and interests; and, finally, an emphasis on 'choices' or 'constraints'. These issues are discussed in ways which stress the advantages of an 'organizing' perspective. Broadly speaking, these advantages accrue from the serious and detailed attention to relations between person and organization, and to the differing contributions of interested participants. Given these qualities, an organizing perspective provides the essential foundations for the model of organizing skills with which this article is primarily concerned.

## *Top-Down or Bottom-Up*

To emphasize the condition of being organized is to treat 'the organization' as an identifiable entity, or unit of analysis, which exists independently of participants' activities and sentiments. Some minimal degree of unity is assumed to follow from shared cognitions, shared goals, and/or shared values. In addition, the 'entity' is typically assumed to be held together by 'organization structures'—again treated as independent of participants. This approach is referred to here as 'top-down' in the sense that the model of organization (top) is separate from, and causally dominant to, the model of person (bottom).

Whether a top-down approach is adopted for pragmatic reasons, or believed to be descriptively valid, organization is treated as 'not merely greater than the sum of its parts, but so superior that it is *effectively divorced from the influence of its parts*' (Georgiou 1973: 77; emphasis added). In other words, the approach results in a sharp divide between person and organization such that the agent, responsible for the latter, is left untheorized as an agent. For this reason, it is perhaps not surprising that relations between leadership and organization have been largely ignored: the definition of the latter has made it independent of, and incommensurate with, leadership.

Rather than direct attention to an assumed whole, a bottom-up approach emphasizes the 'parts' to which Georgiou referred. Of course, these may be conceptualized in various ways. However, since the 'bottom' unit of analysis is person, such a perspective may be judged adequate by the extent to which it reflects a sufficient model of person, and recognizes persons as agents in the achievement of organization. In this way, a bottom-up approach has the advantage of shifting emphasis away from the assumption of a relatively static condition (organization), to the processes in which organizing is manifest—an inherently dynamic perspective.

In conclusion, a bottom-up approach renders amenable to analysis leadership acts and processes as special kinds of organizing: organizing which reflects, and consistently effects, other 'parts'. This makes leadership intrinsic to organization, rather than a mere epiphenomenon, as in a top-down perspective. It is for reasons such as these that an 'organizing' perspective is advocated.

## *Physical and Social Realities*

When the condition of being organized is emphasized, this focuses attention on 'organizational characteristics' in a way which implies that they exist independently of the interactions and sense-making of participants. This has been referred to as a 'physicalist' approach (Allport 1955). For example, it is managers who have typically been requested to describe 'organizational structures'—that is, the 'prescribed framework of organization' (Ranson *et al.* 1980). The accompanying assumption has been that others would provide similar descriptions—as, on the whole, they would—if organization structures were physical objects and if the raters had an equal degree of relevant knowledge. However, different raters provide different descriptions (see e.g. Aldrich 1979). Further, there is often found a degree of consensus within groups of interacting participants which is absent between them. These, along with related findings, reveal the significance of interpretation in perceptual processes, and show that there is an important sense in which they are socially constructed; as was remarked long ago, perception is not an epistemology (Allport 1955).

Here, an approach is argued in which attention is addressed, not to organization structures as outlined above, but to social constructions of organizing. This may be achieved through examination of relationships, interdependencies, influence status, and social order, and could include attention to centralization, standardization, and so on. Such an approach recognized that, through their organizing activities, participants 'assemble ongoing interdependent action into sensible sequences that generate sensible outcomes' (Weick 1978: 3). There is need to study organizing activities in which participants negotiate and enact a sense of 'social order'—that is, an 'adequate guide to the use of knowledge and the conduct of human affairs' (Kelvin 1970: 226). It is important to be clear that organizing is advocated as the focus of analysis, whether or not located in relation to 'an organization' (in the ordinary language sense). For this reason, attention is directed to observed activities, acts, contacts, and relationships, and to participants' constructions of relationships and social order. Illustrations will later be given of these processes, and a model of organizing skills articulated.

## *Unitary or Pluralist Perspective*

A unitary perspective has permeated the characterization of 'organization' as a condition. It has long been apparent in the popular assumption that participants share goals and/or values, and that their activities should reflect this. When this seems not to be the case, explanations have been sought which are consistent with the underlying, unitary assumption. For example, it is suggested that people are imperfect information processors and therefore not very good at acting in rational accordance with their goals.

When organizing is emphasized, activities and relationships provide the starting-point for analysis; for this reason, there is no need to assume shared goals. Instead, more minimal assumptions are possible: for example, the activities and relationships reflect beliefs about interdependence, or what Weick has referred to as 'interlocking means' (Weick 1979). Thus, attention to organizing is attention to activities and relationships and to their connections with sense-making. In particular, considerable importance is attached to participants' beliefs about cause and effect, how these connect with their values and interests, and how they are reflected in action. Again, it is emphasized that 'social order' contributes to, and is evidence of, organizing; further, organizing does not require 'an organization' to be manifest.

## *Choices and Constraints*

Attention to the condition of being organized has typically been accompanied by an emphasis on organization as a source of constraint. Organization structures have been studied as agents of activities and relationships, and, to some extent, sense-making. As has been seen, the emphasis of an organizing perceptive is somewhat different: to emphasize meaningful action is to attend to the actor as an agent, which, in turn, raises the question of choice, and the conditions for its exercise in favour of one line of action rather than another.

When choice is exercised in the context of interdependence, in the context of differences in values, and in the context of differing constructions of social order, consideration of power and influence is irresistible. So too is the need to investigate the conditions of influence as they characterize relationships—what some have called the 'negotiation of order' (e.g. Strauss 1978). For these reasons, organizing activities should be understood as political decision-making in which, to some significant degree, participants negotiate relationships, definitions of social order, and distributions of resources.

### *Organizing: Summary*

It has been argued that there is need for increased attention to organization as a verb, and that organizing should be the recognized 'unit' of analysis—not 'an organization'. Such an approach offers a general framework for the study of organizing, whether or not the actors are legally contracted to the same, or indeed any, employer. It has been argued that what is important is that organizing is performed in interrelated social, cognitive, and political processes: processes which reflect and effect differing values and interests; processes which reflect and create interdependence and inequalities of influence. Later it will be argued that these processes (*a*) can be fruitfully examined as a negotiated order; (*b*) can be conceptualized in relatively novel ways to recognize the differing contributions of persons, and (*c*) depend on leadership processes to facilitate their flexibility and effective long-term promotion of interests.

## Definitions and Perspectives: Leaders and Leadership

'There are almost as many different definitions of leadership as there are persons who have attempted to define the concept' (Bass 1981: 7). Even so, it is possible to identify certain points on which most, if not all, would agree. As with the concept of organization, three elements seem common to most conceptualizations. First, leadership is a fundamentally social phenomenon, and some form of social interaction, usually face to face, is required. Secondly, leadership has the effect of structuring activities and relationships, and related sense-making processes. Thirdly, to be defined as a leader, a participant must be perceived as salient, relative to others; in particular, he or she will be recognized as of higher status in terms of his or her contributions to influence.

It is important to notice that the above elements refer both to 'leader', and to 'leadership'. The first tradition is identified as that which treats these as synonymous, and researches them as though they were properties of an individual. This approach is analogous to the 'entitative' view of organization and therefore referred to in this way. Here the 'entity' is the leader; leadership being treated as a leader characteristic—whether identifiable in what leaders do, or in their underlying characteristics. A second tradition is reflected in the work of a small minority who take seriously the view that leadership is not a personal property, but a process having particular social and cognitive relationship dimensions (e.g. Douglas 1983). This is the view favoured here. Both the entitative and processual approaches will be outlined; however, the latter will be argued for in ways which facilitate later arguments about leadership processes and organizing skills.

As with our discussion of organization and organizing, it is important to emphasize that those who adopt the entitative view may also attend to at least some leadership processes. Similarly, those who emphasize leadership processes may study appointed officials; they may also conclude that, in a given study, a particular individual does, in fact, make the most substantial contributions to leadership processes. None of this, of itself, has direct implications for the underlying constructs of the theorists; as before, what is critical are the different theoretical constructs which underlie the research.

## *Person or process*

The bulk of research claiming to be concerned with leadership has, in fact, focused on appointed officials, managers, and the like. In other words, the approach has largely been top-down, attention being directed to those role occupants who are either assumed to be active in leadership, or assumed to meet some other conceptual requirement. As a result, a considerable portion of research has investigated leaders' characteristics, leadership being treated as though it were one.

In contrast, the bottom-up approach is careful not to conflate the concepts of leader and leadership. Leadership processes are the focus of interests, leaders being identified as those who make especially salient contributions. This is the approach advocated here. Leadership acts are contributed by participants who 'influence their fellows more than they are influenced by them' (Gibb 1969: 212). However, to be defined as leadership acts, it is essential that such influence is acceptable. In other words, when influence is salient, which it will not always be, participants construe it as at least compatible with the means by which they seek to satisfy their values and interests. Leaders are defined as those who 'consistently make effective contributions to social order, and who are expected and perceived to do so' (Hosking and Morley 1985).

It is for the above reasons that leadership is claimed as a certain kind of 'organizing' activity. When leadership is defined in this way it implies: first, that leaders may or may not be appointed officials; secondly, that there may be one or more of them; thirdly, that they can be identified only through the analysis of leadership processes, and, last, that leadership, like organization, is not usefully restricted within the more or less arbitrary bounds of formal organization. When sense-making and social interaction are stressed, as they are here, this provides a way of theorizing 'parts' of organization, and, more importantly, a way of theorizing relations between them. This, in turn, allows the use of a consistent and integrated conceptual framework for locating leaders in different contexts. It is this issue to which we will turn next.

## *Physical and Social Realities*

Those who have focused on leaders, and leadership as a personal characteristic, have paid relatively little attention to the social realities of either leaders or those with whom they interact. For example, just as with organization structures, physicalist assumptions have characterized much of the research on leader behaviours; different sources (leaders, subordinates, superordinates) are expected to produce similar descriptions. Likewise, 'situational' and 'organizational' characteristics have generally been treated as contextual variables, independent of the activities and sense-making of participants (e.g. Fiedler 1967; Meyer 1975). In sum, a physicalist approach has dominated work on leadership, just as it has dominated work on organization. This has been reflected in a person–situation split which treats leaders as entities, leadership as their relatively unbounded acts, and contexts as conditions independent of participants' cognitive-social processes.

An emphasis on social realities directs attention to the sense-making activities of participants. These will be examined here in relation to leadership processes, identifying acts which influence social constructions; those who are perceived to make the most consistent and significant contributions; and why they are perceived to do so. This is a negotiated order perspective which, unlike many others, does recognize inqualities in the influence achieved by different participants (see Meltzer *et al.* 1975).

## *Unitary or Pluralist Perspective*

The entitative approach is unitary in that it minimizes differences in values and interests, particularly as they might exist between interdependent groups 'in' organization. However, when investigating what counts as leadership contributions, and what counts as effective leadership, such differences cannot be ignored (Hosking 1984). More generally, values and interests cannot be ignored, for the reason that they are implicated in participants' constructions of their pasts, presents, and futures, along with understandings of cause-effect relationships, the conditions for acceptance or rejection of influence attempts, and distributions of resources. In sum, values and interests are central to participants' constructions of their social order and the terms on which they will 'do business'.

An implication of these remarks is that the pluralist approach, unlike the unitary, recognizes that leadership is a political process. Leadership is a political matter for the reason that different participants may seek to further different, sometimes conflicting, values and interests; further, leadership is political for the reason that some values and interests are likely to be promoted at the expense of others. Later, a model will be described in which a pluralist approach is taken of leadership as skilful organizing. This will be achieved through a bottom-up approach which stresses interdependence of means, subjective realities, and the conditions of choice.

## *Choices and Constraints*

The top-down approach has largely attended to choice as the prerogative of leaders; they have been examined as they choose their styles of interaction with 'subordinates', and as they might choose their 'situations' (see House and Baetz 1979). In such a perspective, leaders' styles are expected to be constraining, directing and controlling the choices of subordinates.

A bottom-up approach makes no assumptions about who necessarily exercises choice, or who are necessarily constrained; leaders are identified by the effects of their acts, not by the fact of their appointment. The particular approach adopted here locates choice in the wider context of political decision-making. This directs attention to the processes by which certain choices come to be implemented, and why. Leadership is considered as a process in which social order is negotiated, sometimes tacitly, and sometimes explicitly. Those who achieve most influence in the course of negotiations, who do so most consistently, and who come to be expected and perceived to do so, are here defined as leaders.

### *Leadership Processes: Summary and Conclusions*

The approach favoured here has been relatively little researched. The view is taken that leaders emerge in the course of interactions—that is, in the course of political decision processes. These 'organizing processes' involve the more or less collective negotiation of social order, including recipes for action, and the terms of exchange. Further, these processes are not necessarily confined 'within an organization', in the ordinary language sense.

The implications of such a perspective are adequately recognized only when the concept of social order is given its full significance. It has been noted that the concept refers to the degree to which participants have an adequate guide to the use of knowledge and the conduct of human affairs. However, this does not mean that order consists of 'some rigid perpetuation of doing things the way they have always been done' (Kelvin 1970: 226). On the contrary, to have any degree of permanence, social order must be flexible to the degree that relatively enduring changes can be both created and handled. This is a 'dilemma' intrinsic to all social organization (Brown and Hosking 1986). It is a dilemma because an 'uncommitted potentiality for change' (Bateson 1972) must be achieved without the sacrifice of a degree of stability sufficient for participants to experience a sense of identity and continuity. There are various ways of trying to reconcile these conflicting demands; however, only some are effective in the longer term (Weick 1979: 217). The view is taken that the handling of this dilemma is, in some fundamental sense, what leadership is all about; as will be seen, the processes required to achieve this must be very skilful indeed.

## Leaders, Leadership, and Social Skills

Surprising though it may seem, few have seriously considered leadership in terms of skill. Brief mention will be made of relevant work, primarily to show what it does *not* do. As before, the intention is to show what kind of model is being proposed, and how it differs from existing work.

It is possible to identify four lines of approach to the leadership and social skill. Each focuses on leaders as persons, rather than leadership processes, and each locates leaders in 'an organization', rather than examining the skills of organizing. This means that they are largely incompatible with the approach to leadership and organizing adopted here.

## The Regression Approach to Leader Effectiveness

This has dominated theory-oriented research on leadership effectiveness. The general line of argument has been to consider effectiveness as a function of, on the one hand, characteristics of the leader, and, on the other, characteristics of the situation. Skill has effectively been treated as a leader characteristic, rather like behaviour—that is, as an *input* to the effectiveness equation (see Martinko and Gardner 1984). Further, the related practice has been to treat leader characteristics as independent of the situation. In sum, the approach is entitative; leaders and situations are theorized in ways which make them incommensurate.

## Skill as a Personal Resource

The concept of skill has received some prominence in longitudinal studies of decision-making and participation (e.g. Heller 1984). In essence, the approach shares certain similarities with that just described; skill is treated as a personal competence—that is, as an input which may be well or poorly utilized by 'the organization'. Further, interest is directed to decisions *in* organization, rather than to organizing as a more or less skilful decision process.

## Managerial Skills

There is now a considerable literature describing, for example, what managers do, the kinds of relationships they build, the problems they meet, the decisions they take, and so on. Further, some authors at least have begun to note that certain skills seem implied (see Stewart 1976; Kotter 1982). However, little interest has been shown in developing systematic accounts rather than lists, or in developing conceptual bridges between the terms 'manager' and 'leader'.

## Micro-Skills of Interpersonal Communications

Perhaps the most systematic account of social skills has been developed by Argyle and his colleagues, an account in which social skills are represented as analogous to motor skills (Argyle and Kendon 1967). This model is highly circumscribed, in that it focuses on what the performer does, rather than offering a more comprehensive model of performers and performances.

Others have extended this approach by making specific reference to leaders, and by giving more attention to cognitive and motivational aspects of the performer (Alban-Metcalfe 1982; Wright and Taylor 1984). However, these developments have not been of a kind which make it possible satisfactorily to theorize relations between persons and organization.

### *Summary and Comment: Existing Work on Skills*

This literature differs in important ways from the conceptualization of leadership skills shortly to be described. The first is that they are top-down, their scope being restricted to the actions of appointed officials in relation to their subordinates. In contrast, a bottom-up approach will be argued for in which leadership processes are considered as more or less skilful.

Secondly, the literature has tended to concentrate on face-to-face interactions. However, given an interest in the skills of leadership, this is far too restrictive. As will be seen, leadership cannot be understood by exclusive reference to interpersonal and/or within-group processes. Participants are more or less active outside their group, and this has considerable implications for organizing processes and for social order.

Thirdly, in the literature described, the concept of skill has been restricted to a single actor's behaviour, with other social and psychological processes largely being ignored. In contrast, it is here argued that organizing processes can be judged as more or less skilful only when understood in relation to the sense-making of participants, in relation to their values and sense of social order. The model to be presented describes social processes such as networking, in which participants negotiate an account of what is going on, and what needs to be done. The processes are more or less collective, and more or less skilful. The individual enters the analysis through recognition that participants act in different ways, and some contributions achieve more influence than others.

## Social Skills, Leadership, and the Negotiation of Order

It is now possible to outline a systematic and integrative model which combines and implements these critiques of the literature on leadership, skill, and organization. Such a model will require adequate concepts of participants, processes, and contexts. Further, and this is critical, these must be theorized in ways which allow them to be discussed in commensurate terms.

As was mentioned earlier, the view is taken that the skills of leadership are the skills of complex decision-making. Decision-making is understood to begin when one or more participants conclude that the status quo is changing, is likely to change, or is in need of change, and takes action on that basis. Actual and potential events are interpreted in relation to values and interests, and in relation to beliefs about causal connections. Changes may be interpreted as either 'threats' or 'opportunities'—that is, as potential losses or gains for their social order. Decision-making is complex when the consequences of a given course of action or policy are unclear; it is complex to the extent that some consequences seem desirable whilst others do not; it is complex when it is political, when participants disagree about 'the values at stake, the weight to be given to them, the resolution of major uncertainties' (Steinbruner 1974: 18). Organizing processes involve decision-making of this kind (Hosking 1987).

The skills implicated in decision-making can be described using the language of information search, interpretation, influence, and choice, here referred to as 'core processes' (Hosking and Morley 1988). The terms of the model (see Fig. 15.1) have deliberately been made abstract so as to accom-

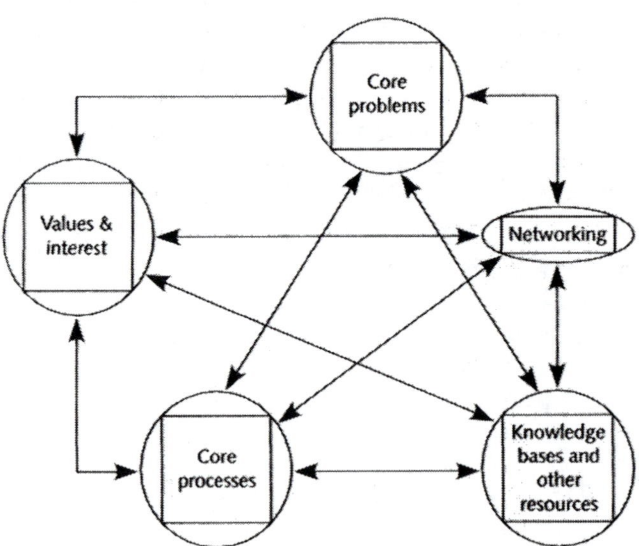


**Fig. 15.1.** Organizing skills.

modate variations in *the content* of the processes discussed. This allows the model to be applied to organizing as it is manifest in relation to diverse 'values and interests', 'knowledge bases', and the like. The use of abstract terms also has the advantage of providing a common language for discussing the three elements in the model, and for discussing their relations.

Last, it should be noted that Fig. 15.1 shows each element to be connected with each other element. This is consistent with the earlier argument that relations between persons and contexts are achieved through the processes of enactment, and social constructions of reality. Despite the difficulties this implies for testing, it seems that these relations are best described as reciprocal and non-contingent, rather than one-way and causal (Gauld and Shotter 1977).

## *Networking, Core Processes, and Core Problems*

Decision-makers may be more or less active in making social contacts and in building relationships. They may do so both within their social order, and with persons 'outside' it. Social contacts may provide information, sponsorship, and other resources, depending on factors such as the strength of direct and indirect relationships, and whether they share the same sense of social order.

Granovetter (1974) is often cited as a seminal study of social networks in transmitting information about employment possibilities. His arguments focused on the relative significance of 'weak' compared with 'strong' contacts—indicated by contact frequency—in the provision of information about employment. His arguments and findings could be very relevant to present interests in networking as a more or less skilful organizing process. However, the perspective and methodology mean that his work is not as relevant as it might be.

Broadly speaking, Granovetter did not investigate 'networking' in the way that the concept is used here. He adopted a methodology in which respondents provided a 'snapshot' of contacts and contact frequency in relation to the one-way 'transmission' of job information. He did not investigate the dynamics of relationships weak or strong, and therefore paid little attention to social exchange, social influence, and associated values and interests. Further, a 'physicalist' model of the actor was adopted, ignoring actors' constructions of 'information', the latter being treated as a fixed commodity. It is central to the present argument that actors are recognized to be more or less active, more or less strategic, and more or less skilful in the cognitive, social processes of reality construction; studies of social networks are of particular value to the extent that they attend to such processes (see Grieco and Hosking 1987).

Other studies have implied (Stewart 1976; Kanter 1983), or argued (Kotter 1982), that 'networking' is an activity which managers (organizers?) perform to varying degrees, with important implications for their effectiveness. However, the concept has yet to be developed in ways which recognize its processual and strategic implications. Further, 'networking' has yet to be recognized as a more or less collaborative process which may reflect varying degrees of skill in the protection and promotion of interests.

The concept of 'networking' is here used to refer to a major organizing activity, one which may make all the difference to whether or not changes in the status quo are understood and handled in ways which protect or further values and interests. Contributions depend on the networking activities of only a few participants in organizing, or on the activities of many. Networking has strategic implications, whether or not it is practised consciously. For reasons that will become clear, leadership processes are more likely to be skilful when one or more participants is active in networking with those on whom the interests of the order most depend.

In ordinary language, networking helps participants (*a*) to build up their knowledge bases and other resources; (*b*) to come to understand the processes through which they can promote their values and interests, and (*c*) to translate their understandings into action. In others words, networking helps participants handle the 'core problems' of working out what is going on (problem identification), what could be done (development of solutions), and what must be done (selection and implementation of policy).

There are two reasons why networking may facilitate the group's handling of their 'core problems'. The first is associated with the development of knowledge and understanding as referred to in (*a*) and (*b*) above. It has already been established that interpretations are social constructions and are, therefore, to some degree negotiated. They are formed by 'moving around' the decision-making environment and talking to people. Interpretations are formed by building relationships in which information, amongst other things, is exchanged. Some people 'move around' more than others. What is more, some are better than others at networking with those on whom they are, or could be, dependent. Similarly, groups differ in the degree to which one or more participants are active in these ways, and are expected to be so (Brown and Hosking 1986).

Networking may also facilitate 'knowledge and understanding' because of its relationship with 'ordinary seeing' (Neisser 1976). To explain, in moving around, participants are less likely to distort, deny, or remain unaware of contradictions (Steinbruner 1974; Nisbett and Ross 1980); further, they can float ideas and get feedback to help them determine what agreements will work and which will be acceptable (see Huff 1984; Wrapp 1984). Networking reduces the likelihood of inflexible, categorical judgements, and, by facilitating the recognition and accommodation of change, facilitates social learning. In other words, networking makes it more likely that participants will build an adequate knowledge base in which they understand threats and opportunities, dilemmas and so on. In general terms, they are more likely to be able to handle the 'core problems' of working out what is going on and what might be done about it (see Fig. 15.1).

The second reason why networking may facilitate the handling of core problems concerns the group's ability then 'to translate their understandings into action', as in (*c*) above. It is through networking that choice and influence come to be associated with information search and interpretation. To explain, networking helps to achieve influence both within the social order and with those 'outside'. With respect to the latter, attempts may be made to influence those on whom the values and interests of the group depend. Whether inside or 'outside' the group, relationships provide channels for achieving direct and indirect influence—that is, for structuring the interpretations and choices of others.

One of the most common ways in which influence is achieved follows from reasons already given: networking facilitates the development of 'knowledge bases', which in turn provide the basis for vivid descriptions, having requisite variety (Weick 1978), and achieving informational influence (Vinokur and Burnstein 1978). Such descriptions, 'scripts', or 'schema' attract commitment because they engage central values and suggest ways in which resources can be mobilized to promote them; they are descriptions of the social order, how it was, is now, and might be. It is by these processes that 'information' is invested with value; it is in these processes that leadership is evidenced, since, as defined earlier, leadership acts are those which most influence what information is used and how. When particular individuals consistently make contributions of this kind, and come to be expected to do so, the term 'leader' is appropriate. For these reasons, leaders are defined as those who have a major impact on the creation of 'social knowledge' (Trujillo 1983).

## *Networking, Negotiation, and Exchange*

It is important to stress again that organizing processes are processes in which order is *negotiated*, both within and between groups. Within the group, core problems are handled by a more or less collective process of negotiation. However, there is evidence to suggest that the processes involved in identification and development are more likely to resemble 'integrative bargaining', whilst those involved in selection are more likely to be 'distributive' (see Walton and McKersie 1966). In addition, groups differ in the degree to which they value particular means, such as 'distributed leadership', and this will also influence the nature and frequency of their negotiations (see Brown and Hosking 1986).

Negotiation characterizes relationships for reasons already given; different people sponsor different 'scripts', and influence has to be acceptable. As has been seen, some participants are more influential than others. This is why organizing skills are to some extent the skills of negotiation. More generally, negotiation characterizes within—and between—group processes in which understandings are built and translated into action. These are the processes in which particular acts achieve influence and come eventually to be associated with particular actors—that is, leaders emerge. This is how policy and social order are negotiated and implemented in the more or less continuous processes of organizing.

Finally, negotiation characterizes relationships because organizing processes are processes of *exchange*. Exchange has long been recognized to be a basic characteristic of social processes (e.g. Homans 1961). Some theorists, of whom Blau is a notable example, have made contributions which are especially relevant to present interests. In *Exchange and Power in Social Life* Blau (1964) emphasized social structures as they emerge through interaction, recognized that relationships should not be reduced to characteristics of individuals, and made explicit attempts to link leadership and organization.

Less attractive, given our present interests, is Blau's distinction between social and economic exchange, his focus on economic exchanges and economic principles, and his emphasis on objective reality. This perspective is related to his rejection of an interpretative approach to social action (Blau 1964: 13). As a result, he fails to give due recognition to symbolic processes and negotiation, and their role in the definition of, for example, status, rewards, leadership, and social order. Even so, the basic foundations of his work can be developed into a more adequate theory of social processes (e.g. Kapferer 1972; Singleman 1972). The implications of such a perspective could then be considered in relation to a revised concept of organization.

The term 'exchange' is here used broadly to include fairly tangible resources of the sort emphasized in economic perspectives, and in discussions of 'transactional leadership' (Burns 1978). However, considerable importance is also attached to symbolic resources as contributed by acts which give meaning and perspective to events (see earlier discussion). A major reason why participants gain power in a system of relationships is because others come to rely on them for contributions of this kind. It seems to be popular to exclude such processes from the range of the exchange concept, defining them as something unusual as 'transformational leadership' (Burns 1978).

However, here the more general concept of exchange is argued to be essential for the understanding of leadership and organizing. Symbolic processes are not rare, they are central to the understanding of long-term relationships, and, in particular, to the understanding of 'flexible' social order.

## *Networking and Knowledge Bases*

Something has already been said of the ways in which networking facilitates the development of knowledge bases. It involves the development and sharing of practical understanding, what others have called 'organizational learning' (see Shrivastava 1983). A key argument has been that those who are more active in networking are more likely to be skilled perceivers; this is how they build their knowledge bases, and, in particular, their understanding of threats and opportunities.

## *Threats and Opportunities*

Those active in networking have more than one account of events, are more likely to know on which issues to focus and so on. More generally, networking facilitates the development of higher order constructs or 'scripts' (Gioia and Poole 1984). These serve 'more or less systematically [to] organize knowledge of the environment and how to work in it' (Hosking and Morley 1985). They exemplify certain kinds of threats and opportunities and how they are handled.

Threats and opportunities may be misinterpreted or neglected. Equally, they may be handled skilfully, increasing the probability that the values and interests of the group will be protected or furthered. Illustrations can be cited from recent studies of family-based networks, some of whom move strategically from one employment setting to another (Grieco 1984; Grieco and Hosking 1987). Network members were found to organize their employment *as a network*. Strategies included locating the members with one employer, or a range of employers, depending on the threats and opportunities understood to be associated with each.

Briefly, family members were found to be employed, not as isolated individuals in different workplaces, but alongside other members of their extended kin group. This was shown to be true over periods of forty or fifty years, even when migration was necessary to achieve a collective presence. Many networks moved in response to the interpretation of changes in the status quo, changes which implied a local threat and/or opportunities elsewhere. In many cases, movement followed the perceived threat of closure. Some members clearly networked more than others and were therefore able to integrate information from different sources, often from other members of the extended kin group. For example, they combined evidence of cutbacks in maintenance programmes with indications that labour was not being replaced, and with knowledge that company properties were being sold. Often, they heard rumours of future redundancies, just as others did, but because of their networking were better able to make sense of what was going on.

## *Capacities and Demands*

Here, the emphasis of the argument shifts from understanding to implementation. The key argument comes from the information-processing paradigm in cognitive psychology, and has been applied to social skills by Welford (1980). At its most general, his argument is that skill is found in the use of 'efficient strategies' to link the 'demands' of tasks with the 'capabilities' of performers. 'Demands' are here conceptualized as core problems, 'capacities' are conceptualized as resources—and resources are limited. Such limitations have especially important implications in relation to understanding threats and opportunities, and in respect of being more or less able to mobilize relationships to achieve influence.

It will come as no surprise that 'efficient strategies' are seen as likely to be most consistently practised by those who are active in networking. This is because they not only have more diverse and/or accurate scripts, but also because they have built relationships within which they can negotiate acceptance of their influence. Returning to the studies of family networks, it seems clear that some participants organized the network more than others, having a major influence over moves to new places of employment and so on. They did so through networking, through their analysis of threats and opportunities, and through arguing in support of scripts that others found persuasive.

'Demands' are met, to a greater or lesser degree, through the development and mobilization of capacities—that is, network resources. In the case of the family networks, once a member had gained access to a workplace, this generated resources to facilitate the employment of other network members. In other words, the network's capacity to meet the threats confronting their values and interests was increased. It should be added that the same small minority were usually the first to achieve family entry into a work site. Once employed, it was they who initially provided 'inside' information on vacancies, job requirements, points to stress in an interview, and so on. It was they who were able to sponsor new entrants from the network, provide food and lodging and other resources. However, once they were employed, other members were also able to contribute to linking the network's capacities and demands.

It is important to appreciate that this reputational resource was dependent on the recognition by all network members of its utility in gaining and preserving employment. The network's reputation was as a source of 'good workers'. Note that, by the perspective adopted here, they sought to preserve this reputation because they found acceptable the terms of exchange negotiated within the family network—terms which, in this area at least, also operated in the interests of the employer.

As has been emphasized, activities of the kind described both supported, and were supported by, a shared sense of social order, and therefore shared understandings about helping, reciprocity of exchange, and so on. Leadership contributions came from many sources over the years. However, only two participants seemed consistently to achieve influence in the strategic handling of core problems, and to have been perceived in this way. It was usually they who were the first to enter and/or leave a new place of employment. It was they who did the most to interpret threats and opportunities, and to link capacities with demands.

## *Dilemmas*

Dilemmas are endemic to the processes of complex decision-making described earlier and, for this reason, endemic to organizational processes. Dilemmas make decision-making difficult and often stressful. They characterize situations of choice whereby selection of a policy—concerning means or ends—rules out an alternative, and in so doing, leaves a problem unresolved. More seriously, there is the type of dilemma which arises when there are major costs if a policy does not change, but there are also major costs if it does (Janis and Mann 1977).

Perhaps the most fundamental dilemma is that which underlies the achievement of 'flexible social order'. The dilemma is how to achieve a degree of order which is sufficient for core problems to continue to be solved, whilst at the same time, not too much, perpetuating a rigid way of doing things as they have always been done (see earlier). This is a dilemma for *all* social organization, however; depending on their values, the dilemma is greater for some than for others. There is evidence to suggest that social-movement groups might be particularly vulnerable (Brown and Hosking 1986). Such groups have to 'keep from degenerating into solely consummatory activities on the one hand, or rationalizing. . . . into too rigid a structure on the other, and in so doing alienating. . . . members' (Freeman 1975: 102).

### *Other Kinds of Knowledge*

A number of authors have noted the extent and significance of knowledge bases in achieving effective organization. For example, certain general managers have been observed to be 'incredibly knowledgeable' about various aspects of their business (Kotter 1982: 126). In particular, they have been found to have a high degree of 'organizational familiarity' and 'industry familiarity' (Gupta 1984). All organizing is dependent on knowledge bases which are in some sense relevant to the core problems shared by participants. Some of this knowledge may be primarily of relevance only to a certain social order—for example, concerning particular interdependencies with other social orders, the requirements of particular jobs in a given labour market, the values, interests and resources of a particular group, and so on. Other knowledge, such as the legal framework of activities, may be of more general relevance.

Knowledge bases of this kind are an essential feature of flexible social order. Their role is especially apparent in the processes by which family-based networks achieve employment for their members. For example, certain networks coordinated the results of members' information-search activities. This information gave the network knowledge of, for example, a wide variety of employers and places of employment, the requirements of particular jobs, where jobs were likely to be lost or gained, and so on (Grieco 1984).

What is important here is that the relevant knowledge was both available and could be mobilized. Those most active in networking are most likely to contribute to, and make sense of, the network's knowledge bases, to have the relationships which will facilitate their mobilization, and, therefore, to be most consistently influential in the structuring of social order. It is in this sense that leaders contribute most to skilful leadership processes.

## Summary

Substantial literature is to be found on 'leadership', 'organization', and, to a lesser extent, social skill. This literature is almost entirely independent—that is, the central concepts are not integrated. It has been argued that the concepts can, and indeed should, be theorized in relation to one another.

A model has been described which does just this. It is believed to represent a truly social psychological approach, combining argument about persons, processes, and contexts. This has been achieved through taking the view that leadership cannot be abstracted from the organizational processes of which it is a part. The study of leadership, properly conceived, is the study of the processes in which flexible social order is negotiated and practised so as to protect and promote the values and interests in which it is grounded. The skills here described are endemic to these processes in that, if they are at a low level, the social order will be unlikely to survive long. Equally, to the extent that organizing processes reflect high levels of these skills, the values and interests of the social order are likely to be protected and promoted. To the extent that particular participants are expected and perceived to make consistent, influential, contributions, leaders are argued to make especially important contributions to skilful organizing.

## Note

This chapter was written whilst Visiting Fellow at the Department of Psychology, University of Warwick, UK, and revised whilst Visiting Fellow, Department of Psychology, Flinders University of South Australia.

## References

Alban-Metcalfe, B. (1982), 'Leadership: Extrapolating from Theory and Research to Practical Skills Training', *Journal of Management Studies*, 19/3: 295–305.

Aldrich, H. (1979), *Organizations and Environments* (Englewood Cliffs, NJ: Prentice-Hall).

Allport, F. (1955), *Theories of Perception and the Concept of Structure* (New York: Wiley).

Argyle, M., and Kendon, A. (1967), 'The Experimental Analysis of Social Performance', in I. Berkowitz (ed.), *Advances in Experimental Social Psychology*, iii. (New York: Academic Press).

Bass, B. M. (1981), *Stogdill's Handbook of Leadership: A Survey of Theory and Research* (New York: Free Press).

Bateson, G. (1972), *Steps to an Ecology of Mind* (London: Intertext).

Blau, P. (1964), *Exchange and Power In Social Life* (New York: Wiley).

Brown, H., and Hosking, D. M. (1986), 'Distributed Leadership and Skilled Performance as Successful Organization in Social Movements', *Human Relations*, 39/1: 65–79.

Burns, J. (1978), *Leadership* (New York: Harper & Row).

Burrell, G., and Morgan, G. (1979), *Sociological Paradigms and Organizational Analysis* (London: Heinemann).

Donaldson, L. (1985), *In Defence of Organization Theory* (Cambridge: Cambridge University Press).

Douglas, T. (1983), *Groups: Understanding People Gathered Together* (London: Tavistock).

Fiedler, F. E. (1967), *A Theory of Leadership Effectiveness* (New York: McGraw-Hill).

Freeman, J. (1975), *The Politics of Women's Liberation* (London: Longman).

Gauld, A., and Shotter, J. (1977), *Human Action and its Psychological Investigation* (London: Routledge & Kegan Paul).

Georgiou, P. (1973), 'The Goal Paradigm and Notes Towards A Counter Paradigm', *Administrative Science Quarterly,* 18: 291–310.

Gibb, C. (1969), 'Leadership', in G. Lindzey and E. Aronson (eds.), *The Handbook of Social Psychology,* iv (2nd edn., Reading, Mass.: Addison-Wesley).

Gioia, D., and Poole, P. (1984), 'Scripts in Organizational Behavior', *Academy of Management Review,* 9: 449–59.

Granovetter, M. (1974), *Getting a Job: A Study of Contacts and Careers* (Cambridge, Mass.: Harvard University Press).

Grieco, M. S. (1984), 'Information Networks and the Allocation of Employment Opportunity' (unpublished thesis, University of Oxford).

Grieco, M. S., and Hosking, D. M. (1987), 'Networking, Exchange and Skill', *International Studies in Management and Organization,* 17/1: 75–87.

Gupta, A. (1984), 'Contingency Linkages between Strategy and General Manager Characteristics: A Conceptual Examination', *Academy of Management Review,* 9: 399–412.

Heller, F. (1984), 'The Role of Longitudinal Method in Management Decision-Making Studies', in J. Hunt, D. M. Hosking, C. Schriesheim, and R. Stewart, (eds.), *Leaders and Managers: International Perspectives On Managerial Behaviour and Leadership* (Oxford: Pergamon).

Homans, G. C. (1961), *Social Behaviour: Its Elemental Form* (New York: Harcourt, Brace and World).

Hosking, D. M. (1983), 'Leadership Skills and Organizational Forms: The Management of Uncertainty', (paper presented to the Sixth Egos Colloquium, Florence).

—— (1984), 'On Paradigms and Pigs', in J. Hunt, D. M. Hosking, C. Schriesheim, and R. Stewart, (eds.), *Leaders and Managers: International Perspectives on Managerial Behaviour and Leadership.* (Oxford: Pergamon).

—— (1987), 'Leadership and Organisational Skills', in A. Keiser, G. Reber, and R. Wunderer, (eds.), *Handbook of Leadership* (Stuttgart: Poeschel Verlag).

—— and Morley, I. E. (1985), *'Leadership and Organization: Processes of Influence, Negotiation, and Exchange.* (unpublished working paper, Warwick).

—— —— (1988), 'The Skills of Leadership', in J. Hunt, R. Baliga, P. Dachler, and C.

Schriesheim, (eds.), *Emerging Leadership Vistas* (Lexington, Mass.: Arlington Heights).

House, R., and Baetz, M. (1979), 'Leadership: Some Empirical Generalizations and New Research Directions', in B. Staw (ed.), *Research in Organizational Behavior* (Greenwich, Conn.: Jai Press).

Huff, A. (1984), 'Situation Interpretation, Leader Behaviour, and Effectiveness', in J. Hunt, D. M. Hosking, C. Schriesheim, and R. Stewart, (eds.), *Leaders and Managers: International Perspectives on Managerial Behaviour and Leadership* (Oxford: Pergamon).

Janis, I. and Mann, L. (1977), *Decision Making: A Psychological Analysis of Conflict, Choice and Commitment* (London: Free Press).

Kanter, R. (1983), *The Change Masters: Corporate Entrepreneurs at Work* (London: Allen & Unwin).

Kapferer, B. (1972), *Strategy and Transaction in an African Factory* (Manchester: Manchester University Press).

Kelvin, P. (1970), *The Bases of Social Behaviour* (London: Holt, Rinehart & Winston).

Kotter, J. (1982), *The General Managers* (London: Free Press).

Lewin, K. (1947), 'Frontiers in Group Dynamics', *Human Relations,* 1: 5–41.

Manning, P. (1982), 'Organizational Work: Structuration of Environments', *British Journal of Sociology,* 33/1: 118–32.

Martinko, M., and Gardner, W. (1984), 'The Observation of High Performing Educational Managers: Methodological Issues and Managerial Implications', in J. Hunt, D. M. Hosking, C. Schriesheim, and R. Stewart (eds.), *Leaders and Managers: International Perspectives on Managerial Behaviour and Leadership.* (Oxford: Pergamon).

Meltzer, B., Petras, J., and Reynolds, L. (1975), *Symbolic Interactionism: Genesis, Varieties and Criticism.* (London: Routledge & Kegan Paul).

Meyer, M. (1975), 'Leadership and Organizational Structure', *American Journal of Sociology,* 81: 514–42.

Meyer, M., Stevenson, W., and Webster, S. (1985), *Limits to Bureaucratic Growth* (New York: Walter De Gruyter).

Neisser, U. (1976), *Cognition and Reality* (San Francisco, Calif.: Freeman).

Nisbett, R., and Ross, L. (1980), *Human Inference: Strategies and Shortcomings of Social Judgement* (Englewood Cliffs, NJ: Prentice-Hall).

Ranson, S., Hinings, C., and Greenwood, R. (1980), 'The Structuring of Organization Structures', *Administrative Science Quarterly,* 25: 1–17.

Shrivastava, P. (1983), 'A Typology of Organizational Learning Systems', *Journal of Management Studies,* 20: 7–28.

Singleman, P. (1972), 'Exchange as Symbolic Interaction: Convergences between Two Theoretical Perspectives', *American Sociological Review,* 37 (Aug.), 414–24.

Steinbruner, J. (1974), *The Cybernetic Theory of Decision* (Princeton, NJ: Princeton University Press).

Stewart, R. (1976), *Contrasts in Management* (New York: McGraw-Hill).

Strauss, A. (1978), *Negotiations: Varieties, Contexts, Processes and Social Order* (San Francisco, Calif: Jossey-Bass).

Trujillo, N. (1983), 'Performing Mintzberg's Roles: The Nature of Managerial Communication', in L. Putnam and M. Pacanowsky (eds.), *Communication in Organizations: An Interpretive Approach* (London: Sage).

Vinokur, A., and Burnstein, E. (1978), 'Novel Argumentation and Attitude Change: The Case of Polarization Following Group Discussion', *European Journal of Social Psychology,* 8: 335–48.

Walton, R., and McKersie, R. (1966), *A Behavioral Theory of Labor Negotiations: An Analysis of a Social Interaction System* (New York: McGraw-Hill).

Weick, K. (1978), 'The Spines of Leaders', in M. McCall and M. Lombardo (eds.), *Leadership: Where Else Can We Go?* (Durham: Durham University Press).

—— (1979), *The Social Psychology of Organizing* (Reading, Mass.: Addison-Wesley).

Welford, A. (1980), 'The Concept of Skill and its Application to Social Performance', in W. Singleton, P. Spurgeon, and R. Stammers (eds.), *The Analysis of Social Skill* (London: Plenum Press).

Wrapp, H. (1984), 'Good Managers Don't Make Policy Decisions', *Harvard Business Review* (July–Aug.) 8–21.

Wright, P., and Taylor, D. (1984), *Improving Leadership Performance* (Englewood Cliffs, NJ: Prentice-Hall).

Zey-Ferrell, M., and Aiken, M. (1981), (eds.) *Complex Organizations: Critical Perspectives* (Greenview, Ill.: Scott Foresman).

# 16 Correspondents' Images of Martin Luther King, Jr: An Interpretive Theory of Movement Leadership

Stephen J. Lilley and Gerald M. Platt

> There were people who maybe didn't go to the mass meetings, who didn't do a lot of other things, but in some way, they contributed to what Dr King was trying to do. When you sent a dollar, when you took your car and drove even to the next door neighbor's to keep them from riding the bus, you participated.
>
> (Mrs Johnnie Carr, former Secretary of the Transportation Committee, Montgomery Improvement Association)[1]

This is a study of the images imparted to Martin Luther King, Jr., during the period 1956 to 1961. These portrayals of King are derived from correspondence sent from people who were more and less active in the movement. Although we focus upon the images these people accorded Dr King, this is also a theoretical essay. We will use correspondents' perspectives to illustrate how participants construct their conceptions of leadership.[2]

We conceive of people in the Civil Rights Movement whether they were vigorously involved in the movement or merely sympathetic to it as engaged in making sense of the movement for themselves. Thus, we suggest that correspondents to King actively interpreted his leadership and the movement's doctrine shaping these to their interests, such as those they may find in their statuses, intentions, beliefs, and values.

Leaders and movement doctrine exhibit many dimensions of expression which the observers may interpretively fit to their interests. This interpretive process results in a diversity of types of portrayals of the leader and a variety

S. J. Lilley and G. M. Platt, 'Correspondents' Images of Martin Luther King, Jr.: An Interpretive Theory of Movement Leadership', In T. R. Sarbin and J. I. Kitsuse (eds.), *Constructing the Social* (London: Sage, 1994), 65–83.

of persons and groups committed to the movement. The evidence is overwhelming that movement adherents are objectively heterogeneous in their social attributes. We will illustrate that these participants also engage in constructing diverse images of movement leadership and more generally participants construct varying conceptions of the movement.

Conventional approaches to social movements such as resource mobilization or traditional collective behaviour theory assume that persons who participate in social movements are more or less homogeneous in their objective characteristics and in their subjective consciousness; that is, they are similar in their class or other statuses, they are committed to the movement for similar reasons, and their conceptions of leadership and doctrine are alike (Morris 1981; Killian 1984; Oberschall 1989).[3] Although social-movements theory has addressed the issue of differences among participants, it has not taken this matter to its theoretical or empirical conclusion (Klandermans and Tarrow 1988; Melucci 1989). We will attempt to show that a close look at movement participants indicates that other approaches are too removed from the subjective experiences of movement participants. A critical problem facing social-movement theory is the explanation of the objective and subjective heterogeneities found among participants in the same movement (Turner and Killian 1972, 1987).[4] How do persons with different background characteristics, expressing varying conceptions of the movement, come together to create collective actions?

## Heterogeneous Movement Participants

The demography of social movements indicates that they are populated with heterogeneous rather than homogeneous persons. Social movements exhibit a spectrum of types of participants from diverse social classes, races, ages, and so on (Traugott 1985; Platt 1987). Similarly, evidence indicates that even ardent followers in movements display varying subjective conceptions of its leaders and its doctrine (Weinstein 1980; Childers 1990).

People in the Civil Rights Movement were exemplary for their objective diversity. At its outset, movement adherents were working black women and men while their leaders were middle-class ministers (Morris 1984). However, as the movement evolved, the Civil Rights participants were drawn from younger black and white men and women, more affluent and educated and from diverse class and cultural backgrounds. Black college youth spearheaded the Student Nonviolent Coordinating Committee lunch-counter sit-ins, voter registration, and education projects in the early 1960s (Childs 1989: 1302) and affluent educated white youth from élite college campuses actively participated in the 1964 Freedom Summer (McAdam 1988). By the mid–1960s the movement was populated with racially, economically, socially, geographically, culturally, and religiously heterogeneous persons.

How did these mixed populations construct the movement for themselves and how did they envision its leaders? These are perplexing questions which only those who were part of the movement can answer. We will concentrate our analysis upon participants' constructions of King's image as a leader.

## Images of Martin Luther King

In 1974 James Hanigan published a paper summarizing the images attributed to King in the popular and scholarly literature. He provides a long list of King images:

> Most observers of King saw some religious significance in his words and work. A great variety of images taken from both of the Old and New Testaments, as well as from secular history, have been used to capture something of this significance: prophet, preacher, apostle, the black Moses, the American Gandhi, a modern-day St Paul, a modern Job, a Socrates, even a Jesus. (Hanigan 1974: 77)

There has been little effort exerted to find out if these were the images of King held by movement participants. In no biography or sociology of King has his image been derived from the perceptions of him acquired from a broad spectrum of movement adherents. There were a very large number of participants, exhibiting a variety of degrees of involvement and activities in the Civil Rights Movement, but only a small portion of those involved in the movement have been interviewed.[5] Almost all of these interviews were conducted with movement 'élites' many years after their participation.[6]

## The So-Called 'Kind' Letters to Martin Luther King

It is possible to approximate a study of movement participants' images of King. During the Civil Rights Movement King's staff retained most of the correspondence to him. Included in the tidal wave of correspondence there were letters from participants in which they proffered their images of King's leadership. For the purpose of this essay, movement participants are defined as those persons who wrote 'kind' letters to Dr King between 1956 and 1961 and whose correspondence are held in the Boston or Atlanta archives. The content analyses in this essay are based on Stephen Lilley's research in the Boston archive (1989); these findings are supplemented by citing from oral histories and correspondence held in the Atlanta archive.

These archives contain thousands of letters, such as, speaking invitations to King, legal and business correspondence, letters from movement notables, hostile letters denouncing the movement and King, and so on. However, only letters from participants referred to by King's staff as 'kind' letters were used in this study. The vast majority of these letters were disqualified because the description of King was too superficial, the letter was illegible, they lacked a date or an address, etc. Thus, the content analysis of participants' perspectives is based upon 621 'kind' letters to King held in the Boston archive.

The correspondents were active in the movement in varying degrees; some walked in the Montgomery Bus Boycott, others were members in the Southern Christian Leadership Conference, still others simply sent money and their support. For example, one woman wrote to Dr King, 'May I add my small voice to the millions who offer you silent encouragement and moral support.' However, another wrote, 'I am a co-worker for the NAACP and I am working just as hard as you are.' Another wrote to King with unqualified admiration for his leadership stating: 'We see why 50,000 people were inspired to follow your leadership in an effort to improve their conditions. I am thoroughly convinced that no one can reach the people . . . and give them unshakable assurance as you can.' Some letters were bold, offering advice and strategies; thus, one correspondent wrote in faltering English: 'You cannot never get full civil rights in the South if you are forever going to be entirely dependent on the ruling class white people in the South for a living, for a job . . . I say colored people must now take a greater share in owning and controlling their own respective communities.' Whether it was through ardent praise, sympathy, advice, or friendly warnings, the correspondents pressured King forward. Ultimately the great civil rights leader confided to his wife: 'People will expect me to perform miracles for the rest of my life. I don't want to be the kind of man who hits his peak at twenty-seven, with the rest of his life an anticlimax. Neither do I want to disappoint people by not being able to pull rabbits out of a hat' (Oates 1982: 149–50).

Mrs Johnnie Carr's introductory remarks ring true for the correspondents: they all 'contributed to what Dr King was trying to do'; they all participated in the movement.

## Analysing Correspondents' Images of King

In the social science literature and in popular media the people in the streets fighting for change are nameless and faceless; they are crowds obedient to leaders. By contrast, the 621 correspondents to King are not anonymous—they left their names, their addresses, and considerably more about their experiences in the movement, such as their feelings and attitudes towards movement doctrine, their reasons for participating, and their perceptions of its leaders. We examine their correspondence to Dr King as an archeological proxy to Civil Rights Movement participants' constructions of King's leadership.

The 621 correspondents' letters to King have been analysed for the writers' objective attributes and subjective attitudes (see Table 16.1.). Among the several objective characteristics that were ferreted out of the correspondence, we will focus upon the effects of race on perceptions of King because the sociological literature suggests race had forceful influences upon Civil Rights Movement participants' consciousness. We were able to discern the race of 391 (63 per cent) correspondents, of which 153 are black (39 per cent) and 238 are white (61 per cent).

**Table 16.1.** Objective characteristics of the 'kind' letter correspondents

| Attributes | Usable cases | | Value name | Frequency of usable cases | Percentage of usable cases |
|---|---|---|---|---|---|
| | No. | % | | | |
| Race | 391 | (63%) | Black | 153 | 39 |
| | | | White | 238 | 61 |
| Region | 562 | (90%) | South | 104 | 19 |
| | | | N. East | 204 | 36 |
| | | | West | 120 | 21 |
| | | | Central | 134 | 24 |
| Gender | 603 | (97%) | Female | 236 | 39 |
| | | | Male | 367 | 61 |
| Year of letter | 621 | (100%) | 1956 | 108 | 17 |
| | | | 1957 | 136 | 22 |
| | | | 1958 | 71 | 11 |
| | | | 1959 | 43 | 7 |
| | | | 1960 | 104 | 17 |
| | | | 1961 | 159 | 26 |
| Degree of activism | 279 | (45%) | Low | 125 | 45 |
| | | | High | 154 | 55 |

Using race to analyse its effects on shaping the images of King permits us to analyse expected projections derived from the status of race and those that vary from expectations drawn from race—the latter an important arena in which our constructive approach will be illustrated. It should be emphasized that all the correspondence is from adherents to the movement, thus, our findings are focused upon portrayals of Martin King's leadership from committed blacks and whites.

## A Content Analysis of 'Kind' Letters to Dr King

The contents of the 621 letters contain twenty-one separate descriptions of King's character and twenty-seven depictions of his performance (Lilley 1989: 80–1, 85–6, 92–3). The distinction between character and performance is based on correspondents' attributions to King as an individual in contrast to their explicitly expressed conceptions of what they thought King was attempting to achieve in his activities.

King's character was described by statements such as a 'prophet sent by God,' a 'true American determined to promote democracy', a 'leader of the Negro race', and an 'advocate of passive resistance'. It was inappropriate to assume all the descriptions intended different meanings. By deriving analytic categories from the literature on leadership and inferring from the descriptions the intended meanings presented in the total contents of the letters, we reduced the portrayals of King's character to four impressions and his performances to five intended attributions. Further reduction would violate the intended meanings of the correspondents.

The four categories describing King's character are: black leader (including such descriptions as 'spokesman for blacks', 'a modern-day Booker T. Washington', etc.), religious leader ('God's instrument', Christ-like'), non-violent leader ('like Gandhi', 'greatest teacher of non-violence today'), and a leader for democracy ('upholder of democracy', 'like Lincoln in your effort to expand democracy'). The five categories depicting his performance are: black goals ('uplifting our race', 'bringing freedom to blacks'), religious goals ('helping to create heaven on earth', 'spreading God's message of love'), non-violent goals ('teaching non-violence', 'demonstrating passive resistance'), democratic goals ('perfecting this democracy,' 'fulfilling the Constitution') and other principled goals ('fight for justice', 'work toward a brotherhood of men').

Even in these reduced forms of character and performance there is considerable perceived variation in the meanings King's leadership had for movement adherents. However, it is necessary to pursue further this analysis to discover the effects of race on correspondents' images of King.[7]

It has been suggested that King was for whites a principled, moral, spiritual, and religious leader, a leader who stressed Christian love and Gandhian non-violence. This has been contrasted with his meaning for African Americans, for whom it has been suggested he played political and practical roles connected with their conditions of oppression and segregation (Meier 1965; Hanigan 1974; Marable 1984).

There is in the correspondence to King an imperfect truth in this last formulation. Among the four characteristics attributed to King, black correspondents more frequently saw King as a 'black leader' than did whites; however, only 41 per cent of the blacks emphasized this theme (see Table 16.2). Fifty per cent of black correspondents stressed his capacity as 'Christian leader', 7 per cent as 'non-violent leader', and 2 per cent as a 'democratic leader', of white correspondents to King, 21 per cent thought of him as a 'leader of blacks', 56 per cent as 'Christian leader', 17 per cent as a 'non-violent leader', and 6 per cent as 'democratic leader'.

If we follow the lead of previous commentators and assume 'black leadership' depicts King in political and practical terms, while 'Christian', 'non-violent', and 'democratic' are principled images of King, we may collapse this analysis still further to uncover the degree to which blacks and whites viewed King as exhibiting practical or principled qualities. Table 16.3 indicates that most of his followers saw principled qualities in King, although blacks stressed his practical side. Thus, there is some truth to perceptual expectations based upon race for black- and white-movement adherents. However, a closer look indicates that a majority of blacks and whites saw King's character in principled terms. Further, 62 black and 27 white correspondents or 38 per

**Table 16.2.** Impressions of King's character, by race

| | Black | | White | | Total | |
|---|---|---|---|---|---|---|
| | No. | % | No. | % | No. | % |
| Black leader | 44 | 41 | 27 | 21 | 71 | 30 |
| Christian leader | 53 | 50 | 72 | 56 | 125 | 53 |
| Non-violent leader | 7 | 7 | 22 | 17 | 29 | 12 |
| Democratic leader | 2 | 2 | 8 | 6 | 10 | 5 |
| Total | 106 | 45 | 129 | 55 | 235[a] | 100 |

Chi square = 16.2, 3 *df*, $p < 0.01$

[a] The number of respondents for each analysis varies with the available information in the letters.

**Table 16.3.** Impressions of King's character (collapsed), by race

| | Black | | White | | Total | |
|---|---|---|---|---|---|---|
| | No. | % | No. | % | No. | % |
| Black leader | 44 | 41 | 27 | 21 | 71 | 30 |
| Principles | 62 | 59 | 102 | 79 | 164 | 70 |
| Total | 106 | 45 | 129 | 55 | 235[a] | 100 |

Chi square = 11.6, 1 *df*, $p < 0.01$
Cross-over = 38%

[a] The number of respondents for each analysis varies with the available information in the letters.

cent did not subscribe to portrayals of King's leadership according to expectations derived from race; they 'crossed over' from expectations inferred from race. More pronounced distributions by expectations are exhibited for blacks and whites regarding King's performance. Tables 16.4 and 16.5 indicate correspondents' conceptions of King's performance. More pronounced distributions by expectations are exhibited for blacks and whites regarding King's performance. Tables 16.4 and 16.5 indicate correspondents' conceptions of King's performance by race; a majority of black correspondents picture King's performance in terms of black goals, and most whites view his leadership performance as expressions of principles. However, even in this distribution, which conforms more closely to race-based expectations, there are signs that show both black and white correspondents see King's leadership performance as practical and principled, thus holding mixed views of what they see King attempting to accomplish.

Collapsing assumed practical and principled categories of performance indicates that 35 per cent of the correspondents do not conform to expectations for perceived performance by race; 35 per cent of both black and white authors of letters to King 'crossed over' from expectations derived from race-based interests (see Table 16.5). More specifically, 30 per cent of the blacks described King's performance in principled terms and 38 per cent of the white followers saw King's performance as directed to practical ends.

Excerpts from the letters contrast the differences between the writers who adhere to the expected racial pattern and those that do not. The excerpts are illustrative; images of King were determined through a scrutiny of the entire letter.

Some black correspondents focused upon the inequalities they faced. They expressed desires for an end to segregation and for freedom and justice for African Americans. They saw King as the instrument to achieve these ends. Thus, a black man wrote:

**Table 16.4.** Impressions of King's performance, by race

| | Black | | White | | Total | |
|---|---|---|---|---|---|---|
| | No. | % | No. | % | No. | % |
| Black goals | 95 | 70 | 82 | 38 | 177 | 51 |
| Christian goals | 17 | 13 | 40 | 19 | 57 | 16 |
| Non-violence | 7 | 5 | 41 | 19 | 48 | 14 |
| Democracy | 1 | 1 | 13 | 6 | 14 | 4 |
| Other principles | 15 | 11 | 39 | 18 | 54 | 15 |
| Total | 135 | 39 | 215 | 61 | 350[a] | 100 |

Chi square = 37.7, 4 *df*, $p < 0.01$

[a] The number of respondents for each analysis varies with the available information in the letters.

**Table 16.5.** Impressions of King's performance (collapsed), by race

| | Black | | White | | Total | |
|---|---|---|---|---|---|---|
| | No. | % | No. | % | No. | % |
| Black leader | 95 | 70 | 82 | 38 | 177 | 51 |
| Principles | 40 | 30 | 133 | 62 | 173 | 49 |
| Total | 135 | 39 | 215 | 61 | 350[a] | 100 |

Chi square = 34.6, 1 *df*, $p < 0.01$
Cross-over = 35%

[a] The number of respondents for each analysis varies with the available information in the letters.

The negroes of Montgomery needed a leader, so you came to lead them, and you did a great job. Now the Negroes of America are at a standstill for the lack of a great Negro leader. . . . You have all the qualities which make a great leader. . . .. You organized the Negroes of Montgomery, why can't you organize the Negroes of America?

Another African American wrote similarly:

I read with consternation the story of your possible resignation from the Dexter Avenue Baptist Church. . . . Freedom from second-class citizenship will not be handed to our race on a silver platter. Under your leadership Montgomery has become a pivotal point of attack. Your greater work remains yet to be done.

However, not all black correspondents emphasized King's indigenous campaign. Some writers viewed his work as transcending racial issues. A black woman wrote to King emphasizing the religious meaning of his leadership for her:

> God gave you many endowments of the spirit to be used in his service . . . Don't let the devil fool you and keep you from the big things God has in store for you. It is ironic that we Colored people who are discriminated, despised, segregated and persecuted should be the ones who through the prompting of the Spirit should hold up to the world, the Lord Jesus Christ, and prove beyond a doubt that God is real.

Another black woman wrote in a similar fashion:

> I view your life and purpose as one sent of the Lord to stand on just such a pedestal for God. . . . When there is a job to be done and God needs a man, He has never lacked a witness. . . . What the world needs is Jesus, His ways, His attributes, His teachings and His life.

While another African American emphasized the principle of non-violence in his letter to King: 'Your successful year of Non-violent resistance was critical and a history-making movement for deprived people everywhere.'

Some white correspondents emphasized aspects of King's work that transcend racial issues, such as the importance of Christian faith in the creation of a more just and holy American community, a theme King frequently emphasized himself in his sermons, speeches, and writings. A white woman wrote to King: 'America needs to be reminded forcefully of Christ's teaching of love to his fellow men! You endeavour to help America turn to Christ and His Word for a pattern of understanding and peace.' While a white man wrote:

> What you are doing is the only forcefully spiritual and Christian movement in the world today. As a northern American white I am truly proud of our American negroes. They have shown a spiritual faith and behavior that should make the world aware of our country's nobler qualities.

And still another white author wrote to stress the significance of non-violence in King's leadership:

> I applaud . . . the remarkable crusade you and your people carried on in Montgomery. This is not simply because it succeeded in doing away with an abominable discrimination but because it demonstrated the Gandhian principle of non-violence. . . . It is a principle which we have to learn to use in international affairs or else the human race is doomed. You have lead the way in a great cause.

However, some white correspondents were concerned with practical matters facing the black community such as their oppression and the welfare. These white correspondents encouraged King to promote freedom and to achieve equal rights for African Americans. They perceived King's work in terms of the advancement of the black community rather than serving transcendent values.

A white man wrote succinctly, 'Thanks from an old white man for your work to promote a better life for your people.' And another wrote:

As a leader and teacher of your people it is probably most assuring that your greatest victory is almost at hand. Montgomery is fortunate that you were on the scene. . . . It is unfortunate that most cities do not have Martin Luther Kings to intelligently lead the colored people successfully through the awkward and difficult days that lie ahead.

While another white woman wrote with a similar theme: 'Your race is proud of you as well as your friends. I commend you for what you have done . . . I believe there is nothing impossible where a people has leader like you.'

We focused upon the effects of race on correspondents' impressions of King because the literature suggests this structural variable influences movement participants' subjective experiences of it and its leadership. From this analysis we might conclude that this suggestion is at least partially correct, because black correspondents did stress King's practical and political leadership. Therefore, we might also infer, as many others have, that black correspondents who perceived King as a practical and political leader were employing race-based interests to interpret King's leadership and his performances. However, not all black correspondents stressed the practical and political qualities of King's leadership; some blacks' images of King emphasized his principled qualities, such as religion, non-violence, and democracy. Were these correspondents using structural bases other than their race to interpret King's meaning for themselves, and if so what were they? Might we assume also that all white correspondents, whose structural circumstances are outside the experiences of black oppression, interpreted King's leadership solely by employing principles? Are the images of King they derived, whether practical or principled impressions, entirely determined by principles, since their structural conditions appear irrelevant to their adherence to the movement?

Structural explanations of black and white correspondents' perceptions of King's leadership are too inconsistent. We will attempt to provide greater theoretical coherence to the findings.

## Interpreting the Findings

How do we interpret for social theory the correspondents' complex conceptions of King as leader? We could simplify the analysis, stressing the statistically significant findings, suppressing the details, underscoring King's essential images to the correspondents. The statistical analyses might suggest that blacks saw King as a leader who served their racial interests and whites perceived him as striving to achieve principles; blacks' perceptions were influenced by race-based interest and whites' images were derived from non-rational beliefs. But this formulation is not universally true; the chi-square analyses shed no light on correspondents' perceptions of King's leadership that do not conform to expectations drawn from race.

Thus, the most interesting inference that one can draw from among these findings is that from 1956 to 1961, while King was an active and visible leader in the Montgomery Improvement Association (MIA) and Southern Christian Conference (SCLC), he bore several meanings simultaneously for both black and white participants in the movement. He was a diverse leader and accomplished different things for the correspondents. King may well have been what he wanted to be for himself, but others committed to the movement found in him what they wanted to see for themselves. Correspondents saw in King and his efforts multiple conceptions of his leadership and performance (Gusfield 1986).[8] King seemed aware of his multiple public meaning, for he once confided, 'I am conscious of two Martin Luther Kings . . . The Martin Luther King that the people talk about seems to be somebody foreign to me' (Oates 1982: 283).

Race may be a significant factor in shaping Civil Rights Movement adherents' impressions of King, but it cannot be the only factor. We eschew, therefore, any attempt at simplifying the findings' complexities and their contradictions by focusing upon statistical significance. In a most important sense King's anomalous images according to race-based interests are decisive, for if taken seriously these perceptions of King recommend theoretical revision. We aspire for a more comprehensive theory—one that subsumes both the central tendencies consistent with expectations drawn from race and the anomalous images of King inconsistent with expectations derived from adherents' race.

## An Interpretive Theory of Leadership: The Movement Constructed

Such a solution resides in reconceptualizing individuals' interpretive processes in relation to: (1) the structural positions they occupy, such as race, class, age, gender; (2) the rational calculations and the non-rational commitments derived from such positions; (3) the beliefs people hold and the emotions they experience resulting from their histories and their immediate circumstances (Platt 1980). We insist that, in describing social structural variables such as race, class, age, gender, etc., their meaning to the individuals occupying them be paramount. Status holders can employ these structures in accord with the imputed cultural, political, and economic meanings embedded in them, and thus these structures constrain volition by reproducing expected social meanings. However, these statuses can be interpreted alternately, creating opportunities for varieties of meanings and for social change (Giddens 1984: 83–6).

In both these circumstances, however, it is the status holders who are engaged in making sense of their social structural positions in relation to their past, present, and future activities, and in connection with their assessments of their immediate circumstances. Different statuses an individual occupies may be used as grounds for action also creating varying evaluative perspectives on the same qualities, statements, and performances expressed by leaders.

The result of this interpretive process is that individuals may devise myriad constructions of leadership by using unexpected bases for creating meaning. The important issue is that persons as active interpreters are continually engaged in fitting and modifying themselves and their social positions to the circumstances they face. They are engaged in constructing their conceptions of the social world and their place in it.

Adherents in social movements engage in these practices similar to persons in any social situation. These individuals can achieve diverse meanings within discourses of race-based interests, they may employ other statuses, or they may rely upon values, beliefs, and the emotions they experience in relation to their historical experiences and the circumstances they face.

For movement adherents, these are alternate ways of interpreting and thereby legitimating their stances against conditions of oppression and injustice. These are alternate ways of making claims for change and providing meaning and legitimacy to the activities in which they engage and in their strivings for freedom, justice, and liberation for black Americans (Spector and Kitsuse 1987: 73–96).[9] These interpretive processes permitted black and white Americans to fit themselves to the movement and to support their strivings for a just society although what a just society, exactly meant was distinct for each correspondent. Analysts may reduce their meanings into coherent categories for presentation to professional audiences as we have done in this essay, but, in truth, adherents' constructions of leadership are private and particular (Geertz 1988: 8–20).

From the subjective perspective of particular adherents there were many different ways of making sense of a movement, of conceptualizing its leadership and justifying adherence. It is appropriate to assume that Civil Rights Movement participants confronted with abstract expressions such as freedom, justice, liberation, a just community, and so on provided unique subjective meanings to these terms which resulted in transcendent but unexamined commitments that bound them together in solidarity.

For movement activists cultural, political, and ideological doctrines are symbolic fabrics from which different threads may be woven into meaningful discourses of private interpretive stances to strive for liberation. Cultural, political, and ideological doctrines are open to interpretations; these are discourses rich with multiple meanings available for adherents' interpretation (Platt and Williams 1988).

In social movements it is especially the case that leaders in their doctrinal expressions may be intentionally ambiguous in order to encourage people to see in the movement aspects of doctrine relevant to their interests whatever these may be (Williams 1977: 39, 40; Kertzer 1988: 11). Leaders may employ rhetorical discourses in order to mobilize larger numbers of disparate persons to find meaning for themselves in the movement.

Thus, we suggest the movement correspondents existed within contexts of privately constructed social worlds to which a distinction can be made between the public appearance of a consensus and *sub rosa* subjective differences. A movement event, no matter how apparently unified, cannot guarantee subjective homogeneity. David Kertzer has highlighted these conditions in political ritual. He notes that rituals and symbols can be ambiguous, therefore, 'ritual action' can foster 'solidarity without consensus' (1988: 69), and 'ritual can serve political organizations by producing bonds of solidarity without requiring uniformity of belief. This is of tremendous political value, since what often underlies people's political allegiances is their social identification with a group rather than their sharing of beliefs with other members' (1988: 67).

However, even when leaders attempt to be deliberately unambiguous, their intentions can be alternately interpreted by adherents who listen to their discourse and observe their activities. Ralph Turner points out that the same role behaviour can be assigned very different meanings. Turner notes, roles 'that convey diametrically opposed evaluations and meanings are often expressed through behaviours that are objectively indistinguishable' (Turner 1985: 30). This was the situation with King, for, as we noted during the period between 1956 and 1961, when King was actively leading the movement, correspondents imputed multiple conceptions to his same performances; their portrayals of his leadership indicated he accomplished distinct things for the different correspondents. It is possible to infer from our findings, as we have, that 'King may well have been what he wanted to be for himself but others committed to the movement found in him what they wanted to see for themselves'.

Thus, movement participants may use leaders' actions and doctrinal expressions combined with personal, political, and cultural commitments to provide meanings relevant to their own interests, such as those that grow out of their race, their beliefs, experiences, and emotions. The self-determined salient aspects of people's material and cultural interests are fitted to leadership's qualities and activities. The specifics of these interpretive processes cannot be determined a priori and certainly not from theorists' preconceptions of what interests are embedded in people's statuses.

For movement participants the substance of these subjective constructions exist along a continuum from relatively coherent formulations about the movement to partial and fragmented notions highlighting dimensions of the movement particularly relevant to them. These privately constructed statements, however, even when subjectively coherent, are not rational deductive portrayals of the movement. Rather they are simply constructed versions satisfying participants' needs to provide for themselves a meaningful place in the movement. Further, for each participant these constructions are unpredictable, because it is impossible to know in advance which factors will be intertwined into their private, complete or fragmented, constructed version of the movement.

This theory calls for an indeterminate interpretive process; it is up to persons in the movement to ascertain its meaning and their place in it for themselves. This is a theory in which volitional interpretive practices are centred, thereby offering explanations consistent with the different images of King's leadership found in the correspondence to him.[10]

There is an analytic coherence to this theoretical formulation. This approach explains the complex constructions of King's leadership and the different attributed impressions of him from both black and white correspondents. It is consistent with the complex subjective experiences and the objective variations found among movement participants. This approach also implies that it is interpretive processes resulting in subjective diversity which influence the objective heterogeneity of movements. The consequence of interpretive processes is that objective and subjective heterogeneities are intertwined—the former in some degree the result of the latter. It is the interpretive processes which make our findings whole by explaining the objective and subjective heterogeneities in relation to the complex constructions of King's leadership.

Much of this approach to leadership is foreshadowed in Max Weber's theory of domination (1978: 212–16; 941–55). Weber well understood that leaders' capacity to command depended upon followers' subjective imputation of authority, whether this meant for followers' power based upon normative legitimacy, expedient self-interest, habit of obedience, or emotional commitments. Weber theorized that there was no single basis for authority, rather that institutional forms of domination depended upon followers' situationally specific subjective imputations. The innovation we have appended to Weber's theorizing is that subjective bases for authority not only vary from situation to situation but vary *within* any particular situation depending upon the interpretive practices in which individuals engage in creating their conceptions of leadership and its bases for authority. We are attempting to add to Weber's formulation of subjective attribution additional degrees of volitional freedom while simultaneously suggesting that social organizations resulting from such personally achieved decisions about authority are more complex than can be inferred from assumptions about the structural aspects of persons (such as, race or class) or from the organizational appearances (for example, rational legal authority) that their subjective decisions create.[11]

## Notes

1. Carr (1972: 34).
2. This approach is derived from Weinstein and Platt (1973), Weinstein (1980, 1990), Platt (1980, 1987, 1991), and Max Weber (1978).
3. For rational-structural analyses of students in sit-ins, see Morris (1981: 744–67) and Oberschall (1989: 31–53). For a spontaneous-heterogeneous conception of sit-ins, see Killian (1984: 770–83).
4. Turner and Killian recognize the diversity of the participants in social movements. They write that people in collective actions 'are heterogeneous in motivation despite the similarity of their behavior' (1972: 27). Further they state: 'we reject the assumption that a social movement is composed of people who are homogeneous in their attitudes and values. Adherents and even the leaders and activists bring divergent conceptions of the situation, the grievance, and the movement goals' (1987: 237).
5. King has been depicted as a charismatic in the sociological literature. Jack Bloom writes of King: he motivated 'blacks . . . enabling them to find inner strength to stand up and fight' (1987: 144). Aldon Morris depicted King as 'able to instill in people a sense of mission and commitment to social change' (1984: 11). Recently Morris depicts King's leadership interactively stressing the input of the black community (1990).
6. Oral History Collections focused upon the Montgomery Bus Boycott and the Anne Romaine Collection of Oral Histories focused upon the Mississippi Freedom Democratic Party. The Anne Romaine Collection was acquired in 1966–7 after the events of the 1964 Democratic Convention. Interviews with Septima Clark (Nov. 1971), John Lewis (June 1970), Ella Barker (Mar. 1967), Fannie Lou Hamer (Nov. 1966), and others of such stature in the Civil Rights Movement, although valuable and significant, should be considered those of 'élites' rather than followers. There are outstanding published oral history anthologies—e.g. Howell Raines (1977) and William R. Beardslee (1977). However, these too focus upon movement 'élites' interviewed years after the events recalled.

7. Correspondents' race was scored on the basis of two types of statements: (1) a clear-cut avowal of race; (2) a contrast or comparison between the writer's race and King's: for example, 'I am delighted to know that you are trying to help our race in the lunch project.'
8. Gusfield suggests temperance movement participants exhibited similar diversities, for example, 'Temperance and Prohibition are also multivalent and polysemous. They have meanings at different levels and different dimensions' (1986: 202).
9. Neither status nor discourse defines the boundaries of interpretation. For example, during the Montgomery Bus Boycott not all the city's black ministers were behind the movement; three were recruited by the city's major to scuttle the boycott in midstream (Morris 1984). Also, southern racists often remarked that King's non-violent philosophy intended quite the opposite; it was meant to provoke violence. The boundaries of interpretation hinge upon membership in terms of publicly expressed commitment to the movement's goals. It was impossible to be defined or to define oneself as a member of the Civil Rights Movement if one's interpretation of the movement did not include something about commitment to 'liberation', 'justice', and 'freedom' for black Americans.
10. Gene Sharp made this point indicating that consent to authority was a volitional condition and could be withdrawn. He also noted people could develop indigenous bases of power for themselves, if they wished to do so (1973: 25–32; 1980: 309–78).
11. This research was conducted in the King Special Collection, the Mugar Library, Boston University, and the Library and Archive of the Martin Luther King Jr. Center for Nonviolent Social Change, Atlanta. We are grateful to Dr Charles Gotlieb, Director, Mugar Library Collection, and Dr Broadus Butler, former Director of the Atlanta Archive, for their assistance. Permission to quote the correspondence to Dr King was granted by the King Center counsel; Dr Butler and Mrs Coretta Scott King made these arrangements possible. Diane Ware, the King Center Reference Archivist, was exceedingly helpful. Danny Bellinger was a thorough research assistant. This research was supported by the Albert Einstein Institution, Cambridge, Massachusetts, and by Glen Gordon, the former Dean of Social and Behavioral Science, the University of Massachusetts. John Kitsuse, Fred Weinstein, Rhys Williams, and Michael Fraser commented on early versions of this paper.

## References

Beardslee, W. R. (1977), *The Way Out Must Lead In: Life Histories in the Civil Rights Movement* (Atlanta, Ga.: Center for Research in Social Change, Emory University).

Bloom, J. H. (1987), *Class, Race and the Civil Rights Movement* (Bloomington, Ind.: Indiana University Press).

Carr, J. M., Mrs (1972), The Martin Luther King Jr., Oral History Project, Martin Luther King Jr. Center for Nonviolent Social Change, Atlanta, Georgia (27 Jan.)

Childers, T. (1990), 'The Social Language of Politics in Germany: The Sociology of Political Discourse in the Weimar Republic', *American History Review*, 95: 331–58.

Childs, J. B. (1989), *Leadership, Conflict, and Co-operation in Afro-American Social Thought* (Philadelphia: Temple University Press).

Geertz, C. (1988), *Work and Lives: The Anthropologist as Author* (Stanford, Calif.: Stanford University Press).

Giddens, A. (1984), *The Constitution of Society: Outline of the Theory of Structuration* (Berkeley and Los Angeles: University of California Press).

Gusfield, J. R. (1986), *Symbolic Crusade: Status Politics and the American Temperance Movement* (2nd edn., Urbana, IU.: University of Illinois Press).

Hanigan, J. P. (1974), 'Martin Luther King, Jr.: The Images of a Man', *Journal of Religious Thought*, 31: 68–95.

Kertzer, D. I. (1988) *Ritual, Politics, and Power* (New Haven: Yale University Press).

Killian, L. M. (1984), 'Organization, Rationality and Spontaneity in the Civil Rights Movement', *American Sociological*, 49: 770–83.

Klandermans, B., and Tarrow, S. (1988), 'Mobilization into Social Movements: Synthesizing European and American Approaches', in B. Klandermans, H. Kriesi, and S. Tarrow (eds.), *International Social Movements Research*, 1: 1–38.

Lilley, S. J. (1989), 'Kind Letters and Support for Dr Martin Luther King, Jr', PhD dissertation (University of Massachusetts/Amherst).

McAdarn, D. (1988), *Freedom Summer* (New York: Oxford University Press).

Marable, M. (1984), *Race, Reform, and Rebellion: The Second Reconstruction in Black America, 1945–1982* (Jackson, Miss.: University of Mississippi Press).

Meier, A. (1965), 'On the Role of Martin Luther King', *New Politics*, 4: 52–9.

Melucci, A. (1989), 'Towards a Theory of Collective Action', in J. Keane and P. Mier (eds.), *Nomads on the Present: Social Movements and Individual Needs in Contemporary Society* (Philadelphia: Temple University Press).

Morris, A. D. (1981), 'Black Southern Student Sit-In Movement: An Analysis of Internal Organization', *American Sociological Review*, 86: 744–67.

—— (1984), *The Origins of the Civil Rights Movement: Black Communities Organizing for Change* (New York: Free Press).

—— (1990) 'A Man Prepared for the Times: A Sociological Analysis of the Leadership of Martin Luther King, Jr.', in P. J. Albert and R. H. (eds.), *We Shall Overcome: Martin Luther King, Jr. and the Black Freedom Struggle* (New York: Pantheon Books).

Oates, S. (1982), *Let the Trumpet Sound: The Life of Martin Luther King, Jr.* (New York: Harper & Row).

Oberschall, A. (1989), 'The 1960 Sit-Ins: Protest Diffusion and Movement Take-Off', *Research in Social Movements, Conflict and Change*, 11: 31–53.

Platt, G. M. (1980), 'Thoughts on Theory of Collective Action', in M. Albin (ed.), *New Directions in Psychohistory* (Lexington, Mass.: D. C. Heath).

—— (1987), 'The Psychoanalytic Sociology of Collective Behavior: Material Interests, Cultural Factors and Emotional Responses', in J. Rabow, G. Platt, and M. Goldman (eds.), *Advances in Psychoanalytic Sociology* (Melbourne, Fl.: Krieger Publishing).

—— (1991), 'An Essay on the History and Epistemology of Weinstein's "History and Theory after the Fall"', *The Psychohistory Review: Studies of Motivation in History and Culture*, 20: 3–20.

—— and Williams, R. H. (1988), 'Religion, Ideology and Electoral Politics', *Society*, 25/5: 38–45.

Raines, H. (1977), *My Soul is Rested: Movement Days in the Deep South Remembered* (New York: Penguin Books).

Sharp, G. (1973), *The Politics of Non-Violence* (Boston: Porter Sargent Publishers).

—— (1980), *Social Power and Political Freedom* (Boston: Porter Sargent Publishers).

Spector, M., and Kitsuse, J. I. (1987), *Constructing Social Problems* (New York: Aldine de Gruyter).

Traugott, Mark (1985), *Armies of the Poor: Determinants of Working Class Participation in the Parisian Insurrection of June, 1848* (Princeton: Princeton University Press).

Turner, Ralph H. (1985), 'Unanswered Questions in the Convergence between Structuralist and Interactionist Role Theories', in H. J. Helle and S. N. Eisenstadt (eds.), *Micro-Sociological Theory: Perspective on Sociological Theory*, ii (London: Sage Studies in International Sociology).

—— and Killian, L. M. (1972), *Collective Behavior* (Englewood Cliffs, NJ: Prentice-Hall).

—— —— (1987), *Collective Behavior* (2nd edn., Englewood Cliffs, NJ: Prentice-Hall).

Weber, M. (1978), *Economy and Society: An Outline of Interpretive Sociology*, ed G. Roth and C. Wittich (Berkeley and Los Angeles: University of California Press).

Weinstein, Fred (1980), *The Dynamics of Nazism: Leadership, Ideology and the Holocaust* (New York: Academic Press).

—— (1990), *History and Theory after the Fall: An Essay on Interpretation* Chicago: University of Chicago Press).

—— and Platt, G. M. (1973), *Psychoanalytic Sociology: An Essay on the Interpretation of Historical Data and the Phenomena of Collective Behavior* (Baltimore, Md.: Johns Hopkins University Press).

Williams, R. (1977), *Marxism and Literature* (Oxford: Oxford University Press).

# 17 Voicing Seduction to Silence Leadership

Marta B. Calás and Linda Smircich

> Everything is seduction and nothing but seduction. They wanted us to believe that everything was production. The leitmotive of world transformation, the play of productive forces is to regulate the flow of things. Seduction is merely an immoral, frivolous, superficial, and superfluous process; one within the realm of signs and appearances; one that is devoted to pleasure and to the usufruct of useless bodies. What if everything, contrary to appearances—in fact according to the secret rule of appearances—operated by (the principle of) seduction?
>
> (Baudrillard 1988: 162)

> '. . . If you cannot give something up for something of like value, if you consider it nonsubstitutable, then you do not possess it any more than it possesses you. So the father must not desire the daughter for that threatens to remove him from the homosexual commerce in which women are exchanged between men, in the service of power relations and community for the men.'
>
> (Gallop 1982: 76)

Following from the epigraphs above, we want to reflect on the meanings(s) of leadership for our own time and place. Joining other authors (e.g. Burrell 1984; Hearn and Parkin 1984, 1987; Acker 1987; Botti 1988; Pivy 1988; Billing and Alvesson 1989; Hearn *et al.* 1989) who observe the pervasiveness of sexuality in organizational life, we propose that the myth of leadership and its associated romantic appeal (Meindl *et al.* 1985) create the most vital

M. B. Calás and L. Smircich, 'Voicing Seduction to Silence Leadership', *Organization Studies*, 12/4 (1991), 567–602.

sexuality in the organizational literature. These authors, however, discuss organizational practices without reflecting upon the 'seductive effects' of organizational *writings*. Our focus in this paper on *textual analysis* emphasizes the social role played by organizational research and theory (writings) as another form of organizational practice: that of the academic community, whose purpose is the creation of *knowledge* for other members of society, (e.g. Calás and Smircich 1988).

In these writings, we argue, leadership feeds on the denial of consummation while constantly playing on the edges of transgression. Rather than suppressing desire—overcoming immoral and illegal acts by heroic denials of instinct—leadership works because it embodies desire, while covering its traces with the sign of truth (e.g. Lewicki 1981). As a form of seduction, there is nothing profound about leadership. It is a game, all there on the surface. Meanwhile we theorists of leadership have worked hard—and, of course, in vain—to penetrate its depth and to erase it gaps. We hope to expose, in this paper, some of the rhetoric that has created this seductive game, and at the same time articulate its limitations.

Our analyses are inspired by poststructuralist approaches to cultural analysis (e.g. Calás 1987; Cooper and Burrell 1988). These analytical strategies focus on elements of signification through which specific societies inscribe what they designate as *knowledge*. Poststructuralist analyses are of particular value in understanding the cultural limits of knowledge at times when innovations in theory and research are expected, but do not seem to be happening (e.g. Webster and Starbuck 1988; *Academy of Management Review* 1989).

We consider the leadership literature to be a prime example of this condition. While it seems that organizational research and theory keep on asking for new approaches and innovation, and that reconceptualizing leadership has been a focal point of these endeavours (e.g. International Leadership Symposia, 1971–85; Standing Conference on Organization Symbolism, 1989; and sessions on leadership at every Academy of Management meeting in the USA), it also seems that the more things change, the more they remain the same. Thus, in this paper, we are concerned with what is claimed to be knowledge about leadership. What prevents us from saying something different from what can be said as *knowledge* about leadership in our society? What might make it possible to say something different?

In addressing these issues here, we employ three different poststructuralist approaches—Foucault's genealogies, Derrida's deconstruction, and feminist poststructuralism—to reread four classic texts of the organizational literature: Barnard's *The Functions of the Executive*, McGregor's *The Human Side of Enterprise*, Mintzberg's *The Nature of Managerial Work*, and Peters and Waterman's *In Search of Excellence*. These texts have a common claim of being written more for organizational practitioners than for the scholarly community, but they have been influential in both communities. While written in different time periods, each text offers a definition and a prescription for effective organizational leadership.

We draw from Foucault's archeologies and genealogies (e.g. Foucault 1973, 1979, 1980, 1986, 1988; Davidson 1986) to underscore that, while on the surface our cultural discourses of knowledge appear to differ across disciplines and to change over time, they are embedded together in the modern *episteme*. Foucault's work uses historical analyses to underscore that different modalities of power are capable of producing a net-like organization of practices and discourses that society ends up calling *knowledge*. From this point of view, knowledge is produced by heterogenous practices of power rather than from the discovery of *truth*, the traditional dictum in science and philosophy. In our analyses of organizational writings, we show how each text appears to promote change from prior works regarding what should be considered 'leadership', but each, at the same time, maintains a specific set of practices and discourses in place—the basic power-relations network on which 'leadership' has been constituted and re-constituted.

We also draw on Derrida's deconstruction (e.g. Derrida 1976, 1978, 1982, 1986). This approach allows us to retrace how the rhetorical and linguistic forms used to signify 'knowledge' work under the assumption that they represent a referent which is external to language. Deconstruction helps us to understand how this assumption masks the play of textual signification where words are meaningful, not because of their external referents, which are also linguistically constituted, but because of the existence of an oppositional term over which each apparently 'self-standing' terms stands to differentiate itself from the other, and become meaningful.

Our focus in this paper, on the leadership/seduction opposition, illustrates this point. Leadership, as a theoretical concept which claims to represent 'knowledge' about an external referent, i.e. what leadership in organizations really *is* and what organizational leaders really *do*, is constructed over an opposite concept, 'seduction', which it devalues and tries to make invisible in relation to 'leadership'. Deconstructing 'leadership' helps to analyse the dependency of supposedly opposite concepts on one another and shows how rhetoric and cultural conditions work together to conceal this dependency. Deconstruction, then, is not a way to destroy the concept of leadership. Rather, it is an analytical strategy that permits us to question the limits that may have been imposed upon discourses of *knowledge*, and opens the possibility of enacting other, different, discourses.

Since deconstructive readings may appear unusual to the typical reader of organizational texts, we offer some guidance for following what we are trying to accomplish. First, the deconstructive strategies we use are intended to enhance the doubleness in every discourse. That is, what we do emphasizes that writings and words are polysemous—they have multiple meanings—and that the standard interpretation of those meanings within a particular community of knowledge (e.g. organizational scholars) is just an arbitrary limit imposed upon writings, which does not always succeed in limiting the meanings. For example, using the *Oxford English Dictionary* we start with an etymological analysis to demonstrate how leadership and seduction are alike and also to reveal the possible, concealed, genderedness (rather than neutrality) of both terms.

Secondly, and following from the first point, our reading approach in this paper focuses on the sexual meanings of standard organizational writings. We make these other meanings explicit, and show how the apparently covert sexuality of leadership discourses was, in fact, never covert: the term 'leadership' is an almost euphemistic usage. Our readings subvert the positive meaning of leadership versus the negative meaning of seduction by proposing that seduction, rather than leadership, has been the dominant term all along. By so doing, we underscore the importance of ambiguity (rather than preciseness) for any discourse (and for any discourse of *knowledge)* by making the sexuality and seductiveness *already embedded* in the discourses of leadership explicit. That is, leadership is seduction not by what it says but by what it does not say, or by the undecidability of what it may be saying. Once we make it openly sexualized, it loses its (sex) appeal as 'knowledge'.

Thirdly, the form in which we make these arguments is not typical argumentative logic—in fact, *unreal argumentative logic* is the discoursive form that attempts to cover 'seduction' with 'leadership'. Instead, consistent with the interest of current poststructuralist theorizing in the body, sexuality, gender, and their intersections with representation and rhetoric (Foucault 1980; Irigaray 1985*a*; Hunter 1989*a*, *b*), what we do in this paper, our *reading effects,* is to present leadership discourses in juxtaposition with other discourses about sexuality. Our readings suggest that both types of discourses are actually equivalent, and change together from time to time. To create *reading effects*—rather than *assertive arguments*—we use an array of deconstructive strategies including intertextualizations in parallel and interweaving forms, marginal conversations, iterations, and mimicry, which we will explain further in each section.

These deconstructive strategies displace the taken-for-granted meanings of typical leadership writings and exploit the possibilities of other meanings. They attempt to disseminate, to open to excess, the possibilities of signification in any organizational discourse. Dissemination, more than polysemia, accounts for the impossibility of a final interpretation. It allows us to question the forms by which closure has been imposed over organizational theorizing and the implications of such closure.

Derrida (1981) contrasts 'polysemia' with 'dissemination', indicating that the former suggests many meanings in one, and the possibility of collecting and recuperating all those meanings. Dissemination, on the other hand, is generative and promotes, endlessly, the possibility of other meanings (e.g. Krupnick 1987). Here we should also emphasize the difference between the poststructuralist approaches we are using in this paper and more typical interpretive approaches (e.g. the organizational symbolism literature). While both interpretive and poststructuralist approaches would consider phenomenological philosophy among their intellectual forebears, interpretivism is more likely to be associated with polysemia. Interpretive approaches, in general, resort to subjective and intersubjective understandings (e.g. social constructions) to posit both the possibility of multiple meanings but also the possibility of *real, final understandings* located in subjectivity. Since poststructuralist approaches *problematize* the notion of subjectivity (i.e. denying the possibility of a subject located outside language and, therefore, constituted by the same language whose meanings 's/he' is trying to recover), they make suspect the interpretivists' claims to knowledge. Said differently, from a poststructuralist perspective, the interpretive act of recovering meaning is, in itself, another creation of meaning—and the interpretive 'researcher' is an illusion, a reflection, or his/her/our own ability to observe/name the world outside endless language—therefore *dissemination*. For more detailed discussions on this point regarding organizational literature we refer the reader to other citations in this paper, particularly Calás (1987: chs. 1, 3), Cooper and Burrell (1988), and Martin (1990).

Finally, we also draw from feminist poststructuralism to add other specific political dimensions to our analyses. While Foucauldian genealogies enhance our understanding of how dominant and oppressed groups are accomplices in maintaining the complex network power/knowledge in which we are all embedded, and Derridian deconstruction furthers our understanding of the constitutive role of language beyond any claim of mere representation for 'what is', neither approach focuses on the particular role played by the signifier *gender* in the formation of current conditions of knowledge in modern Western society.

Feminist poststructuralism(s), inspired by various forms of poststructuralism (e.g. Irigaray 1985*a*, *b*; Jardine 1985; Cixous and Clement 1986; Diamond and Quinby 1988; Hunter 1989a; Flax 1990), posit, in general, the importance of the structure masculinity/femininity in sustaining the durability of practices, discourses, and forms of signification that allow certain activities the claim of *knowledge*, while disallowing others. Organizational analyses based on feminist poststructuralism(s) focus on the intersections between patriarchy and organizational knowledge, and the social/discursive relations which sustain these intersections (e.g. Calás and Smircich 1989; Martin 1990).

Thus, we follow our deconstructive *reading effects* with reinterpretations of each book's meanings based on feminist poststructuralist analyses of Freud's work. Our reinterpretations emphasize that Freud's notion of masculine seduction—the real existence of which, he eventually denied, has never been eliminated, but, rather, has been rearticulated as 'leadership'. Leadership, however, is only capable of articulating a form of seduction which thrives on *sameness*. That is, leadership as leadership seduces only those who are of the same kind—masculine or masculine-identified—and promotes, as 'leadership knowledge', only a homosocial system of organization, i.e. based on the values of masculinity, including masculine definitions of *femininity*.

In the final section, we try to break the narrow circle of masculinist seduction which seems to be identified as 'leadership knowledge'. What, we might ask, are the implications for organizational knowledge of accepting that leadership is homosocial seduction? What other seductions may be possible, and with what consequences? We cannot tell you at this point. Instead, we ask you to stay with us throughout the text and experience the seduction of leadership. At the end, we hope that you and we can come together and explore some answers.

Before we start, however, a note of caution is in order. While some may (and do) quarrel with us over our 'obscene' distortions of Barnard's, McGregor's, Mintzberg's, and Peters and Waterman's innocent writings, we want to emphasize that we are not commenting upon these authors as persons, nor questioning their good intentions in writing these books. What we are doing here is reappropriating public documents—their texts—to show the multiplicity of language at work. Embedded in the multiple meanings of discourses—including ours—are already the traces of other plausible interpretations.

## How is it that Seduction is Leadership and Leadership is Seduction?

In our typical way of thinking about organizations, 'leadership' is something good, something needed. 'What we need around here is some leadership' we say when things are not going right, but rarely (ever?) have we heard a call for some 'seduction'. Why is that? How is it that leadership is good and seduction is bad? An etymological investigation illustrates this point.

*From the dictionary*

LEAD: to guide on a way, esp. by going in advance; to direct on a course or in a direction, to serve as a channel for, to have charge; to go at the head of; to be first in or among; to have a margin over to begin to play with (— trumps); to aim in front of a moving object (— a duck); to direct (a blow) at an opponent in boxing.

syn: see GUIDE, LEAD, STEER, PILOT, ENGINEER

GUIDE implies intimate knowledge of the way and of all its difficulties and dangers; LEAD implies a going ahead to show the way and often to keep those that follow under control and in order; STEER implies an ability to keep to a chosen course and stresses the capacity of manœuvring correctly; PILOT suggests guidance over a dangerous, intricate or complicated course; ENGINEER implies guidance by one who finds ways to avoid or overcome difficulties in achieving an end or carrying out a plan. (*Oxford English Dictionary,* 1989: viii. 744–7).

SEDUCE: [L *seducere* to LEAD away, fr. *se-* apart + *ducere* to lead]: to persuade to disobedience or disloyalty; to lead astray; to entice into unchastity; attract.

syn: see LURE, ENTICE, INVEIGLE, DECOY, TEMPT, SEDUCE.

LURE implies a drawing into danger, evil, or difficulty through attracting and deceiving; ENTICE suggests drawing by artful or adroit means; INVEIGLE implies enticing by cajoling or flattering; DECOY implies a luring into entrapment by artifice; TEMPT implies the presenting of an attraction so strong that it overcomes the restraints of conscience or better judgment, SEDUCE implies a leading astray by persuasion of false promises. (*Oxford Eglish Dictionary,* 1989: xiv. 860–2)

Notice the contrasts sustaining the meaningfulness of these terms: lead/seduce; guide/lure; correctly/false; good/bad.

Notice, however, that seduction includes leadership: seduction means to lead (astray); to mis-lead [mis: badly, wrongly]. Seduction has a bad reputation. Seduction is leadership gone wrong.

Notice also that leadership includes seduction: to lead is to attract and stimulate, to overcome. Thus, to seduce is to lead wrongly, and it seems that to lead is to seduce rightly.

Why don't we call the leader a seducer? Again, from the dictionary, we learn:

SEDUCER: One who tempts or persuades (another) to desert his allegiance of service. Now rare or obsolete.

SEDUCTOR: Obsolete. A male seducer. [Obsolete means no evidence of standard use since 1711].

SEDUCTRESS: fr. L. to LEAD away: a female seducer. (*Oxford English Dictionary,* 1989: xiv. 861–2).

One who seduces, lures, induces, entices, presents an attraction so strong that it overcomes restraints. One who seduces is a seductress: a female seducer. Seductors (male seducers) no longer exist. Thus, many can be a 'leader' but only a woman can be a 'seductress'. No need for the term 'seductor' when 'leader' will do.

## A Genealogy of Leadership / Seduction

Let's now find what we can learn about seduction, when reading about leadership. By calling this main section of the paper a 'genealogy'—following the Foucaldian usage—we are pointing to the fact that the four organizational 'classics' we are analysing cover a time period of almost fifty years of organization theorizing without showing development or progress, despite their claim to the contrary. Rather, through our readings we show how these texts trace a circle—*a circle of seduction*—that is quite narrow in what it includes. While practices and discourses of leadership change, together with other discourses and practices of their time, they maintain specific power / knowledge relationships.

## What is Leadership? As Answered by Chester Barnard in *The Functions of the [Seductive] Executive*

Barnard (1938) addressed the question 'What is the essence of leadership?' With the aid of the dictionary, we reread Barnard's answer:

| *Barnard* | *Dictionary* |
| --- | --- |
| The CREATIVE function as a whole is the ESSENCE of leadership. | CREATIVE: productive; having the quality of something created rather than imitated. |

ESSENCE: the permanent as contrasted with the accidental element of being, the individual, real, ultimate nature of a thing esp. as opposed to its existence.

It is the highest test of executive RESPONSIBILITY [*note*: elsewhere in his text, p. 261, Barnard defines executive responsibility as the tendency to inhibit, control, or modify inconsistent immediate desire, impulses, or interests] because it requires for successful accomplishment that element of CONVICTION that means IDENTIFICATION of personal codes and organization codes in the view of the leader.

RESPONSIBILITY: moral, legal accountability.

CONVICTION: the act or process of convicting of a crime, esp. in a court of law; the act of convincing a person of error or of compelling the admission of a truth, the state of being convinced of error or compelled to admit the truth, a strong persuasion or belief.

IDENTIFICATION: evidence of identity orientation of the self in regard to something (as a person or group) with a resulting feeling of close emotional associations.

This is the COALESCENCE that CARRIES CONVICTION to the personnel of organization, to that informal organization underlying all formal organization that senses nothing more quickly than INSINCERITY.

COALESCENCE: to grow together, to unite into a whole: fuse.

CARRY: transport, convey, take, conduct, escort, to influence by mental or emotional appeal, sway, to get possession or control of: capture.

CONVICTION: the state of being convinced of error or compelled to admit the truth.

INSINCERITY: hypocrisy, playing a part on the stage, feigning to be what one is not, or to believe what one does not; esp. the false assumption of an appearance of virtue or religion.

Without it, all organization is dying, because it is the INDISPENSABLE element in creating that DESIRE for ADHERENCE—for which no INCENTIVE is substitute—on the part of those whose efforts WILLINGLY contributed constitute organization.' (Barnard 1938: 281).

INDISPENSABLE: not subject to being set aside or neglected, absolutely necessary.

DESIRE: to long or hope for; to express a wish for;

> syn: wish, want, crave, covet—desire, wish, want are often interchangeable though
>
> DESIRE or wish is often chosen as giving more dignity or a more respectful tone to a request.
>
> DESIRE: conscious impulse toward an object or experience that promises enjoyment or satisfaction in its attainment, longing, craving, sexual attraction or appetite.
>
> ADHERENCE: steady or faithful attachment, fidelity, applied chiefly to mental or moral attachment.
>
> INCENTIVE: stimulating: something that incites action.
>
> WILLING: ready, without reluctance readiness/eagerness to accede to or anticipate the wishes of another. (*Webster's Ninth New Collegiate Dictionary*, 1988)

What is Barnard saying? Table 17.1 rearticulates *The Functions of the [Seductive] Executive*. The deconstructive strategy we have used in this case, iteration, explicitly removes the 'original text' by displacing its context. Using the multiple meanings available, the rearticulation 'uncovers' another plausible text inscribed in the apparently straightforward and unequivocal descriptions of 'what is leadership'.

As if self-conscious about the sexual themes in his text, Barnard also elaborates a discourse of morality over his discourse of desire. Here, rather than just citing Barnard, we have juxtaposed his words with those of M. J. Exner's in *The Sexual Side of Marriage* (1932), a sex manual contemporaneous with *The Functions of the Executive*. In this parallel intertextualizaion, illustrated in Table 17.2, we see that leadership is like sexual passion in that it energizes and satisfies. Leadership like sexual passion can have its ups and downs, but organization and our entire social structure rest upon their capacity to arouse and express that which is higher—morality. We recommend that you read the table back and forth, from Barnard to Exner, in order to experience the full effect of this juxtaposition.

Table 17.1. Leadership is the creation of desire

| |
|---|
| Leadership is the absolutely necessary creation of desire, a longing, wishing, craving—the creation of sexual attraction that promises to be satisfied through faithful attachment. There are no substitutes for gaining the willing contribution of efforts. Leadership/desire is the life force of organizations, without it, organization/the species dies. |
| How does a leader create desire? First the leader must achieve a state of 'conviction'—an act of self-seduction, where his feelings of separation from the group are totally overcome and he truly believes that he and the group are one. He must truly assume the appearance of virtue and not feign belief. |
| This is an executive's hardest ordeal for it means inhibiting, controlling, or modifying his own inconsistent impulses and intensifying those which are consistent. The fusion in the leaders' mind, of himself and the group, lures, sways, influences mentally or emotionally, and captures [Seduces?] the personnel of the organization, but only if the leader is a true believer, for organization personnel can tell when you're faking it. |
| This creation, the production of himself-fused-with-personnel, is the real creativity of leadership. No imitations will be accepted. The seduction that is leadership depends on truth. Thus, in order to create and sustain organization—Barnard's leader seduces. |

## The Carnal Pleasures of the Priestly Executive

Now, what was that all about? Interweaving the words from both sides of Table 17.2 we find that:

'So among those who cooperate' (the mating parents, the family, the clan, the tribe, the state, the nation, our entire social structure) 'the things that are seen' (appreciation, companionship, sympathy, love, devotion, protection, service, sacrifice, chivalry, honour, etc.) 'are moved by' (find their fullest satisfaction in) 'the things unseen' (the self-centred physical attraction).

Both Exner and Barnard speak in dignified tones about the ultimate goodness and morality of sexuality/leadership. Sex yields supreme ecstasy, it is food for the soul, the spur of creative endeavour. Leadership is vitality, the catalyst for organization. The sparks of sexuality ignite sympathy and sociality, the sparks of leadership ignite cooperation, uniting two into coordination; they enable the progressive forms of social structures.

Whereas Exner considers 'mating parents' to be the foundation of social structure, Barnard's world depends on 'binding the wills of men', a form of non-heterosexual reproduction (e.g. Kanter 1977; Burrell and Hearn 1989). He is explicit in this point as he says: 'Executive responsibility, then, is that capacity of leaders by which, reflecting attitudes, ideals, hopes, derived largely from without themselves, they are compelled to bind the wills of men to the accomplishment of purposes beyond their immediate ends, beyond their times' (Barnard 1938: 283). While, earlier, he had said: 'Responsibility is the aspect of individual superiority in determination, persistence,

Table 17.2. The higher ends of leadership and sexuality

| Barnard (1938) | Exner (1932) |
|---|---|
| 'Leadership, of course, often is wrong, and often fails.' (p. 283). | 'On the purely physical level it (sexual passion) may carry man to the lowest levels of degradation.' (p. 48) |
| 'But until that happens—as perhaps it inevitably does in time to all leaders—until that happens the creation of organizational morality is the spirit that overcomes the centrifugal forces of individual motives.' (p. 283) | 'In an ideal sex relationship we do not set apart in opposition the physical and the psychic . . . They become fused in the total experience of love. The physical and the emotional in sexual love at its best all become spiritual together, and irradiate and energise the total life of the partners.' (p. 46) |
| 'Without leadership in this sense the inherent difficulties often cannot be overcome even for short periods . . .' (p. 283) | 'As an integral constituent of love it makes for healthy personality; it yields supreme ecstasy; it feeds the soul; and it spurs life to creative endeavour.' (p. 46) |
| 'the vitality is lacking, there is not enduring cooperation, without the creation of faith, the catalyst by which the living system of human efforts is enabled to continue its incessant interchanges of energies and satisfactions'. (p. 259) | 'Human sympathy in all its wide range of affectional and social expression undoubtedly had its starting point in the first spark of sexual sympathy which arose to assure the mating of parents . . . The sympathetic and social qualities and relationships developed in the family gradually extended beyond the family in turn to the nearest of kin, the clan, the tribe, the state, the nation. They underlie our entire social structure. In this social zone of sex are found the higher affectional attractions between male and female—as contrasted to the self-centred physical attraction—including appreciation, companionship, sympathy, love, devotion, protection, service, sacrifice, chivalry, protection, service, sacrifice, chivalry, honour, etc. . . . these qualities are psychic and social. They are other-seeking, other serving qualities which find their fullest satisfaction in the happiness and service of others.' (pp. 38–9) |
| 'Cooperation, not leadership, is the creative process; but leadership is the creative indispensable fulminator of its forces.' (p. 259) | 'Out of the self-centred physical base of sex there gradually developed the higher psychic, aesthetic and social elements which have so greatly enlarged and enriched human life and made an organized soical world possible.' (p. 38) |
| 'For the morality that underlies enduring cooperation is multidimensional. It comes from and may expand to all the world; it is rooted deeply in the past, it faces towards the endless future. As it expands, it must become more complex, its conflicts must be more numerous and deeper, its call for abilities must be higher, its failures of ideal attainment must be perhaps more tragic; but the quality of leadership, the persistence of its influence, the durability of its related organizations, the power of the coordination it incites, all express the height of moral aspiration, the breadth of moral foundations.' (p. 284) | |
| 'So among those who cooperate the things that are seen are moved by the things unseen. Out of the void comes the spirit that shapes the end of men.' (p. 284) | |

endurance, courage . . . which is most inferred from what is *not* done, from abstention, which commands respect, reverence . . .' (Barnard 1938: 260, emphasis in original)

Seduction as seduction is necessarily excluded from both Barnard's and Exner's discussions for it is dangerous to the maintenance of social structure, organization, and the succession of leadership. In Barnard, particularly, the language of morality that he uses to describe the leader (faith, sacrifice, abstention, reverence) calls to mind images of a priest (usually called

'Father')—an individual of superior determination, whose endurance and courage is more inferred from what he avoids (*does not* do): succumbing to temptation, and engaging in sexual intercourse. Seduction, as seduction, is inimical to orderly relations of men/human life.

In these concerns, we hear the echo of another famous practitioner-theorist, Sigmund Freud, who, in his paper 'Femininity' (1933) reported: 'an interesting episode in the history of analytic research which caused me many distressing hours. In the period in which the main interest was directed to discovering infantile sexual traumas, almost all my women patients told me that they had been seduced by their father' (1965: 120).

Freud felt compelled to reject the first version of the seduction theory because of his 'surprise at the fact that in every case the father, not excluding my own, had to be blamed as a pervert' (Freud 1897; quoted in Bernheimer and Kahane 1985: 14). Unable to accept the possibility of so many perverse fathers, Freud ended up proposing an infantile polymorphous perverse sexuality where children were the ones who fantasized seduction by the father (e.g. Gallop 1987; Hunter 1989*a*, *b*). However, this different theory of seduction did not focus solely on children. Gallop observes that:

> It has become a commonplace of the history of psychoanalysis to mark as a turning point the moment in the 1890s when Freud stopped believing in 'real' seduction at the origin of hysteria and realized that the source of neurosis is the child's fantasies . . . But here, in a 1931 text, Freud is talking about 'actual seduction'. The father cannot be a seducer; that would undercut his upright position as patriarch. Even the mother only seduces unwittingly in the execution of her proper duties. The 'actual seduction', intentional seduction, can only be the act of another child (children, not parents, are perverse) or a nurse. The servant, member of a lower class, like a child, is capable of perversion. (Gallop 1987: 214)[1]

This is also the case with Barnard's executive. The executive cannot be a seducer; that would undercut his upright position. So, Barnard makes his leader into a Father/priest, incapable of seduction and close to God, but with the mandate to attract his flock of sinner-seducers (perverse children, nurses, mothers, and other organizational participants) to confession and absolution. Denying that seduction is part of his craft, the leader can take pleasure in voyeuristic activities promoted by his absolute dedication to his responsibilities.

At the same time, the executive must be a seducer . . . that's where the desire for adherence comes from. What is Barnard's way out of this? The only way out is to call seduction something else: 'leadership'.

## Who Can be a Leader? As Answered by Douglas McGregor in *The [Seductive] Side of Enterprise*

This book, published in 1960 and still widely cited, inaugurated the emphasis on humanistic psychology discourses within the managerial literature. It is addressed to the top management of American corporations, and it promotes a change in traditionally held assumptions about who can be a leader.

McGregor's approach to leadership seems to be discontinuous from Barnard's—as McGregor stresses a more egalitarian, relational, and situational stance for his leader in contrast with Barnard's moral loneliness in the empty room at the top. Our argument claims that McGregor's approach actually furthers Barnard's seductive homosocial logic (of the Father). In our readings, we argue that the changes in assumptions which McGregor espoused were not only from Theory *X* (or classical management theory) to Theory *Y* but a move away from the conventions of *X*/*Y* to a desire for *YY*, i.e. a homosocial order. That is, we propose that this text has a riddle written on its surface which plays on the conventional biological sex notations: female *XX*; male *XY*, and tries to eliminate any vestige of *X* while wondering about the possibility of an all *Y* world.

This 'wild speculation' on our part may not be so wild after all. Why do the *X*/*Y* notations signify theoretical differences? Why not *A*/*Z*, if the author's interest was to indicate widely divergent viewpoints? An interesting coincidence (?): at the time that this book was written, 1959, women were defined as having two *X* chromosomes, while men were defined as having an *X* and a *Y*, according to the adopted scientific notations.

The deconstructive strategies we follow in this section, illustrated in Tables 17.3 and 17.4, intertextualize McGregor's discourse on leadership by emphasizing the *monologic* it shares with a textual cohort. This other text, *The American Male* by Myron Brenton (1966), explicitly addressed the social and sexual fears which assaulted the American male population in the early 1960s, and suggested a possible resolution for those fears. Notice how McGregor's arguments about leadership and Brenton's resolution of issues around male sexuality share 'a manner of speaking' and can be reconfigured into a very consistent *monologue*. Our recommendation to the reader is to follow the sequence of our intertextual weavings by reading McGregor's and Brenton's texts as if they were a single text.

Our 'conversation' in the right-hand margin may be read after the central text (McGregor's/Brenton's). Or you may dash back and forth, from 'margin to centre', as if the margin were the commentary of someone who, on overhearing the main conversation, wonders about its meaning. Regardless of the way you read it, we have positioned the materiality of this column—its physical form on the page—to illustrate the outsidedness and marginality of those others who cannot engage with the *mainstream* discourse: they are left out, invisible, unheard, but still capable of breaking the orderly surface of the central text through a *playful absent presence*. The presence on the page of the typically absent 'other' is a reminder that dominant knowledges pretend to rest on their own essence, or self-identity, while being nothing more than a play of differences over the voices they deny or silence.

The marginal 'conversation' uses specific deconstructive arguments from Derrida (1976) and Irigaray (1985*b*) to wonder about the (il)logic within the main conversation. It points to the ways in which McGregor's and Brenton's texts betray their main assumptions on issues such as the relational and egalitarian nature of leadership/sexuality, and about the leadership/sexual roles that 'the diverse' can play in organizational/personal relations.

These arguments unfold from one table to the other, as if there were a riddle which is solved at the end. The solution reveals the phallogocentric order that rules leadership and sexuality. Please read (and play with) these two tables now. In the next section we will discuss them further.

## The [Seductive] Side of Enterprise: The Text as a Sexual Joke

We would like to discuss our reading in Tables 17.3 and 17.4 as a particular instance of seduction within the discourses of leadership: leadership as a sexual joke. Gallop's (1988) commentary on Freud's analysis of the sexual joke emphasizes how these jokes—which in theory are smut uttered by a man in order to seduce a woman—would only occur between males and females of the lower social classes. At the higher social level, the sexual joke would not take place between men and women. Rather, it will be a typical scene among *gentlemen*, and will exclude the *ladies*.

Gallop equates the *telling* of sexual jokes with the institution of marriage in that in both cases their purpose is to initiate men into an exchange which strengthens the bonds among them: a male economy. Through their *content* sexual jokes either transform women into objects of circulation or perform, more immediately, in the conservation of a homosocial dominant order. That is, the seductiveness of the sexual joke among men is that it positions women

Table 17.3. The logic of supplementarity defines the texts

| McGregor (1960) | Brenton (1966) | Our Conversaton |
|---|---|---|
| 'It is quite unlikely that there is a single basic pattern of abilities and personality traits characteristic of all leaders. The personality characteristics of the leader are not unimportant, but those which are essential differ considerably depending upon the circumstances.' (p. 180) | | IT ALL HINGES ON *ABILITIES*<br>(*ability*: capacity fitness or tendency to act or be acted on in a specified way).<br>THUS ANYBODY CAN BE A LEADER!<br>BUT WAIT—DOES THIS MEAN THAT *THE SAME* CAN BE LIKE *THE OTHER?*<br>(*same*: resembling in every relevant aspect).<br>(*other*: opposite or excluded by something else).<br>(*same/other*: tendency in Western discourse which privileges masculine 'sameness-unto-itself').<br>BUT OH! HERE WE GO AGAIN! THAT WONDERFUL LOGIC OF THE *SUPPLEMENT* . . .!<br>(supplement: something that completes or makes an addition).<br>TO MAKE US THINK THAT THE WEAK REQUIRES THE POWER OF THE STRONG . . .<br>BUT WHY WOULD THE STRONG REQUIRE THE LACK OF THE WEAK? WHO IS THE ORIGIN? WHO IS THE SUPPLEMENT? Jacques Derrida found out about Rousseau in *OF GRAMMATOLOGY* but it is all over the logocentric order. |
| | 'Leadership, dominance and dependency—all shift with the particular needs and abilities of the marital partners and with the requirement of the situation.' (p. 215) | |
| 'The same is true of leadership at different organizational levels. A very successful foreman would not make a successful president (or vice-versa!). Yet each may be an effective leader.' (p. 181) | | |
| | 'This doesn't preclude a division of labour and a decision-making, of course. Whenever two persons of the same or opposite sex live together, such a division, based on interest and competence, comes into being.' (p. 215) | |
| 'On the other hand, leaders who differ notably in abilities and traits are sometimes equally successful when they succeed each other in a given situation. Within rather wide limits, weaknesses in certain characteristics can be compensated by strength in others.' (p. 181) | | |
| | '[I]t allows each of the partners the freedom and the scope to expand, to unfold their personalities, to realize their particular potentials . . .' (p. 216) | |
| 'This is particularly evident in partnerships and executive teams in which leadership functions are, in fact, shared. The very idea of the team implies different and supplementary patterns of abilities among the members.' (p. 181) | | |
| | '[I]t affords each partner recognition and acceptance of his or her particular strengths, weaknesses, and needs . . .' (p. 216) | |

**Table 17.4.** But it is the homosocial that solves the riddle

| McGregor (1960) | Brenton (1966) | Our Conversation |
|---|---|---|
| | '[F]ew contemporary cultures are as hostile to homosexuality as America's is . . . It's significant that society is much more tolerant of female than of male homosexuality . . .' (p. 32) | Luce Irigaray says that the possibility of our social life, or our culture, depends upon a HOM(M)OSEXUAL monopoly because the law that orders our society is the exclusive valorization of men's needs and desires, of exchanges among men. THUS, THE DEVALUATION OF *MALE HOMOSEXUALITY* CAN UPSET THE SOCIAL AND ECONOMIC ORDER. NOW, HOW SHOULD THE RIDDLE BE SOLVED? Do deviants pose/possess a THREAT?<br>(*threat*: from *trudere*: to push, thrust)<br>IN SPITE OF SOCIAL SCIENCE RESEARCH, THE CHANGES WITH TIME REDUCE PREDICTABILITY IN THE *RELATIONSHIP*<br>(*relationship*: connection by blood or marriage)<br>WITH *RESOURCES*<br>(*resource*: re-again + sourdre- to spring up = something that lies ready for use; supply of something to take care of a need). Luce Irigaray says that patriarchal societies might be interpreted as functioning in the mode of 'semblance' or based on an analogy. WHO WOULD BE *SELF-FULFILLED?*<br>(*self*: identity, of the same kind; fulfilment: to carry out; obey; complete) WHO ARE THE *WE?*<br>(*we*: I and the rest of the group that includes me; *I* as used by sovereigns). |
| 'An important point with respect to these situational influences on leadership is that they operate selectively . . . to reward conformity with acceptable patterns of behaviour and to punish deviance from these . . . One consequence of this selectivity is the tendency to "weed out" deviant individuals some of whom might nevertheless become effective, perhaps outstanding leaders.' (pp. 183–4) | | |
| | 'Such animosity creates a vicious circle in which both homosexual, and heterosexual males become victims . . . This hostility produces defensive reactions in homosexuals, who now feel free enough to become militant, forming their own social and political action groups . . .' (p. 32) | |
| 'What is the practical relevance for management of these findings of social science research in the field of leadership? First, if we accept the point of view that leadership consists of a relationship . . . we must recognize that we cannot predict the personal characteristics of the managerial resources that an organization will require a decade or two hence.' (p. 185) | | |
| | 'In such a society the artistically gifted man and the man who is a gifted sportsman would be equally valued in terms of their maleness . . . Why not tap all out societal and temperamental resources to create an atmosphere in which all kinds of ways are possible and in which self-fulfilment becomes more than a pretty word?' (p. 217) | |
| 'Some people in some companies will become outstanding leaders as foremen, or as plant superintendents, or as professional specialists. Many of these would not be effective leaders in top-management positions . . . If we take seriously the implications of the research findings in this field we will place high value on such people. We will seek to enable them to develop to the fullest of their potentialities in the role they can fill best . . . and persuade them that we consider outstanding leadership at any level to be a precious thing.' (pp.188–9) | | |

and working-class men as objects of desire of the ruling class. However, women in these jokes perform as 'currency' and maintain their otherness, while 'lesser' men function to reiterate the *sameness* of the ruling order.

More specifically, often the subjects of the sexual jokes analysed by Freud were male homosexual servants. In these stories, the servant would perform some special service for his master, who, in gratitude, would then elevate the servant to become the master's peer. The punch line tells otherwise, because, in fact, the master has used the servant one more time. He has maintained the servant in his humiliated and debased position while fooling him into believing that he has become his equal. In general, homosexual servant jokes play on the multiplicity of those who are the same, while being different. Similar to those where women are the objects, these jokes exploit *double entendre* and domination, but they perform primarily in the transference of homosexual desires while enhancing the hierarchical order of a homosocial libidinal economy.

McGregor's—and Brenton's—texts could be read as sexual jokes of the 'servant' type. The seduction of these texts hinges on the way in which they appease the ambivalence felt by those in dominant positions—American corporate bosses and American heterosexual males—when the winds of equality (of women and other non-dominant people) blow too close for comfort. In Table 17.3, both books constantly touch upon 'the same' and 'the other' as a way to remark the existence of *differences*. At the same time, they use a logic of *supplementarity*—playing with the notion of opposites needing each other—to make explicit the existence of weaknesses in 'the other' and their need to stay attached (maintain relationship) with the strong/same/dominant group.

The constant talk about egalitarianism has the doubleness of the homosexual joke. Both texts were written to circulate among men. It is clear from their contents that their intended public was not women, nor just any men, but a certain higher class male population. For example, Table 17.4 shows that, for McGregor, it is important to acknowledge those others who *manage* in the organization, such as foremen and superintendents, while reminding us of the distance between them and those at the top. Thus, this book is a riddle about the servant who becomes elevated by his master, for the master's pleasure (as his equal, capable of leadership). In the end the master is not humiliated by having descended, and partaken, at such low levels (after all, it all happened only *in the text/joke*). Rather, the remarks serve to maintain everybody *in their proper place*.

Brenton's book may now easily be understood as the intertext in McGregor's work. *The American Male* openly recognizes the fears of homosexuality in the male population during the early 1960s. It is also explicit in indicating the pervasiveness of this fear among the middle class, and the relationship of their fear to 'the many homosexual jokes that keep making the rounds' (Brenton 1966: 182). The central message calls attention to the intolerance of society for male homosexuality as this intolerance ends up disrupting the homosocial order. Male homosexuals separate from this order and create another dominant economy, much to the dismay of heterosexual males, who lose their 'servants'. The 'punch line' ends up evoking those situations where male could be with male, or play alternative non-traditional male roles, and still be dominant members of society.

McGregor's/Brenton's discourse is a mouthful of dominant males' desire for the selfsame, who entertain themselves in remaking the hierarchical order that they purport to abolish. Their texts tease the reader to think about the different *positions* that any one member of the organization/society can take—and play on the seduction of this *double entendre*—but, in every instance, they close off any possible change for the 'servants', convincing them that they will benefit by remaining in their lower position. In the end, the 'central text' accomplishes little more than to make more explicit and well defined the libidinal economy of the dominant groups.

## How is a Manager also a Leader? As Answered by Henry Mintzberg in *The [Seductive] Nature of Managerial Work*

Originally published in 1973, and very slightly revised in 1980, Henry Mintzberg's book *The Nature of Managerial Work* claims to describe the actual makings of everyday managerial activities. This text tries to answer the question: As a leader, what does a manager do?

Mintzberg's writings have inscribed a discourse that seduces us into believing 'this is leadership'. Our re-readings of the role of the manager as leader—one of ten managerial roles in the book—re-mark the sexuality in these descriptions:

| *Mintzberg* (1980) | *Dictionary* |
|---|---|
| 'The organization looks to its formal HEAD for guidance and motivation. In his *leader* role, the manager defines the atmosphere in which the organization will work.' (p.60) | HEAD: the upper or principal extremity of various things, esp. when rounded, projecting or of some special shape. The top, summit, upper end (of an |

eminence, or erection, as a pole, pile, mast, sail, staircase, ladder).

'The tone of the organization is usually SOUNDED by its top executive, and the success of the enterprise may well depend on

SOUND(ED): to order, signal; an elongated instrument for exploring surgically body cavities.

whether he INFUSES the whole hierarchy with energy and vision or whether, through

INFUSES: introduces, insinuates, implies a pouring in of something that gives new life or significance.

ineptness or NEGLECT, he allows the organization to stagnate. (Harbison and Myers 1959: 15–16, in Mintzberg, p. 60)

NEGLECT: giving insufficient attention to something that has a claim to one's attention.

'Leadership involves interpersonal RELATIONSHIPS between the leader and the led. In the informal group, the leader is usually followed because of his PHYSICAL

RELATIONSHIP: dealings, affairs, sexual intercourse.

PHYSICAL: concerned or preoccupied with the body and its needs: carnal, marked by sexuality.

or CHARISMATIC power.

CHARISMATIC: favour, gift.

In analyzing the activities that make up the leader role, we must note first that leadership PERMEATES all activities; its importance would be underestimated if it were judged in terms of the proportion of a manager's activities that are strictly related to leadership. Each time a manager ENCOURAGES or criticizes a

PERMEATE: to diffuse through or penetrate something—permeable: penetrable.

ENCOURAGE: to spur on: stimulate to excite to activity or growth: arouse.

subordinate he is acting in his CAPACITY as *leader*

CAPACITY: potentiality, a position assigned or assumed.

. . . the manager's actions are screened by subordinates searching for leadership clues. In answering a request for authorization, he may ENCOUNTER or INHIBIT a subordinate, and even in his form of greeting, messages (perhaps non-existent ones) may be read by ANXIOUS subordinates.' (p. 61)

INHIBIT: a restraining of the function of a bodily organ

ANXIOUS: ardently or earnestly wishing.

In addition to these activities, one finds another set in which the manager PROBES

PROBE: a slender surgical instrument for examining a cavity.

(one might say 'MEDDLES' into the actions of his 'subordinates'. The manager is able to PROBE freely because he alone is not constrained by well-defined bounds of authority within his organization. He is the only one in the organization with a very broad mandate—to put this another way, he is the only one who can MEDDLE at will—and his activities clearly reflect this. (pp. 61–2)

MEDDLE: to interfere without right of property—officiously intrusive—to thrust or force in or upon without permission, welcome or fitness.

'In concluding the discussion of the *leader* role, two points should be noted. First, the key purpose of the *leader* role is to effect an INTEGRATION between individual needs and organizational goals. The manager must concentrate his efforts so as to bring subordinate and organizational needs into a common accord in order to promote efficient operations. Second, it is the *leader* role that managerial power most clearly manifests itself. Formal authority vests the manager with great POTENTIAL power; leadership activity determines how much of it will be realized. (p. 62)

INTEGRATION: to form into a whole, to unite into something.

POTENT(IAL): existing in possibility, capable of developing, potent: bridegroom, husband, master, able to copulate as male.

Thus, through the *leader* role, the manager WELDS diverse elements into a cooperative enterprise. (p. 62)

WELD: to unite closely or intimately.

*The Manager as* LIAISON

LIAISON: a close bond or connection, an illicit sexual relationship.

One of the major findings of the empirical studies of managerial work is the significance of HORIZONTAL relationships. While vertical or authority relationships have received much attention in the literature—specifically in terms of the *leader* role—HORIZONTAL relationships have been largely ignored.' (p. 63)

HORIZONTAL: lie, recline, supine. (*Webster's Ninth Collegiate Dictionary,* 1988)

What is Mintzberg saying? Table 17.5 rearticulates the *Seductive Nature of Managerial Work* from our readings above. Again, as with Barnard's text, we rely on the strategy of iteration to 'uncover' another plausible text inscribed in the apparently straightforward and unequivocal descriptions of 'the manager as leader'.

## The Narcissistic Seduction of Mintzberg's Leader

After the 'true confession' in Table 17.5 one must ask: What has happened in the few years that have lapsed between the publication of McGregor's (1960) and Mintzberg's (1973) work? How has McGregor's relationship-oriented leader, with all his seductive talk about the equality of inequality, been transformed into Mintzberg's solitary and narcissistic, but omnipotent, leader with no patience for anything but the most direct activities?

Some answers are again provided by the intertext of contemporaneous works. In *Footholds: Understanding the Shifting Family and Sexual Tensions in our Culture* (Slater 1977), the author explores issues of sexuality in the USA during the 1970s. This text is openly preoccupied with the possible ills that 'narcissism' could bring to the fabric of complex societies. However, this work is

**Table** 17.5. The manager as seducer

| |
|---|
| The organization looks at the projection of an erection for its guidance and motivation. The *leader* introduces and insinuates by pouring that which gives new life. He will never give insufficient attention to that to which he claims. |
| He will develop sexual affairs and will be preoccupied with the body and its carnal needs. |
| He will bestow his favours and gift to those placed into his possession. |
| He will constantly stimulate, excite, arouse and penetrate. He will do so because he is potent in every position. Thus he will never restrain the function of the bodily organs from those who are ardent with earnest wishes. |
| With his slender instrument he will examine every cavity even if he has to be intrusive, thrusting or forcing in without permission, welcome, or fitness. |
| He will unite and form into a whole, developing that which exists in possibility. Like a bridegroom, husband, and master, he will produce pregnancies when using his ability to copulate as a male. |
| He will unite closely and intimately with those that are not the same. However, he would not conceal any longer the illicit sexual relationships he carries on with those who are like him, and with whom he lies down. |

very explicit when rescuing narcissism from a totally 'bad press'. The following passages are particularly relevant to our discussion:

> 'If we view sexual energy, or libido, as being able to expand and contract, then we can throw some light on a familiar process—the withdrawal of energy from larger groups to smaller and more exclusive ones . . . The most extreme form [of libidinal contraction] we will call narcissistic withdrawal . . . Narcissistic withdrawal is often tolerated in people who are expected to be of great benefit to society: leaders, prophets, shamans . . . The basis of this tolerance is perhaps some vague awareness that great enterprises require an abundance of libidinal energy, which must be withdrawn from the usual social objects . . . The person who has stored up energy will attract the energy of others to him, after the physical principle that the greater the mass the greater the attraction. A person of this kind can be a focus for group loyalty. (Slater 1977: 114–121)

Slater informs us about our need for, and acceptance of, narcissistic leadership. It is good for us and, as a passing remark, we want to remind the reader of the central position taken by discourses of narcissism during the 1970s in the USA. For example, Lasch's *The Culture of Narcissism* (1979) was a nationwide best seller which identified narcissism in—among other social activities—corporate and managerial structures. It singled out Maccoby's (1976) view of desirable organizational leadership—'the gamesman', boyish, playful, and seductive who maintains an illusion of limitless options—as a fitting embodiment of narcissistic tendencies.

Ironically, Lasch's strong critique of USA society at the time brought back to him major proof of the accuracy of his assessment—fame and fortune derived from the ultimate narcissistic object, 'the mirror'—as readers flocked to look at their own images represented in this book. At the same time, this commentary on our part is a remark on a favourite image in postmodernist arguments, where the endless repetition provided by mirror reflections on other mirrors makes it impossible to separate 'originals' and 'copies'—i.e. the contiguity of Lasch's textual representation of society and the social act, seemingly provoked by the text, which reverts back to the textual representation in an endless 'chicken-and-egg' game. Consider the effects of this form of thinking over our typical notions about organizational knowledge.

Mintzberg's narcissistic leader, then, is a good representative of the discourses of his time, but what does it mean to perform as a leader under narcissistic premisses, and how do these changes still maintain the continuity of the homosocial order?

If we accept Slater's interpretation of narcissism (and its seductiveness) as a tenable form of leadership, there is no reason to believe that it will exclude women leaders. Narcissistic tendencies, after all have been presented in traditional Freudian analysis as plausible stages of infantile sexual development, regardless of gender (e.g. Badcock 1988). However, Karen Horney's reinterpretation of Freud's theory of seduction (Westkott 1986) may shed a different light on this issue.

According to Westkott, Horney argues that narcissistic and seductive activities carry over into adulthood, and are related to each other. However, these activities are qualitatively different in males and females. Horney describes men's sexualizing behaviour from the perspective of the endangered female, who is the object of compulsive masculinity. Through compulsive masculinity—the never-ending pursuit of sexual conquest and seduction—men devalue women as a way of maintaining their own sense of superiority. Men define their self-esteem and affirm their power through this form of domination, reasserting the narcissistic belief about their superior position in society.

At the same time, feminine seductiveness is, in Horney's view, the conversion of fear into desirability. It is a way of promoting a submissive identity informed by sexuality to avoid aggression. The distinction between submission and sexuality allows Horney to show feminine seductiveness—and the apparent female desire and forms of making herself desirable—as the response of women resigned to the inevitability of violence in sexualization. Thus, feminine narcissism—which promotes sexual attractiveness—is interpreted as a form of avoiding mistreatment by getting to be among 'the chosen few' who are perhaps more used, but less abused.

These male–female sexual relations are seen by Horney as an unavoidable condition of Western society where pervasive competitiveness forms a normal pattern of social relations. The predominant values of competition and success foster the cultivation of a grandiose image, of superiority—and generate feelings of hostility and fear—primarily in those most likely to be in the public male eye.

Horney decries that these historically situated male narcissistic tendencies create very precarious conditions for women's expression of self. Under these conditions, women may be able to express their social sense of self only through the already mentioned submission-seduction, or through an equally undesirable alternative: emulating traditional male values, celebrating risk-taking in violence, and in success over others.

Thus, under these premisses, the space for women—and other 'feminized' non-dominant members (e.g. Ferguson 1984)—in the social arrangements of modern Western society is either subordination or emulation of the competitive and glory-oriented masculine narcissistic order. In either case, feminine narcissistic activities will maintain—through submission or cloning—the homosocial order.

In this regard, then, Mintzberg's leader—compulsively masculine in its narcissistic seduction—plays on the conditions of modern Western society.

Under Mintzberg's leader, those for whom compulsive masculinity is not a value will still submit to its ruling. Lacking other options within the system, they will perpetuate the conditions they may be wishing to escape. Violence here will always be covered by 'acquiescence'.

## Back to the Future—What is Leadership? As Answered by Peters and Waterman in *In [the Seductive] Search of Excellence*

Few texts would serve us better than this one as 'end-point' for our genealogical investigations. As we understand it, this work closes the *circle of seduction* which defines both the concept of leadership and the possibility of *modern* organizational theorizing. In the introductory chapter, the authors confess their original intention to discount leadership as an important element of organizational success. They soon correct themselves. Their assumption that leadership was an overrated and reductionist concept that covered up other more important organizational attributes had to be dropped because 'what we found was that associated with almost every excellent company was a strong leader (or two) who seemed to have a lot to do with making the company excellent in the first place' (Peters and Waterman 1982: 26).

Representative of organizational discourses of the 1980s, the text is self-conscious in using differentially gendered nouns and pronouns in reference to organizational activities. Throughout the book, it is clear that the authors recognize that there is diversity in organizational constituencies, and that women may be occupying positions of organizational leadership.

Has the homosocial order been broken by the inclusion of women into positions of authority? We became uneasy when observing that the first definition of leadership in the text followed Mintzberg's definition very closely. We questioned whether these assumed 'neutral' practices, which Peters and Waterman presented as 'the necessary activities of the leader that take up most of *his or her* day' (Peters and Waterman 1982: 82; emphasis added) would reveal the compulsive male and the alienated female selves decried by Horney. Our uneasiness was compounded by the fact that the chapter where this discussion occurs is titled 'Man Waiting for Motivation'.

So, we have tried another deconstructive strategy. We questioned whether a different kind of leadership is even possible, one which would be defined by traditional feminine imageries. For this purpose, we follow Luce Irigaray's approach, mimicry, where:

> One must assume the feminine role deliberately. Which means already to convert a form of subordination into an affirmation, and thus to begin to thwart it . . . [it means] for a woman, to try to recover the place of her exploitation by discourse, without allowing herself to be simply reduced to it. It means to resubmit herself . . . to 'ideas', in particular to ideas about herself, that are elaborated in/by masculine logic, but as to make it 'visible', by an effect of playful repetition, what was supposed to remain invisible: the cover-up of a possible operation of the feminine in language. (Irigaray: 1985*b*: 76)

For this purpose, we took Peters and Waterman's first definition of leadership and 'fantasized' in Table 17.6 the subtext that it would have if pronounced—alternatively—by male and female leaders. For the full effect of our mimicry read consecutively the similar sentences in each column.

## The Seductive Travesty of a Moral Leader

Now, in Table 17.6 the 'male subtext' seems to reiterate and even reinforce the leadership imagery and its seductiveness. The 'female subtext' creates a 'motherly' feeling. It promotes a solid context but neither an exciting nor a seductive one. It will be difficult to identify either leadership or seduction in a second reading.

It is important to notice, however, that we have deployed both those columns with our subtexts to show that they are nothing more than diverse views *from within the phallic order*—that is, a masculinist view of 'the feminine' including 'the stoic mother' and 'the fickle male'. They bespeak of 'the old dream of symmetry' (Irigaray 1985*a*) where parallel, but different, male and female forms of leadership may be possible (e.g. Loden 1985; Rosener 1990), but which doesn't question whose idea is the notion of 'symmetry'. Whose concept of the world would symmetrically 'gendered' leadership represent and reproduce? Wouldn't 'feminine leadership' be an oxymoron?—not because of 'feminine' but because of 'leadership'? (e.g. Calás 1988).

Even if we promoted the view that both male and female forms of leadership are possible (which we do not), it would be difficult to find these arguments within Peters and Waterman's text. In subsequent paragraphs, the authors promptly inform us that the activities described by their words in Table 17.6 are what Burns (1978) calls 'transactional leadership'. The authors

**Table 17.6.** Leadership as seductive travesty

| Peters and Waterman (1982) with a [male subtext] | Peters and Waterman (1982) with a [female subtext] |
|---|---|
| Leadership is many things. It is patient, usually boring coalition building *[or the game of courting your prey]*. | Leadership is many things. It is patient, usually boring coalition building *[or the careful sewing of a family quilt]*. |
| It is the purposeful seeding of cabals that one hopes will result in the appropriate ferment in the bowels of the organization *[to impregnate for the moment of production/reproduction]*. | It is the purposeful seeding of cabals that one hopes will result in the appropriate ferment in the bowels of the organization *[to mother the beauty of a bountiful field of flowers and grain]*. |
| It is meticulously shifting the attention of the institution through the mundane language of management systems *[to cover the doubleness of your intentions]*. | It is meticulously shifting the attention of the institution through the mundane language of management systems *[to keep alive hope in the moments of despair]*. |
| It is altering agendas so that new priorities get enough attention *[you know, that cute one in the typing pool]*. | It is altering agendas so that new priorities get enough attention *[to change one's career/mind for the sake of your children]*. |
| It is being visible when things are going awry, and invisible when they are working well *[you only press in your advances if she doesn't fall for your words]*. | It is being visible when things are going awry, and invisible when they are working well *[but you still know I am here, to give you a hand or dry your tears]*. |
| It's building a loyal team at the top that speaks more or less with one voice *[so that she, at the bottom, can be kept silent in her pain]*. | It's building a loyal team at the top that speaks more or less with one voice *[full of cacophonies, and always sustained by cries and laughter]*. |
| It's listening carefully much of the time, frequently speaking with encouragement, and reinforcing words with believable action *[yes, I'll say 'I love you' every time I possess you]*. | It's listening carefully much of the time, frequently speaking with encouragement, and reinforcing words with believable action *[yes, I love you and do come back if you need my help]*. |
| It's being tough when necessary, and it's the occasional naked use of power *[you pitiful thing, daring to oppose me, feel all the weight of my rage . . .]*. | It's being tough when necessary, and it's the occasional naked use of power *[you won't snatch my children away from me. Don't even come close, I'll kill you first.]* |

go on to indicate that these are just the everyday necessary activities of the leader, that he/she must not fail to perform. However, the authors' real interest in leadership is centred on Burns's 'transforming leadership', that occurs less frequently and 'builds on man's [*sic*] need for meaning, leadership that creates institutional purpose . . .' (Peters and Waterman 1982: 82)

Soon the authors recite the marvels of this personage as follows:

> The transforming leader is concerned with minutiae, as well. But he is concerned with a different kind of minutiae; he is concerned with the tricks of the pedagogue, the mentor, the linguist—the more successfully to become the value shaper, the exemplar, the maker of meanings . . . No opportunity is too small, no forum too insignificant, no audience too junior. (Peters and Waterman 1982: 82–3)

How naïve of us to think that Peters and Waterman's discourse would provide us with an opening for arguing *against* the fiction of 'female leadership' and the old dream of symmetry! There is no way to enter the sign 'woman' in this discourse, not even in an essentialist symmetric manner. Suddenly, we remember Gallop's (1982) commentary on Luce Irigaray's readings of Freud, which remarks that there is a certain pederasty implicit in pedagogy (. . . the mentor? . . . the linguist?) because a greater man penetrates a lesser man with his knowledge. This (male) homosexuality in the structures of society includes everybody. It is the male standard of knowledge—the apparently sexually indifferent logos, science, logic—which measures all members of the structure along a predefined agreement over what knowledge is. That is all there is to know about 'leadership'.

Thus to experience the full force of this knowledge here, we have the 'Transformational [travestite?] Leader', in all his socratic exhibitionism, when Peters and Waterman quote directly from Burns:

> Transforming leadership occurs when one or more persons engage with others in such a way that leaders and followers raise one another to higher levels of motivation and morality. Their purposes, which might have started out separate but related, in the case of transactional leadership, became fused . . . Various names are used for such leadership: elevating, mobilizing, inspiring, exalting, uplifting, exhorting, evangelizing [pederastic?]. The relationship can be moralistic, of course, but transforming leadership ultimately becomes moral in that it raises the level of human conduct and ethical aspirations of both the leader and the led, and thus has a transforming effect on both . . . (Burns 1978: 20, quoted in Peters and Waterman 1982: 83)

We noticed, as did Peters and Waterman, the familiarity of that discourse, but, different from Peters and Waterman, who exalted the *truthfulness* in these 'universal words' as first uttered by Chester Barnard, we felt how these words closed the homosocial *circle of seduction* for organizational leadership.

The supposedly innovative text of Peters and Waterman, and its celebrated *transcendent leader*, could do nothing more than repeat one more time the old signifiers. Under the guise of 'newness', the authors could do no more than articulate some empty discourses for the 1980s, while returning to the beginning of the circle. There is no other possibility for the paragraph than its capacity to transport us back, in a flash, through the parlours and gymnasiums permeated by sexual/homosexual jokes, and then to make us repent and pray 'in-the-Name-of-the-Father', kneeling in front (in whatever way) of 'Barnard-the-priest'. We also sensed, if ever so slightly, the sadness of an exhausted old satyr inside those words.

## Summary

What have we achieved as a result of these rereadings of classic commentaries on leadership? In them we see three images of leadership. Barnard's leader is a superior person, a priest/saint whose concerns for morality bring him close to God, but, as a man, he is still tied to his carnal needs. The minute human flesh is put onto leadership we have a man trying to perform like God, but who constantly commits seduction of his adoring flock.

McGregor gives up the image of godly leadership. Theocracy is exchanged for democracy, and the rule of God becomes the rule of the people. The shrewd Douglas is able to recognize the joke implicit in both cases. Neither God nor the people can rule, but the privileged class can make the populace, the flock, believe and follow their apparent representatives. Both the flock and the populace need to give their 'selves' to the leader in order to feel that they are somebody. McGregor is ready to produce an egalitarian trickster/leader holding out a promise of a new value system—but it is only a seductive joke!

With Mintzberg, there is no longer any pretence. At the dawn of the sexual revolution, emerging from the promiscuous discourses of the 1960s, anything goes! The oversexed, narcissistic leader is a permissible figure, under the illusion that others are equally empowered to counteract his advances: would they do it if they didn't want to? The thought that seduction may be happening out of fear is discounted.

Finally, we can repeat our previous lines about Peters and Waterman and close the *circle of seduction*. However, if we want to do justice to this text, one more commentary is in order. Rather than propose *In Search of Excellence* as a poor contribution to the tradition of leadership literature—which could not do anything new and had to go back to Barnard—we want to call attention to a very important way in which it differs from that tradition: the difference between modern and postmodern organizational writing. As a postmodern text this book falls under that variety which Jameson (1983) calls *pastiche* and he defines as parody without humour.

Parody, as critique, mimics with humour and irony some serious subject. Parody, as a modern genre, is supposed to make us smile/laugh when we notice the absurdity in the comparison between the serious subject and its parodic double. When the serious subject no longer exists, the humour behind the parody gets lost. Unable to laugh/critique, what remains with us in pastiche is our inability to stop thinking about that non-existent subject and to get it out of our cultural space. In pastiche—as postmodern genre—

repetition becomes the only mode of engagement, as we become unable to separate 'the original' from 'the copy'.

Peters and Waterman's return to Barnard via Burns illustrates this point well. The recycling of old discourses is not a rediscovery of 'eternal verities'. Rather, it is a reflection of how the organizational field, in its quest for *knowledge*, has impoverished what can be said as organizational research and theory. Because we have ignored the petty institutional game—the homosocial libidinal economy of competitiveness and glory—that has provoked this condition, we keep repeating 'the copy' as if it were 'truth'.

We argue that, at this point in time, leadership research/literature—as we know it—cannot be other than pastiche. Perhaps the only reality left in the homosocial libidinal economy represented in these writings is in the text, in 'the copy'. What *seductiveness* does 'leadership' hold for those who *dominate* the *writing scene,* that they must keep on repeating its name in a constant recycling of a masculine self-image? We posit that it is in that *act of repetition* that 'the original' and 'the copy' become juxtaposed. Researchers and theorists of leadership may be *saying/doing* about leadership very different things from what actual managers are *saying/doing* about it, but one and the other constantly reproduce strong manifestations of the homosocial order by repeating seduction as truth.

In the meantime, we ask, is this homosocial, élitist, monologic leadership the desired seduction for the organized life of the present—an organizational life of companies without offices (e.g. Marshall 1984) behind the screen of PCs and VTRs and of 'telecommuting' activities (e.g. Zuboff 1988; Perin 1990)? Is it desired by people connected through telemarketing, electronic mail, and computer networks, and whose lives have taken on the mark of 'global technologies'? Is leadership a desirable seduction for a post-Fordist, post-industrial society and an increasingly female labour force? Are other seductions possible?

## Different Pleasures

To summarize what we have been trying to show so far with this text, at first we set up the opposition between the signifier 'leadership' and the signifier 'seduction'. We noted that organizational writers have valued 'leadership' over 'seduction'. Leadership is upright, but seduction has gone astray. Leadership has come to be associated with the maintenance of orderly relations among men, beyond the bounds of time. Leadership is socially acceptable, but seduction is not. It seems that seduction is a problem that could bring about the downfall of men.

Through our rereadings of 'the classics' we noticed that the 'problem' has been there all along. Without seduction, the leadership literature wouldn't have been possible, it would have lost its (sex) appeal. However, we also noticed that leadership writings in the organizational disciplines have so far been limited to forms of seduction associated with homosocial *domination* and *servitude*.

Still, in our introduction, we said we wanted to explore different models of seduction—perhaps to let the seductress define organizational life and change that life beyond what has been possible with 'leadership'. This is proving difficult. As we performed our analyses we realized that, similar to 'leadership', our images of 'seduction' also emanated from a male-dominated culture. When we thought of 'seduction' and seduction 'scenes', we got a very limited set of images: perverse children and lower-class people; homosexual servants; 'Lolitas' and sirens on the cliffs—images of corruption rather than morality, as practised by the 'lesser ones'.

How then does one go further than the limited, univocal leadership-seduction? Is there a more open signifier for describing human desire? We decided that the signifier we were after was 'pleasure'. Pleasures beyond leadership-seduction may provide the bases for other types of social relations and new forms of organizational knowledge. What different pleasures can we imagine? Since we have criticized the masculine orientation of the leadership-seduction literature, we must consider sources that try to free themselves from the phallocentric influence. For inspiration, we turned to Utopias imagined by feminist authors.

## Utopia One

In *Herland* (Gilman 1979) we find a world pervaded by the pleasures of community, the pleasures of friendship, the pleasures of motherhood, and the pleasures of work. Herland is a world of only women. When the males of their civilization were killed in a series of wars and when, due to a natural disaster, their country was sealed off from the rest of the continent, one woman developed the capacity for parthenogenesis. She gave birth to five daughters who inherited her power. Herland was repopulated from this First Mother. The country is a genuine community where notions of individuality and the limitations of a wholly personal life were inconceivable.

In this book, Herland is described by a male narrator from the USA who, with two buddies, has managed to invade the country and ends up staying there for a year. This narrator just happens to be a sociologist and so we—the readers—expect him to give us a good participant observer account. He does. For example:

> We had expected a dull submissive monotony, and found a daring social inventiveness far beyond our own, and a mechanical and scientific development fully equal to ours.
>
> We had expected pettiness, and found a social consciousness besides which our nations looked like quarrelling children—feebleminded ones at that.
>
> We had expected jealousy, and found a broad sisterly affection, a fair-minded intelligence, to which we could produce no parallel.
>
> We had expected hysteria, and found a standard of health and vigour, a calmness of temper, to which the habit of profanity, for instance, was impossible to explain—we tried it. (Gilman 1979: 81)

Despite all his words of admiration for this society—and after many months in Herland—the narrator reflects upon his own culture.:

> You see, with us, women are kept as different as possible and as feminine as possible. We men have our own world, with only men in it: we get tired of our ultra-maleness and turn gladly to the ultra-femaleness. Also in keeping our women as feminine as possible, we see to it that when we turn to them we find the thing we want always in evidence. Well, the atmosphere of this place was anything but seductive. The very number of these human women, always in human relation, made them anything but alluring. (Gilman 1979: 129–30).

Does *Herland* represent an alternative model to be emulated? To us it does not: rather, it illustrates the illusion of 'alternative worlds' when they are placed in opposition to a dominant one. All that *Herland* accomplishes is to repeat the notion of pleasure along patriarchal lines, since all that is admirable in the society (first quote) and all that is undesirable (second quote ) is defined under masculine standards.

It reminds us of some women-in-management literature, where women's differences/no differences in organizational behaviour are assessed under standards assumed to be neutral. It is seldom mentioned that the 'standards' were defined by the original 'inhabitants' of managerial and academic positions—who were not women.

## Utopia Two

Another Utopia is seen in *Women on the Edge of Time* (Piercy 1976), when a modern-day woman, Connie Ramos, is transported into a community in Massachusetts in the year 2137. In the future the category *gender* has lost significance. A single pronoun, 'per', has replaced her/his and he/she. The categories of *race* and *class* are also gone. Babies are produced technologically in special brooders, and all people can be mothers.

Connie—who, in her own time, is a mental patient with a personal history of abuse and penury—questions the social arrangements of the future:

> How can men be mothers! How can some kid who isn't related to you be your child? . . . It was part of women's long revolution. When we were breaking up all the old hierarchies. Finally there was the one thing we have to give up too, the only power we have had, in return for no more power for anyone. The original production: the power to give birth. Cause as long as we were biologically enchained, we'd never be equal. And males never would be humanized to be loving and tender. So we all became mothers. Every child has three. To break the nuclear bonding. (Piercy 1976: 105)

In spite of her marginal position in her own society, Connie cannot accept the 'loss of motherhood' as a social improvement. Upon her discovery that men could also breastfeed:

> She felt angry. Yes, how dare any man share that pleasure. These women thought they had won, but they had abandoned to men the last refuge of women. What was special about being a woman here? They had given it all up, they had let me steal from them the last remnants of ancient power, those sealed in blood and milk. (Piercy 1976: 135)

Now, while the first Utopia illustrated the limits of alternative views under oppositional premisses, the very different alternative offered by this second Utopia doesn't fare much better. In this case, rather than an alternative female-dominated world, the text provides a world beyond androgyny, which works against every possible known structure of domination. It does so by collapsing for the readers many of these known structures and reconverting them into unknown ones. For example, motherhood is such a valuable condition for the society that it is offered to everyone, but is also taken away from everyone (i.e. brooders).

This is an ambiguous world where our typical concept of 'progress' breaks down because our notions past/present/future become unintelligible, and that is the main impediment for understanding this world as an alternative. Under our current notions of *knowledge*, we are likely to react like Connie

Ramos, who couldn't accept a world without oppression because it didn't look like what she—the oppressed—expected the future to be.

Like Connie Ramos, our modern (mono)logic already has a known blueprint (an evaluation standard) for the 'unknown'—what we can say/think as 'the progress of knowledge'—which, paradoxically, would make us oppose different knowledges, even when we may be clamouring for them.

## Utopia Three

In trying to articulate here, in our text, different pleasurable practices of organizing, we have engaged in another utopia. Utopia three is our dream that Utopias one and two would have solved our problem, and they do not. Can we learn anything from having tried? Is there anything which can help us turn leadership-seduction into other pleasures of organization?

By voicing this third Utopia as our own fiction—in having written this whole paper *as if* we were going to be able to articulate an alternative for the dilemma leadership/seduction—we can tell you now that finding an alternative was never our purpose. Our purpose, rather, was *the very action of writing this improbable paper.*

Throughout the paper we were calling attention to another pleasure, the 'pleasure of the text' (Barthes 1975) and what can be done with it. Similar to other writers, we writers of organizational matters can 'do' with texts. How can we make some different pleasures out of this 'doing'? Unless we spend some time meditating on this point we risk staying caught in our impoverished and repetitious organizational research and theory—unable to say *differently* in our writings.

To clarify, our utopias serve to emphasize how naïve it is to try to propose 'alternative organizations' without questioning the logic, the metaphysical assumptions, which inform our current thinking and writing about organizations. Before any real alternative becomes possible—outside the current monologic—it is necessary to question the limits of what we have taken for granted so far. 'Analytical strategies' like the ones deployed in this paper, in their own experimental form and farfetchedness, are attempts to reflect upon the limits of the *normal* logic.

For us, deconstructing 'leadership' has been an occasion for arguing against closure over what we—organizational scholars—could think and say as organizational theory and research, in this case represented by the discourses of 'leadership'. Deconstructing 'leadership' dislodges the *masculinist monologic* in which we have encased our organizational signifiers because it allows for *absurdity* to appear. Through *textual exercises* of this nature we might be able to observe, eventually, the absurdity of other currently acceptable organizational theorizing and understand how rhetorical-cultural structures perpetuate discourse under the rubric of 'research/theory/knowledge'.

Our recourse to *gender* in this questioning is in recognition of the role of patriarchy in our current structures of knowledge. The 'women's voice' that we have enacted here as our 'outside' from where to question is only a temporary site for noticing the limits of modern knowledge. Perhaps, by having been outside the dominant academic order, some women's writing and thinking has been more adventurous, as they didn't have to conform to the modern tradition of knowledge. In this paper we have been particularly inspired by Irigaray's more recent writings where:

> To be sure, such writing is deliberately unstable, rejecting the necessity for a solid ground beneath its own slipperiness. Like Derrida, Irigaray refuses the demand for fixed philosophical positions in what can only be described as a highly performative kind of writing. Such writing can also be said to be seductive, if by this word one understands a certain deliberative reversibility. Readers may respond with fascination, bafflement, or anger, depending upon their willingness to be led astray . . . The appeal of such writing derives, in large part, from its transgressive nature and its promise of forbidden pleasures. . . (Burke 1989: 236)

Thus, as we revert here to a playful discourse and imagine worlds of possibilities otherwise forbidden, we hope to open spaces for others to enact different worlds in ambivalent spaces which are not yet inside or outside the organizational texts. As we make available these spaces as another form of discourse about organizations, we deny to them any claim of solid ground or final word. Instead, we use them as an occasion to mark, in organizational theorizing, *the need to accept the temporality of our knowledge and the need to write and rewrite organizations and organizational theory as we move along in an ever-changing world.*

Rather than *fixing* ourselves in the text (the typical imagery of 'universal truth-knowledge' in modern metaphysics) we prefer the imagery of a transient subject, never to be captured, always on the move, as so many points of pleasure on a woman's body. As we write these words, we recognize that this is all that we (Calás and Smircich) have been doing so far, but, at the same time, this form of writing ourselves into the organizational text has provided us with the pleasures of resistance and activism (Diamond and Quinby 1988), while maintaining an awareness—so often forgotten in the dominant order—of the limits of human agency.

What other pleasures for the 'organizational text' can our friends and colleagues inscribe . . .? What is your pleasure?

## References

*Academy of Management Review* (1989), 'Special Forum on Theory Building', 17: 486–594.

Acker, J. (1987), 'Hierarchies and Job: Notes for a Theory of Gendered Organization' (paper presented at the American Sociological Association annual meetings, Chicago, August).

Badcock, C. (1988), *Essential Freud* (Oxford: Basil Blackwell).

Barnard, C. (1938), *The Functions of the Executive* (Cambridge, Mass.: Harvard University Press).

Barthes, R. (1975), *The Pleasure of the Text*, trans. R. Miller (London: Jonathan Cape).

Baudrillard, J. (1988), 'On Seduction', in *Selected Writings*, trans. and ed. M. Poster (Stanford, Conn.: Stanford University Press).

Berhheimer, C., and Kahane, C. (1985) (eds.), *In Dora's Case: Freud-Hysteria-Feminism* (New York: Columbia University Press).

Billing, Y., and Alvesson, M. (1989), *Kon, ledelse, organisation (Gender, leadership, organization)* (Copenhagen: Djofpforlaget).

Botti, Hope (1988), 'Portare le differenze sul lavoro: due utopie a confronto' (paper presented at the conference Gestire le Differenze, sponsored by CISL, Milan, 1–2 June).

Brenton, M. (1966), *The American Male* (New York: Coward-McCann).

Burke, C. (1989), 'Romancing the Philosophers: Luce Irigaray', in D. Hunter (ed.), *Seduction and Theory* (Urbana, Ill.: University of Illinois Press, 226–40).

Burrell, G. (1984), 'Sex and Organizational Analysis', *Organization Studies*, 5/2: 97–118.

Burns, J. M. (1978), *Leadership* (New York: Harper & Row).

Burrell, G. and Hearn, J. (1989), 'The Sexuality of Organizations?' in *The Sexuality of Organization*, J. Hearn, D. Sheppard, P. Tancred-Sheriff, and G. Burrell (eds.), (Newbury Park, Calif.: Sage), 1–28.

Calás, M. B. (1986*a*), 'The Unavoidable Contextual and Cultural Bases of Attribution of Leadership Research: A Literary/Literature Review', (paper presented at the Academy of Management meeting, Chicago, August).

—— (1986*b*), 'Cultural and Contextual Grounds for Leadership: A Mosaic of Leadership Theories' (paper presented at the Southern Management Association meeting, Atlanta, November).

—— (1987), 'Organization Science/Fiction: The Postmodern in the Management Disciplines (unpublished doctoral dissertation, University of Massachusetts, Amherst, Mass.).

—— and Smircich, L. (1988), 'Reading Leadership as a Form of Cultural Analysis', in *Emerging Leadership Vistas*, J. G. Hunt, R. D. Baliga, H. P. Dachler, and C. A. Schriesheim (eds.), (Lexington, Mass.: Lexington Press), 201–26.

—— —— (1989), 'Using the F word: Feminist Theories and the Social Consequences of Organizational Research' (paper presented at the Academy of Management Meeting, Washington, August).

Cixous, H. and Clement, C. (1986), *The Newly Born Woman* (Minneapolis: University of Minnesota Press).

Cooper, R., and Burrell, G. (1988), 'Modernism, Postmodernism and Organizational Analysis: An Introduction', *Organization Studies*, 9/1: 91–112.

Davidson, A. I. (1986), 'Archaeology, Genealogy, Ethics' in D. C. Hoy (ed.), *Foucault: A Critical Reader*, (Oxford: Basil Blackwell), 221–3.

Derrida, J. (1976), *Of grammatology*, trans. G. C. Spivak (Baltimore: Johns Hopkins University Press).

—— (1978), *Spurs* (Chicago: University of Chicago Press).

—— (1981), *Positions*, trans. A. Bass (Chicago: University of Chicago Press).

—— (1982), *Margins of Philosophy* (Chicago: University of Chicago Press).

—— (1986), *Glas* (Lincoln, Neb.: University of Nebraska Press).

Diamond, I. and Quinby, L. (1988), *Feminism and Foucault: Reflections on Resistance* (Boston, Northeastern University Press).

Exner, M. J. (1932), *The Sexual Side of Marriage* (New York: Norton).

Ferguson, K. E. (1984), *Thinking Fragments: Psycho-Analysis, Feminism and Postmodernism in the Contemporary West* (Berkeley and Los Angeles: University of California Press)

Flax, J. (1990), *Thinking Fragments: Psychoanalysis, Feminism, and Postmodernism in the Contemporary West* (Berkeley and Los Angeles: University of California Press).

Foucault, M. (1973), *The Order of Things* (New York: Vintage Books).

—— (1979), *Discipline and Punish* (New York: Vintage Books).

—— (1980), *The History of Sexuality* (New York: Vintage Books).

—— (1986), *The Uses of Pleasure*, trans. R. Hurley (New York: Vintage Books).

—— (1988), 'On Power', in *Michel Foucault: Politics, Philosophy Culture* ed. L. D. Kritzman (New York: Routledge), 96–109.

Freud, S. (1965), 'Femininity' (1933), in *New Introductory Lectures on Psychoanalysis* (New York: Norton).

Gallop, J. (1982), *The Daughter's Seduction: Feminism and Psychoanalysis* (Ithaca, NY: Cornell University Press).

Gallop, J. (1987) 'French Theory and the Seduction of Feminism', in A. Jardine and P. Smith (eds.), *Men in Feminism* (New York: Methuen) 111–15.

—— (1988), *Thinking through the Body* (New York: Columbia University Press).

Gilman, C. P. (1979), *Herland* (New York: Pantheon Books; first published, 1915).

Hearn, J. and Parkin, W. P. (1984), 'Women, Men and Leadership: A Critical Review of Assumptions, Practices and Change in the Industrialized Nations', *International Studies of Management and Organizations*, 14: 38–60.

—— —— (1987), *'Sex' at Work* (New York: St Martin's).

—— Sheppard, D. L., Tancred-Sheriff, P. and Burrell, G. (1989) (eds.), *The Sexuality of Organizations* (Newbury Park, Calif.: Sage).

Hunter, D. (1989*a*) (ed.), *Seduction and Theory: Readings of Gender, Representation, and Rhetoric* (Urbana, Ill.: University of Chicago Press).

—— (1989*b*), 'Introduction', in D. Hunter (ed.), *Seduction and Theory: Readings of Gender, Representation and Rhetoric* (Urbana, Ill.: University of Chicago Press), 1–10.

Irigaray, L. (1985*a*), *The Speculum of the Other Woman*, trans. G. G. Gillman (Ithaca, NY: Cornell University Press).

—— (1985*b*), *This Sex which is not One* (Ithaca, NY: Cornell University Press).

Jameson, F. (1983), 'Postmodernism and Consumer Society', in H. Foster (ed.), *The Anti-Aesthetic: Essays on Postmodern Culture* (Port Townsend, Wash.: Bay Press) 111–25.

Jardine, A. A. (1985), *Gynesis* (Ithaca, NY: Cornell University Press).

Kanter, R. M. (1977), *Men and Women of the Corporation* (New York: Basic Books).

Krupnick, M. (1987), 'Introduction', in M. Krupnick (ed.), *Displacement: Derrida and after* (Boomington, Ind.: Indiana University Press), 1–17.

Lasch, C. (1979), *The Culture of Narcissism* (New York: Warner Books).

Lewicki, R. J. (1981), 'Organizational Seduction: Building commitment to Organizations', *Organizational Dynamics* (Autumn), 5–21.

Loden, M. (1985), *Feminine Leadership or How to Succeed in Business without being One of the Boys* (New York: Times Books).

Maccoby, M. (1976), *The Famesmen* (New York: Bantam Books).

Marshall, J. (1984), *Woman Managers: Travellers in a Male World* (Chichester: Wiley).

Martin, J. (1990), 'Deconstructing Organizational Taboos: The Suppression of Gender Conflict in Organizations', *Organization Science*, 1/4: 339–59.

McGregor, D. (1960), *The Human Side of Enterprise* (New York: McGraw Hill).

Meindl, J., Ehrlich, S. B., and Dukerich, J. M. (1985), 'The Romance of Leadership', *Administrative Science Quarterly*, 30: 78–102.

Mintzberg, H. (1973/1980), *The Nature of Managerial Work* (2nd edn., Englewood Cliffs, NJ: Prentice Hall).

*Oxford English Dictionary* (1989), 2nd edn. (Oxford: Oxford University Press).

Perin, C. (1990), 'The moral fabric of the office: Panopticon discourse and schedule flexibility' in *Research in the Sociology of Organizations*. Special volume: *Organizations and professions*. Pamela S. Torbert and Steven R. Barley (eds.), 243–270. (Greenwich: JAI Press).

Peters, T. J. and Waterman, R. H. (1982), *In Search of Excellence* (New York: Harper & Row).

Piercy, M. (1976), *Woman on the Edge of Time* (New York: Fawcett).

Pivy, P. (1988), 'Towards a Dynamic Management of the Differences between Men and Women in Organizations' (paper presented at the conference Gestire le Differenze, sponsored by CISL, Milan, 1–2 June).

Rosener, J. B. (1990), 'Ways Women Lead', *Harvard Business Review* (Nov.–Dec.), 119–25.

Slater, P. (1977) *Footholds: Understanding the Shifting Family and Sexual Tensions in our Culture* (Boston: Beacon Press).

Webster, J., and Starbuck, W. H. (1988), 'Theory Building in Industrial and Organizational Psychology', *International Review of Industrial and Organizational Psychology*, 93–137.

*Websters Ninth New Collegiate Dictionary* (1988) (Springfield, Mass.: Merrian-Webster).

Westkott, M. (1986), *The Feminist Legacy of Karen Horney* (New Haven: Yale University Press).

Zuboff, S. (1988), *In the Age of the Smart Machine: The Future of Work and Power* (New York: Basic Books).

# References


Ackerson, L. (1942), *Children's Behavior Problems: Relative Importance and Intercorrelation among Traits* (Chicago: University of Chicago Press).

Adams, S. (1996), *The Dilbert Principle* (New York: Harper Business).

Barthes, R. (1990), *S/Z* (Oxford: Blackwell).

Bass, B. M. (1985), *Leadership and Performance beyond Expectations* (New York: Free Press).

—— (1990), *Bass and Stogdill's Handbook of Leadership: Theory, Research and Managerial Applications* (New York: Free Press).

BBC2 (1995), *My Brilliant Career: Ratner, Lord of the Rings* (London: BBC; 4 Jan.).

Braverman, H. (1974), *Labor and Monopoly Capital* (New York: Monthly Review Press).

Bryman, A. (1992), *Charisma and Leadership in Organizations* (London: Sage).

Burns, J. M. (1978), *Leadership* (New York: Harper & Row).

Chandler, A. D., Jr (1962), *Strategy and Structure* (Cambridge, Mass.: MIT Press).

Cole, R. E. (1980), *Work, Mobility and Participation: A Comparative Study of American and Japanese Industry* (Berkeley and Los Angeles: University of California Press).

Colley, L. (1992), *Britons: Forging the Nation, 1707–1837* (London: Pimlico).

Cronin, V. (1971), *Napoleon* (London: Fontana).

Dixon, N. (1976), *On the Psychology of Military Incompetence* (London: Futura).

Donaldson, L. (1995), *American Anti-Management Theories of Organization* (Cambridge: Cambridge University Press).

Fiedler, F. E., and Garcia, J. E. (1987), *New Approaches to Effective Leadership: The LeaderMatch Concept* (New York: Wiley).

Gannon, M. J. (1994), *Understanding Global Cultures* (London: Sage).

Gardner, H. (1995), *Leading Minds* (London: HarperCollins).

Grint, K. (1995), *Management: A Sociological Introduction* (Cambridge: Polity Press).

—— and Gill, R. (1995) (eds.), *The Gender-Technology Relation* (London: Taylor & Francis).

—— and Willcocks, L. (1995), "Business Process Re-Engineering in Theory and Practice: Business Paradise Regained? *New Technology, Work and Employment*, 10/2: 99–109.

—— and Woolgar, S. (forthcoming), *The Machine at Work: Technology, Work and Organization* (Cambridge: Polity Press).

Hamilton, P. (1975), D101, *Making Sense of Society* (Unit 28; Milton Keynes: Open University Press).

Hampden-Turner, C., and Trompenaars, F. (1993), *The Seven Cultures of Capitalism* (New York : Doubleday).

Heifetz, R. A. (1994), *Leadership without Easy Answers* (Cambridge, Mass.: Belknap Press).

Hemphill, J. K. (1949), *Situational Factors in Leadership* (Columbus, Oh.: Bureau of Educational Research, Ohio State University).

Hersey, P., and Blanchard, K. H. (1982), *The Management of Organizational Behaviour* (Englewood Cliffs, NJ: Prentice Hall).

Hofstede, G. (1980), *Culture's Consequences: International Differences in Work-Related Values* (California: Sage).

Howe, M., Davidson, J. and Sloboda, J. (1996), 'It ain't what you do, it's the way that you do it—that's what gets results', quoted in *Observer*, 13 April.

Kaplan, R. E. (1996), *Forceful Leadership and Enabling Leadership: You can be Both*, (Greensboro, NC: Center for Creative Leadership).

Kenny, D. A., and Zaccaro, S. J. (1983), An Estimate of Variance due to Traits in Leadership', *Journal of Applied Psychology*, 68/4: 678–85.

Kertzer, D. (1988), *Ritual, Politics, and Power* (New Haven: Yale University Press).

Kouzes, J. M., and Posner, B. Z. (1987), *The Leadership Challenge* (London: Jossey-Bass).

Krause, D. G. (1995), *The Art of War for Executives* (London: Nicholas Brealey).

Latour, B. (1988), '*The Prince* for Machines as well as Machinations', in B. Elliott, (ed.), *Technology and Social Process* (Edinburgh: Edinburgh University Press).

—— (1995), *We Have Never Been Modern* (Hemel Hempstead: Wheatsheaf).

Lord, R. G., De Vader, C. L. and Alliger, G. M. (1986), 'A Meta-Analysis of the Relation between Personality Traits and Leadership Perceptions: An Application of Validity Generalization Procedures', *Journal of Applied Psychology*, 71/3: 402–410.

Machiavelli, N. (1981), *The Prince* (Oxford: Oxford University Press).

Manz, C. C. and Sims, H. P. (1991), 'Superleadership: Beyond the Myth of Heroic Leadership', *Organizational Dynamics* (Spring), 18–35.

Marx, K. (1954), *Capital*, i (London: Lawrence & Wishart).

Nathan, B. R., Hass, M. A., and Nathan, M. L. (1986), 'Meta Analysis of Fiedler's Leadership Theory: A Figure is Worth a Thousand Words' (paper, American Psychological Association, Washington).

Nethaway, R. (1996), 'Mystery of Clinton's Sex Appeal Solved', *Guardian* (4 June).

Newstetter, W.I., Feldstein, M. J., and Newcomb, T. M. (1938), *Group Adjustment: A Study in Experimental Sociology* (Cleveland, Oh.: Western Reserve University).

Pareto, V. (1966), *Sociological Writings*, ed. S. Finer (London: Pall Mall Press).

Peter, L. (1978) (ed.), *Quotations for our Time* (London: Souvenir Press).

Peters, J. J., and Waterman, R. H. (1982), *In Search of Excellence* (New York: Harper & Row).

Plato (1941), *The Republic* (Oxford: Oxford University Press).

Roberts, N. C., and Bradley, R. T. (1988), 'Limits of Charisma', in J. A. Conger, and R. N. Kanungo (eds.), *Charismatic Leadership* (San Francisco: Jossey-Bass).

Rosener, J. B. (1990), 'Ways Women Lead', *Harvard Business Review* (Nov.–Dec.), 119–160.

Scott, W. R., and Meyer, J. W. (1994), *Institutional Environments and Organizations* (London: Sage).

Starhawk (1986), *Truth or Dare* (New York: Harper & Row).

Stogdill, R. M. (1948), 'Personal Factors Associated with Leadership: A Survey of the Literature', *Journal of Psychology* 25: 35–71.

—— (1950), 'Leadership, Membership and Organization', *Psychological Bulletin*, 47: 1–14.

Storr, A. (1996), *Feet of Clay: A Study of Gurus* (London: HarperCollins).

Sun Tzu (1963), *The Art of War* (Oxford: Oxford University Press).

Tolstoy, L. (1991), *War and Peace* (Oxford: Oxford University Press).

Thucydides (1972), *The Peloponnesian War* (Harmondsworth: Penguin).

Useem, M. (1996), 'Do Leaders Make a Difference?' *Financial Times*, 8 March.

Weber, M. (1968), *Economy and Society* (London: University of California Press).

Wilkinson, H. (1996), 'Cracks in the Glass Ceiling', Observer (2 June).

Williamson, O. E. (1970), *Corporate Control and Business Behaviour* (Englewood Cliffs, NJ : Prentice Hall).

Woodward, J. (1965), *Industrial Organization: Theory and Practice* (London: Oxford University Press).

Wright, P. (1996), *Managerial Leadership* (London: Routledge).

# Index

# Index